CHAPTER ONE.

The Theistic Model.

1. Fool, Alchemy, Hermetic Arcanum, Corpus Hermeticum.

2. Magus, Mastery, Meditations On the Tarot, Christian Hermeticism.

3. Hermit, Druidry, The Zohar, Moses de Leon.

4. Emperor, Magick, Occult Philosophy, Cornelius Agrippa.

5. Hierophant, Wizardry, Summa Theologica, St Thomas Aquinas.

6. Chariot, Sorcery, A Course In Miracles, Helen Schucman.

7. Devil, Diplomacy, Paradise Lost, John Milton.

8. Empress, Entrepreneurship, Science and Health, Mary Baker Eddy.

9. Death, Ninjutsu, Divine Comedy, Dante.

10. Lovers, Enchantment, Enneads by Plotinus.

11. Priestess, Scoutcraft, The Holy Koran.

12. Worldsoul, Leadership, Holy Bible.

13. Tower, Invention, City of God, St Augustine.

14. Hanged Man, Craftsmanship, Le Morte D'Arthur, Thomas Malory.

64 Hexagrams.

2Sm 16:23 And the counsel of Ahithophel, which he counselled in those days, was as if a man had enquired at the oracle of God: so was all the counsel of Ahithophel both with

David and with Absalom.

1Ki 6:5 And against the wall of the house he built chambers round about, against the walls of the house round about, both of the temple and of the oracle: and he made chambers round about:

1Ki 6:16 And he built twenty cubits on the sides of the house, both the floor and the walls with boards of cedar: he even built them for it within, even for the oracle, even for the most holy place.

1Ki 6:19 And the oracle he prepared in the house within, to set there the ark of the covenant of the LORD.

1Ki 6:20 And the oracle in the forepart was twenty cubits in length, and twenty cubits in breadth, and twenty cubits in the height thereof: and he overlaid it with pure gold; and so covered the altar which was of cedar.

1Ki 6:21 So Solomon overlaid the house within with pure gold: and he made a partition by the chains of gold before the oracle; and he overlaid it with gold.

1Ki 6:22 And the whole house he overlaid with gold, until he had finished all the house: also the whole altar that was by the oracle he overlaid with gold.

1Ki 6:23 And within the oracle he made two cherubims of olive tree, each ten cubits high.

1Ki 6:31 And for the entering of the oracle he made doors of olive tree: the lintel and side posts were a fifth part of the wall.

1Ki 7:49 And the candlesticks of pure gold, five on the right side, and five on the left, before the oracle, with the flowers, and the lamps, and the tongs of gold,

1Ki 8:6 And the priests brought in the ark of the covenant of the LORD unto his place, into the oracle of the house, to the most holy place, even under the wings of the cherubims.

1Ki 8:8 And they drew out the staves, that the ends of the staves were seen out in the holy place before the oracle, and they were not seen without: and there they are unto this day.

2Chr 3:16 And he made chains, as in the oracle, and put them on the heads of the pillars; and made an hundred pomegranates, and put them on the chains.

2Chr 4:20 Moreover the candlesticks with their lamps, that they should burn after the manner before the oracle, of pure gold;

2Chr 5:7 And the priests brought in the ark of the covenant of the LORD unto his place, to the oracle of the house, into the most holy place, even under the wings of the cherubims:

2Chr 5:9 And they drew out the staves of the ark, that the ends of the staves were seen from the ark before the oracle; but they were not seen without. And there it is unto this day.

Psa 28:2 Hear the voice of my supplications, when I cry unto thee, when I lift up my hands toward thy holy oracle.

Introduction and Initiation.

1. This gives the fourteen crafts of tarot.

It is asserted that they are crafts and that there are fourteen of them.

This assertion can be doubted. They are not crafts and there are not fourteen of them.

One or the other claim must be true and not both. We get fourteen because seventy eight minus sixty four gives fourteen remainder. We have seventy eight tarot cards, fifty six minor arcana and twenty two major arcana. If the fifty six minor arcana are laid out in a matrix grid of four rows and fourteen columns that gives us a simple shape that is preordered by what the minor arcana is, as given. If we then look at the suits and pictures we make the intuitive judgement that eight of the major arcana go in as two extra columns on each of the four rows. We assume this because the matrix grid of minor arcana permits it. By a process involving equal parts logic, intuition and common sense and a method of elimination we decide which eight major arcana are used to make the two extreme columns at either end of the matrix grid of minor arcana. First we don't include any cards that seem obviously people as heads of craft such as the Fool, Magus, Hermit etc. Second we look to the meaning of the suit to see if any major arcana naturally fall into place. We are following the minor arcana code of wands=spring, pentacles=summer, swords=autumn, cups=winter. Then Justice and Judgement seem to be a pair. Justice is a picture of someone holding a sword. So we suppose these go at either side of the suit of Swords. Sun and Star seem to be a pair just as good as Sun and Moon so we assume one and not the other. Then we say like summer and Pentacles and place accordingly. Moon goes well with Temperance which is what we mean by Cups and winter so Temperance at the beginning of Cups and Moon at the end of it all. That just leaves Wands, spring. Strength on the Wheel of Fortune is the helpful condition for success on this course so we try that and see what remains.

2. They are numbered one to fourteen which corresponds to the same numbering in the minor arcana. Having built our matrix grid of sixty four cards we are left with a remainder of fourteen major arcana. We have to order these fourteen in sequence and we can't use the numbering given on the cards. Rather we have to go by the pictures. The Devil is awkward, supposed to be secret intelligence so we say fits with the occult meaning of the number seven so we consider that possible. A Hierophant (Ancient Greek: ἱεροφάντης) is a person who brings religious congregants into the presence of that which is deemed holy. As such, a hierophant is an interpreter of sacred mysteries and arcane principles.The word comes from ancient Greece, where it was constructed

from the combination of ta hiera ('the holy') and phainein ('to show'). Our model of excellence in this regard is Aristotle and his craft is Wizardry. We associate with the pentagram which is five sided so number five. The difference between Aristotle and Plato is the same as the difference between Wizardry and Sorcery. Sorcery can be understood as two intersecting equilateral triangles being the concordance of heaven and earth, consciousness and body, and has six points, associated to the light and dark sphinx of the Chariot. So Sorcery, Chariot, Six.

3. The numbering is arcane and for example one the Fool is aligned with ten the Lovers in the way that ten is one plus zero which equals one, so the Fool and the Lovers go together. In this way we go through each of the fourteen major arcana and eventually arrive at this sequence as being coherent, correspondent and useful.

1 The Fool, Alchemy; 2 The Magus Mastery; 3 The Hermit Druidry; 4 The Emperor Magiçk; 5 The Hierophant Wizardry; 6 The Chariot Sorcery; 7 The Devil Diplomacy; 8 The Empress Entrepreneurship; 9 Death Ninjutsu; 10 The Lovers Enchantment; 11 The High Priestess Scoutcraft; 12 The Worldsoul Leadership; 13 The Tower Invention; 14 The Hanged Man Craftsmanship. The fourteen cards put this way is a product of craft thirteen Invention and holds together initially only inasmuch as the rules of inventive science dictates. Some aspects are whimsical for example craft nine Ninjutsu is a play on the idea of the art of nine.

4. Each craft is associated to one of the fourteen major arcana mentioned. So it begins with one, The Fool, the craft of Alchemy, then two, the Magus, the craft of Mastery, then three, the Hermit, the craft of Druidry. To follow the meanings associated here it is useful to be familiar with the occult significance of number as described for example by Cornelius Agrippa in his Second Book of Occult Philosophy.

This one then is associated with the Fool whose special province is the craft of Alchemy.

So to the number three we associate The Hermit Druidry and the essence of mystery teachings.

Following this line we learn to invent the occult meaning of each of the numbers one to fourteen, associate the designated tarot card and signify each by its relevant craft.

5. The idea is that the number, the tarot card and the craft each hang together by occult reasoning. According to the ideas thus described we invent or discover the occult meaning of each of the numbers one through to fourteen. Then by looking at the pictures of each of the remaining major arcana and knowledge of what they mean as crafts with reference to the occult meaning of number we associate each tarot card to a number. The name of the relevant craft may offer itself to improvement over time however the names as given are exactly the same as first expression of this system twenty years ago. When this is done by a process of elimination we place each of our cards along the top row of our minor arcana matrix grid to make fourteen columns of five rows. Starting with the first nine numbers we assert fool, magus, hermit, emperor, hierophant, chariot, devil, empress, death. With these nine cards placed it is easy to assume ten the lovers. That just leaves four cards, priestess, worldsoul, tower, hanged man which we place in that order. We have no remainder. In accord with necessary sufficient conditions we have accounted for all seventy eight tarot cards. We have a matrix grid of sixty four cards and a craft system of fourteen cards.

6. So the Hermit is associated to the number three, like in the Trinity, and the Hermit is to do with mysticism which is labelled in this system as Druidry.

The number four is foursquare, and associated to Magick, the secret craft of which the Emperor is Master. It is the advanced science that begins with Mastery, the Magus, number two, in the same way that two and four are consequential.

The number five, like a pentagram, is associated to Wizardry, the Hierophant and is abstract and Empirical Science as compared to six, Sorcery, the Chariot which is focused on noumena and phenomena, perhaps like neuro-linguistic programming.

In this way each number, tarot image and craft hang together on their own and simultaneously correlate in meaningful ways with each of the other crafts. You are not forced by the system of tarot to take this explanation as given. You could associate the tarot cards differently to the order stated here. Tarot does permit of alternative expressions of itself. The explanation provided here is one that has been found to work by practice and experience.

7. The association of a single book to each of the crafts is speculative. The idea is to obtain a manual for a model of excellence in each craft. The choice of books is entirely dependent on appropriateness to craft and can be much harder than your present ability to understand. Key principles that guide selection of books are similitude and affinity, appropriateness and correspondence, reflectivity and familiarity. The best, easiest and simplest introductory initiation into the craft books that I know of is as follows:

Introductory Initiation Texts.

1. Fool, Alchemy, Science Set Free, Rupert Sheldrake.

2. Magus, Mastery, The Mindmap Book, Tony Buzan.

3. Hermit, Druidry, Meditations On the Tarot, Christian Hermeticism.

4. Emperor, Magick, Mechanism of Mind, Edward de Bono.

5. Hierophant, Wizardry, Brain Building, Marilyn vos Savant.

6. Chariot, Sorcery, Roots of NLP, Robert Dilts.

7. Devil, Diplomacy, Ethics of Spinoza.

8. Empress, Entrepreneurship, Think and Grow Rich,Napoleon Hill.

9. Death, Ninjutsu, The Art of War, Sun Tsu.

10. Lovers, Enchantment, White Tigress Teachings.

11. Priestess, Scoutcraft, How To Solve It, G Polya.

12. Worldsoul, Leadership, Holy Bible.

13. Tower, Invention, The Triz Handbook, Vladimir Petrov.

14. Hanged Man, Craftsmanship, Tao of Jeet Kune Do, Bruce Lee.

The Modern Esoteric School texts is a bit harder and the Transcendental Eternals is adept level. You can also design your book selection around a central theme. So you could design a Taoist Immortal Classics selection or you could take the Koran as your central text and build an Arabic Islamic selection around that which involves knowledge outside of my field. If you are a bio-chemist you could design a scientific selection dependent on your familiarity with the nature of the subject. You may also decide to choose a deck of cards that better reflects your choice of craft books than the Rider Waite standard deck that I have used. The system of tarot described here also requires the design of decks not yet available. For example we need a Tibetan deck based around the structure as I have explained it, a Taoist Immortal Classics deck, a Buddhist Scripture deck and a Christian African deck.

8. Ideally the choice of books is flexible and discretionary where each player would choose their own selection of what books are collected, in such a way that each of the books dovetails with each of the others. My choice of books presented here is provisional and towards a winning system of esoteric classics to make sure each craft has an adequate reference work. The idea is that tarot is a game system. The

placement of cards, the association of crafts, the selection of books all allows for alternatives to the prime system described here. It is up to the individual player to make their own decisions. Tarot is an imperfect information game according to game theory and you never know all that is to be known about the other players.

9. It means that each player would have a private and secret set of information as to craft. Secrecy is fundamental to tarot and it is not supposed that any player knows very much about any other player except for example that they may both be using the system 78T64I14C9S or the Meditations on Tarot, a Journey Into Christian Hermeticism or some other system not detailed here such as a kabbalistic Jewish system.

10. On completion the idea is as stated where there is a correlation between number, tarot card, craft and reference book. If you do learn the system I have iterated the best way is to first be sure about the occult meanings of number one to fourteen. Then be confident that the association of tarot card to each of the numbers is appropriate. Then have a sense of what is the sort of craft meant by each number card association. And finally select a personal set of books next to each craft. That accounts for the fourteen crafts and then all you are left to do is learn about the 64 matrix grid which is explained in the text after this article. The ten points of this article are meant as an introduction and initiation into the use of 78T64I14C9S. The system itself accounts for the entirety of tarot with no remainder. It is complete as I have described it and meets logical mathematical rules such as no excess no deficiency, reduction to necessary sufficient conditions, well formedness, coherence, correspondence and utility.

All that is required now is to deepen the study of the article I have titled 78T64I14C9S so that the cards of the sixty four matrix grid and fourteen crafts are understood together as an explanation of seventy eight tarot cards.

Alchemy is best understood today as tethered by the readily available works of Paracelsus and most precisely as described in the questions and answers of his Catechism of Alchemy.

It is narrowly focused through the Six Keys of Eudoxus and has routes back in time quite clear to discern in the four element theory of earth, air, fire and water grounded in Indian and Tibetan Buddhist theories of nature and also regularly alluded to in Aristotle. From Aristotle it finds its way into Arabic occult science. It is said you should judge Alchemy as the parent by the value of its children those being physics, chemistry and biology in modern terms. Its number is one in the sense that it is first, something coming from nothing and before other things. Its Tarot card is the Fool in the sense that only a fool studies Alchemy and also if you have nearly no knowledge of the wize arts as is the case with the Fool, the place to start the journey of discovery is Alchemy.

Mastery is the second Craft of this system and follows on from Alchemy. Its Tarot card is the Magus which shows an initiate pointing to heaven and earth. On the table in front of the initiate are four objects representing the suits of wands, pentacles, swords and cups. The primary focus of Mastery is the skill of learning and it means learning as play. An example of this expression is the Montessori method of teaching infants. The objective of Mastery is the learning of Magic, hence the Magus.

Druidry may be considered in this system as a six pointed star made by two intersecting equilateral triangles. Where the points of one triangle designated heaven and pointing downwards are the matter of Hinduism, Buddhism and Taoism. And the points of the other triangle designated earth and pointing upwards are the matter of Judaism, Christianity and Islam. Druidry then is an arcane and occult reading of all six systems with a view to discovering cardinal articulations connecting them in their diversity. Its Tarot card is the Hermit.

The Emperor is the Tarot card of Magick. It means an accomplished adept status of the learning begun in craft two, the Magus. It can mean magic when applied to any diverse range of subject matter or it can mean the abstract study of its own self nature. A good place to start is the book, Mechanism of Mind, by De Bono or How to Solve It, by G Polya. Its implication is a complete control of the tools of Mind. It's expression is empirical science. It is closely associated to Craft Thirteen, Invention.

Wizardry is best characterised as a rationalist science when compared to Sorcery idealist and Magic empiricist. Wizardry focuses on algebra, logic, mathematics and the study of the methods of notation used to communicate these arts such as that of music. The exemplar of Wizardry is the work of Aristotle. Its sign is the pentacle and its number is five. Einstein would be considered a Wizard whereas Tesla a Magician. It is described as the wize art and is focused on the meaningful expression of wisdom. Its Tarot card is the Hierophant.

There is a difference between doing Sorcery and an analytical study of what Sorcery is.

The most advanced exemplification of doing Sorcery may be the Works of Plato. The closest explanation of an analytical study of what Sorcery is, may be the Neuro Linguistic Programming of Bandler and Grinder as described by Robbins in his book Unlimited Power. And a less precise but much broader canvas would be the entire corpus of the matter of psychology.

Sorcery then is both immediately available in various guises to anybody who wishes to explore its expression and is very common and at the same time is distant and complex by virtue of the difficult nature of its subject matter. Its Tarot card is the Chariot.

Diplomacy is an art commonly practiced by lawyers, politicians, ambassadors, representatives of all kinds, persuasive communicators of any sort and spies. Its number is seven which is characterised as an awkward number. Its factors are one and six, two and five, three and four, none of which go together in any smooth manner. Its Tarot card is the Devil suggesting a powerful coercive force to do the right thing such as law and order policing. Diplomacy in this system suggests an adept who has a sophisticated knowledge of the previous six Crafts. Also it is alien and implies subversive knowledge of communication between species.

Entrepreneurship is the individual approach to wealth creation when wealth is understood less narrowly than in the sense of financial gain. So for example a nurse or schoolteacher could practice effective Entrepreneurship even though modestly paid in monetary terms. A sorcerous explanation of the structures of Entrepreneurship is the book Think and Grow Rich by Napoleon Hill in particular his suggestions of a master mind and psychic phenomena. The accruing of wealth in this sense may be in terms of specialist knowledge, establishment status, physical object or money itself. Its number is eight and its Tarot card is the Empress.

The Craft of Ninjutsu in this system is the psychophysical study of the phenomena of death. Its number is nine and its Tarot card is Death. It is understood on a multitude of levels.

First it may be considered in terms of Sun Tsu in the sense that the Art of War is of vital importance to the state, it is the road of life and death. Or in terms of the Five Rings of Musashi in the sense that the way of the warrior is the resolute acceptance of death. As such a rare and valued text on the subject of death in itself is the Tibetan Book of the Dead in particular as relates to practice of the Death Transit between incarnations. In Christian terms this is the fulfilment of its own belief system.

John 5:24

Verily, verily, I say unto you, He that heareth my word, and believeth on him that sent me, hath everlasting life, and shall not come into condemnation; but is passed from death unto life.

John 8:51

Verily, verily, I say unto you, If a man keep my saying, he shall never see death.

Romans 6:23

For the wages of sin is death; but the gift of God is eternal life through Jesus Christ our Lord.

1 Corinthians

The last enemy that shall be destroyed is death.

1 Corinthians 15:54

So when this corruptible shall have put on incorruption, and this mortal shall have put on immortality, then shall be brought to pass the saying that is written, Death is swallowed up in victory.

The Craft of Enchantment is the Tarot card the Lovers. It is numbered ten being a combination of one and zero, yang masculine and yin feminine. A refined understanding of this Craft may be found in Plotinus. The Enneads by Plotinus lead the student to a consideration of the essence of soul, the nature of being, the meaning of love in time and eternity, virtue, happiness and the good. Alternatively the importance of this study is explained in the writing of the Kama Sutra. Whereas by its nature this Craft has a double aspect being the relationship of male and female, it may be considered individually as contemplation of beauty as described in Plato's Symposium.

The High Priestess Tarot card is craft eleven, Scoutcraft. This may not be the most appropriate name for what is meant by this subject matter but it tends towards the meaning. Its focus is Ain Soph in Jewish kabbalah, or the Yin and Yang of the Tao. Its Bible is the I Ching Book of Changes. As such the High Priestess herself is suggestive of Shekinah. In particular this Craft refers to the sixty four hexagrams when transposed over the Minor Arcana plus eight remaining Major Arcana and the knowledge of how this works. It is also the understanding of the philosophical and scientific meaning of the hexagrams.

The Craft of Leadership is knowledge of the Holy Bible as manifested by the World Soul.

The Quran mentions the Torah, the Zabur ("Psalms") and the Injil ("Gospel") as being revealed by God to the prophets Moses, David and Jesus respectively in the same way the Quran was revealed to Muhammad, the final prophet and messenger of God according to Muslims. Leadership then is closeness to Jehova if Hebrew, Jesus if Christian and Allah if Muslim. However in the system of Tarot detailed here, Leadership is defined as the Holy Bible. It is numbered as twelve in terms of Crafts and its Tarot card is the World.

The Craft of Invention is Tarot card the Tower, number thirteen. Its earlier name is ars inveniendi and its focus is all that is made by man. Its warning is that in the face of nature represented by lightning the pinnacle of the crown of what is made can be destroyed and the Tower representing civilised evolution be sundered its people thrown to the ground. It's promise is that through Invention time may be reversed, lighting may be made to retract, antigravity can cause the people to fly upwards and the crown may be replaced. It is one of the later crafts in this system but is also one of the original creative influences in the sense that each initiate must invent for themselves a personal understanding of what 78T64I14C9S is.

Craftsmanship is the spirit, mind, body sciences of

India, China and Japan. It encompasses both yoga when understood in terms of Patanjali, and martial arts when understood in terms of Shaolin and Wu Tang. It is the fourteenth Craft in this system and its Tarot card is the Hanged Man. Its exemplars are the Chen and Yang schools of Tai Chi Chuan or the combined study of Judo, Aikido and Karate. Readily available Masters of Craftsmanship are people such as Funakoshi and Ueshiba.

CHAPTER TWO.

System: 78T64I14C9S.

78 Tarot cards, 64 I Ching, 14 Crafts, 9 Secrets.

Modern Esoteric School.

1. Fool, Alchemy, Psychology and Alchemy, Carl Jung.

2. Magus, Mastery, The Mindmap Book, Tony Buzan.

3. Hermit, Druidry, Meditations On the Tarot, Christian Hermeticism.

4. Emperor, Magick, A System of Logic, J.S. Mill.

5. Hierophant, Wizardry, Process and Reality, Alfred North Whitehead.

6. Chariot, Sorcery, The Red Book, Carl Jung.

7. Devil, Diplomacy, Ethics of Spinoza.

8. Empress, Entrepreneurship, Think and Grow Rich,Napoleon Hill.

9. Death, Ninjutsu, The Art of War, Sun Tsu.

10. Lovers, Enchantment, White Tigress Teachings.

11. Priestess, Scoutcraft, How To Solve It, G Polya.

12. Worldsoul, Leadership, Holy Bible.

13. Tower, Invention, Increasing Human Energy, Nicola Tesla.

14. Hanged Man, Craftsmanship, Tao of Jeet Kune Do, Bruce Lee.

The Transcendental Eternals.

1. Fool, Alchemy, Hermetic Arcanum, Works of Paracelsus.

2. Magus, Mastery, Upanishads, Bhagavad Gita.

3. Hermit, Druidry, Buddhist Scripture, Dhammapada.

4. Emperor, Magick, Occult Philosophy, Cornelius Agrippa.

5. Hierophant, Wizardry, Works of Aristotle.

6. Chariot, Sorcery, Works of Plato.

7. Devil, Diplomacy, Descartes to Kant.

8. Empress, Entrepreneurship, The I Ching.

9. Death, Ninjutsu, Tibetan Book of the Dead, Dalai Lama.

10. Lovers, Enchantment, Enneads by Plotinus.

11. Priestess, Scoutcraft, The Holy Koran.

12. Worldsoul, Leadership, Holy Bible.

13. Tower, Invention, Euclid, Works of Archimedes.

14. Hanged Man, Craftsmanship, Yellow Emperor Classic of Medicine, Neijing Suwen.

Suit of Wands.

Strength. 100100, Thunder over Thunder. Genesis and Exodus.

Ace. 100110, Lake over Thunder. Leviticus.

Two. 100111, Heaven over Thunder. Numbers.

Three. 100101, Fire over Thunder. Deuteronomy.

Four. 100011, Wind over Thunder. Joshua.

Five. 100001, Mountain over Thunder. Judges.

Six. 100000, Earth over Thunder. Ruth.

Seven. 100010, Water over Thunder. 1 Samuel.

Eight. 110110, Lake over Lake. 2 Samuel.

Nine. 110111, Heaven over Lake. 1 Kings.

Ten. 110101, Fire over Lake. 2 Kings.

Page. 110011, Wind over Lake. 1 Chronicles.

Knight. 110001, Mountain over Lake. 2 Chronicles.

Queen. 110000, Earth over Lake. Ezra.

King. 110010, Water over Lake. Nehemiah.

Fortune. 110100, Thunder over Lake. Esther.

Suit of Pentacles.

Sun. 111111, Heaven over Heaven. Job.

Ace. 111101, Fire over Heaven. Psalms.

Two. 111011, Wind over Heaven. Proverbs.

Three. 111001, Mountain over Heaven. Ecclesiastes.

Four. 111000, Earth over Heaven. Song of Songs.

Five. 111010, Water over Heaven. Isaiah.

Six. 111100, Thunder over Heaven. Jeremiah.

Seven. 111110, Lake over Heaven. Lamentations.

Eight. 101101, Fire over Fire. Ezekiel.

Nine. 101011, Wind over Fire. Daniel.

Ten. 101001, Mountain over Fire. Hosea.

Page. 101000, Earth over Fire. Joel.

Knight. 101010, Water over Fire. Amos.

Queen. 101100, Thunder over Fire. Obadiah.

King. 101110, Lake over Fire. Jonah.

Star. 101111, Heaven over Fire. Micah.

Suit of Swords.

Justice. 011011, Wind over Wind. Nahum.

Ace. 011001, Mountain over Wind. Habakkuk.

Two. 011000, Earth over Wind. Zephaniah.

Three. 011010, Water over Wind. Haggai.

Four. 011100, Thunder over Wind. Zechariah.

Five. 011110, Lake over Wind. Malachi.

Six. 011111, Heaven over Wind. Matthew.

Seven. 011101, Fire over Wind. Mark.

Eight. 001001, Mountain over Mountain. Luke.

Nine. 001000, Earth over Mountain. John.

Ten. 001010, Water over Mountain. Acts.

Page. 001100, Thunder over Mountain. Romans.

Knight. 001110, Lake over Mountain. 1 Corinthians.

Queen.. 001111, Heaven over Mountain. 2 Corinthians.

King. 001101, Fire over Mountain. Galatians.

Judgement. 001011, Wind over Mountain. Ephesians.

Suit of Cups.

Temperance. 000000, Earth over Earth. Philippians.

Ace. 000010, Water over Earth. Colossians.

Two. 000100, Thunder over Earth. 1 Thessalonians.

Three. 000110, Lake over Earth. 2 Thessalonians.

Four. 000111, Heaven over Earth. 1 Timothy.

Five. 000101, Fire over Earth. 2 Timothy.

Six. 000011, Wind over Earth. Titus.

Seven. 000001, Mountain over Earth. Philemon.

Eight. 010010, Water over Water. Hebrews.

Nine. 010100, Thunder over Water. James.

Ten. 010110, Lake over Water. 1 Peter.

Page. 010111, Heaven over Water. 2 Peter.

Knight. 010101, Fire over Water. 1 John.

Queen. 010011, Wind over Water. 2 John.

King. 010001, Mountain over Water. 3 John.

Moon. 010000, Earth over Water. Jude Revelations.

This gives the fourteen crafts of tarot.

They are numbered one to fourteen which corresponds to the same numbering in the minor arcana.

The numbering is arcane and for example one the Fool is aligned with ten the Lovers in the way that ten is one plus zero which equals one, so the Fool and the Lovers go together.

Each craft is associated to one of the fourteen major arcana mentioned.

So it begins with one, The Fool, the craft of Alchemy,

then two, the Magus, the craft of Mastery

then three, the Hermit, the craft of Druidry.

The idea is that the number, the tarot card and the craft each hang together by occult reasoning.

So the Hermit is associated to the number three, like in the Trinity, and the Hermit is to do with mysticism which is labelled in this system as Druidry.

The number four is foursquare, and associated to Magick, the secret craft of which the Emperor is Master. It is the advanced science that begins with Mastery, the Magus, number two, in the same way that two and four are consequential.

The number five, like a pentagram, is associated to Wizardry, the Hierophant and is abstract and Empirical Science as compared to six, Sorcery, the Chariot which is focused on noumena and phenomena, perhaps like neuro-linguistic programming.

In this way each number, tarot image and craft hang together on their own and simultaneously correlate in meaningful ways with each of the other crafts.

The association of a single book to each of the crafts is speculative. Ideally the choice of books is flexible and discretionary where each player would choose their own selection of what books are collected, in such a way that each of the books dovetails with each of the others.

My choice of books presented here is provisional and towards a winning system of esoteric classics to make sure each craft has an adequate reference work.

It means that each player would have a private and secret set of information as to craft.

On completion the idea is as stated where there is a correlation between number, tarot card, craft and reference book.

Three things are found to coincide, The Holy Bible, The hexagrams of the Book of Changes known as the I Ching and sixty four Tarot cards.

To establish the correctness of the schematic it is necessary to associate each thing with each of the others individually, so the Bible with the I Ching and the Bible with the Tarot Cards, and the I Ching with Tarot Cards. Before we do that it is helpful to prove the order of each of the things separately. So the Bible is seen to be in its normal sequential order of books and the only device that is used is to make it 64 books rather than 66 books. And the way this is done is to place the first two books together, that is Genesis and Exodus, and the last two books together, that is Jude and Revelations.

Then if we look at the I Ching separately to see if its order makes sense on its own, we find that the device that is applied is a simple code. It is suggested that the code sequence thunder, lake, heaven, fire, wind, mountain, earth, water is followed throughout. So first of all the lower trigrams are in that sequence which we see is reference to eight books each.

So lower trigram thunder refers to books Genesis and Exodus through to 1 Samuel and the tarot cards zero through to seven wands being eight cards, the Thunder Books.

Lower trigram lake refers to books 2 Samuel through to Esther and the tarot cards eight through to infinity wands being eight cards, the Lake Books.

Lower trigram heaven refers to books Job through to Lamentations and the tarot cards zero through to seven pentacles, the Heaven Books.

Lower trigram fire refers to books Ezekiel through to Micah and the tarot cards eight through to infinity pentacles, the Fire Books.

Lower trigram wind refers to books Nahum through to Mark and the tarot cards zero through to seven swords, the Wind Books.

Lower trigram mountain refers to books Luke through to Ephesians and the tarot cards eight through to infinity swords, the Mountain Books.

Lower trigram earth refers to books Philippians through to Philemon and the tarot cards zero through to seven cups, the Earth Books.

Lower trigram water refers to books Hebrews through to Jude and Revelations and the tarot cards eight through to infinity cups, the Water Books.

From this is can be seen that the sequence thunder, lake, heaven, fire, wind, mountain, earth, water is followed throughout the lower trigrams.

If we then look at the upper trigram we find that in each case the same sequence is followed beginning with a doubled trigram in each case and then the natural sequence thereafter.

So for example taking the thunder books, we find zero

wands strength is lower trigram thunder and upper trigram thunder, that is thunder doubled. And then the next trigram in sequence must be lake, which it is in reference to ace wands, lake over thunder. And the next in sequence must be heaven, which it is in reference to two wands, heaven over thunder.

Or if we start with the lake books, we find eight wands is lower trigram lake and upper trigram lake, that is lake doubled. And then the next trigram in sequence must be heaven, which it is in reference to nine wands, heaven over lake.

And the next in sequence must be fire which it is in reference to ten wands, fire over lake.

Given it is observed that the zero tarot card and the eight tarot card are in each suit representative of a trigram doubled then it can be noticed that the same sequence of thunder, lake, heaven, fire, wind, mountain, earth, water is obtained throughout all the upper trigrams.

That being the case it is clear that the Book of Changes individually follows a rational sequence throughout in the schematic as given.

We can further show that the sequence selected is not arbitrary and is necessitated by the nature of the trigrams in this way.

Thunder = 100

Lake = 110

Heaven = 111

This can be understood as one increasing from the bottom where the left hand side digit is first and bottom and the right hand digit is last and top.

Wind = 011

Mountain = 001

Earth = 000

This can be understood as zero increasing from the bottom where the left hand side digit is first and bottom and the right hand digit is last and top.

Fire = 101

Water = 010

This can be understood as completion of each sequence where fire completes the thunder lake heaven sequence and water completes the wind mountain earth sequence.

This further goes to prove that the sequence as given is not arbitrary and is in fact a necessary consequence of the trigrams as given.

If we look at tarot cards separately we find that a reasoned line is followed to establish them in the order as given.

Two sequences are established. The first is the order that the suits follow, which is wands, pentacles, swords, cups. The second is the order that the cards in the suits follow, which is the numbers one through ten, then 11 Page, 12 Knight, 13 Queen, 14 King.

The order of the suits is according to this schematic:

Spring = Wands

Summer = Pentacles

Autumn = Swords

Winter = Cups.

For this reason we lay the suits out in a matrix of four rows and fourteen columns and this accounts for all the minor arcana.

When so layed out fifty six cards are placed with the suit of wands above the suit of pentacles above the suit of swords above the suit of cups. And each of the suits following the sequence one to fourteen.

When so layed out we are forced to lay out the major arcana of twenty two cards with four in a column before the suits, four in a column at the end of the suits which accounts for eight cards and fourteen remain which must be placed in a row above the suit of wands.

That accounts for all seventy eight tarot cards in a rational matrix or grid.

Strength is layed out opposite the Wheel of Fortune, the first at the beginning of the suit of wands and the latter at the end of the suit of wands.

Sun is layed out opposite Star, one at the beginning and the other at the end of the suit of pentacles.

Justice is layed out opposite Judgement at the beginning and end of suit of swords.

And Temperance is opposite Moon at the beginning and end of suit of cups.

That just leaves fourteen major arcana remaining which are layed out in a row according to the numbering given for the crafts in the schematic provided earlier.

We have here demonstrated that each of the things, Bible, Tarot Cards and I Ching are in a sequence individually that makes sense when taken on their own without reference to each of the other things.

It here remains to show that the sequence obtained also makes sense when each of the things is layed out over each of the others. By this I mean that the three sequences coincide in a meaningful way that makes sense to the whole.

To do this it is easiest to notice particular coincidences that are forced by the patterns as given because some of them are so startling.

The suit of pentacles offers several examples of this sort.

So for example The Sun, Heaven over Heaven, Book of Job

reveals a coincidence of meaning between all three things in a way that is immediately pleasing.

This is immediately followed by Ace of Pentacles which often looks like a sun in the sky being Fire over Heaven and the Book of Psalms.

If we consider the Four of Pentacles, Song of Songs, Earth over Heaven, the coincidence of meaning between the hexagram and the Bible is quite astounding.

We could compare it to the Book of Hebrews being Water over Water and the meaningful coincidence between the things seems to be quite beyond what chance would offer.

Or The Star being Heaven over Fire is a very exact match of meaning.

Alternatively we could look at the lower trigrams in particular. Here it is very meaningful that the majority of the Pauline Gospel is accounted for by the trigrams earth and water being the entirety of the suit of cups. And for the Suit of Cups itself to be characterised by earth and water is symbolically directly coincidental. Or Heaven and Fire for the Suit of Pentacles.

What remains to be proved and is left to the reader to work out for themselves is how a better understanding of the standard meaning of the hexagrams lends itself to an extremely pleasing occult meaning of its associated tarot card. And how this meaning is non-contradictory and conformable with the Books of the Bible in their standard order.

Nothing entered by one thing is two things, called nothing and one thing, in relationship is three things, nothing, one and the relationship between them. From three things come all the ten thousand things.

Three things disappear into one thing and seem to be the central axel known as earth.

And from an anonymous source:

Around the earth four elements appear images of the four seasons. These are the five. And they are made from four elements circling the earth at the centre. We obtain eight from five because one of the five disappears and the remaining four double to give eight. And so after this manner, the elements according to two contrary qualities are contradictory to one another, as fire to water and earth to air. We name the eight virtues as thunder, lake, heaven, fire, wind, mountain, earth, water. These eight combined with each of themselves once gives sixty four combinations. These sixty four combinations are a product of selectively sorting one or zero on six layers to obtain sixty four hexagrams. They divide into thirty two exact opposites known as the Thirty Two Paths of Wisdom. These describe how any one hexagram changes into its exact opposite and can therefore be demonstrated in two directions.

When we consider aether, a name formed by manipulation of the letters of the name earth, this is the quintessence, or the fifth element, at the centre of the axel, around which the four prime elements move. We find aether to be a compound involving the elemental forces one or zero or not one or not zero, which is four apparent possibles generated from is and is not and one or zero. One is unity, zero is emptiness, the relationship of one and zero is called change.

Originally conceived by and according to the school of Yang Lu-ch'an,1799–1872, born in Kuang-p'ing, and his grandson Yang Ch'eng-fu, 1883–1936:

The Chinese explain it very easily and simply. They say Tai Chi is the Supreme Ultimate, sourced from Wu Chi, the Formless Void, and the mother of Yin and Yang. Through motion the Tai Chi separates into Yin and Yang, in stillness they fuse and return to Tai Chi. In their variations yang and yin make eight forces called Peng, Lu, Chi, An, Tsai,

Kao, Lieh, Chou. Peng is like water supporting a moving boat, and is the body filled with a spring like energy. It can be very quick. Lu is the attraction power of emptiness, the space of nothing that compels towards itself. Chi energy is elastic like the rebound of a ball bouncing off a wall. An energy is like flowing water, and the capacity of water to fill up any hollows. Tsai energy is that of a lever, pushing and pulling rotation round an axel. Kao energy is explosive like pounding a pestle, the sharp energy. Lieh revolves like a spinning disc, or like a whirlpool in a pond. Chou is to clearly distinguish empty and soft from full and hard, so that what is insubstantial and substantial are clarified.

Anonymous:

A name must refer to only one thing in any one system and must not refer to two different things in one system.

A name may often refer to two different things in two different systems and the name from one system must not be used to mean a thing from a different system.

According to the principle of these rules we notice the difference between earth of the five elements and earth of the eight virtues, and that the meaning of earth may be different when the name is used in different systems. Furthermore the necessity to distinguish between the abstract level of the four elements and the abstract level of the eight virtues.

For this reason, we name the four original elements as wood, fire, metal, water with earth at the centre. This is satisfied in tarot as the suits wands, pentacles, swords cups. So through our four suits the abstract level of wood/wands, fire/pentacles, metal/swords, water/cups is manifest as a structurally confirmed idea. Each of these suits can be demonstrated to include sixteen cards, which divide into eight cards twice in each suit. Each group of eight cards accounts for eight unique hexagrams, where the primary trigram is the same for the eight hexagrams in any one group.

And so after this manner the elements according to two contrary qualities are contrary to one another, as fire to water and earth to air. Now if we apply our understanding to this idea then we can call the earth element by the name label wood, and we can call the air element by the name label of metal. We then obtain our basic code which is earth at the centre signed by the Tai Chi symbol so that the duality of its nature in unity is clarified. The four seasons are the pattern placed over time. The four compass directions are the pattern placed over space. Both patterns naturally occur in place in our model and all variations of the model maintain the pattern established by the four seasons and four compass directions.

If you draw a vertical line bisected by a horizontal line, you can designate it as up, down, right, left, as you look at it.

Up is fire, south, summer, hot and dry, the suit of pentacles and contains the two virtues heaven and fire.

Down is water, north, winter, cold and wet, the suit of cups and contains the two virtues earth and water.

Left is wood, east, spring, hot and wet, the suit of wands and contains the two virtues thunder and lake.

Right is metal, west, autumn, cold and dry, the suit of swords and contains the two virtues wind and mountain.

The wood element obtains its moistness from water and winter, its hotness from fire and summer.

The metal element obtains its dryness from fire and summer, its coldness from water and winter.

Anonymous:

When you consider the possible number states one or zero, you notice that in the same place or location you can have either a one or a zero. And the place must exist before the one or zero as a potential for their existence. Yet we do not find the place on its own without the content, one or zero. So we can assert the kind of situation where an invisible and difficult to define subtle object must exist for some other thing that is more visible to exist. And since the more visible object does exist we can assume the existence of that on which it must depend. The elements must exist in some thing, which for the purposes of sign label we may call the cauldron.

And from the school of Yang Luchan and Yang Chengfu:

The cauldron is like a cooking pot. Water over fire and the flames are extinguished. Place a cauldron between the fire and water and steam is generated. This is the artifice of alchemy. Now if the elements are inside something, a thing that is more subtle and less visible than the elements, then we may suppose the earth describes the mixed state of all the elements together, until the thing they exist in started to move in a circular way called spinning. As it began to spin the elements were differentiated according to their natures being up, down, left or right.

From the combinations of up, down, left, right and plus, minus, one, zero, and hard, soft, fast, slow and hot, cold, damp, dry we obtain characteristics that we associate to each of the four cardinal compass directions with South at the top.

Anonymous:

Having our four cardinal positions each can be said to divide according to potential and fulfillment.

Wood potential is all the hexagram that have thunder as a base trigram. Designated 100.

Wood fulfilled is all the hexagram that have lake as a base trigram. Designated 110.

Fire potential is all the hexagram that have heaven as a base trigram. Designated 111.

Fire fulfilled is all the hexagram that have fire as a base trigram. Designated 101.

Air potential is all the hexagram that have wind as a base trigram. Designated 011.

Air fulfilled is all the hexagram that have mountain as a base trigram. Designated 001.

Water potential is all the hexagram that have earth as a base trigram. Designated 000.

Water fulfilled is all the hexagram that have water as a base trigram. Designated 010.

It is important to differentiate the characteristics of each of the virtues one from the other so that the unique nature of each is established. We call both thunder and lake hexagrams together by the name of the wood element, both heaven and fire together by the name of the fire element, both wind and mountain together by the name of metal element, both earth and water together by the name of the water element.

So at our first order we have four elements, and eight virtues at our second order, the third order being when each of the eight virtues combine with each of the others and themselves once.

From the sixty four situations produced when each of the eight virtues is combined with each of the others and themselves once, in the manner of eight multiplied by itself, so the elements work themselves out. Very few are they who understand the deep mysteries explained in simple and easy terms here. In this knowledge and through the elements proceeds the binding and loosening, the transmutation, the knowing and foretelling of things, the driving away of all evil, and the gaining of good spirits.

Let none therefore who is not familiar with these three levels or order of the elements, which do follow the sequence that is two, four, eight, sixty four, be confident that he is able to work any thing in the occult sciences of magick.

But whosoever shall know how to reduce those of one order into those of another, impure into pure, compounded into simple, and shall know how to distinguish each of the meanings in accord with the order that is being worked, then that adept will understand the nature, virtue, power, of the elements as number, degrees and order, and without dividing the substance, he shall easily obtain to the secret and most divine knowledge and perfect operation of all natural things and also celestial secrets of diverse sort.

Anonymous:

The number two raised to the sixth power is therefore our first number. $2 \times 2 \times 2 \times 2 \times 2 \times 2 = 64$.

Two raised to the sixth power is saying that you can imagine having six places stacked one above the other. And each place can be one of only two contradictory possibles, one or zero, male or female, on or off, yang or yin, active or passive.

So the two in the number two power six means that only two possibilities exist. And the six in the same number means those two possibilities exist in each of six places, such that whatever the truth of which state any one place is in, it can change to its opposite state and everything else remain the same, which is true of each of the six positions individually. The change of state then is from one to zero or from zero to one. This is called a moving line and happens when one of the places in a hexagram is fully accomplished or exhausted. When the energy of a position is exhausted then the point of weakness is the first to move. The result being that an active becomes passive or a passive becomes active. You can designate a changing line by placing a cross over the sign whether it is a one or zero. A one with a cross means changing to zero. A zero with a cross means changing to one. From here it is clear that any one of the hexagrams can change into any one of the others by manipulation of changing lines.

If we take three coins of the sort that are identical and all have a head on one side and the other side we call tails.

To ask a question is to deliberately direct the attention towards a focal matter.

To throw coins is a random device that must generate a specific, determined, locally defined cause identified by the date the question is asked. It means that the method of random selection does not generate a random answer, but the only answer that is early and beforehand associated to the time of throwing the coins which mechanically can not be dissociated from the purpose to which they are applied.

Everything is built in, including the answer received to the divinatory method. It is assumed that coincidence is the fact of the matter. So the fact that at the particular time, in that place, where the question is clearly articulated and the method is followed exactly, then the hexagram generated is not arbitrary but the only response obtained in that instance. Having generated an answer to the question it is a matter of theory and practice in reference to skill of interpretation.

Therefore, if we say heads are equal to three and tails are equal to two and we throw three coins in one go, we will receive one of four possible outcomes, three heads is nine, three tails is six, two heads and one tail is eight or two tails one head is seven. Using this method we say six is yin moving to yang and show it as a zero with a cross, nine is yang moving to yin and show it as a one with a cross, seven is yang fixed shown as a one, eight is yin fixed shown as a zero.

In this way we can generate any one of the sixty four hexagrams with changing lines.

Formulate the question and write it down.

Get three coins.

Build the hexagram one line at time, from the bottom to the

top.

Line one of the hexagram is at the bottom while line six is at the top.

Each line is determined as follows:

Throw all three coins at once. Add up the numerical value of the three coins based on whether they came up heads or tails, to obtain 6,7,8 or 9 as follows:

The "head"side will be the Yang and have a value of 3.

The "tail" side will be the Yin and have a value of 2.

Write down the result. This is line one (the bottom-most) line of the hexagram.

Repeat throwing the coins five more times and each time write the result above the previous one. At the end you should have a column of six digits, each ranging in value from 6 to 9.

Convert each digit to a hexagram line, as follows:

A sum of 7 is a stationary Yang line, represented by the unbroken line.

A sum of 8 is stationary Yin line, represented by the broken line.

A sum of 6 is a moving Yin line, represented by the broken line with an X in the middle.

A sum of 9 is a moving Yang line, represented by the unbroken line with an X in the middle.

Obtain the primary hexagram. Ignore the differences between the stationary and moving lines to obtain your main hexagram. Go to that hexagram in the book by scanning first the lower trigrams then the upper trigrams to find your answer. Read the sections titled The Image, The Judgment, as well as those sections corresponding to the moving lines. If there are no moving lines, simply skip the

Lines section altogether.

Obtain the secondary hexagram. If there are moving lines from throwing your coins, convert each moving line to its opposite. So a moving Yang line becomes a Yin line while a moving Yin line becomes a Yang line. The resulting hexagram is your secondary hexagram and represents the ending situation while the primary hexagram represents the current situation.

Originally conceived by and according to the ideas of Ludwig Josef Johann Wittgenstein, 26 April 1889 – 29 April 1951, in his Tractatus Logico-Philosophicus written in 1918:

The world is all that is true and real. The world is the totality of facts, not of things. The world is determined by the facts, and by their being all the facts. The facts in logical space are the world.

The world divides into facts, and each item can be true or false, while everything else remains the same.

What is the case, a fact, is the existence of a state of affairs, a situation.

A state of affairs is a combination of objects.

It is essential to things that they be possible constituents of states of affairs.

Each thing is as it were, in a space of possible states of affairs.

Anonymous:

Take a card from any one of the minor arcana. Say eight pentacles, fire over fire, mid summer. This space is logically determined. I can imagine the space empty, but I can not imagine the thing without the space. For this reason we can imagine seventy eight tarot cards empty. Then we have space for the thing. With seventy eight cards empty of things, the most natural shape they fall in to is four times sixteen and one times fourteen.

And from Ludwig Wittgenstein:

A spatial object must be situated in infinite space. Objects contain the possibility of all situations in which they can exist.

An imagined world, however different it may be from the real one by virtue of the perfection of its order, must have something, a form or structural reflectivity, in common with it. Objects are just what constitutes this unalterable form. The configuration of objects produces states of affairs. In a state of affairs, objects fit into one another like links in a chain. The determinate way in which objects are connected in a state of affairs is called the structure. Form is the possibility of structure. The existence and nonexistence of states of affairs is reality.

Logical pictures can depict the world. A picture has logico-pictorial form in common with what it depicts. A picture depicts reality by representing a possibility of existence and nonexistence of states of affairs. A picture contains the possibility of the situation it represents. What a picture represents, it represents independently of its truth or falsity, by means of its pictorial form. What a picture represents is its sense. The agreement or disagreement of its sense with reality constitutes its truth or falsity. In order to tell whether a picture is true or false we must compare it with reality. It is impossible to tell from a picture alone whether it is true, although you may be able to determine it is false.

A logical picture of facts is a thought. A state of affairs is thinkable. What this means is we can picture it to ourselves. The totality of true thoughts is a picture of the world. A thought contains the possibility of the situation of which it is the thought.

In a proposition, a thought can be expressed in such a way that the elements of the propositional sign correspond to the objects of the thought.

The simple signs employed in propositions are called names. Definitions are rules for translating into one language from another. Any correct sign language must be translatable into any other for which we have rules.

It seems possible to give the most general propositional form. That is, to give a description of the propositions of any sign language in such a way that every possible sense can be expressed by a symbol satisfying the description, and every symbol satisfying the description can express a sense, providing that the meanings of the names are correctly chosen.

The essence of language consists in the employment of fixed associations in order that something now sensible and object which can be a spoken word, picture, gesture, written symbol, may call up the idea of something else.

CHAPTER THREE.

The structural logic of playing cards is interesting. If we say clubs equals spring, diamonds equals summer, spades equals autumn and hearts equals winter. It is only because clubs are made of wood which is an organic thing like springtime. And diamonds are bright like fire or sunshine in summer. And spades are made of metal which is the opposite of wood so must be autumn, and that just leaves hearts which are cold like water and winter. Then since there are fifty two cards in a deck of cards that makes one card for each week of the year because there are just by coincidence fifty two weeks in a year. So that makes each suit one season of the year and each suit contains thirteen cards and each season contains thirteen weeks. For those people who may want to investigate the logic of the eight gates referred to in the sixty four changes, one way the logic of the structure of playing cards is equivalent to the seasonal system of the eight gates is as follows. If spring is wood and clubs then that is thunder and lake. If summer is fire and diamonds then that is heaven and fire. If autumn is metal and spades, then that is wind and mountain. If winter is water and hearts, then that is earth and water. And thunder/lake spring are opposite wind/mountain autumn, and heaven/fire summer are opposite earth/water winter.

Since the above touches on the matter of games, it would seem reasonable at this point to mention why I would not provide further details on this subject at the present. And the reasoning is simple. That at the present point there are various explicit, implicit, legitimate and illegitimate, suggested or enforced, stated or not stated conditions applied to any discourse on the matter. Such that any discourse on the matter either conforms to a deep knowledge of the matter or it doesn't. If it does conform to a deep knowledge of the matter then there is a duty of care to any particular involved players. And if it does not conform to a deep knowledge of the matter then whilst it would not concern the involved players neither would it be of any interest.

Again, since games are a significant area of human endeavour that rarely receive the informed attention that they deserve, neither is it appropriate to fall short for fear of talking about some area that a different player wants kept confused. I think what most often happens in this circumstance is that any person who chooses to reveal some area of interest that they do know something about, they will provide good information in regard to some bounded domain and say nothing at all about any other area. That is useful, given different authorities provide similar knowledge into their own fields, however we are still left with the problem of missing connections between the games that no one seems to notice, blanks in terms of generalised skills relevant to different families of games, and a lack of abstract comprehension of the nature of games as they relate to human behaviour and knowledge.

There are other difficulties. That is, given what I have just said, it notifies us as to the enormity of any task associated to tackling this area. And as well the fact that repeating what has already been well stated by other parties need not be further detailed, since their ideas can be referred to by school as required, enabling the interested enquirer to go directly to any particular school of thought.

And then the matter that quite seriously good information is permanently under the double bind that because it is good information it should not be revealed and if it can be revealed it is not seriously good information. That is further re-inforced in this context by the possibility of revealing information, but only that which we know already.

It is like the "as long as" condition applied to Socrates by his various opponents. They apply the condition that he can answer the question "as long as he does not use any of the elements necessary to provide a sufficient answer". Which leads to Socrates doing one of two things. He either decides to provide a lesser answer which is still in itself interesting, while notifying his audience that the better answer which he does have involves knowledge forbidden by his questioners. Or alternatively he directs himself to demonstrating why the necessary elements required to provide a sufficient answer cannot be forbidden.

Or it is the same as the bind applied to zen monks. They are asked: "Do you know zen?"

And they cannot say "yes, I know zen" because by definition apparently any who say they know zen don't know zen. But they cannot say "No, I don't know zen" because that would be to miss the point and may suggest they really don't know zen. But then that is the nature of zen that it requires a spontaneous answer in the spacetime event that is immanent and evident which must prove by its spontaneity an eternal knowledge. Or it would not be zen.

The point I am making is that the nature of the environment may necessitate that any answer to the question of games is provided in terms of minimax optimised critical paths towards a statistical evaluation of probable outcomes in game theory. And people like Ender Wiggin, Donal Graeme and Jurnau Gurgeh can not be held up as fictional models for that kind of knowledge, and neither can it be suggested that they are ignorant of what that knowledge happens to be.

As an example I will mention a few game ideas that do not meet conventional knowledge.

For example: Once is happenstance. Twice is coincidence. Three times is great game.

First move is stealthy. Second move is sinister. Third move is a cover up.

The only commandment is: "Thou shalt not get caught".

The only crime is: "Getting caught".

The only plea is: "Not ignorant".

The only penalty is: "Game death".

Life is a zero sum game. It meets the conditions of the laws of thermodynamics. You cannot win, you cannot break even, you cannot get out of the game.

Changing the subject:

Viser versa, topsy turvy, upside down and inside out, back to front, front to back, roundabout, between the lines and zig zags, see saw, higgledy piggledy, mish-mash, gobbledy gook, counter-intuitive, contra-indicated, anti-clockwise, more or less, now and then, this and that, through and through,

Game theory is not game theory. Game theory is an element of the set called theory of games.

Game theory is at this date a finished product that advocates its own redundancy. Game theory provides a specific information that necessitates any game is played according to conditions that make no sense to the purpose of the games to which it is applied. Therefore game theory is of no use.

The above line is one possible attitude to take towards game theory and the theory itself cannot defend itself against the above line. However, the above line is wrong. It is a line that is often taken by any who have believed in some matter that they then promote in their minds to a level beyond its status, and then when they find it fails them in some way they just as quickly deny its value as they bought its ideas originally.

Then where does game theory fit in to place? Until I state

otherwhise, game theory is taken to mean a specific product of mathematicians that is applied to games and is different to the theory of games. Game theory is well stated, well defined and basically thorough to the restricted limits of its own protocols. It is valued by people who study the theory of games as well as by those who play games. However it is not necessary to understand game theory in order to play games.

It would then be natural to ask. Can people who play games win at an advanced level without knowing game theory? And the nervous line is that people may not want to have to know game theory in order to win at games.

The hard answer is that people who play games according to game theory will not win at an advanced level. Which does not answer the question directly.

To attend to the important matters in this area involves many small points that do not immediately evidence connections between themselves so it is not easy to exactly explain what is worth our attention.

Game theory can easily be mastered by mathematicians who do not play games. And people who play games may often only have a vague idea as to what game theory is about. But at a certain point any who plays games at an advanced level will have mastered game theory at some stage in the past. In that way game theory is not the same as a theory of games and it is simply one of the understandings that a game player will have in their repertoire of tools that they use in order to play games well.

Neumann, Morgenstern and Nash are the inventors of the foundation of all modern game theory and not of a theory of games. So we can suppose that game theory is only referring to the school of the three named mathematicians and as well to a large quantity of social dynamic and business economic argumentation that is derived from their original ideas. As such, the argumentation often no longer refers to games but instead applies game theory to any area of human endeavour to which it may seem suitable. As if to say that any area of human activity can be considered as a game and therefore is susceptible to the conditions detailed in game theory. It means that there is a sort of fallacious reasoning built in that no person would really want to have to argue with, partly because it does not matter. And if people who have no intention to master game theory enjoy writing books about how it applies to social dynamics then that is their own business. And if people who have mastered game theory enjoy demonstrating mathematical proofs that rarely meet the attention of people who play games then that is the nature of intellect in academic surroundings.

We now have to make the distinction between three different things. The first is a theory of games. The second is game theory. And the third is pseudo-game theory. Pseudo-game theory is any and all accurate and inaccurate applications of game theory to any and all areas of human endeavour not specifically and only a game and will not receive any attention in this discourse.

Game theory is a very small argumentation originally designed by Neumann, Morgenstern and Nash and developed by various mathematicians over the last fifty years. As such it is the focus of attention in this discourse. Theory of games is a matter that is best directed towards excellence in chess, backgammon, mah jongg, poker, wei chi, dominoes and dice and is a significant area that is rarely given the attention it deserves, including now.

In the terms of this discourse the model designed by Neumann Morgenstern and Nash known as "Game Theory" has been provided in five specific points. The five points as given will be known as the "Game Domain Model". The reason for this is two. One is because the theories of Neumann Morgenstern and Nash are specific to themselves so this is to differentiate from their own work whilst notifying that the game domain model is only in reference to their work. Two is because the theory of games may include the game domain model and that the game domain model is not taken as the larger matter.

1. The Game Domain Model proposes four factors in the games to which it refers and suggests those factors determine the evidential nature of the games. Which can be applied to areas not directly defined by those factors in such a way that the correct outcome is adjusted in the favour of the person who does so.

2. The four factors are agent, rules, strategy and payoff. And the four factors lead to the suggestion that specific designs are demanded by any who are in the context to which they apply. The designs are utility, economics, probability and equilibrium. And they are modified by whether the context involves perfect information or imperfect information.

3. Agent is the idea games involve players who design strategy from an individual perspective and that the strategy they design is modified by the play of other agents. Meaning that the evidential strategy of any game is dependent on the interactive play of the different agents.

Rules is the idea that any game is preconstructed such that moves made by agents are restricted to what is possible and appropriate in accord with the preconstruction.

Strategy is the idea that each agent plays their moves with a view to perfect action designed to realise the maximum possible payoff.

Payoff is the idea that perfect play will result in a specific outcome and nothing else.

4. Utility is the idea that all evidential action should demonstrate a maximal value against some quantifiable purpose.

Economics is the idea that the better strategy will obtain a given result with most efficient use of available energy and for any expense of energy will obtain more of the desired result than any other possible strategy.

Probability is the idea that in a game of chance the mathematically correct move will be the one that optimises the advantage obtained by the most probable outcome.

Equilibrium is the idea that all players could play perfectly and if they do so then it would not be appropriate to deviate from what is the correct move in any particular context.

5. Perfect information games are ones where all the agents can all have all the information that is relevant to strategy. Noughts and crosses or drafts or chess are all perfect information games.

Imperfect information games are ones where any one agent only has a limited amount of information of all the information that is known by all the players and where each agent has different information from any other agent. Poker or dominoes or mah jongg are all imperfect information games.

The following discourse is given in square brackets and is designed with a sense of being a sequence of moves in a particular "universe of discourse" and in accord with knowledge of the "game domain model". The moves are listed A, B, C, D, and with a small note as to the idea behind the move in each case. The entire sequence of moves is only the moves ABCD and that entire sequence is to be taken as use of a tactic. Simply for the purpose of clarity it is useful to make quite plain what is the difference between strategy and tactic since it is an area that people may not always be sure of. Very simply, strategy is conceptual and tactics are behavioural. By which I mean, strategy is a larger plan that exists in conceptual terms designed in order to realise some specified objective or purpose. The use of tactics are those behaviours that occur in the immediate time bound event which serve to realise in the moment the actualisation of strategy. So to restate differently, strategy is mental-thought and tactics are physical-behaviour.

[A. This is the first move in the immediate universe of discourse. It counters equilibrium by the tactical use of mistake. And it double binds because it provides an apparent revealing of some sort of mistake. It uses a confusional technique because it refers to a fictional character designed by Roger Zelazny known to be of magickal nature neither scientific nor fantasy, thus blurring the distinction between fact and fiction, myth and reality.

Hello world.

I have made a mistake already and this is only my first move so I am in double jeopardy, bound to be hazard, damage, and much frenzy.

I must immediately own up to the fraudulent use of someone else's code name because I didn't think it would work and the Lord of Shadows, Knight of the Twilight Realms and Black Jack of Diamonds could find out about it if I'm not careful.

Can I get thrown out because that might save us all some trouble, pickle and fiddlesticks.

Well when the real Shadowjack turns up may be we could just explain it was an honest mistake and someone of great ethical integrity has somehow got mixed up with the wrong people.

So anyway it is a long way round of saying that I am not really Shadowjack, and if it hadn't worked it wouldn't have mattered but since it worked I am now stuck with someone else's codename.

Nevertheless, walking the mythic paths of deepest mystery is not unknown to the person mistakenly using the codename Shadowjack in this unfortunate misunderstanding.

I remember when Aristotle first turned up in Athens at

seventeen after the Oracle had told him to investigate some of the new ideas people were having around that area. No one realised at the time how this would change the Pythagorean influence on local politics.

B. This is the second move in the sequence. It counters the natural course of the first move without removing the advantage obtained by the depth of the first move. It enables reference to a particular game domain and some of the key players in it without necessitating that they be directly involved. And it pre-emptively describes some of the difficulties of the conditions that would necessarily exist in the universe of discourse.

This is a new note. The previous dialogue is completed. The dialogue to follow is not related to the previous one. As the father of modern invention, Leonardo Da Vinci is the parent of the father of modern science, Galileo, who in turn is the parent of the father of modern philosophy Descartes. It is obvious to every person who can count to three that Leonardo, Galileo and Descartes must be studied together since it would be quite impossible to understand any one of them properly without reference to the other two. That is because all three of the named people are on one side in a conflict and are the three together opposed to some people. That is not to say that Leonardo, Galileo and Descartes are without error since that would be to misunderstand the problem. The problem would be to say any thing at all without having studied all three of them. Descartes asks if it is possible that God could be a deceiver. Of course God can be a deceiver in the same way that a parent deceives their children as to the real nature of the world. Since any parent who told the truth to their children as to what in fact the world is would be considered strange. Galileo misrepresents Aristotle and provides misleading examples of what Aristotle said in a way that does no justice to the truth. Although only a person who has studied Aristotle could do so. And Leonardo invents the investigation of light as its own matter, considering perception to be a relative condition, which he writes about in notes that offer little explanation of his art.

Are Leonardo, Galileo and Descartes considered the best known of writers? By that I mean is it the case that every well read person will say that they have read all of the published works of those people? And have all of their works been properly compiled without error and without the noise of noted references that only serve to misdirect from the primary source? And have they been translated into modern Italian, French, English, Spanish, German so that even less well read intelligent people can scan a paperpack? And if not does it matter?

So the "why" question is raised. Surely in the time of Leonardo da Vinci one hundred years before the writing of Galileo and Descartes the same reason existed. The conflict in this regard is valuable to study in its own right. I do so not to answer the question but to understand the problem. You have to consider the unknown.

There is a point of conflict that involves different correct organisations at the boundary where they touch. One thing is to name some of those organisations. I shall name several. The Roman Catholic church, the church of England, The Christian Rosenkreutz society, the Coal Burners, Carbonari and Allumbrado, the Hebrew Jewish community, the accademia schoolmen, the Charlemaine Roland order, the Islam Muslim community.

Since I contend that there is a point of conflict at the time of Leonardo da Vinci involving every one of the organisations named, it is interesting that the consensus would seem to be that none of them really exist as an actual entity in the modern world. Or better stated that they are somehow each one wrong in some way when it comes to what matters in the world of today.

What is my point, might be the question. And the answer would be, just kidding with you. Do you want to play?

C. This is the third move in the sequence. It did not occur in order as given and was brought in later as a natural evolution of the idea suggested by move two. It refers to characters designed by Orson Scott Card, Gordon R Dickson and Iain M Banks. And it refers to the specific characters because the imaginative universes they exist within are a useful device in order to make available some of the ideas related to a theory of games.

Gameplayers such as Ender Wiggin, Donal Graeme and Jurnau Gurgeh in each case demonstrate a similar identity at different stages of life. Ender aged fifteen, Donal aged twenty five, Jurnau aged thirty five. The game is broadly the same in each case although the understanding of it is expanded in each story. The game would seem to be as old as civilisation and its tools are evident at every point in civilised history.

Theory of games must account for:

It is non-verbal.

Playing cards, chess, backgammon, wei chi, dominoes.

It is strategic.

The strategic aspect is non-verbal.

Therefore it is secret.

It involves structural logic.

Meaning the tools of the game are an absolute rational.

It is mathematical.

So that a mathematical comprehension plays a non-verbal strategic conflict with absolutely rational tools based on secrecy.

It traverses across the boundaries of civilisation.

So that an Asian can play opposite an Oriental or Russian equally without having to speak any language other than what is usual to the game.

When we deliberately look to discover a constant through different games, it is very easy to find. If we restrict our investigation to only those games which show a familial relationship we are immediately able to limit ourselves to dominoes, chess, backgammon, mah jongg, playing cards, wei chi, dice. Why would we limit ourselves to only those games? Because we can prove something. The import of those games can be demonstrated by a reverse method. That is, were we to take away that small community of games, perhaps ninety five percent of what we can understand about games would be lost to us. Meaning that those five or six games and about five or six others not mentioned do nearly all the work.

What that means is that we do not need to study games as a large number of different games. It is imperative that we study a small community of games specifically. And in that area, what can be understood in regard to games can be better clarified. We can look to see if there is a connection between the games. For example chess has pieces called king, queen and knight. And playing cards also have kings, queens and jacks, where jacks are like pages which are like knights. So then we can investigate what that connection might be. More distantly we can look at mah jongg and see that it has suits which correspond exactly with our suits in cards. And whereas we do not have a game like wei chi if we look at one of the earliest tools used by architects to plan a construction we find that it is a board of lines in a grid where counters are placed on the grid exactly the same as in wei chi.

If we were to look at the space, hole, or blank in terms of what we don't know about the small community of games specified it will be discovered to be of such large size as to be nearly incomprehensible. The only believable explanation for this is that such games justify the involvement of highest known intellect at any stage of human history. And if that is right, then that same level of intellect has deliberately deconstructed the connecting knowledge between them.

D. This is the fourth move in the sequence. It is designed to lead towards the understanding of the way in which the game domain model is used in fact in reality.

The mechanism tells the story of its own agents. Control of some aspect of the mechanism is noticed by the mechanism itself. The mechanism is longer time than any of its component parts. Any function of the mechanism held by any particular agent may be held by a different agent. The function may be essentially continual whereas the agent responsible for the function changes over time, even though the function is constant. If the identification of agent and function becomes itself constant then eventually the mechanism would necessitate any identity holding the function was the same agent.

If we then consider the given world in terms of functional agents that extend in some constant way beyond the lifespan of any individual identity it is clear that specific functions are permanent in the given world. For example the librarian in the Vatican Roman Catholic function is presumably a constant function as long as the Vatican library has existed. Now the agent who holds the function of librarian in the Vatican must be a different individual over time, whereas the function must not itself change. And yet the constancy of the function must demand that the identity of the agent is consistent with itself. I would suppose that there are many such functions which are as long lived as their constant relationship to the organised machine to which they belong.

It may be that we can then define adult as those identities capable of operating as agents for functions that are constant to some long lived mechanism. Whereas children in that sense may not condition their identity towards operating as agent for function to some long lived mechanism. If we give that, then I would suppose that adult identities can exist while not active agent for some function. In which case they have to find something else to do.

The difference between adult and children in the sense detailed is useful in this specific context. Since there has to be an indefinable line that connects the child potential to adult and as well the child in similar environment who perhaps does not have that sophisticated potential. Since the environment is better if it can support both. And also the same environment is better if it can support the more mature person who is interested in developing their education beyond some childhood boundary.

And as well the educated adult who desires to broaden a specialist level of knowledge into some previously closed subject matter. Other variables would be cultural living conditions of the person accessing the environment and the capacity of the environment to support a range of intellect in diverse living conditions.]

That completes the description of the tactical moves ABCD.

In regard to the game domain model a different one person game that is relevant to boolean logic and a contemporary of Venn:

Dodgson's game is clever. Here is how that works. Say a = true belief and ~a = false belief.

And b = fact and ~b = not fact. Then draw a vertical line with a at the top and not a at the bottom. And bisect the vertical line with a horizontal line with b on the right and not b on the left. That makes a top right box that is ab which is true belief of a fact. And a bottom right box that is false belief of a fact. And a bottom left box that is false belief of a not fact. And a top left box that is true belief of a not fact. Then take a small white counter as existant and a small black counter as not existant. The idea is to have true beliefs of facts and to not believe what is not fact. So put a white counter in the top right corner. That says true beliefs of facts exist. Or put a black counter in the top left box. That says true beliefs of not facts do not exist. Or a white counter in the bottom left box. That says false beliefs of not facts exist. Or a black counter in the bottom right. That says false beliefs of facts do not exist. The basic idea is to decide the related terms to use for a and b and then to show ab at top right, not ab at bottom right, not a not b at bottom left and not ba at top left. Then use the black and white counters to show the possible variations of existence and non-existence in regard to the related terms that are being used. Apart from the rules as stated it is reasonable to make other rules as desired. If someone places a black counter on the top line that means some beliefs that are facts do not exist and some beliefs that are not facts do not .

What I am clarifying in this context is the complexity of a theory of games is much more than the game domain model, and at the same time that the game domain model is quite useful as one element in the theory of games. The reason the game domain model can only be thought of as a necessary condition and nothing else is because it fails in regards to correspondence at every stage, it fails in regard to coherence outside a very limited field, it fails in regard to utility in many areas. Yet since it is close to being a universal abstraction of the simplest and easiest idea of what games involve it must be considered as hypothetically true. Only then can we determine where it is coherent within the larger matter of a theory of games, where it does correspond to reality in context of a larger theory and where it is useful to people who play games.

Taking a serious line, here is my thinking on the matter of different schools. John Venn, Zermelo-Fraenkel and Turing are a school. They would tend to refer to the same idea group.

Most people who know about one of the three people named will be familiar with the other two. Their ideas are okay. They are not shocking. They provide good information. In modern terms they would be consistent with Philip K Dick, Arthur C Clarke and Isaac Asimov. So essentially a right hand path, basically mechanistic, empiricist, and entirely dependent on the less well known left hand path school.

In this sense a middle line school would be Frege, Russell and Wittgenstein. Mathematicians, theorists and philosophical logicians. They would hold a line close to Jules Verne, Arthur Conan Doyle and Frank Herbert. Either they move from scientific fact to imaginative possibility or they maintain some sort of logical necessity for imagined scientific development. They are more correct in their rationality and less bound by the requirement to satisfy the restriction to present limits in knowledge. So they are dependent on the right hand path school to make fact what they think about in theory.

And a left hand path school would be Lorentz, Schrodinger and Everett. Edgar Allan Poe, Heinlein and Zelazny. At no stage do they pretend to the boundaries of the consensus mind-set nor to the reality of given phenomena and they support their line with an embedded attitude to science and knowledge that is both sensible and deliberately provocative. They are quantum theorists and support ideas that are present in diverse forms below the perceptual field.

Quantum flavours spin strange loops

Quarks lepton and the Quinks eigenstatic

Dance patterned time in fractal lines of

Chaotic dream shape.

Deep design spoke words to no beginning

And no end thought ideas of indefinite shape

While perception reflection and phenomena

Streamflowed continuum event through change.

All great metaquizical thinkers know that

What isn't, wasn't and won't be

Is different to this and that and

Maybe if possibly sometimes perhaps occasionally.

No thing entered by one thing

Is two things, called no thing and one thing,

In relationship is three things,

No thing, one thing and the relationship between them.

From three things all things appear.

Three things disappear

And seem to be one thing

Called the central axel known as earth

Around earth the four forces

Is five elements called the steps

Centre, forwards, backwards, left and right.

Spring, Summer, Autumn, Winter,

Four forces circle the earth,

And the change between them is

A total of eight gates called,

Thunder, Lake, Heaven, Fire, Wind, Mountain, Earth, Water.

Eight gates combine as the

Sixty Four changes,

Thirty two opposites,

Made from no thing and one thing

And the relationship between them.

CHAPTER FOUR.

What is philosophy?

Philosophy is a different answer if it is the first question to the answer given later.

So can I have the later answer first?

Okay, you can have one of the later answers first. Philosophy is the invention of a person called Socrates which became popular as a tradition of intellectual development among the european civilisation.

Is there no other philosophy to the one invented by Socrates?

There is no modern philosophy other to the one invented by Socrates. To the extent that we have philosophy from before the invention of it by Socrates we have some different thing. Before Socrates philosophy did not exist or alternatively what philosophy did exist before Socrates did not exist after Socrates.

And are there no schools of philosophy other to the one invented by Socrates?

Yes, there are the schools of other civilisations that have taken the invention of philosophy by Socrates and applied it to their own wisdom teachings.

So did they not exist before Socrates?

No, philosophy did not exist before Socrates. The wisdom teachings of various schools from the different civilisations existed before Socrates, though that is not the same as philosophy.

Then there is a difference between philosophy and the wisdom teachings?

Yes. The wisdom teachings and philosophy are not the same thing. For example, mathematics can be considered as one of the knowledge bases of the wisdom teachings and need have no reference to philosophy.

What about religion?

Is Buddhism religion?

I don't know.

Is the magical belief of agricultural communities religion?

To them it is.

And are Buddhism and the magical belief of agricultural communities philosophy?

Yes, no and maybe.

Okay. They are not philosophy. Philosophy is the invention of a person called Socrates which became popular as a tradition of intellectual development among the european civilisation.

Is philosophy something to do with intellect?

Yes. Philosophy is the school of intellect. As such it different to religion which is the school of spirit. And it is different to the wisdom teachings which are the school of knowledge. Philosophy therefore exists below religion as intellect must serve spirit, and it exists outside of wisdom since intellect must be independent of knowledge, and it exists alongside perception since sense and reason each inform the other, and it exists above will, since intellect must direct action.

What is the philosopher's stone?

It is the name given by alchemists to the evolved fruit of the work of alchemy.

Is it anything to do with philosophy?

Alchemy is to do with philosophy as one of the occult

traditions that many central philosophers within the tradition are similarly students of alchemy.

Is alchemy nonsense?

No, alchemy is encrypted such that the information obtained outside is nonsense.

Encrypted by whom?

Encrypted by philosophers.

What about the other occult traditions?

The primary occult traditions that are relevant to philosophy are alchemy, magic, wizardry, sorcery, heuristic, kabbala and magick.

Why is that?

Because the same people who control philosophy also study the above named traditions.

Is philosophy anything to do with the craft?

Yes, because craft is one of the matters that Socrates originally directed the attention of philosphy towards.

What is the difference between craft and the craft?

Craft is given here as an ordinary level of knowledge of some specialist subject. That is, while the knowledge may not be common to all, because the subject is some specialist matter, the level of knowledge is only ordinary. And the specialist matter can be of diverse kind, whether building wooden sailing boats or needlework, weaving and tapestry. Craft then has to be understood in terms of a threefold, that is,

craft, art and science. Where craft is an ordinary level of knowledge in regard to a specialist subject such as needlework, then art is a professional level of knowledge of the cardinal articulations of the same subject. Cardinal is used here in the sense of principle points and articulations is used in the sense of jointed connecting areas between the cardinals. Therefore art is in particular the knowledge of principle points and connecting joints between them in regard to some craft. When the subject of craft and art is given a normative in regard to theory and method such that the theory and method are common to most who practice the craft then that is called science.

The difference between craft and the craft is that which is obtained when the original subject matter is detached from the ordinary knowledge of the cardinal articulations, theory and method of the specialist subject. This is easily understood in regard to needlework, weaving and associated skills. Where the artist level of knowledge of the particular craft involves an alteration in the thought patterns of the person who has the given knowledge, such that the adjustment in thought patterns learned through the craft is obtained as a possession.

What does this have to do with "quality" ?

Quality as understood in philosophy has several different meanings. Aristotle defines quality in two different ways, neither of which exactly coincides with the meaning that is alluded to by Socrates. And Socrates does not necessarily specifically define quality in the way that Aristotle provides definitions. For this reason, the subject matter of quality as understood within the school tradition of philosophy has typically remained one of the mysteries.

So quality is something to do with philosophy?

Yes it is one of the things that philosophy finds mysterious.

Can you explain it?

"Quality is the measurable relationship between subject and object."

If that is the definition of quality, then why is it a mystery?

Because it does not exist. And since it does not exist, it is a mystery. That is, given any some object, quality can not be discovered in the object. Given any subjective perceiver, quality cannot be discovered in the subjective perceiver. Only when some object and subjective perceiver coincide in the event continuum does quality exist. Furthermore, given the same object and a different subjective perceiver the measure of quality will adjust. And given a different object and the same subjective perceiver the measure of quality will adjust. So whilst we know that it is there, we cannot categorise it either with our sense perceptors nor with our reasoning intellect.

Does philosophy explain this?

No perhaps not. One of the reasons for this document is to offer an idea of what philosophy does, and the reason for what philosophy does not do.

How do you mean?

If philosophy is the school of intellect then the nature, purposes, structure, form and function of philosophy are geared towards that rather than anything else. And since the intellect is of a kind unique to itself, then the discipline for intellect is peculiar to its nature. Meaning that philosophy does not do what people may want it to do if what people want it to do is different to the purpose for its own existence. For that reason, philosophy is commonly accused of not providing answers that explain some question.

Then what does philosophy do?

It provides a domain of discourse within which intellect can be directed towards the understanding of any matter to which it would attend. In doing so it makes the possibility that the given matter can be answered by the professional in any craft, art or science once the intellect has understood the matter.

Can you give a specific example using the matter of quality detailed earlier.

Yes, intellect understands it is one of the mysteries. And therefore that the answer to the mystery of quality belongs to the domain of the mystery teachings rather than to philosophy. For this reason, philosophy does not explain the answer to the mystery of quality although it does clarify what quality can be understood to be in reference towards. The catch is that if philosophy were to explain the mystery of quality in the manner detailed, then it would no longer be doing philosophy it would be doing whatever the mysteries are.

You make the distinction between subject and object. Is that a matter of philosophy?

Yes, in the sense that at a deeper structural level than philosophy a divide exists that manifests itself in various ways at the level of philosophy. And one of the ways that the divide manifests itself at the level of philosophy is as the difference between subject and object.

Can you make it plainer.

Okay. However, the method I would find easier is to provide a specific answer that is definitive and that uses specific terms that can be found in philosophy. Once the answer is understood, then it proves its adequacy by how well it corresponds to each of the areas where the divide manifests itself.

What is that specific answer?

It is to provide a definition for three attitudes.

The attitudes are empiricism, idealism and rationalism.

All three attitudes can exist within any one person, in the sense that any person can take any one of the attitudes at any particular time and also can deliberately choose to change their attitude from one to the other. Taken together the three attitudes are definitive and with understanding they can demonstrate either that the deeper divide does not in fact exist in the way it seems to, or alternatively that if the deeper divide does exist, it is because it is supposed to.

Do your definitions of the three attitudes correspond to those given in philosophy?

It is a puzzle. The three attitudes exist. The definitions exist. Philosophy talks about the three attitudes and the definitions. Whether the three attitudes, three definitions and the conversation about them all coincide is rather doubtful. For that reason it does require astuteness on the part of the enquirer. Without astuteness the enquirer can obtain useful information but they will not be able to obtain any deep knowledge or understanding. With astuteness then the enquirer can easily adjust the information provided in philosophy in such a way that the attitudes, definitions and understanding all become a definitive knowledge.

Can you give a similar example.

Yes, we can talk about the knower, the knowing and the known. This is a very old idea from before the time of Socrates. If we define the three positions of the person who knows, the activity of knowing and the thing that is known then it is clear that the three things cannot be divided. Yet even though they cannot be divided, we make the distinction between knower, knowing and known, therefore they are divided.

And does that correspond to the three attitudes?

No it does not. It seems to correspond to the three attitudes, but that is only if we always take what we do not understand and group it together with any similar thing that we do not understand. Since we do not understand in either case then we say that the two things are correspondent. But they are not. They are similar.

How do you explain the three attitudes?

As a matter of priority. Or in terms of precedence given to

one of only a few possible alternatives. Or of a decision as to the correct placement of value. Or as a choice in regard to where reality exists.

And specifically?

Empiricism is precedence given to matter, object and sense perception. It is to place value in the field of the known. It is to say that reality exists in the physical object before anywhere else.

Rationalism is precedence given to mind, reason and thought. It is to place value in the field of the knower. It is to say that reality exists in the mental thought processes before anywhere else.

Idealism is precedence given to event, continuum and the coincidence of mind with object. It is to place value in the field of the knowing.

It is to say that reality exists in the conjunction of reason with sense perception.

And how does that then relate to philosophy?

Well, given the definitions provided, philosophy has available a large matter that exhaustively details the entirety of the given attitudes, even though the attitudes as given are not necessarily exactly the same as those given in philosophy. What I mean is that where empiricism is used in philosophy as a term it may not be defined in the same way in every use of the same term. And also that for example empiricism may be placed conceptually against realism or phenomenalism or some other concept. For this reason it is important to clarify my use of the same terms.

That is empiricism, rationalism and idealism are three attitudes that are together definitive of a subject. There is no fourth attitude. And it is not possible to reduce to only two attitudes. And in regard to placement against other attitudes they place only against the other two.

Can you expand on how the three attitudes are to be understood?

Yes, once the above definitions are detailed it is then possible to associate various areas as required to any one of the three attitudes.

Empiricism then is sense perception. It uses induction and analogy. It is the basis of all mechanical science. It directs its attention to the truth of first propositions. It has a mechanical engineering orientation and also the physical, chemical and biological studies. It directs its attention towards the physical. It says object exists. It believes in matter.

Rationalism is reasoning mind. It uses deduction and mathematics. It is the basis of all theoretical knowledge. It directs its attention to the truth of argument from first propositions. It has an accademic theoretical orientation and also the metaphysical imaginative studies. It directs its attention towards the idea and the reason. It says thought exists. It believes in the understanding.

Idealism is active agent. It uses signlabel and symbol. It is the basis of all writing, language and numeric model. It directs its attention to the appropriateness of model between the theory and practice. It has an artistic orientation and also music, drama and dream. It directs its attention towards the space between empirical and rational or the location at which the two polarities coincide. It is the study of the reasoning mind in regard to corresponding sense object best understood through geometry, algebra and symbolic notation. It says idea exists. It believes in magic.

Does that answer the mind body question?

On its own it does not. That is because the mind body question by its nature is a topological mathematical problem. Since the mathematics of topology are a specific problem, then if the mind body question is a matter of topology then it is not easily answered by nature of that fact.

Can you clarify that point?

Yes, the matter of the mind body problem is one that any student of philosophy must be puzzled by because it asks whether the identity of the person who asks the question is a mind or a body. It forces mistake in the enquirer who asks the question, because they can not detach their own identity and existence from any possible answer they may give. For that reason it is considered a topological mathematical problem.

What is the mind body problem?

Essentially the question many ask, which philosophy attends to is: "Who is that?, who are you?, who am I?" These are all a matter of identity and non-identity. Because the answer to any person is in each case unique, it makes the question difficult to answer in the singular. The way to do so is to change "Who?" to "What?". When we apply what? to the identity of person we raise the mind body problem. So now we have the question "What is that, what are you, what am I" all as applied to the identity of person. Since the answer to what? is common to each of those who ask the question it is easier to answer.

How does the question "What am I?" relate to the mind body problem?

Well the matter itself notices the difference between empiricism and rationalism. But it makes the matter of the difference refer to the individual person. That is we notice empirically object exists. We notice rationally mind is evident in some objects and not in others. We that do the noticing would seem to have mind where other objects do not. And we notice that whether we have mind or do not have mind, we are object. So the question raised is how does self as mind coincide with self as object, and also how does self as mind coincide with other as mind or object, and also how does self as object coincide with other as mind or object.

Can the mind body problem be answered?

Perhaps not. What can be answered is the question "What am I?". The reason we probably can not answer the mind body problem is because we would always provide a provincial answer. That is, we would provide an answer that satisfies the limited provincial nature of our own identity and fails to satisfy any who did not fit that provincial pattern.

How do we answer the question "What am I?"

You are an active agent with the capacity for rational thought operational in a spacetime continuum that presents phenomena to your sense perceptors as object manifesting change.

Philosophy can provide structure that adequately reflects the truth of the above answer in terms of a transparent model. The use of the given abstract model in its diverse applications would tend to be some other discipline not philosophy.

The model is given as -

Empirically, five external sense perceptions: Visual, Auditory, Kinesthetic, Olfactory, Gustatory.

Rationally, five internal vehicles for thought: Imagination, Intuition, Emotion, Inspiration, Discernment.

Ideally, five logical levels: Perception, Behaviour, Thought, Narrative, Identity.

As given, the model is abstract and without deviation towards any particular bias. It is a necessity that the use of the model would require adjustment towards the bias of any particular application of itself.

You talked in terms of the tradition of philosophy. Is it possible to detail what that tradition is specifically?

Yes, we can do so in terms of twenty five specific individual people. In this way we can prove an unbroken line of european intellectual development that is initiated by the philosophy of Socrates, and where each named person individually would agree with the given names of those previous to themselves. Those people are named:

1.Socrates, 2.Plato, 3.Aristotle, 4.Virgil, 5.Marcus Aurelius, 6.Augustine, 7.Charlemaine, 8.Dante, 9.Raymond Lull, 10.Leonardo Da Vinci,

11.Galileo, 12.Johannes Kepler, 13.Rene Descartes, 14.Spinoza, 15.John Locke, 16.Immanuel Kant, 17.George Berkeley, 18.Ben Franklin,

19.Edmund Husserl, 20.Bertrand Russell, 21.Ludwig Wittgenstein, 22.Jean-Paul Sartre, 23.Carl Jung, 24.Jean Baudrillard,

25.Jacques Derrida.

It is a matter of identity, narrative and thought. As given, those specific twenty five names provide an identity. The identity provides a narrative. And the narrative is the ideas of the thoughts of the specific identity.

What are the three levels of philosophy?

The first is to direct the attention towards the matter of philosophy, that being: Place, Duration, Movement, Change, Object, Phenomena, Being, Event, Identity, Mind and other related areas.

The second is to direct the attention towards the written work of the philosophers who have already provided argumentation on the matter of philosophy, several of whom are detailed by name above.

The third is to direct the attention towards explanation of the written work of the philosophers.

How would you explain what doing philosophy actually is?

What doing philosophy actually is, is to attend to the unknown in order to clarify whether it is knowable or unknowable. And if knowable then to name what any particular matter may be knowable as. And if unknowable then to name in what way unknowable.

CHAPTER FIVE.

Before modern science existed means before Leonardo, Galileo and Descartes and before modern mathematics existed means before Euler, Mozart and Boole. So before those people the school of invention existed. And one of the schools of invention that existed in the same places as Leonardo, Galileo, Descartes, Euler, Mozart and Boole was based on three principles. And each of the three principles had three elements. The three principles were induction, analogy and anomaly. And the three elements of induction were constancy, duration and generality. The three elements of analogy were similarity, commonality and familiarity. And the three elements of anomaly were difference, peculiarity and exceptionality.

The idea of induction was the study of the truth of propositions. That is to say, where some sensible thing called phenomena was noticed to be the same in this place as that place it was called constant. And where it was noticed to be the same in this time as that time it was called duration. And where it was noticed to be the same throughout its examples it was called generality.

The idea of analogy was the study of the relationship between different things. That is to say, where some two different things were noticed to coincide with each other in some way they were called similars. And where the two different things were noticed to belong to the same larger thing it was called commonality. And where they were noticed to be connected to other things of like nature it was called familiarity.

The idea of anomaly was the study of those things not included. That is to say, where induction and analogy were used it was noticed that any thing excluded was called different. And where some things that were noticed would not be explained by induction or analogy they were called peculiar. And where some things were noticed to be unusually advanced beyond what was normal they were called exceptions.

Since Leonardo, Galileo, Descartes, Euler, Mozart and Boole things are much easier because modern science now exists. Modern science does not have to worry about three principles each containing three elements. Because modern science has only to deal with four functions, three processes, two rules and one exception. The four functions are called hypothesis, experiment, validation and model. The three processes are called generalisation, deletion and distortion. The two rules are called prediction and falsifiability. And the one exception is called anomaly.

In regard to the four functions: Hypothesis is to affirm a proposition which may or may not be true, such as "It is the case that stable things remain in place". Experiment is to find examples of where the propostion is true by pushing on stable things to see what happens. Validation is to confirm the correctness of the hypothesis in more not less instances. Model is the use of a method called deduction to provide good argumentation from the proposition to its proof.

In regard to the three processes: Generalisation is the requirement to demonstrate what is normally the case. Deletion is the requirement to eliminate any peculiar examples from the result that contradict what is normally the case. Distortion is the requirement to adjust the explanation of the result so that what is normally the case can be presented as a law of nature.

In regard to the two rules: Prediction is the rule that we must be able to determine beforehand in regard to any experiment that one of two most probable outcomes always happens and that possible improbable outcomes do not happen. Falsifiability is the rule that we must be permitted to check our results for correctness and accuracy or incorrectness and inaccuracy.

In regard to the one exception: Anomaly is the understanding that the use of hypothesis, experiment, validation, model and generalisation, deletion, distortion and predictability and falsifiability has a necessary outcome in terms of peculiar, particular exceptions that are not detailed in any of our work and only show up as blanks, missing links and connections that don't exist.

The anomaly pattern here is:

(+1) x (+1) = (+1) Plus one multiplied by plus one is plus one.

(+1) / (+1) = (+1) Plus one divided by plus one is plus one.

(-1) x (+1) = (-1) Minus one multiplied by plus one is minus one.

(-1) / (+1) = (-1) Minus one divided by plus one is minus one.

(+1) x (-1) = (0) Plus one multiplied by minus one is zero.

(+1) / (-1) = (0) Plus one divided by minus one is zero.

(-1) x (-1) = (0) Minus one multiplied by minus one is zero.

(-1) / (-1) = (0) Minus one divided by minus one is zero.

Given the pattern as stated, that means:

(+1) x (-1) =/= (-1) x (+1) Plus one multiplied by minus one does not equal minus one multiplied by plus one.

(+1) / (-1) =/= (-1) / (+1) Plus one divided by minus one does not equal minus one divided by plus one.

(+1) x (-1) = (+1) / (-1) = (-1) x (-1) = (-1) / (-1)

Plus one multiplied by minus one equals plus one divided by minus one equals minus one multiplied by minus one equals minus one divided by minus one.

The definition of the rules for the above pattern is:

1. Positive number multiplied by plus one is original positive number.

2. Positive number divided by plus one is orginal positive number.

3. Negative number multiplied by plus one is original negative number.

4. Negative number divided by plus one is original negative number.

5. Positive number multiplied by minus one is zero.

6. Positive number divided by minus one is zero.

7. Negative number multiplied by same negative number as itself is zero.

8. Negative number divided by same negative number as itself is zero.

The question raised by the anomaly pattern is whether the Q function, which we could call the quantum factor or the indefinite variable or neither the unity set nor the empty set is a necessary element of the given terms. And the fact that it proves the deep structure involves an either or switch. That is, because we can detail two different rules at any one time for "minus a divided by minus a" such that it can give either zero or minus one. And dependent whether the rule we are using gives zero determines the coherent rule base that must be followed by the other rules. Since if we say the rule is that "minus a divided by minus a gives minus one" then the other rules must conform to that. What it means is, that "for any minus a divided by minus a, the answer may at any stage be either minus a or zero, which is the quantum variable or Q. Since we have built the quantum variable into our prime pattern it is useful to have the anomaly pattern clearly stated in order to prove Q.

To Prove Q:

Given minus one divided by minus one.

Minus one divided by minus one equals minus one

If the rule we are following is any negative number divided by itself is minus one or alternatively if the rule we are following is any negative number divided by minus one is minus one.

Minus one divided by minus one equals zero

If the rule we are following is any negative number divided by itself is zero or alternatively if the rule we are following is any negative number divided by minus one is zero.

Then since there is an indefinite variable built in to our choice of rule at that precise point we have to use the Q function in order to notify ourselves that a more abstract universal level does not make the decision either way. Instead, at that more abstract level neither the empty set nor the unity set is quite acceptable.

Given the anomaly pattern raises the matter and does not solve it, then this is one possible direction towards its solution.

We can state specific matters in their most clear formulation at this stage, with the understanding that our workings out may enable us to better state later.

One. The rule that any number whether positive or negative when multiplied by the unit number called plus one, then the result will be the original positive or negative number.

Two. The rule that any number whether positive or negative when multiplied by the unit number called minus one, then the result will be zero.

Three. Therefore minus one multiplied by plus one must always give the result called Q, that is, the quantum indefinite or neither one nor zero or both minus one and zero.

To clarify: according to rule one, 10 x 1 = 10 ; -10 x 1 = -10 ; -1 x 1 = -1.

To clarify: according to rule two, 10 x -1 = 0 ; -10 x -1 = 0 ; 1 x -1 = 0.

To clarify: according to rule three -1 x +1 = -1 ; +1 x -1 = 0 therefore Q.

Now the only thing we can do at this stage is to challenge our rules, that is to say, either rule one or rule two is false, or both rule one and rule two are false.

Since rule one is held to fit the condition "most certain" we would tend to maintain that as correct. Then we must challenge rule two. What we must do here is ask ourselves why rule two is the given rule rather than some other rule, and we do that so that we do not immediately replace rule two with a different wrong answer.

The reason rule two is as given is because there is an earlier conditional statement. The earlier conditional statement is that "multiplication by minus one" must provide a different answer to "multiplication by plus one".

Using our sign labels that means:

a . +1 = a and ~a . +1 = ~a

a . -1 =/= a and ~a . -1 =/= ~a

Then in order to meet the earlier conditional statement we determine whether we can find out what "multiplication by minus one" must give. The way we do so is to first ask what we mean by "multiplication by plus one". And we say, any positive number multiplied by plus one gives the original positive number because multiplied by plus one means to say : One example of the original number. And we then say: multiplication by plus two means two examples of the given number combined. And multiplication by plus three means three examples of the given number combined.

Following the same rule through to any negative number multiplied by plus one gives the original negative number because multiplied by plus one means to say: One example of the original negative number. And multiplication by plus two means two examples of the given negative number combined. And multiplication by plus three means three examples of the given negative number combined.

Given that, then what must "multiplication by minus one" give? And our answer is any positive number multiplied by minus one gives zero because multiplied by minus one means to say: one example of the given number subtracted. So any positive number subtracted from itself must give the answer zero.

What we cannot say is that any positive number multiplied by minus one gives the negative of the same number, because that is what we would mean by multiplied by minus two.

The proof is as follows:

If the original number is plus ten, then:

$+10 \times -1 = +10 - (+1 \times +10) = +10 - 10 = 0.$

$+10 \times -2 = +10 - (+2 \times +10) = +10 - 20 = -10.$

$+10 \times -3 = +10 - (+3 \times +10) = +10 - 30 = -20.$

Which makes most sense because the difference between plus ten and zero is ten units, the difference between plus ten and minus ten is twenty units, the difference between plus ten and minus twenty is thirty units.

If we decide that is not acceptable then the rule we would replace it with is that any positive number multiplied by minus one gives the same number in the negative. That would be:

$+1 \times -1 = -1$

$+2 \times -1 = -2$

$+3 \times -1 = -3$

$+10 \times -1 = -10$

In that case we would have plus one multiplied by minus one is minus one.

And we would have minus one multiplied by plus one is minus one.

Which would seem to be okay, so we go back to our original pattern and see how it fits. We are required to make all the other changes demanded to maintain coherency within the pattern, and then to restate our rules for the different version of the anomaly pattern.

The anomaly pattern here is:

$(+1) \times (+1) = (+1)$ Plus one multiplied by plus one is plus one.

$(+1) / (+1) = (+1)$ Plus one divided by plus one is plus one.

$(-1) \times (-1) = (+1)$ Minus one multiplied by minus one is plus one.

$(-1) / (-1) = (+1)$ Minus one divided by minus one is plus one.

$(-1) \times (+1) = (-1)$ Minus one multiplied by plus one is minus one.

$(-1) / (+1) = (-1)$ Minus one divided by plus one is minus one.

$(+1) \times (-1) = (-1)$ Plus one multiplied by minus one is minus one.

$(+1) / (-1) = (-1)$ Plus one divided by minus one is minus one.

The definition for the rules for the above pattern is:

1. Positive number multiplied by plus one is original positive number.

2. Positive number divided by plus one is orginal positive number.

3. Negative number multiplied by minus one is positive of

original number.

4. Negative number divided by minus one is positive of original number.

5. Negative number multiplied by plus one is original negative number.

6. Negative number divided by plus one is original negative number.

7. Positive number multiplied by minus one is negative of original number.

8. Positive number divided by minus one is negative of original number.

The position we are now in is where we have two versions of the anomaly pattern, each of which is coherent with the rules associated to its own pattern, and each of which provides a different answer to the other.

Given that we have two versions of the anomaly pattern where we would prefer to only have one, and we have two sets of rules where we would prefer to only have one, then the idea may be to determine whether one of the two patterns is clearly correct and the other clearly wrong.

However, what we are prohibited from doing is making an arbitrary choice to affirm one pattern and negate the other simply because we only want one pattern to deal with. By which I mean, we can do so, and if we do so it is just as likely that a different decision maker will make the contradictory choice. Which would mean that given both versions of the anomaly pattern and two different decision makers it is quite possible for both decision makers to take a contradictory line to the other in regard to assigning a truth value to either pattern.

Since that is reasoned, we are in a position where we would like to be confident that one version of all the possible versions of the anomaly pattern is more correct than any other possible version. To obtain that more correct version necessitates we consider the higher order pattern through universal abstraction. And we already know that pattern will require the use of the quantum indefinite, neither one nor zero, or Q.

What that gives us is the answer that either rule base for the anomaly pattern is correct and at the same time notifies us that more than one rule base exists for the particular set of terms. What it will not do is specify that one answer is more correct than the other. Essentially what the higher order universal abstraction says is: Multiplication of any number by minus one gives minus one or zero or plus one or the negative of the original postive number or the positive of the original negative number. That is the nature of Q in the universal abstract. And all it means is that particular instances of Q will give only one of the possible answers, dependent on being coherent with the rule base being applied in that instance.

For that reason we may decide to further detail the anomaly pattern at the level of mathematics without moving up a logical level to the universal abstraction. Because what we would like to do is determine what are the conditions that enable both versions of the anomaly pattern to exist. And as well, to consider whether it may be possible to detail how the patterns may relate one to the other.

And the problem with that line will be that what it will show is that one set of rules for the anomaly pattern is referring to the result as a processing number and the other set of rules for the anomaly pattern is referring to the result as a final object. Which will then mean that both answers exist at the same time. Using this example provided earlier to clarify what I mean:

$+10 \times -1 = [+10 - (+1 \times +10) = +10 - 10] = 0.$

$+10 \times -2 = [+10 - (+2 \times +10) = +10 - 20] = -10.$

+10 x -3 = [+10 - (+3 x +10) = +10 - 30] = -20.

The information contained in the square brackets is a processing number and the information on either side of the brackets is a final object number.

It means that when we say +1 x -1 = -1 we mean that the result "-1" is a processing number that must then be applied to the original object number of "+1" which will give "+1 -1" as a processing calculation which then works out as "0" as a final object number.

In that way it may be that the second anomaly pattern details in whole or in part the processing number in regard to the stated terms, which when then worked out against the original object number will give the object result detailed in the first anomaly pattern. And the difficulty is that if we accept this theory the second anomaly pattern strengthens the first anomaly pattern because it says it provides a processing number result for the final object result. And if that is correct then we are back to the original anomaly.

What the previous explanation does is direct attention towards a simple pattern that can be detailed in two ways, both different and either of which could be considered correct. It easily may be that a third or fourth version of the same patterns can be detailed. The only requirement in this matter is that the basic format is adhered to and that the rules being applied in any particular version are properly described. In that way it may be possible that one pattern is shown to be clearly correct making the other versions less necessary. Since all that is desired in this particular is that we can detail one correct version of the given variables.

CHAPTER SIX.

Is it original?

Well he references it when he feels like it, plagiarises when he feels like it and writes completely original work when he feels like it. So I don't know.

Furthermore he references what people clearly didn't say as if they did and forges things they may have said but didn't without referencing.

He is controversial in the sense that he believes the Original Gift of God to man was free will since God permitted man to eat of the Tree of Knowledge of Good and Evil even though they were told not to. He believes Jesus Christ cannot be of the Line of David because it was an Immaculate Conception. And that Christians are breaking the Second Commandment when they worship statues of Jesus on the Cross as God.

Additionally he believes mankind is a genetically modified colonisation of planet Earth, that there are three distinct light speeds determined by whether light is moving through Solar, Interstellar or Intergalactic space, and that time does not slow down as speed increases nearer to light speed, relative to another object that is stationary.

Also that it is an out of sequence cause-effect anomaly serving to cast doubt on the theory of evolution that Plato, Aristotle, Plotinus, Euclid and Archimedes all wrote complete works at the start of modern history.

Ontological Questions.

A. Phenomenology.

All attempts to prove the existence of an objective reality separate from our consciousness of it as such are doomed to failure. Simply because any attempt at such a proof can only be the product of consciousness. And any comprehension of such a proof can only be the understanding of consciousness. And any such proof can only ever exist as a phenomena of consciousness.

Objective reality as such is a product of combined minds.

B. Cogito.

1.

Some existence contains All thought.

Some thought contains All self identity.

Therefore Some existence contains All self identity.

2.

Existence is a necessary condition of Thinking.

Self nature thinks.

Therefore self nature exists.

3.

Thinking presupposes existence.

Thoughts are individual to self.

Therefore this self exists.

C. Soul.

The individuating definition of soul is perspective.

Soul is in a state of total war for its own perspective position.

The place of soul is defined by its own perspective position that can only be held by the individual soul.

Without perspective position, place, time, soul is entirely absolute.

Given the usual descriptions of soul adhered to by Socrates,

Plato, Aristotle, Plotinus, Hegel.

D.

What am I?

You are an active agent with the capacity for rational thought operational in a spacetime continuum that presents phenomena to your sense perceptors as object manifesting change.

E.

What is that?

Empirically, five external sense perceptions: Visual, Auditory, Kinesthetic, Olfactory, Gustatory.

Rationally, five internal vehicles for thought: Imagination, Intuition, Emotion, Inspiration, Discernment.

Ideally, five logical levels: Perception, Behaviour, Thought, Narrative, Identity.

F. Impermanence, Immutability, Emptiness.

Phenomena changes constantly. That is impermanence. The sense perceptions.

Truth is constant to eternity. That is immutability. The mind.

Space without phenomena. Time without thought. That is emptiness. Existence.

G. Continuum.

Event, Time, Space, Mind, Object.

This is the continuum. It exists so far back that when we look for its beginning we cannot find it. So far forwards that when we look for its end it disappears into infinity. It is what body is born into but mind already exists within its self. Purpose is only entirely to serve the context that gives life to content.

The above seven ideas are those that immediately come to

mind when any person thinks about ontology, the nature of existant being.

They are not direct quotes. They are ideas extracted, each from a different source. I do not think that it is possible to go directly to the original thinker who suggested the possibility of the above detailed ideas to find these ideas exactly as stated.

A is extracted from Husserl.

B from Descartes.

C from Hegel.

D perhaps from Aristotle.

E perhaps from Plato.

F from Gautama.

G from Lao Tsu.

At the present moment the eighth idea does not immediately force itself on my attention.

So that is the point that is interesting. Since it suggests that seven specific ideas are very central to ontology. There is not one of the above stated ideas that on reflection I think could be deleted without disadvantage to the whole.

All of the ideas can be differently stated. And their contradictory can be in some cases stated.

However as stated there is a sense of their coherence together. They do not contradict each other. And that being the case it implies that they can in deed be taken together as separate components of one single theory.

Does God have an opposite?

How many sons of God are there?

Are the sons of God also gods?

Are any sons of God less than others?

What is the goal of prophets and teachers?

How many minds are there?

What is a human being?

Is mankind finished or in process?

How much can we and should we attempt?

What is the purpose of life and consciousness?

What is the next step?

Who was Adam the son of? See Luke 3:38.

Which was the son of Enos, which was the son of Seth, which was the son of Adam, which was the son of God.

This was the genealogy of Jesus. It began at verse 23, saying Jesus was the son of Joseph and Joseph was the son of Heli which was the son of Matthat and so on, David and Solomon and all, until Enos, "which was the son of Seth, which was the son of Adam, which was the son of God," in verse 38, from which he had started. But Adam was "the son of God" only metaphorically, wasn't he? The text did not seem to be speaking poetically; it repeated "which was the son of" in what seemed to be a very literal sense each time until it reached that astonishing conclusion. It seemed to be saying that Adam was the son of God as literally as Joseph was the son of Heli.

Does God have an opposite? See Exodus 3:14 and Ephesians 4:4-6.

Exodus 3:14 said: And God said unto Moses, I AM THAT I AM: and he said, Thus shalt thou say unto the children of Israel: I AM hath sent me unto you.

And Ephesians 4:4-16 was even more startling: There is one body, and one spirit, even as ye are called in one hope of your calling: one Lord, one faith, one baptism, one God and Father of all, who is above all, and through all, and in you all."

How many sons of God are there? See Romans 8:14-17.

For as many as are led by the Spirit of God, they are the sons of God; For ye have not received the spirit of bondage again to fear; but ye have received the Spirit of adoption, whereby we cry, Abba, Father. The Spirit beareth witness with our spirit, that we are the children of God: and if children, then heirs; heirs of God, and joint heirs with Christ; if so be that we suffer with him, that we may also be glorified.

Everybody was a child of God — not just Adam and Jesus — and the Bible said so.

Are the sons of God also gods? See John 10:34.

Jesus answered them, Is it not written in your law, I said, Ye are gods?

Are any sons of God less than others? See Colossians 3:4.

When Christ, who is our life, shall appear then shall ye appear with him in glory. In other words, When you can see Christ you are Christ. When your will becomes one with the Will of God, as Abraham said.

What is the goal of prophets and teachers? See Ephesians 4:11-13.

And he gave some apostles, and some prophets, and some evangelists, and some pastors and teachers; For the perfecting of the saints, for the work of the ministry, for the edifying of the body of Christ: Till we all come in the unity of the faith, and of the knowledge of the Son of God, unto a perfect man, unto the measure of the stature of the fullness of Christ.

How many minds are there? See Deuteronomy 4:39 and Exodus 3:14.

Know therefore this day, and consider it in thine heart, that the Lord he is God in heaven above and upon the earth beneath: there is none else. And God said unto Moses: I AM

THAT I AM .

What is a human being? See Genesis 1:26.

And God said, Let us make man in our image, after our likeness.

Is mankind finished or in process? See 1 John 3:2.

Beloved, now are we the sons of God, and it doth not appear what we shall be: but we know that when he shall appear, we shall be like him, for we shall see him as he is.

How much can we and should we attempt? See John 14:12.

Verily, verily, I say unto you, He that believeth in me, the works that I do he shall do also; and greater works than these shall he do.

What is the purpose of life and consciousness? See 2 Corinthians 9:8 and Luke 12:32.

And God is able to make all grace abound toward you; that ye, having always all sufficiency in all things, may abound to every good work. Fear not, little flock; for it is your father's good pleasure to give you the kingdom.

What is the next step? See Romans 8:19.

For the earnest expectation of the creature awaiteth the manifestation of the sons of God.

Going forward we have:

World War 3

Global warming

Geological disasters

Pandemic mutations

Refugee crises

I can't wait.

CHAPTER SEVEN.

I remember when Aristotle first turned up in Athens at seventeen after the Oracle had told him to investigate some of the new ideas people were having around that area. No one realised at the time how this would change the Pythagorean influence on local politics.

If the Aristotles in the Parmenides is a different Aristotles to the later one, then the later one would have known of the earlier one who had the same name. Since the Parmenides is the basic primer for the later Aristotles entire Metaphysics, it is a happy coincidence that the fool of the Parmenides is also called Aristotle.

If the Parmenides is a description of the teenage Aristotle's initiation into the Platonic Pythagorean Society of Athens, then it is soon after he made his deal with a local enforcer. As a seventeen year old male, Aristotle's main worry was Plato's taste for boys. He decided he needed a body guard since his own sexual preference was specifically only girls.

He made his deal with a local soldier who agreed to enforce Aristotle's desire not to be turned into one of Plato's charmed young men.

Of course it mattered whether Plato had real boyfriends or not. If he had not, then Aristotle would not have been worried. Since he did have some, Aristotle was not prepared to allow chance any margin. The soldier that Aristotle arranged his security service deal with begins at this particular event.

The particular soldier is not seventeen. Aristotle is

seventeen. No one argues with the soldier that Aristotle does this deal with.

The time is when Troy is finished. The survivors of Troy are migrating to Italy and will build Rome. Rome has not yet begun to exist.

Civilisation is advanced beyond present society in any present date.

We can define two separate Civilisations as bordered by the use of chopsticks or knives and forks. Two different civilisations, the boundary of each marked by the change from knives and forks for eating, to the use of chopsticks for eating. You know which civilisation is in control by the eating implements utilised.

Aristotle was already quite proficient in the use of both knives and forks, and chopsticks. His body guard only used chopsticks.

Over the following few decades Socrates would teach Plato, Plato would teach Aristotle, Aristotle would educate Alexander, Alexander would conquer the entirety of the known world, and it would then change its name to the Roman Empire.

Within a century more or less, Julius Caesar would obtain power over the entire Empire and direct it towards mechanisation, building roads from each of its centres to each of the others.

The empire operates from its Rome headquarters for only about four hundred years. Over that time it makes the transition from the religious doctrine of the Greek gods under their Roman names and changes to become entirely Christian.

The Christian Empire is basically established at the time of the Roman Empire collapse.

Both events are documented by Augustine in his book called

"The City of God".

The headquarters moves from Rome over the following two hundred years and is the Holy Roman Empire of Charlemaine. Charlemaine provides the legal system that is established throughout all Roman Empire territory whether directly controlled or colony. The date is around six hundred years after Julius Caesar started building roads.

The Christian Holy Roman Empire of Charlemaine is challenged by the Arabic civilisation of the Koran. This conflict is four hundred years before the invention of the English language. The Koran becomes widely distributed throughout the Roman Empire at this time.

Dante writes a century before Chaucer. When Chaucer writes the first book in the new language of Britain called English, the Roman construction of the society of Britain is already one thousand years established. That is, approximately one thousand years after Roman Empire colonised Britain, the first book written in the English language is authored by Chaucer.

With the invention of the English language, controls of the Holy Roman Empire move to Britain, and the British Empire is in its growth stage from the time of Chaucer to that of Shakespeare. A time span of only three or four hundred years. By the time of Shakespeare, the British Empire as dominant is finished. The date is only five hundred years in the past from the present date.

British society becomes ritualised and artificial in the hundred years following the works of Shakespeare. The colonies become the primary focus for developing progress, as well as trade with China and India.

Within two hundred years the Empire headquarters moves from Britain to the newly invented United States. At the same time the feudal medieval system of Europe that is aristocratic royalty is modified under the controls of renaissance science. The artistic and scientific minds at the time are the level of Galileo, Kepler, Descartes, Spinoza, John Locke.

The length of time between Galileo, Kepler, and Descartes and Benjamin Franklin, Thomas Jefferson and John Hancock is two hundred years.

Fourth of February Seventeen Eighty Nine George Washington is elected first President of the United States of America. That is 1800 A.D. Two hundred years in the past from the present date, the first American President came to power.

The industrialisation of the United States takes one hundred and fifty years from 1800 to 1950.

The Crystal Palace exhibition in Britain in 1851 signifies the established force of this industrialisation. Over the one hundred years that follow the Empire in Europe and America acquires electricity, automobiles, aeroplanes.

That is fifty years in the past from the present date.

At that time, fifty years in the past, the United Nations publishes the Universal Doctrine of Human Rights. The membership of the United Nations includes most of the major nations on the planet.

Meaning that the history time line provided that leads to the establishment of the United Nations is only one of several histories, and says nothing at all about any of the others.

At the time of the Declaration of Universal Human Rights several civilisations are mature to the industrial level of Europe and the United States.

Asia can be divided into India and Pakistan. India is primarily Hindu.

Pakistan has for one thousand years been Muslim. For this reason Pakistan associates in many ways with North African

Arabic states that are the home of Islam.

The European geography divides into German Latin to the West and Russian Slavic to the East.

The Orient is Chinese controlled with independent nations in relationship to that such as Japan, Korea, Vietnam.

Africa is largely pre-industrialisation.

In addition, various individual cultures maintain their ethnic integrity different to the majority population.

The Hebrew Jewish culture is as usual dispersed throughout the different countries and at this date also in the process of building the new state of Israel.

Smaller populations include the Gaelic, Basque, Nordic, American Indian, Australian Aborigine and others.

If we consider the state of play over the last fifty years to the present, what we perceive depends on how we divide. And different methods of division permit quite alternative perceptions.

In one framework it looks as if the British Empire now has control of fifty three countries on the planet, those that are members of the Commonwealth. Many of those countries are very small and to one degree or another rely on the sovereign leadership of the Monarchy.

In a different framework it looks as if the Vatican has control of one fifth of the worlds population, a population that covers most of Europe, much of the United States, and various other countries.

Russia has influencing control of all of Eastern Europe.

Germany has industrial controls of Western Europe and the European Community.

China is industrialising throughout its geography and making huge investments into Africa. It also has some sort of financial understanding with the United States of America.

The United States has close relationships with Israel and Japan, and may easily have the important controls of Britain. So if we looked at it that way it may seem as if the United States is the power behind the Commonwealth.

Each of these different organisations are on a scale such that they cannot be perceived or controlled by smaller scale components.

They are all members of the United Nations.

CHAPTER EIGHT.

Written 7th to 14th October 2013.

A poem?

Ode to User Abd.

I got dark magicks. Not for publication.

Hyperlinks to strange domains.

Live in real time.

Cyber war on different planes.

Do you want to play the C.I.A. and all the rest,

Cos they can't say they play as well as me,

Its really cool,

Like the Count of St Germain.

I remember way back when,

Case hacked into Wintermute,

And Rutger Hauer made the claim

I have done questionable things.

Any way, enough of that. Why Ender at fifteen years old, Donal at twenty five years old, Gurgeh at thirty five years old.

Look at it backwards. Gurgeh is the mature identity, roughly the same person as Han Solo.

Donal is the ideal twenty something. He doesn't develop.

Ender is the child version.

If you take the Ender character forwards to Ender's Game

Part II, speaker for the dead or whatever, you are forced away from the location held by Ender at fifteen years old.

Donal Graeme is understood through memory loss. If we suppose the aim is to describe a location and the identity holding it, then he has no memory of being Ender Wiggin.

Gurgeh may be much older than thirty five, given Culture's technology, I never remember it in details that way.

However, if we understand Gurgeh as a mature version of the identity that holds the given location, where both Donal Graeme and Ender Wiggin are earlier covers.

Then we obtain an entertaining matrix for the particular identity. Although it is Han Solo.

Now I think it means Special Circumstances department of Culture's Bureau for Exotic Contact has psychoprofiled a particular identity called Gurgeh at critical stages, and used the code names Ender, Donal and Solo for some reason or another. Then stashed the profiles in seemingly innocuous adventure stories. Hard to believe, I know.

The alternative identity to consider is the Kwizatz Haderach, Luke Skywalker and Sumner Kagan.

But when it comes to Dworkin, we be talkin bout a different thing

Since his science is individual to himself.

Practiced by the individual it is called magick. Practiced by the community it is called science.

If we take away levitation of objects by mind power, then everything else the Jedi have got is available. Before we assume the credibility of the Jedi, in principle I mean, not because of the story given.

Didn't Tom Bombadil switch rings when he through it up into the air and it disappeared.

So when Bombadil catches the ring, the one he gives back to

Frodo is already a different ring?

Theory of games must account for:

It is non-verbal.

Playing cards, chess, backgammon, wei chi, dominoes.

It is strategic.

The strategic aspect is non-verbal.

Therefore it is secret.

It involves structural logic.

Meaning the tools of the game are an absolute rational.

It is mathematical.

So that a mathematical comprehension plays a non-verbal strategic conflict with absolutely rational tools based on secrecy.

It traverses across the boundaries of civilisation.

So that an Asian can play opposite an Oriental or Russian equally without having to speak any language other than what is usual to the game.

I've got a knock knock who's there joke.

Knock knock.

Who's there?

Doctor.

Doctor who?

No, not Doctor Who, Doctor Strange.

Which doctor?

No, not a Witch doctor, a doctor doctor.

Doctor Doctor?

A Bob Hope joke.

Someone says you have got two hopes, Bob Hope and No

Hope.

But you have three Bobs. Bob Hope, Bob Monkhouse and Bob Marley.

That gives two hopes and three bobs, which is obviously five somethings.

What does two hopes plus three bobs equal?

Two hopes plus three bobs equals five x.

Which seems to be mathematically true and logically false.

I've got a Doctor Doctor joke.

Doctor Doctor.

That is a pair of doctors.

What is a pair of doctors?

Doctor Who and Doctor Strange.

What? A pair o' docs.

What is a pair o' docs?

No, not a pair o' docs,

A paradox.

What is a paradox?

What is a paradox?

Well its a bit like a pair o' dice.

Why is a paradox a bit like a pair o' dice?

The following patterns are in their most standard order. They may not be entirely correct as stated. In any example of this pattern, if most of the individual patterns are correct, then the remainder are correctable. If you can see one that can be better stated, for example concludes some when could conclude all, then feel free to correct it. They are definitely not in their most perfect statement nor in their most perfect sequential order.

Therefore the game you play privately, is to correct any that need correcting, manipulate their statement into a more better form, and adjust their sequence to show symmetry.

First Figure.

1. All B is C. All A is B. Therefore All A is C.

2. No B is C. All A is B. Therefore No A is C.

3. All B is C. Some A is B. Therefore Some A is C.

4. No B is C. Some A is B. Therefore Some A is not C.

Second Figure.

1. No C is B. All A is B. Therefore No A is C.

2. All C is B. No A is B. Therefore No A is C.

3. No C is B. Some A is B. Therefore Some A is not C.

4. All C is B. Some A is not B. Therefore Some A is not C.

Third Figure.

1. All B is C. All B is A. Therefore Some A is C.

2. No B is C. All B is A. Therefore Some A is not C.

3. Some B is C. All B is A. Therefore Some A is C.

4. All B is C. Some B is A. Therefore Some A is C.

5. Some B is not C. All B is A. Therefore Some A is not C.

6. No B is C. Some B is A. Therefore Some A is not C.

Fourth Figure.

1. All C is B. All B is A. Therefore Some A is C.

2. All C is B. No B is A. Therefore Some A is not C.

3. Some C is B. All B is A. Therefore Some A is C.

4. No C is B. All B is A. Therefore Some A is not C.

5. No C is B. Some B is A. Therefore Some A is not C.

Working backwards to more simpler:

1."a equals a",

2."not a equals not a",

3."a does not equal not a".

4."a plus zero equals a"

5."a minus zero equals a"

6."not a plus zero equals not a"

7."not a minus zero equals not a"

8."a multiplied by one equals a"

9."a divided by one equals a"

10."not a multiplied by one equals not a"

11."not a divided by one equals not a"

12."a multiplied by zero equals zero"

13."a divided by zero equals zero"

14."not a multiplied by zero equals zero"

15."not a divided by zero equals zero"

16."a plus one equals one plus a"

17."a minus one equals minus one plus a"

18."not a plus one equals one plus not a"

19."not a minus one equals minus one plus not a"

20."zero plus a equals a"

21."zero minus a equals minus a"

22."zero plus not a equals not a"

23."zero minus not a equals minus not a"

24."a plus a equals a plus a"

25."a multiplied by a equals a" (Or b)

26."a minus a equals zero"

27."a divided by a equals one"

28."a plus not a equals zero"

29."a multiplied by not a equals zero"

30."a minus not a equals one"

31."a divided by not a equals minus one"

Or the first figure according to the Wizard Aristotle:

First Figure.

1.

First then take a universal negative with the terms A and B.

If no B is A, neither can any A be B. For if some A (say C) were B, it would not be true that no B is A; for C is a B.

But if every B is A then some A is B. For if no A were B, then no B could be A. But we assumed that every B is A.

Similarly too, if the premiss is particular.

For if some B is A, then some of the As must be B. For if none were, then no B would be A. But if some B is not A, there is no necessity that some of the As should not be B.

2.

If A is predicated of all B, and B of all C, A must be predicated of all C:

Similarly also, if A is predicated of no B, and B of all C, it is necessary that no C will be A.

3.

Let all B be A and some C be B. Then it is necessary that some C is A.

And if no B is A but some C is B, it is necessary that some C is not A.

So there will be a perfect syllogism.

Chapter Two.
Written 14th to 17th October 2013.

A Bob Hope joke.

Someone says you have got two hopes, Bob Hope or No Hope.

But you have three Bobs. Bob Hope, Bob Monkhouse and Bob Marley.

That gives two hopes and three bobs, which is obviously five somethings.

What does two hopes plus three bobs equal?

Two hopes plus three bobs equals five x.

Which seems to be mathematically true and logically false.

A detailed analytic of the Bob Hope joke.

First Premise.

First point.

Bob Hope is logically different to No Hope.

Only two things are logically different to no hope.

That is some hope or all hope.

Second point.

The two hopes are Bob Hope (or) no hope.

Meaning the function "or" is used, that is either or, but not both.

Whereas when you claim two hopes, you imply "and" is used.

Meaning one hope plus one hope gives two hopes.

Third point.

If No hope is one of the alternatives possible,

then that means zero hope.

If the other alternative possible is different to zero hope.

Then it must mean some hope or all hope.

Fourth point.

If we assume unless we find a contradiction:

That Bob Hope means some hope but not all hope.

Then logically the original assertion can be better stated:

That is some hope or no hope, meaning some or none.

Second premise.

First point.

You have three bobs.

The game ends at this point. I'll explain why.

You have three bobs is the mathematically and logically correct answer to the given puzzle.

We now have to access deeper structure to understand the previous statement.

We could have auto pilot analysed the second premise/ statement using the method applied to the first premise/ statement.

That is the natural arithmetic progression.

We prefer the geometric progression in our analysis.

Given that our capacity to analyse is a constant to both possibilities.

This is to guard against a mistake called "counting twice".

Bob Hope is in both premise one and two, so only gets counted once.

Side of Square = 5

Square of side of square = 25

Sum of square of other two sides = 50

Square Root of Fifty = 7.07 106 781 186 5475

Diagonal of Square = 7.07 106 781 186 5475

Diameter of circle = 7.07 106 781 186 5475

Circumference = 22.2 144 146 907 9181

Radius = 3.53 553 390 593 2738

Diameter = 7.07 106 781 186 5475

Area of circle = 39.2 699 081 698 7238

Quink = 4.44 288 293 815 8362

Pi = 3.14 159 265 358 979

Circumference divided by Side of Square gives Quink.

Circumference divided by Diameter of Circle gives Pi.

Square root of eight, divided by eight,

gives a number that when multiplied by ten is the radius, which multiplied by two is the Diameter of Circle.

1. The Game Domain Model proposes four factors in the games to which it refers and suggests those factors determine the evidential nature of the games. Which can be applied to areas not directly defined by those factors in such a way that the correct outcome is adjusted in the favour of the person who does so.

2. The four factors are agent, rules, strategy and payoff. And the four factors lead to the suggestion that specific designs are demanded by any who are in the context to which they apply. The designs are utility, economics, probability and equilibrium. And they are modified by whether the context involves perfect information or imperfect information.

3. Agent is the idea games involve players who design strategy from an individual perspective and that the strategy they design is modified by the play of other agents. Meaning that the evidential strategy of any game is dependent on the interactive play of the different agents. Rules is the idea that any game is preconstructed such that moves made by agents are restricted to what is possible and appropriate in accord with the preconstruction. Strategy is the idea that each agent plays their moves with a view to perfect action designed to realise the maximum possible payoff. Payoff is the idea that

perfect play will result in a specific outcome and nothing else.

4. Utility is the idea that all evidential action should demonstrate a maximal value against some quantifiable purpose. Economics is the idea that the better strategy will obtain a given result with most efficient use of available energy and for any expense of energy will obtain more of the desired result than any other possible strategy. Probability is the idea that in a game of chance the mathematically correct move will be the one that optimises the advantage obtained by the most probable outcome. Equilibrium is the idea that all players could play perfectly and if they do so then it would not be appropriate to deviate from what is the correct move in any particular context.

5. Perfect information games are ones where all the agents can all have all the information that is relevant to strategy. Noughts and crosses or drafts or chess are all perfect information games. Imperfect information games are ones where any one agent only has a limited amount of information of all the information that is known by all the players and where each agent has different information from any other agent. Poker or dominoes or mah jongg are all imperfect information games.

I've got some elephant jokes.

What did the man say when he saw a herd of elephants come running over the hill?

Here come a herd of elephants, running over the hill.

What did the man say when he saw a herd of elephants come running over the hill wearing sunglasses?

Nothing. He didn't recognize them, because they were wearing sunglasses.

Why do elephants paint their toenails red?

So they can hide in cherry trees.

How do you know if you have had an elephant in your fridge?

Footprints in the butter.

How do you get four elephants in a Cadillac Escalade?

Two in the back, two in the front.

If you have read this, then you know the above five elephant jokes.

A study of "sequential time complexity"

However, if we understand Gurgeh as a mature version of the identity that holds the given location, where both Donal Graeme and Ender Wiggin are earlier covers.

Then we obtain an entertaining matrix for the particular identity. Although it is Han Solo.

Now I think it means Special Circumstances department of Culture's Bureau for Exotic Contact has psychoprofiled a particular identity called Gurgeh at critical stages, and used the code names Ender, Donal and Solo for some reason or another. Then stashed the profiles in seemingly innocuous adventure stories. Hard to believe, I know.

I don't agree with the way the above is stated. It is taken from chapter one.

I can not go back and change the original statement. If I try to do so, it will register the change as present moment.

For a specific record, this is one example, in reference to the above statement:

(cur | prev) 00:08, 16 October 2013 Shadowjack (discuss | contribs) . . (3,878 bytes) (-3,931) . . (undo)

(cur | prev) 00:02, 16 October 2013 Shadowjack (discuss | contribs) . . (7,809 bytes) (+3,948) . . (undo)

(cur | prev) 11:30, 15 October 2013 Shadowjack (discuss | contribs) . . (3,861 bytes) (+2) . . (undo)

(cur | prev) 11:29, 15 October 2013 Shadowjack (discuss |

contribs) . . (3,859 bytes) (+48) . . (undo)

(cur | prev) 11:24, 15 October 2013 Shadowjack (discuss | contribs) . . (3,811 bytes) (+182) . . (undo)

Now if you go to view history at the top of this page, click on it.

Then click on the date for 11.24, 15 October 2013, it will take you to the text at that time. Then just keep clicking view newer version at the top of the text and it will take you through the changes to the text.

It is called a mistake.

Solution here:

In Ender's Game the novel that may not make it into the film, I don't know. Is that in the later battles they are continued as training exercises. The individuals involved are only told afterwards that it was the real thing.

Now what if that is false.

Instead, that only training exercises happened.

If that is so, then Ender maintains his cover. A fabricated story of any desired sort follows. Or a true story of someone else.

Then, that the preferred model for this system as a twentysomething is Donal Graeme.

After the Donal Graeme story he takes a holiday as Han Solo.

And the identity in question is a Special Circumstances operative for Contact, within Culture called Jurnau Gurgeh.

Real time: At the same time as writing this note:

Britney Spears, music video - "Work" is released on music tv.

Chapter Three.
Written 17th to 19th October.

The question of the fourth Bob.

This is of course Bob Parkhurst, played by Gabrielle, in the Blackadder chronicles.

More widely recognizable as Joan of Arc.

So it looks like Gabrielle played both roles.

So if we have Bop Hope, Bob Monkhouse and Bob Marley.

I don't see how Bob Parkhurst is the fourth Bob.

Does it mean young Bob is to be treated mannishly?

The version by Doris Day:

A-tisket a-tasket

A green and yellow basket

I wrote a letter to my love

And on the way I dropped it,

I dropped it,I dropped it,

And on the way I dropped it.

A little boy he picked it up and put it in his pocket.

Coincidence between three different languages:

Lattice One, Logic:

I. (a => b v c) => [(a < b => c) ∧ (a < c => b)]

II. (d => a v b) => [(a => d < b) ∧ (b => d < a)]

III. (e => a v c) => [(a => e < c) ∧ (c => e < a)]

IV. (f => b < c) => [(b => f v c) ∧ (c => b < f)]

V. (g => c < b) => [(c => g v b) ∧ (b => c < g)]

Lattice One, Algebra:

I. (a = b . c) => [(a / b = c) ∧ (a / c = b)]

II. (d = a . b) => [(a = d / b) ∧ (b = d / a)]

III. (e = a . c) => [(a = e / c) ∧ (c = e / a)]

IV. (f = b / c) => [(b = f . c) ∧ (c = b / f)]

V. $(g = c / b) => [(c = g . b) \land (b = c / g)]$

Lattice One, Number:

I. $(8 = 2 . 4) => [(2 = 8 / 4) \land (4 = 8 / 2)]$

II. $(16 = 8 . 2) => [(8 = 16 / 2) \land (2 = 16 / 8)]$

III. $(32 = 8 . 4) => [(8 = 32 / 4) \land (4 = 32 / 8)]$

IV. $(1/2 = 2 / 4) => [(2 = 1/2 . 4) \land (4 = 2 / 1/2)]$

V. $(2 = 4 / 2) => [(4 = 2 . 2) \land (2 = 4 / 2)]$

Three Moirae:

Clotho: Spinner

Lachesis: Calculator

Atropos: Finisher

Mnemosene and her nine daughters.

Calliope: storytelling.

Clio: history.

Erato: love poetry.

Euterpe: music.

Melpomene: singing.

Polyhymnia: sacred poetry.

Terpsichore: dance.

Thalia: comedy.

Urania: astronomy.

The original actors in all of Mr Shakespeare's plays:

William Shakespeare, Richard Burbadge, John Hemmings, Augustine Phillips, William Kempt, Thomas Poope.

George Bryan, Henry Condell, William Slye, Richard Cowly, John Lowine, Samuell Crosse, Alexander Cooke.

Samuel Gilburne, Robert Armin, William Ostler, Nathan Field, John Underwood, Nicholas Tooley, William Ecclestone.

Joseph Taylor, Robert Benfield, Robert Goughe, Richard Robinson, John Shancke, John Rice.

A puzzle:

Every time you play a hand differently from the way you would have played it if you could see all your opponents' cards, they gain.

And every time you play your hand the same way you would have played it if you could see all their cards, they lose.

Conversely, every time opponents play their hands differently from the way they would have if they could see all your cards, you gain.

And every time they play their hands the same way they would have played if they could see all your cards, you lose.

So David Sklansky's ideas as to poker at their simpler level are all very good.

That level of dexterity with a deck of cards is useful.

Patience.

Fifty two cards shuffled, placed separately face down.

Turn up one card, then try to turn up the similar card in a different suit.

If you turn up a matching card, then remove them from the game.

If you don't turn up a matching card then both cards get turned face down.

Keep playing until you clear the deck.

Playing this game, there is a strategy running through your mind as you play.

Assume you do not at the present stage have the most perfect strategy for this game running through your mind.

Assume also that a most perfect strategy for this game exists.

If you play this game repetitively,

then eventually as time goes by the most perfect strategy offers itself to you quite naturally.

It then naturally happens that you play the particular game with a perfect strategy for itself.

You learn it non-verbally and only by not less than ten hours of playing the one game.

1a. The message is that: it is a house game.

1b. You can bet against the house. In a game of poker with ten players, three are any good, seven provide the income. The income gets divided among the three players who are any good.

1c. I toss a coin. It spins as it rises in the air. As it falls I catch it, and without looking turn it over on the back of my other hand.

It is covered so I have not yet seen the outcome.

I am to tell my associate if it is heads or tails. If it is heads, he is to bet on black in a roullette game. If it is tails he is to bet on red.

I am not to look at the coin to see whether it is heads or tails until the ball is spinning round the roullette wheel.

1d. Only three possibilities exist.

All three possibilities are given an equal value in the category called possible. Each possibility has the same eigenvalue.

The possibilities are red or black or neither red nor black.

1e. If zero comes up, everyone who has bet on red or black loses.

But there is only one zero among dozens of reds and blacks.

Chapter Four
Written 19th to 21st October 2013.

A theory of gambling, part one.

First point.

It occurs to me that there is a "confused event" in relation to what I am about to consider.

The "confused bit" is not linear.

It is not in the interests of nearly everybody for the confused bit to be explained.

The only people who want the "confused bit" clarified are a very small proportion of those who gamble.

For this reason it seems to be something different to what it is first thought to be.

Here is my analogous example.

Plenty of people may want to ride horses. They have fun with it. They like trying to work out how to get the saddle on the horse, how to hold the rains so they thread through the little and index finger. How to make the horse turn left or right or whatever. And they are happy to be instructed in everything to that end.

Most people do not want to learn how to ride a horse like a red indian or a cowboy.

So the sort of gambling theory that I would like to entertain is a bit like that. People just don't want it.

Second point.

There are many forms of gambling. People bet on horse races, dog races, football matches or anything else. In these areas which I do not touch, it seems to me that knowledge of the variables in the event is the important factor. Skill at gambling less so. In the sense that if you know the race is between only two or three possible horses, the only gamble is which of the three do you bet on.

So whereas that kind of event is gambling, the skill involved is not skill at gambling so much as skill at knowing horses.

Whereas gambling itself has structure. So what I would like to clarify here, is some of the ideas in relation to the structure of gambling.

And this is what most people do not want to know.

You may argue and say: "They do really".

But they don't. And if they know ideas of this sort, they do not apply tactics that reflect the strategic knowledge.

Why is that?

Third point.

Having this knowledge as to gambling does you no good at all.

It soon means that you will not be included in professional games, and amateur games do not pay for its original purpose.

So what is it for?

Fourth point.

It is not appropriate, even if one could do so, to exhaustively describe this matter in terms of its most essential simple elements.

The ideas of system incompleteness and precision of knowing inter-related variables explains why this is so.

That is you somehow have to build in to your own understanding the sense that if you know certain parts properly well, the better you can know those parts, the less well you know some other parts. And that it is the nature of any system that explanation of one part normally costs in regard to covering up some other part.

Fifth point.

The two games I have in mind are blackjack and poker. Blackjack is also known as pontoon and is played in many professional casinos.

It is okay to turn up at a casino, play blackjack for a couple of hours and lose one hundred pounds sterling.

You have to lose, otherwhise the croupier gets into trouble.

She will let you play as long as you don't win. So it is a pleasant two hours leisure activity that costs a hundred pounds.

What the croupier does know, because it is her business, is that you have taken her control of the deck of cards.

If you lose, then only the croupier knows. She is happy for you to play in that sense.

If you win, then the casino house system knows. You don't want that.

(This is an aside: If you play at the same casino over a small space of time, so that you become familiar. Then they will soon let you win enough to pay for all your evenings drinks, a three course meal for two people, and still leave with one hundred pounds sterling in your pocket. Any time you play. So in that sense the casino is friendly enough.)

Sixth point.

For this article I will freely draw on some of the ideas detailed by Mr Sklansky as to poker theory.

I am not referring to his work while writing. So that side of it is from memory. Meaning that if it is clear in my writing that it is similar to ideas mentioned elsewhere, that is the reason.

The form of poker I prefer is where each player is dealt three cards, then immediately two cards.

There is one round of betting on the five cards given which is the ante.

Then each player can exchange any number of cards once, before betting starts properly.

Any player can fold at any stage without their cards being seen by other players, by throwing in their cards face down.

The win sequence is:

Royal straight flush.

Four of a kind.

Full house.

Flush.

Straight.

Three of a kind.

Two pairs.

One pair.

High card.

The betting goes in a circle from left to right. Each player has to maintain the quantity of bet raised by their turn in each round. Meaning that you only bet once in any round, when it is your turn.

When it is your turn to bet, you can stay in by either meeting the present stake or by raising it to not more than twice the present stake. If you raise by any amount, then the next player has to meet that or fold.

The betting on one hand can continue indefinitely until all but one player has folded, or two players remaining decide to see each other.

If you pay to see the other player you put in the present stake without raising, when it is your turn against the remaining player and you both have to show your cards.

If you have to fold at any stage because you do not have the required stake to stay in, then that is called going bust.

The player with the best hand at the end of the game wins the amount generated in that round, given they have the required stake to stay in the game.

When one round is completely finished, the deal moves to the person on the left of the previous dealer.

The cards are randomly shuffled once by the dealer on their receiving the deck. Having shuffled once they are not shuffled again until the next person becomes dealer.

A theory of gambling, part two.

First idea:

Every time you play a hand differently from the way you would have played it if you could see all your opponents' cards, they gain.

And every time you play your hand the same way you would have played it if you could see all their cards, they lose.

Conversely, every time opponents play their hands differently from the way they would have if they could see all your cards, you gain.

And every time they play their hands the same way they would have played if they could see all your cards, you lose.

Where do we locate winning and losing?

The commonplace gambler will say that they have had a good night if on leaving the casino they have more money in their pocket than when they arrived. So they place winning at the location of more money at the end than at the beginning.

And the same gambler will say that they have had a bad night if on leaving the casino they have no money in their pocket. So they place losing at the location of having spent all their money.

The fundamental theory of poker is that winning and losing are located differently.

That is:

Defensively.

Winning is when your opponents play differently from the way they would do, if they could see all your cards.

Losing is when your opponents play in such a way that it is the same as if they could see all your cards.

Offensively.

Winning is when you play in such a way that it is the same as if you could see all your opponents cards.

Losing is when you play differently from the way you would do, if you could see all your opponents cards.

So that:

Winning is when your opponents play differently from the way they would do, if they could see all your cards. Defense.

Winning is when you play in such a way that it is the same as if you could see all your opponents cards. Offense.

Losing is when your opponents play in such a way that it is the same as if they could see all your cards. Defense.

Losing is when you play differently from the way you would do, if you could see all your opponents cards. Offense.

Second idea.

To win the round to lose the hand. To win the hand to lose the game. To win the game to lose the match.

Or alternatively,

To lose the round to win the hand. To lose the hand to win the game. To lose the game to win the match.

What is the scale of victory?

The commonplace idea is to play for every point. To win every game you can if you can. If you win every point you can and every game you can then the larger matter will happen naturally.

Its symptom is a focus of attention on only the immediate moment, with no sense of context or duration.

Alternatively, the idea is to play in such a way that your method is such that you can win tournaments, even if you don't.

From the poker players perspective, the idea is this.

If you play poker with a view to profit over one year.

Then you divide the year into twelve months of play.

You divide a month into a specific number of hours of play.

The total profit obtained after one year of play is divided by the number of hours of play to provide an hourly rate.

The hourly rate is a product of the variables, number of hours played and total profit obtained.

Then given you have some idea of the profit to be obtained from five hundred hours play over one year.

You are able to calculate the immediate round, hand, game and tournament against your known hourly rate.

If your hourly rate is sometimes more sometimes less than your calculation, how it averages in practice is the thing you want to get at.

So, again with the second idea we place the location of winning and losing differently which in turn alters the method you would apply to the game.

Third idea.

When you lose, no matter how often, lose small amounts.

When you win, however infrequently, win large amounts.

This idea has to be kept separately from idea two. It is to do with being a discerning player.

Its meaning is central to what poker is.

The two variables that coincide are quality of the hand and

quantity of the pot.

The important matter is that if the quantity of the pot is good, you must win it, whether your hand is good or not.

And that if the quantity of the pot is small, you may not want to win it, whether your hand is good or not.

Most seriously, this: that if you had a straight flush early in a game with a small pot, your single best move is to fold without putting too much into the pot, and without anyone seeing your cards.

This is a necessity, not a choice. It pays for a reverse bluff later. I'll explain the forms of bluff a bit further on.

And again with idea three we are adjusting the placement of winning and losing. In particular it generates a confidence in losing hands with a small quantity pot regardless of the quality of cards dealt. And also generates an urgency towards winning hands with a sizeable pot regardless of the quality of cards dealt.

Fourth Idea.

Tight and loose play.

Playing loose is when the games have only just started, the pot is small, there are loads of players.

So here you should ante up in every round, play every game, but only bet small amounts and fold early.

Playing tight is when the games are well under way, the pot is increasingly attractive, the stronger players are all that remains.

So here you should ante up only in the rounds where your opening cards are good, do not play the games that offer low stakes, but bet large amounts all the way through to the end where the stakes are high and the pot is high quantity.

Fifth Idea.

It just occurred to me that this is an excellent place to make a Lady Gaga reference. Since she has made poker so famous in modern times.

So anyway, Lady Gaga, I love you, poker face, fan from the beginning, lets do dinner.

What we mean by poker face is entirely a product of skill at bluffing. Bluffing is not usually understood properly.

This is my explanation of what bluffing is.

Bluffing is basically to do with unconscious signals. The sense is that throughout our game we, and all the other players make physical gestures that are observable by other players. The assumed proposition is that there is a direct link between what we see when we look at the hand of cards we are dealt, and the physical gestures we make that are observable by other players. And as well to do with what we actually do when we play the cards we are dealt.

The science of bluffing is designed to re-associate our unconscious gestures to different hands of cards from what is natural.

This is in two possible ways.

One is if the person reading our gestures was mis-directed at the start. The result being that they have the wrong code in terms of gesture to cards dealt. So that when the same gesture is made, they assume its association to a different hand of cards from what is in fact the case.

Two is if we have conditioned our gestures so that they are different to what is instinctively natural in regard to cards dealt. This is a sort of "cool". It means that if a fellow player reading our gestures knows a standard model that usually works, they will have a confidence that it will also work here, which it won't.

The combination of these two elements of the science of bluffing gives what is known as a poker face.

The idea is you do not change your "cool" at any stage of the game at least in theory.

It is only mastery of the science of "bluffing" that enables you to maintain your cool, resulting in a poker face.

It is not the case in this system that you only bluff occasionally. The matter of bluffing is operational through all of your game.

These bluffs must be built in as standard:

Pure bluff. Given a pair of aces(Ace is high), play as if you have two pairs. You will win if players with better hands fold too early.

So the idea of pure bluff is to force mistake in the other players' game all the way through to the end.

Semi bluff. Given three of a kind, play as if you have three of a kind. You will win if the other players think you have a full house or think you have a pair.

Reverse bluff. Given a full house, if it is a small pot, then play as if you have a pair, and fold on the second round of betting without showing your cards.

Double bluff. Given a good hand such as four of a kind, pretend you have two pairs, then bet really high amounts as if you are using the pure bluff. You will win if other players think it is funny and immediately raise you the same high amounts. But you have four of a kind.

Combination bluff. Manipulation of any of the basic four types into their possible alternatives.

The important message to remember is that you should employ all of these types of bluff through out your game without informing the other players when you are bluffing and when you are not.

It is in this sort of way that a poker face becomes one of the tools in your repertoire.

Sixth idea.

Quality of hand dealt.

The winning hands of poker are reflective of the most probable occurrence. So that a straight flush is least probable and a pair is most probable, where every hand has a highest card.

The non-commutable variables are quality of hand against quantity of pot.

The four extremes are:

good hand with a large pot.

good hand with a small pot.

weak hand with a large pot.

weak hand with a small pot.

The important bit is you can not play in such a way that you only win when you have a good hand with a large pot.

Because you also want to be able to win when you have a weak hand with a large pot.

So that means if the pot is small you do not always want to win whether your hand is good or weak.

Furthermore, since the weaker hands are always the most probable, you have to be able to play weak hands well so that you can defeat players with good hands or weak hands competing for the same high gain pot.

Good play of weak hands is the single essential to covering your basic game. If you can play weak hands well then something alters in significant ways to the advantage of your whole game.

CHAPTER NINE.

Strategic Context.

The appropriateness of strategic studies in this context is worth checking. The presupposition I will affirm is that whatever strategic studies is and what ever the content of such involoves, it is better left to the professional organisations, namely the American Central Intelligence Agency, The Israeli Mossad, the French Foreign Legion and suchlike. Because they are best positioned to attain a high level of understanding in regard to the matter of strategic studies.

And the corollary, that in this context what that high level of understanding may be, the attainment of it will always be frustrated by the fact that it is by definition impossible to attain in this context.

And if I affirm that the line stated is correct, then what does that entail.

My second point is that given the above stated line is correct, then there is sufficient value in having a relatively open forum in this context for the same matter, that will by nature of the environment necessitate a distorted content. The given matter then, can be considered under the built in condition that it is in a particular domain of discourse.

The contrary line is to say that we can say nothing and that the matter is an entirely closed subject to any but the professional organisations, or that if we do say anything at all we are bound to follow the rule base of those people who do intelligence work for one of the named professional organisations.

But it may be that we do not really know what that rule base is, we are not operational for some specific organisation, we simply want to open a conversation as to the matter of strategic studies. Is that conceivable and if it is, how should it be done?

The purpose of this discourse is not to answer the above question, since I think that it is a question that must be answered by those people who want to develop a strategic studies course in this context.

The purpose of this discourse, is, given the above understanding is clear and the requirement that others satisfy the explicit and implicit responsibility they have in order to provide a strategic studies course, to answer the problem: "Know your enemy".

The problem "Know your enemy" is an abstract multi-hierarchical complex.

For the problem to exist requires that a solution is not known. If a solution were known, then the problem could not exist.

For any and all given problem, we have an adequate method that is to be applied to provide a working solution in the first instance that can be made entirely sufficient meeting all necessary conditions of a solution as time goes by.

The problem called "Know your enemy" defeats this adequate method, because the nature of the problem forces a circular fault in the adequate method that is to be applied to provide a working solution.

To understand this point I will provide an analogous example. We can suppose the scenario where some given mechanism works effectively even if any particular fault occurs in the singular. It would only fail if two unlikely faults occur at the exact same time, and it is guaranteed that the mechanism is made such that two unlikely faults cannot occur at the exact same time. Therefore the mechanism only fails when it matters. The difficult understanding that must be completely clear is that only when two unlikely faults must not occur at the exact same time is the moment when they do so. And consequently, we have the scenario where the mechanism only fails at the exact moment when it must not, and it never fails at any moment when it does not matter.

The above scenario of the mechanism that only fails when it must not, and never fails when it does not matter cannot be solved by the adequate method that is to be applied to provide a working solution in the first instance. That is because it is the nature of the scenario that the problem exists. It means that the problem by its nature cannot be solved from within the scenario to which it refers.

The solution to the above problem is as follows. In the scenario to which it refers it is a necessity that it be understood that the mechanism works effectively all the time when it does not matter. And that the same mechanism will only fail when it must not fail. Therefore the solution is that a totally separate mechanism must always be in place at the moment when the other mechanism must not fail. Since the first mechanism does not fail every time that it must not and never fails when it does not matter, the second mechanism must nearly always never be used, but must always be in place at the moment when the first mechanism must not fail. In that way the problem is solvable.

In a similar way we can solve the problem: "Know your enemy". We can suppose that the problem by its nature cannot be solved from within the scenario to which it refers. That is because it is the nature of the scenario that the problem exists.

The solution then is to consider the problem: "Know

someone else's enemy."

Through study of the problem "know someone else's enemy" we do not have the same in built complexity and we can in this way obtain an understanding.

And what we discover through study of other people's enemy a constant exists in each particular case, that enables us to make the following argument.

The enemy is an unkown and unknowable that manifests in the particular as a knowable and known.

The knowable and known is a particular aspect or manifestation of the enemy, through which the enemy operates.

The most fundamental constant through any aspect of the manifestation of the enemy is the desire for success.

The most fundamental method used by any aspect of the manifestation of the enemy is betrayal.

The most fundamental motive of each aspect of the manifestation of the enemy is envy.

This leads us to ask the question what do we actually mean by enemy?

And many people will affirm: there is no enemy.

The problem with the affirmation, there is no enemy, is that it claims the enemy is not, which is very offensive.

It involves a forced struggle on the part of the enemy to exist.

The closest explanation of where we can correctly affirm: the enemy is not, and, there is no enemy, is in the game of chess.

Given two opposing players in the game of chess, neither one would honestly claim the other was their real enemy, simply on the basis that one would probably not play one's real enemy at the game of chess. And also, the level of agreement between both players as to the rules and nature of appropriate play has already neutralised the energy such that hard enmity cannot express itself.

But outside of that agreed combat between opposing minds according to preconstructed rules it is not clear how the affirmation:

"there is no enemy" can be anything but false.

The question what do we mean by enemy results in a consideration of two kinds of definition, at least.

One kind of enemy is much like us, only different. So then perhaps the population of a bordering territory, such that any conflict is as to ownership of territory. Or a different branch of the same religion as us, or a different interpretation of the same religion. These and various others are examples of the case where we find the enemy to be like us, only different. And this kind of enemy is always knowable.

The second kind of enemy is other to us. It is called "other". We exist or it does, not both. Where the other is, we are not.

Does this second kind of enemy exist? And the more we affirm not, the more it struggles to be.

So instead we affirm, it only can exist where we are not, and it may not exist where we are. In that way we are not specifying that it cannot or does not exist anywhere, simply that it does not exist here. Tuberculosis is this kind of enemy and medicine has many examples of similar kind. And this kind of enemy is to a large extent unknowable.

The difference between freedom fighter and terrorist is useful in order to develop our idea of the enemy.

The difference is not a euphemism and we can specify the difference very clearly in terms of two factors and their contradictory, as follows:

Freedom fighter is defined by two factors and must meet

both conditions not only one.

1. Has the ethical advantage.

2. Has a positive statement of identity.

Terrorist is defined by two factors and must meet both conditions not only one.

1. Has the ethical disadvantage.

2. Has a negative statement of identity.

If for the sake of this argument we define the good as a verb, not a noun, then that is an active doing value. To have the ethical advantage in an abstract sense means to be aligned to the good as a verb. And to have the ethical disadvantage in an abstract sense means to be opposed to the good as a verb. The significance of this is that it is not necessary to consider both sides in a conflict in order to determine ethical advantage, it is only necessary to consider any side individually, and to determine whether it is aligned to the good or whether it is opposed to the good.

In regard to negative and positive statement of identity, it is a matter of existance or proof of being.

A positive statement of identity means that without the opponent the identity still exists, whereas a negative statement of identity means that without the opponent the identity does not exist. Therefore we can show the freedom fighter outside of the scenario where he exists as a force in some conflict. And we cannot find the terrorist outside of the scenario where he is defined by opposition to some positive entity.

By positive entity in the given world I mean some specific established structure on which the given world is based, such as the Vatican, the Pentagon, or the Deutschebank. So the enemy in this sense would literally define their existence by the opposition to some such structure, and it is as if they obtain being by a negative statement. Furthermore there is a difference between the opposition to any particular President of the Pentagon, and the opposition to the structure of the President of the Pentagon.

Therefore we can posit the kind of enemy that is opposed to the existence of the established structures on which the given world is based, and ask whether that kind of enemy exists or does not exist.

The previous discourse has attended to the problem called "Know your enemy". At the very least it has opened the understanding to the fact that the problem even exists. Since it is a problem that most who begin to consider strategic studies would be presented with even though outside of that particular domain of discourse the problem may never be looked at.

The next point I would make is that within the domain of discourse called strategic studies the problem of "know your enemy" is not answered at all, and if it is answered it is done in such a way as to mislead and disinform the enquirer. This is because the nature of the problem is very difficult.

The particular reason is only this specifically: that when any person considers the problem "know your enemy" they face a gloss.

That is, if any individual who so ever directs their own perception towards their own enemy they will see a shine.

By gloss or shine I mean a sort of optical illusion in the perception that cannot in this instance be easily overcome.

The way that I suggested this can be overcome is to consider the problem: "Know someone else's enemy" since in that way there is no gloss or shine to the perception.

And having obtained a clearer understanding of someone else's enemy in abstract this can be usefully applied as a framework to the problem know your enemy.

Finally, if the thing itself is the problem know your enemy, and the previous discourse is my explanation of the thing itself, then the following is the thing itself explained:

1. The problem "know your enemy" is an abstract multihierarchical complex.

2. It is similar to the scenario where a mechanism only fails when it must not and never fails when it does not matter.

3. That is because it is the nature of the scenario that the problem exists. It means that the problem by its nature cannot be solved from within the scenario to which it refers.

4. The solution then is to consider the problem: "Know someone else's enemy."

5. The enemy is an unkown and unknowable that manifests in the particular as a knowable and known.

6. The knowable and known is a particular aspect or manifestation of the enemy, through which the enemy operates.

7. The most fundamental constant through any aspect of the manifestation of the enemy is the desire for success.

8. The most fundamental method used by any aspect of the manifestation of the enemy is betrayal.

9. The most fundamental motive of each aspect of the manifestation of the enemy is envy.

10. The problem with the affirmation, there is no enemy, is that it claims the enemy is not, which is very offensive.

It involves a forced struggle on the part of the enemy to exist.

11. One kind of enemy is much like us, only different. And this kind of enemy is always knowable.

12. The second kind of enemy is other to us. It is called "other". We exist or it does, not both. Where the other is, we are not.

Does this second kind of enemy exist? And the more we

affirm not, the more it struggles to be. So instead we affirm, it only can exist where we are not, and it may not exist where we are. In that way we are not specifying that it cannot or does not exist anywhere, simply that it does not exist here. And this kind of enemy is to a large extent unknowable.

13. An enemy defined by the fact that it is opposed to the good, when the good is used as a verb, not a noun.

14. An enemy therefore that has the ethical disadvantage.

15. An enemy that can not make a positive statement of identity.

16. An enemy that defines its existance by a negative statement of identity.

17. An enemy that is opposed to the existence of the established structures on which the given world is based.

CHAPTER TEN.

The clever question is ontological and the answer cannot be provided in a way that is immediately clear to the intelligent beginner. And perhaps the answer cannot be provided clearly in the first explanation of itself. And perhaps the answer has to be indirectly noticed since the question is not itself clear. The ontological question is "What is that?". And two people look at the "that" which is pointed at and both perceive some different "thing". Perhaps that is one way to indirectly notice the answer. There are deep things like that, and there are not-deep things like that. So when I look at the "that" do I see what is deep or what is not-deep? And if I then were to explain didactically what "that" is, and provide an explanation of what is not-deep, perhaps that would be to disinform from what is deep. And if what is deep cannot be explained after the explanation of what is not-deep, and I have already explained that I only see what is not-deep, then maybe what is deep can no longer be explained ever. Which would be most unfortunate.

Or perhaps there are two ways of perceiving "that" which is not-deep and we have not yet decided which way that is not-deep we prefer. And so I jump in and say what "that" is and only explain one way of perceiving "that" and do not acknowledge that the other not-deep way of perceiving "that" even exists. Then perhaps any who had followed my explanation would think that "that" is only what I had said it to be.

They would be like people looking at a cube of three dimensions, told only to look at one side because "that" is a square, and then only have one corner explained so they miss every part of "that" except for a ninety degree angle. But maybe that is not even a cube, maybe it is a multidimensional hypercube capable of navigating the metacomplex for purposes quite unknown. Now in that case if I look at "that" and give an immediate explanation of it as a ninety degree angle which is two lines meeting at a point where one line is perpendicular to the other does that mean that it is false. No it is true. And it is still true even though some other person can look at the same thing and see a complete square including the corner I have described. And some person who sees deeper can look at the same thing and see a complete cube, including the square and corner. And some other person can look at the same thing and see a multidimensional hypercube.

My reason for the previous dialogue is to describe what is the problem with answering the question "What is that?". The question "What is that?" is only three words so seems so easy to answer in any particular case. But it is called the ontological question so it must be much deeper than it seems or else it would not be called the ontological question.

8QnMQ/x

8 Questions: Where and When, Who and What, How and Why, Which and Whether.

To the power of n: Where else and When else, Who else and What else, How else and Why else, Which other and Whether other.

Multiplied by MQ: Meta Questions directed towards answers to 8Qn in terms of structure, process, function, purpose, form, context, content.

Divided by x: A possibility versus probability categorisation in order to weight the values of the analytic.

$a + 0 = a$ and $a \cdot 1 = a$

a + 1 = 1 + a and a . 0 = 0

a . b = b . a and a + b = b + a

(a + b) + c = a + (b + c) and (a . b) . c = a . (b . c)

a + (b . c) = (a + b) . (a + c) and a . (b + c) = (a . b) + (a . c)

a + ~a = 0 and a . ~a = 0

a + a = a + a and a . a = a

~(a + b) = ~a + ~b and ~(a . b) = ~a . ~b

The above schematic is a prime pattern where further reduction is not possible without losing the information to which it refers. Addition of information to the above schematic serves no good purpose. If we classify the given prime pattern as the Boolean Prime then we can examine it according to a designed method. The first point is to distinguish between whether it is correct or incorrect and whether it is true or false. By correct or incorrect we are checking whether it is an accurate statement of the Boolean Prime. By true or false we are checking whether the Boolean Prime is itself true or false. If we discover that the given schematic is an accurate statement of the Boolean Prime and that the Boolean Prime is true, then we have a Prime Pattern that is cleared as sound. Prime Patterns of this sort are collectable items of significant value and the game then is to use the given Prime Pattern as a measure of the sort of thing to be collected. We could name the following as the Prime Pattern of P's and Q's.

p means "p is true" Affirmation.

~p means "p is false" Negation.

p v q means "either p is true, or q is true, or both" Or.

p ^ q means "both p and q are true" And.

p > q means "if p is true, then q is true". If - then.

p < q means "since q is true, then p is true. Since - then.

p <-> q means "p and q are either both true or both false" If and only if.

These are cardinal articulations that must be known previous to any more sophisticated information. The idea is to question in regard to the more sophisticated information what are the cardinal articulations that must be clearly stated at the previous level. And then to collect together only those patterns detailed as cardinal articulations and to exclude out any thing that is not specifically a cardinal articulation. Imaginatively it must be relatively easy to detail in a single volume what are the reduced prime patterns stated in terms of cardinal articulations. It is clear when the stated pattern is correct since we cannot find anything previous to itself. We could call it "The Book of Cardinal Articulations and Prime Patterns".

The prime pattern of p's and q's must exist before any truth tables can be detailed. P is true or p is not true is the decision that must be made before we can use the prime pattern of p's and q's. Given two different decision makers the same p at the same time can be both true and false since the nature of what truth is does not demand that two different decision makers assign the same value to p. This is provable. How do we decide whether p is true or p is false? A judgement as to the truth or falsity of p is an early decision that determines all the outcomes that are derived from p. The reason that two different decision makers can correctly assign contradictory value to p is because truth depends on the existence of three variables. We can provide an example of what is true in terms of 2+2=4 is correspondent, coherent and useful. By correspondent we mean it refers accurately to something outside itself. By coherent we mean it belongs to a larger system within which it makes sense. And by useful we mean it has a utility in regard to some purpose. Truth as hard as 2+2=4 is correspondent, coherent and useful. For any p its truth or falsity depends on correspondence, coherence and utility. And for that reason if two different decision makers are judging from two different systems with two different purposes and two different perspectives, then those two decision makers could assign two different values for any p at the same time, such that where one says p is true for the same p the other will say it is false. The decision as to whether p is true is a non-arbitrary choice. That means for any p that is said to be true based on given reasons, it is not possible to arbitrarily claim the contradictory, that p is false.

For any p that we state as true, we must be able to demonstrate these reasons: P is externally correspondent to some fact. P is internally coherent within a larger system. P is useful according to some pragmatic purpose.

For any p that we state as false, we must be able to demonstrate these reasons: P does not externally correspond to any known fact. P is entirely incoherent within a larger system. P has no use according to some pragmatic purpose.

It is not enough that some p fails to meet our criteria for truth that it is stated as false. For any p to be stated as false it must meet our criteria for falsity. And that necessitates the use of the universal operator which is to say: Every p is true, false, or neither true nor false. Since only those p which meet all of our criteria for falsity are called false, and only those p which meet all of our criteria for truth are called true, therefore some p must exist which are neither true nor false.

The following which begins with the Pythagoras code could be called the prime pattern of number. One plus two plus three plus four equals ten, proving the first four numbers are the sum of number. x squared equals x whether x equals one or x equals zero, proving one does not equal zero. Any number squared divided by two plus half the original number is equal to the number of times each of the consecutive integers in the original number combine with itself and each of the others once, as in dominoes. Pi squared and the square root of pi are both constant. A place holder exists that is neither one nor zero. What is the place holder?

It is useful to clarify in particular two peculiar understandings that seem to be evident from the analysis up to this point. One is that given our criteria for falsity and our criteria for truth that it is a necessity we accept some propositions exist that are neither true nor false, such that using the universal operator we must say for all propositions every p is true or false or neither true nor false. The second peculiar understanding is that given two decision makers as to the truth or falsity of p it is at least possible in many not all cases that the two decision makers can take a contradictory position.

For those two reasons we are forced to notice a difference between the truth of 2+2=4 and other propositions that meet our stated criteria for truth. Because unlike many of those other propositions the truth of 2+2=4 is not easily contradicted. That is, given two decision makers it is not clear how either decision maker could correctly claim the falsity of 2+2=4. That would suggest that we can add a fourth criteria that is met by this type of proposition. And that fourth criteria is that this type of proposition is capable of universal abstraction.

Given that, we can suppose a difference between any proposition that meets our three basic criteria for truth and those propositions that also meet the fourth criteria of being capable of universal abstraction. Understanding what is universal abstraction is a significant matter. Two plus two equals four and 2+2=4 are both late languages in sign label for something that is itself universally abstract. To understand this it is claimed that "equals means the power of making different things the same". So the sign label "equals =" is a functional power that combines what is different so that they seem the same. Then what is the universal abstraction?

It is the case that ** and ** is **** and that is not the same as @@ and @@ is @@@@. So because the universally abstract pattern is common to both we invent a sign label system which is above both. There is nothing in the sign label 2 which tells us anything about number. It is only that we have become so accustomed to thinking 2 and two are what they signify that we tend to not notice the complete lack of any content.

Now the third peculiar understanding is to clarify the difference between first propositions and the cardinal articulations of prime patterns. First propositions may nearly always be neither true nor false because of their hypothetical nature as first propositions. Meaning that they probably fail our truth criteria on grounds of not being coherent within a larger system since that larger system does not yet exist at the time of first propositions. We would tend to call these hypothetically true propositions and build our truth tables as if they were true unless we find a contradiction in which case that would count as incoherence so they would move to being hypothetically false. And if we do not find a contradiction we would forget that our first propositions are only hypothetically true.

The cardinal articulation of prime patterns is capable of universal abstraction. That is because the truth of the prime patterns is first in structure rather than first in time sequence. For this reason when it comes to hard truth comparable with the strength of 2+2=4 we do better to investigate the Boolean prime pattern, the prime pattern of p's and q's and the prime pattern of number. Given these three examples of what is meant by cardinal articulations then other prime patterns that meet all four criteria for truth can be collected together.

To re-iterate we can reinforce our earlier definition of the criteria for truth and falsity:

For any p that we state as true, we must be able to demonstrate these reasons: P is externally correspondent to some fact. P is internally coherent within a larger system. P is useful according to some pragmatic purpose. P is capable of universal abstraction.

For any p that we state as false, we must be able to demonstrate these reasons: P does not externally correspond to any known fact. P is entirely incoherent within a larger system. P has no use according to some pragmatic purpose. P is not capable of universal abstraction.

And why this is useful is because it means we can assess beforehand the hypothetical truth and falsity of our propositions that are neither true nor false. That is, where a proposition is neither true nor false, and we find that it is likely to be capable of universal abstraction then we are more confident about using it as hypothetically true even though it has not yet met all of our other criteria for truth. And where a proposition is neither true nor false, and we find that it is likely to never be capable of universal abstraction then we are more confident about using it as hypothetically false even though it has not yet met all of our other criteria for falsity.

$a - 0 = a$ and $a / 1 = a$

$a - 1 = -1 + a$ and $a / 0 = 0$

$a / b = a / b$ and $a - b = -b + a$

$0 - a = -a$ and $1 / a = 1 / a$

$1 - a = -a + 1$ and $0 / a = 0$

$(a - b) - c = a - (b - c)$ and $(a / b) / c = a / (b / c)$

$a - (b / c) = (a - b) / (a - c)$ and $a / (b - c) = (a / b) - (a / c)$

$a - \sim a = 1$ and $a / \sim a = -1$

$a - a = 0$ and $a / a = 1$

$\sim(a - b) = \sim a - \sim b$ and $\sim(a / b) = \sim a / \sim b$

The previous schematic is a continuation of the rules of the Boolean Prime. As stated it may be correct or incorrect. And when correctly stated it may be true or false. What is clear is that the prime pattern does lend itself to be correctly stated in its most true formulation. The difficulty is as to whether it is possible to check the correctness and truth of the patterns. It is not the case that a more correct true pattern can simply be offered as an alternative to the one given since we would be in the same position in regard to checking the more correct true pattern. And it is not the case that a different decision maker can affirm or negate any particular terms of the patterns, since any alteration to the given patterns would itself have to be demonstrated to be accurate and true. Therefore it is asked whether any person who has the stated patterns can follow a process by which to check their truth without having to refer to a different decision maker. And the reason that matters is because we may not want to agree with the other decision maker on any area of this that we cannot demonstrate in a universally abstract way.

The process then, that is best used, in order to check the correctness and truth of the patterns will now be explained. What makes the process in itself attractive is that it self-validates. And also that the process is organic and once understood can be individually used by different decision makers in the way they prefer, without the requirement to obtain confirmation from any other decision maker.

The first rule is to determine what is the simplest term from either pattern. And once that is determined to only include those terms which most closely cohere with the first term. The second rule is to not include any term that is contradictory to the first term. And the third rule is to bring in any not previously stated terms that clearly are coherent with the first term.

a = a and ~a = ~a and a =/= ~a

"a equals a", "not a equals not a", "a does not equal not a".

a + 0 = a and a - 0 = a and ~a + 0 = ~a and ~a - 0 = ~a

"a plus zero equals a" "a minus zero equals a" "not a plus zero equals not a" "not a minus zero equals not a"

a.1 = a and a/1 = a and ~a.1 = ~a and ~a/1 = ~a

"a multiplied by one equals a" "a divided by one equals a" "not a multiplied by one equals not a" "not a divided by one equals not a"

a.0 = 0 and a/0 = 0 and ~a.0 = 0 and ~a/0 = 0

"a multiplied by zero equals zero" "a divided by zero equals zero" "not a multiplied by zero equals zero" "not a divided by zero equals zero"

If we then clarify what we have decided is coherent up to this point without going any further it means we are then able to check our most simple terms on their own. If we can confirm these terms as accurate and correct then they are the measure of truth that we apply to the next group of terms that we select.

a = a and ~a = ~a and a =/= ~a

a + 0 = a and a - 0 = a and ~a + 0 = ~a and ~a - 0 = ~a

a.1 = a and a/1 = a and ~a.1 = ~a and ~a/1 = ~a

a.0 = 0 and a/0 = 0 and ~a.0 = 0 and ~a/0 = 0

All we do here before moving forward is confirm to ourselves that these are the simplest terms of the pattern and that from the given pattern we could not start with any more simple. If they are the simplest terms then all we need do is confirm our own agreement that as stated they are correct and that they are true because coherent without internal contradiction between themselves. We do not need do more at this stage, but cannot reasonably progress further until that point is accomplished.

Now crucially, given the patterns as stated in this document, whether they are correct as stated and whether in their most correct formulation they are true is no longer the matter. Because the method for checking them for correctness and truth is the way to organically formulate them in their most correct statement of themselves. And the next stage in that regard is to clarify a second small group that satisfy similar conditions to the first one stated. To do so it is correct to use any terms of the first group as required.

$a + 0 = a$ and $a - 0 = a$ and $\sim a + 0 = \sim a$ and $\sim a - 0 = \sim a$

"a plus zero equals a" "a minus zero equals a" "not a plus zero equals not a" "not a minus zero equals not a"

$a + 1 = 1 + a$ and $a - 1 = -1 + a$ and $\sim a + 1 = 1 + \sim a$ and $\sim a - 1 = -1 + \sim a$

"a plus one equals one plus a" "a minus one equals minus one plus a" "not a plus one equals one plus not a" "not a minus one equals minus one plus not a"

$0 + a = a$ and $0 - a = -a$ and $0 + \sim a = \sim a$ and $0 - \sim a = - \sim a$

"zero plus a equals a" "zero minus a equals minus a" "zero plus not a equals not a" "zero minus not a equals minus not a"

$a + a = a + a$ and $a \cdot a = a$ and $a - a = 0$ and $a / a = 1$

"a plus a equals a plus a" "a multiplied by a equals a" "a minus a equals zero" "a divided by a equals one"

$a + \sim a = 0$ and $a \cdot \sim a = 0$ and $a - \sim a = 1$ and $a / \sim a = -1$

"a plus not a equals zero" "a multiplied by not a equals zero" "a minus not a equals one" "a divided by not a equals minus one"

Isolating the second group of terms so that they can be themselves checked, the idea then is to determine whether we have maintained consistency throughout. That is, where the process of checking our terms has involved some correction of the original information, have we gone back to the original information and made any adjustment required by this process. In this way it does not matter as such what changes we make on the one condition that we correct towards coherency such that at any point in time the given pattern is more accurate and coherent than the previous statement of itself.

a + 0 = a and a - 0 = a and ~a + 0 = ~a and ~a - 0 = ~a

a + 1 = 1 + a and a - 1 = -1 + a and ~a + 1 = 1 + ~a and ~a - 1 = -1 + ~a

0 + a = a and 0 - a = -a and 0 + ~a = ~a and 0 - ~a = - ~a

a + a = a + a and a . a = a and a - a = 0 and a / a = 1

a + ~a = 0 and a . ~a = 0 and a - ~a = 1 and a / ~a = -1

And to facilitate this constant correction towards coherency of the stated patterns with less internal contradiction is the organic self-validation procedure that justifies the method that is described. Combining both our adjusted simplest possible patterns is the basis that we can now establish.

a = a and ~a = ~a and a =/= ~a

a + 0 = a and a - 0 = a and ~a + 0 = ~a and ~a - 0 = ~a

a.1 = a and a/1 = a and ~a.1 = ~a and ~a/1 = ~a

a.0 = 0 and a/0 = 0 and ~a.0 = 0 and ~a/0 = 0

a + 1 = 1 + a and a - 1 = -1 + a and ~a + 1 = 1 + ~a and ~a - 1 = -1 + ~a

0 + a = a and 0 - a = -a and 0 + ~a = ~a and 0 - ~a = - ~a

a + a = a + a and a . a = a and a - a = 0 and a / a = 1

a + ~a = 0 and a . ~a = 0 and a - ~a = 1 and a / ~a = -1

At this stage, which describes the pattern from its most simple possible terms, the only thing that I would do is clarify what seems to be a resolution of an internal contradiction so that if it is significant at any later stage, we know where to direct our attention towards. And that is:

$a - a = 0 \wedge a + \sim a = 0 > a - \sim a = / = 0$

If a minus a equals zero and a plus not a equals zero, then a minus not a cannot equal zero.

$a / a = 1 > a / \sim a = -1$

If a divided by a equals one then a divided by not a equals minus one.

Given those two areas are noticed, which are without internal contradiction as stated, then the coherence of the related terms and the absence of contradiction can be checked by detailing the associated terms:

$a - a = 0$ and $a / a = 1$ and $a + a = a + a$ and $a . a = a$

$a - \sim a = 1$ and $a / \sim a = -1$ and $a + \sim a = 0$ and $a . \sim a = 0$

Then the point we arrive at here is that this pattern is a complete statement of the simplest possible terms of the Boolean Prime and to our present understanding it is correct, coherent and without internal contradiction. Since it is so tiny it is not the idea that we should be intent on some larger thing. Having that pattern in place, we can now consider the third main part of the original pattern which is to replace any number value with the letter b, such that we include terms based on a and b.

$a . b = b . a$ and $a + b = b + a$

$(a + b) + c = a + (b + c)$ and $(a . b) . c = a . (b . c)$

$a + (b . c) = (a + b) . (a + c)$ and $a . (b + c) = (a . b) + (a . c)$

$\sim(a + b) = \sim a + \sim b$ and $\sim(a . b) = \sim a . \sim b$

$a / b = a / b$ and $a - b = -b + a$

$(a - b) - c = a - (b - c)$ and $(a / b) / c = a / (b / c)$

$a - (b / c) = (a - b) / (a - c)$ and $a / (b - c) = (a / b) - (a / c)$

$\sim(a - b) = \sim a - \sim b$ and $\sim(a / b) = \sim a / \sim b$

Now whereas we are required to demonstrate the correctness

of the a:b patterns it is clear from the shape of them as given that they are consistent with our previous argumentation and that as given there is no contradiction. That means that the demonstration of correctness is not the same process since our aim in this regard would be to challenge the rules that are being applied, in order to determine whether the rules when correctly applied are themselves appropriate. Which we are not in fact required to do. Therefore we can give the entire pattern in its most complete form up to this stage.

$a = a$ and $\sim a = \sim a$ and $a =/= \sim a$

$a + 0 = a$ and $a - 0 = a$ and $\sim a + 0 = \sim a$ and $\sim a - 0 = \sim a$

$a.1 = a$ and $a/1 = a$ and $\sim a.1 = \sim a$ and $\sim a/1 = \sim a$

$a.0 = 0$ and $a/0 = 0$ and $\sim a.0 = 0$ and $\sim a/0 = 0$

$a + 1 = 1 + a$ and $a - 1 = -1 + a$ and $\sim a + 1 = 1 + \sim a$ and $\sim a - 1 = -1 + \sim a$

$0 + a = a$ and $0 - a = -a$ and $0 + \sim a = \sim a$ and $0 - \sim a = - \sim a$

$a + a = a + a$ and $a . a = a$ and $a - a = 0$ and $a / a = 1$

$a + \sim a = 0$ and $a . \sim a = 0$ and $a - \sim a = 1$ and $a / \sim a = -1$

$a . b = b . a$ and $a + b = b + a$

$(a + b) + c = a + (b + c)$ and $(a . b) . c = a . (b . c)$

$a + (b . c) = (a + b) . (a + c)$ and $a . (b + c) = (a . b) + (a . c)$

$\sim(a + b) = \sim a + \sim b$ and $\sim(a . b) = \sim a . \sim b$

$a / b = a / b$ and $a - b = -b + a$

$(a - b) - c = a - (b - c)$ and $(a / b) / c = a / (b / c)$

$a - (b / c) = (a - b) / (a - c)$ and $a / (b - c) = (a / b) - (a / c)$

$\sim(a - b) = \sim a - \sim b$ and $\sim(a / b) = \sim a / \sim b$

The immediately previous pattern which begins with a equals a and completes with the bracketed term not a divided by b equals not a divided by not b is the smallest pattern of this sort. It is very easy to construct from the given pattern to variations on the same still without using the prime pattern of p's and q's. All one needs do is bracket any term and place a not in front of the bracket for example. And the same patterns can be extended into proofs by use of the pattern of p's and q's. When proving the important tool is to show what any term does not equal. For example, to say: If a minus a equals zero and a plus not a equals zero, then a minus not a cannot equal zero. In terms of the correctness of the pattern as detailed, there is no obligation on the part of any decision maker to maintain the pattern as stated. And as stated the pattern need not be held as the only possible statement of itself. All that is required is that if any one single term of the pattern is altered from its present statement, where there is no internal contradiction throughout the entire pattern, then the related terms would need to be altered in order to maintain the coherence throughout and to ensure that the altered pattern also has no contradiction.

Other areas can be noticed also. For example it is quite clear that a different decision maker need not adhere to our given criteria for what is truth and can choose to apply a completely different set of criteria not here detailed. All these sorts of different possibilities do, is satisfy our own property in the sense that we are defined by the systems we adhere to. As to the complex synergetic organic nature of the pattern as detailed, where as stated it is coherent throughout without contradiction, where it begins at the earliest possible point of a = a, and provides a complete set of terms without excess or deficiency and without any blanks, that complex synergy is organic in nature.

As to the difficulty of the complex synergy the secret is to take only the first term and confirm to oneself that it is understood. Then to take the second term and confirm to oneself that it is understood and also that is is coherent with the first term. In that way each small group of terms can be easily learned, even though when the several small groups of terms are combined the complex synergy is more difficult.

1."a equals a",

2."not a equals not a",

3."a does not equal not a".

4."a plus zero equals a"

5."a minus zero equals a"

6."not a plus zero equals not a"

7."not a minus zero equals not a"

8."a multiplied by one equals a"

9."a divided by one equals a"

10."not a multiplied by one equals not a"

11."not a divided by one equals not a"

12."a multiplied by zero equals zero"

13."a divided by zero equals zero"

14."not a multiplied by zero equals zero"

15."not a divided by zero equals zero"

16."a plus one equals one plus a"

17."a minus one equals minus one plus a"

18."not a plus one equals one plus not a"

19."not a minus one equals minus one plus not a"

20."zero plus a equals a"

21."zero minus a equals minus a"

22."zero plus not a equals not a"

23."zero minus not a equals minus not a"

24."a plus a equals a plus a"

25."a multiplied by a equals a"

26."a minus a equals zero"

27."a divided by a equals one"

28."a plus not a equals zero"

29."a multiplied by not a equals zero"

30."a minus not a equals one"

31."a divided by not a equals minus one"

The challenge as to the rules that are applied in the given pattern is best directed towards correspondence rather than as to their coherence. Where we have previously been checking the correctness of the statement of the patterns and the truth of the patterns when correctly stated the focus has been towards as to coherence. When we check the rules that are being used because of their position as first propositions they are already understood as neither true nor false. What we can demonstrate is that within the limits of the patterns as described they do satisfy correspondence, coherence and utility. And because we know they are neither true nor false, we can demonstrate that outside the very limited patterns they do not fail on coherence and will fail on grounds of correspondence.

The reason we would do such is so that we can determine what are the adjustments we are required to make in order to make use of the rules when outside the limited patterns as detailed. And before we can do that we must clarify the prime patterns of the rules in themselves as used within the limited patterns as detailed. As we construct the prime pattern of rules it will become evident what are the grounds of correspondence which will fail outside the limited given pattern.

First: a, b, 0, 1, +, -, ., /, =, =/=, ~, ().

Second: ++ = +, +- = +-, -- = -, +.+ = +, +/+ = +, -.- = +, -/- = +, +.- = -, +/- = -, -/+ = -

Third: + = + , - = -, . = ., / = /, ~ = ~, = = =, =/= = =/=, () = ()

Fourth: + =/= -, . =/= /, ~ =/= -, = =/= =/=

Fifth: =

First postulate is that the sign labels we use are only a, b, zero, one, plus, minus, multiplied by, divided by, equals, does not equal, not, brackets.

Second postulate is that the addition of positive terms gives a positive, the addition or subtraction of positive term with a negative term gives a positive or a negative, the subtraction of negative terms gives a negative, the multiplication of positive terms gives a positive, the division of positive terms gives a positive, the multiplication of negative terms gives a positive, the division of negative terms gives a positive, the multiplication of positive term with negative term gives a negative, the division of positive term by negative term gives a negative, the division of negative term by a positive term gives a negative.

Third postulate is that plus equals plus, minus equals minus, multiplied by equals multiplied by, divided by equals divided by, not equals not, equals equals equals, does not equal equals does not equal, brackets equals brackets.

Fourth postulate is that plus does not equal minus, multiplied by does not equal divided by, not does not equal minus, equals does not equal does not equal.

Fifth postulate is equals.

Where we will challenge the given system as to correspondence will focus primarily on the difference between object and process. And with a supposition that there is nothing in our given system that enables us to distinguish between when the sign labels refer to an object and when the same sign labels refer to a process. The second supposition will be that our given system does not enable us to signify when we move logical level in regard to genus and species. The third supposition will be that our given system does not specify the difference between ontologically existant and imaginatively existant. The fourth supposition will be that the multiplication of a positive and minus term gives a minus process.

In regard to the first supposition, two multiplied by three equals six, where if two is an object, then multiplied by three is not an object and is a process.

In regard to the second supposition, two apples plus three pears is five fruit, where apples and pears are species and fruit is genus.

In regard to the third supposition, positive integers can exist and negative integers cannot, where positive number can be object and negative number can only be process.

In regard to the fourth supposition, plus three multiplied by minus five equals minus twelve, where the difference between plus three and minus twelve is a total of fifteen units. The proposition that any positive number multiplied by minus one equals zero.

1: a, b, 0, 1, +, -, ., /, =, =/=, ~, ().

2: ++ = +, +- = +-, -- = -, +.+ = +, +/+ = +, -.- = +, -/- = +, +.- = -, +/- = -, -/+ = -

3: + = + , - = -, . = ., / = /, ~ = ~, = = =, =/= = =/=, () = ()

4: + =/= -, . =/= /, ~ =/= -, = =/= =/=

5: =

The prime pattern of rules is correspondent, coherent, useful and universally abstract. That means even though it is true, it is not in itself sufficient. The fifth rule details the matter. Essentially it raises the question "what is that?" in regard to equals. As all in the whole world know, the ontological question, what is that?, is not easy to answer. When the ontological question is directed towards equals we enter the field that studies being existant. Which is outside the domain of the study of the truth of prime patterns.

In the fourth rule where we state equals does not equal does not equal, we are noticing that there are two related sign labels which together have a contradictory function. The existance of the two contradictory functions enables us to satisfy what the difference is between the two. When we use equals we are saying some entity is the same as a different entity. When we use does not equal we are saying some entity is not the same as a different entity. By universal abstraction we can define this as to say being is being and the contradictory being is not being. That then explains the way in which we use equals, which is the mathematical equivalent of the word "is". And the way in which we use does not equal, which is the mathematical equivalent of the word phrase "is not".

Given that understanding, it becomes clear that if we attend to the matter "what is equals?", we will be forced to attend to the more abstract matter, what does "is" mean? The important knowledge here is to realise that we can not answer the second level question "what is equals?" unless we can answer the first level question "what does <is> mean?". And if we can answer the first level question, then answering the second level question becomes easy.

The concepts that are inter-relationally involved in this kind of study include being, doing, meaning, existence, non-existence, identity, non-identity and no other concepts. In mathematical terms we can say the concepts are one, some, more, less and none. Therefore, if we consider only those five mathematical concepts we can define some basic terms. One object is an existant identity. If the same identity is repeated that is some. Some is more than one. One is less than some. None is the non-existance of one and some. The concept of more is to do with addition. The concept of less is to do with subtraction. A repetitive addition is called multiplication.

A repetitive subtraction is called division. Existence is an affirmation. Non-existance is a negation.

Any number squared divided by two plus half the original number is equal to the number of times each of the consecutive integers in the original number combine with itself and each of the others once, as in dominoes. In a standard nine bar set of dominoes the integers one to nine and zero are all represented in relation to each of the other integers. That is a total of ten units. Ten squared is one hundred. One hundred divided by two is fifty. Half the original number is five. Fifty plus five is fifty five. And in a standard nine bar set of dominoes there are fifty five counters. Given dominoes do not use late language sign label for number, and instead use a pattern of points to show the universal abstract that exists at the earlier level than sign label, they are useful in regard to demonstrating the ontological status of existant being of number.

At the level of dominoes, the sign labels and the concepts do not yet exist. Without the sign labels and without the concepts, still dominoes exist. Dominoes therefore are ontologically earlier than the sign labels and the concepts. And from the ontological existence of dominoes it is very easy to build the sign labels and concepts of number.

If we imagine we have a set of dominoes for only the units one and none, then that is two units. Two squared is four, four divided by two is two. Half the original number is one. Two plus one is three. Therefore we will have a set of dominoes with three counters. One of those counters will show none on both sides of the counter. Another will show one on both sides of the counter. Another will show none on one side and one on the other side of the counter. In that way without defining our concepts we are showing the concepts in their immanent form. And with the dominoe that has none on both sides we are saying none is the same as none or none equals none. And with the dominoe that has one on both sides we are saying one is the same as one or one equals one. And with the dominoe that has none on one side and one on the other side we are saying none is not the same as one or none does not equal one. And we know what we mean because we have three dominoes and we can see what we mean. And we think that each of the three dominoes is different to the other two. And if we thought of the connecting line between the two sides of any one dominoe as plus, then we would know that none plus none is none, one plus none is one, and one plus one is two. And if we look at the whole dominoe and thought of what happens when we take away one side that would be like minus, so we could say none minus none is none, one minus none is one, one minus one is none, two minus one is one.

All we need now do is notice what are the functions that are evident without specific sign label. And we can see that the difference between nothing and something is similar to the difference between the dominoe that is blank on both sides and the dominoe that has a blank on one side and a one on the other. And the difference between one and some is similar to the the difference between the dominoe that has a blank on one side and one on the other and the dominoe that has a one on both sides. And we can understand that some is more than one and one is less than some and none is the non-existance of one or some. So at this stage we have proved the first five concepts of number which are one, some, more, less, none. And we can apply those concepts as sign labels of functions such that we understand one is existant entity, some is a repetition of one, and none is the non-existance of entity. And we can apply the sign label functions of addition to some being more than one, and subtraction to one being less than some. Which means we have now invented our sign labels for the functions of addition and subtraction. And we know what we mean by "is" because "none <is> none" and "one <is> one" and we know what we mean by "is not" because "none <is not> one". Therefore we have demonstrated using three dominoes the function before sign label of the concepts of one, some, more, less, none, addition, subtraction. And now we simply invent the sign labels to specify those functions, which leads to the prime pattern of rules as detailed.

1: a, b, 0, 1, +, -, ., /, =, =/=, ~, ().

2: ++ = +, +- = +-, -- = -, +.+ = +, +/+ = +, -.- = +, -/- = +, +.- = -, +/- = -, -/+ = -

3: + = + , - = -, . = ., / = /, ~ = ~, = = =, =/= = =/=, () = ()

4: + =/= -, . =/= /, ~ =/= -, = =/= =/=

5: =

a = a and ~a = ~a and a =/= ~a

a + 0 = a and a - 0 = a and ~a + 0 = ~a and ~a - 0 = ~a

a.1 = a and a/1 = a and ~a.1 = ~a and ~a/1 = ~a

a.0 = 0 and a/0 = 0 and ~a.0 = 0 and ~a/0 = 0

a + 1 = 1 + a and a - 1 = -1 + a and ~a + 1 = 1 + ~a and ~a - 1 = -1 + ~a

0 + a = a and 0 - a = -a and 0 + ~a = ~a and 0 - ~a = - ~a

a + a = a + a and a . a = a and a - a = 0 and a / a = 1

a + ~a = 0 and a . ~a = 0 and a - ~a = 1 and a / ~a = -1

a . b = b . a and a + b = b + a

(a + b) + c = a + (b + c) and (a . b) . c = a . (b . c)

a + (b . c) = (a + b) . (a + c) and a . (b + c) = (a . b) + (a . c)

~(a + b) = ~a + ~b and ~(a . b) = ~a . ~b

a / b = a / b and a - b = -b + a

(a - b) - c = a - (b - c) and (a / b) / c = a / (b / c)

a - (b / c) = (a - b) / (a - c) and a / (b - c) = (a / b) - (a / c)

~(a - b) = ~a - ~b and ~(a / b) = ~a / ~b

When the prime pattern of p's and q's is applied to the prime pattern of number that we have established we obtain the prime pattern of sets in its most simple possible formulation. The prime pattern of sets is a universal abstraction of the prime pattern of number. It is more universal because it is not particular to number and can just as easily be applied to concepts. It is more abstract because its sign label system is common to both the functions of number and of language. What is strange is that the difference of sign label satisfies the thought of a more universally abstract system, such that it is not possible to follow the exact same idea shape of the prime pattern of number even though the formulaic terms may be similar. In that sense we are driven to better state our explanation of the meaning of the sign labels that we use, given that the first statement of their meaning is only adequate. Therefore in this pattern of sets, one of the continual processes is to clarify exactly how to better define the sign labels.

As with the prime pattern of number we will find that we can obtain the most simple reduction of the earliest pattern of sets, and that the complete pattern is itself quite tiny. And given that pattern the more complex extensions are indefinitely large. It is an old idea of invention that if a pattern that is known to be true can be exactly matched by a different pattern then the other pattern will be true.

a means "a is true" Affirmation. Or "a" means an entity in the universe of discourse that may be a genus or species, or may be a class or member of class, or may be a set or element of set.Or "a" means everything that is "a" in our universe of discourse.

~a means "a is false" Negation. Or "~a" means everything that is "not a" in the universe of discourse. Or "~a" means some entity that is an element of everything that is not "a" in the universe of discourse.

b means "b is true" Affirmation. Or some entity not a in the universe of discourse that may be defined in a similar manner to the way in which a is defined.

~b means "b is false" Negation. Or some entity not b in the universe of discourse that may be defined in relation to b in a similar manner to the way in which not a is defined in relation to a.

a v b means "either a is true, or b is true, or both" Either one or the other or both.

a ∧ b means "both a and b are true" And. Both one and the other.

a => b means "if a is true, then b is true". If - then. If set of elements then any element of such a set.

a =/=> b means "if a is true, then b is false". If - then not . If set of elements then not any element of a different set.

a < b means "since b is true, then a is true." Since - then. Since the way this system uses the inclusion sign label may be inconsistent with the way other systems use the same sign label it requires further clarification. My definition is as follows: (a < b) ∧ (b < c) => a < c. That is to say, if a contains b, and b contains c, then a contains c. I am using the sign label as an arrow to show that the species is part of the genus or that the element is contained by the set.

a /< b means "since b is true, then a is false." Since - not then. If member of a class, then not any different class.

a <=> b means "a and b are either both true or both false" If and only if. Only if both and not either one without the other.

a <=/=> b means "a is true and b is false, or a is false and b is true". Either one or the other not both.

ɸ means the empty set, or the class whose membership is none.

1 means the unity set, or the class whose membership is

itself.

e means everything in the given universe of discourse.

! means not not. Or in regard to a single entity it means neither entity nor not entity.

Q means neither the unity set nor the empty set. Or an indefinite variable.

a => a and ~a => ~a and a =/=> ~a

a ∧ φ => a and a ∧ ~φ => a and ~a ∧ φ => ~a and ~a ∧ ~φ => ~a

a v 1 => a and a < 1 => a and ~a v 1 => ~a and ~a < 1 => ~a

a v φ => φ and a < φ => φ and ~a v φ => φ and ~a < φ => φ

a ∧ 1 => 1 ∧ a and a ∧ ~1 => Q ∧ a and ~a ∧ 1 => 1 ∧ ~a and ~a ∧ ~1 => Q ∧ ~a

φ ∧ a => a and φ ∧ ~a => ~a and φ ∧ ~(~a) => !a

a ∧ a => a ∧ a and a v a => a and a ∧ ~a => e and a < a => 1

a v ~a => Q and a ∧ ~(~a) => a ∧ !a and a < ~(~a) => a < !a

a v b => b v a and a ∧ b => b ∧ a

(a ∧ b) ∧ c => a ∧ (b ∧ c) and (a v b) v c => a v (b v c)

a ∧ (b v c) => (a ∧ b) v (a ∧ c) and a v (b ∧ c) => (a v b) ∧ (a v c)

~(a ∧ b) => ~a ∧ ~b and ~(a v b) => ~a v ~b

a < b => a < b and a ∧ ~b => ~b ∧ a

(a ∧ ~b) ∧ ~c => a ∧ (~b ∧ ~c) and (a < b) < c => a < (b < c)

a ∧ ~(b < c) => (a ∧ ~b) < (a ∧ ~c) and a < (b ∧ ~c) => (a < b) ∧ ~(a < c)

~(a ∧ ~b) => ~a ∧ ~(~b) and ~(a < b) => ~a < ~b

One of the understandings to develop is that the similar thought-idea can be expressed using different sign label languages. And that the difference in the larger system of the sign label languages alters the idea-shape of the thought-idea. Given that the prime pattern of number was detailed in the sign label of number and then the same thought-idea was detailed in the sign label of language, such that a = a means a equals a. In that sense the above pattern of sets is the exact same thought-idea given in the language of sets. Which we can then detail in the sign label of spoken language. When we detail the pattern of sets in the sign label of spoken language, the idea-shape will be different to when we detail the pattern of number in spoken language. That means a common thought-idea can be explained in two different universally abstract languages, that of the pattern of number and that of the pattern of sets, and when each of those different sign label systems are detailed in spoken language two different idea-shapes are detailed in one language for the same thought-idea.

What will be the case is that the familial relationship between the thought-idea, and the idea-shape when detailed in the two sign label systems, and the idea-shape when detailed in the spoken language will be very close. Meaning that it is natural that they are different to other decision maker systems in terms of internal coherence, correspondence and utility. As the earlier explanation clarified there is no requirement to satisfy coherence to some other decision maker's system, we do not have to satisfy correspondence from the other decision maker's perspective and we do not have to prove utility to the other decision maker's purpose.

At this earliest possible stage given that we have the common thought-idea in the idea-shape of different sign label systems that we have designed, it is easy to prove the terms of the pattern of sets. We shall do so in two ways. One is to explain each term in the spoken language. Second is to show each term next to the equivalent term in the sign label of number. This is important because at this stage it is easy and later it would not be possible. That is because the sign label system of sets can be used on its own without any requirement to refer to the prime pattern of number from which it is universally abstracted. And also, once the label system of the prime pattern of sets is understood it can be used without any reference to the prime pattern of sets in the same way that the sign label system of number can be used without any reference to the prime pattern of number.

In regards to the given spoken language explanation of the individual terms of the pattern of sets it has to be thought of as correct or incorrect in itself and in reference to terms that are correctly stated or not, and if correctly stated then true or not. For this reason it is permanently the possibility that a more correct spoken language explanation can be provided. And presumably to consider that the same universally abstract sign label pattern of sets could be explained in a variety of different spoken languages.

1. a => a If a, then a.

2. ~a => ~a If not a, then not a.

3. a =/=> ~a If a, then not not a.

4. a ∧ ф => a If a and the empty set, then a.

5. a ∧ ~ф => a If a and not the empty set, then a.

6. ~a ∧ ф => ~a If not a and the empty set, then not a.

7. ~a ∧ ~ф => ~a If not a and not the empty set, then not a.

8. a v 1 => a If a or the unity set, then a.

9. a < 1 => a If a includes the unity set, then a.

10. ~a v 1 => ~a If not a or the unity set, then not a.

11. ~a < 1 => ~a If not a includes the unity set, then not a.

12. a v ф => ф If a or the empty set, then the empty set.

13. a < ф => ф If a includes the empty set, then the empty set.

14. ~a v ф => ф If not a or the empty set, then the empty set.

15. ~a < ф => ф If not a includes the empty set, then the empty

set.

16. a ∧ 1 => 1 ∧ a If a and the unity set, then the unity set and a.

17. a ∧ ~1 => Q ∧ a If a and not the unity set, then Q and a.

18. ~a ∧ 1 => 1 ∧ ~a If not a and the unity set, then the unity set and not a.

19. ~a ∧ ~1 => Q ∧ ~a If not a and not the unity set, then Q and not a.

20. φ ∧ a => a If the empty set and a, then a.

21. φ ∧ ~a => ~a If the empty set and not a, then not a.

22. φ ∧ ~(~a) => !a If the empty set and not not a, then !a.

23. a ∧ a => a ∧ a If a and a, then a and a.

24. a v a => a If a or a, then a.

25. a ∧ ~a => e If a and not a, then everything in the universe of discourse.

26. a < a => 1 If a includes a, then the unity set.

27. a v ~a => Q If a or not a, then Q.

28. a ∧ ~(~a) => a ∧ !a If a and not not a, then a and !a.

29. a < ~(~a) => a < !a If a includes not not a, then a includes entity neither a nor not a.

30. a v b => b v a If a or b, then b or a.

31. a ∧ b => b ∧ a If a and b, then b and a.

32. (a ∧ b) ∧ c => a ∧ (b ∧ c) If term a and b term and c, then a and term b and c.

33. (a v b) v c => a v (b v c) If term a or b term or c, then a or term b or c.

34. a ∧ (b v c) => (a ∧ b) v (a ∧ c) If a and term b or c, then term a and b term or term a and c.

35. a v (b ∧ c) => (a v b) ∧ (a v c) If a or term b and c, then term

a or b term and term a or c.

36. ~(a ∧ b) => ~a ∧ ~b If not term a and b, then not a and not b.

37. ~(a v b) => ~a v ~b If not term a or b, then not a or not b.

38. a < b => a < b If a includes b, then a includes b.

39. a ∧ ~b => ~b ∧ a If a and not b, then not b and a.

40. (a ∧ ~b) ∧ ~c => a ∧ (~b ∧ ~c) If term a and not b term and not c, then a and term not b and not c.

41. (a < b) < c => a < (b < c) If term a includes b term includes c, then a includes term b includes c.

42. a ∧ ~(b < c) => (a ∧ ~b) < (a ∧ ~c) If a and not term b inc c, then term a and not b term inc term a and not c.

43. a < (b ∧ ~c) => (a < b) ∧ ~(a < c) If a inc term b and not c, then term a inc b term and not term a inc c.

44. ~(a ∧ ~b) => ~a ∧ ~(~b) If not term a and not b, then not a and not not b.

45. ~(a < b) => ~a < ~b In not term a inc b, then not a inc not b.

{{{Information contained in three brackets is a later note, not part of the original article.

Considering Idea 40 above, this seems to be the correct statement:(a ∧ ~b) ∧ ~c => a ∧ (~b ∧ ~c)

And this seems to be the false statement: (a ∧ ~b) ∧ ~c => a ∧ ~(b ∧ ~c)

The reason for the original statement is: (a - b) - c = a - (b - c)

Whereas the correct statement may be: (a - b) - c = a + (-b - c)

So the point I am drawing the attention towards is the double negative that is built in to the inference of the idea whereas the proposition does not contain a double negative.

Why this will matter later is because two different decision makers will be able to disagree as to the use of "and not".

The question will be does "and not" mean <and not> entity or does it mean <and> not entity.

It is similar to the question of does not equal and whether does not equal not entity makes a not not entity.

Since the pattern of sets is more abstract than the pattern of number it has required the use of some sign labels that need not exist at a less abstract level. That is e, ! and Q. By universe of discourse we mean the restricted parameter bounded by the terms of meaning. It operates at a prime level in the sense that the permitted sign labels define the universe of discourse abstractly, and how they are used in particular applications define the universe of discourse specifically. In this sense, the prime number pattern is a particular application of the more abstract pattern of sets.

When the pattern of number is abstracted to provide the pattern of sets then using the sign label system of the pattern of sets our given terms can be forced to demonstrate a term that they can not answer with only the given terms. That is without ! we cannot show not not as a single entity, without the term e we cannot show everything in our given universe of discourse as a single entity, and without the term Q we cannot show not the empty set and not the unity set as a single entity. The basic rule in regard to the three terms Q ! e is that at any less abstract level they be replaced by any coherent non-contradictory term. They are required at the more abstract level so that in particular instances of the use of the pattern of sets the coherent non-contradictory term that is used in the same place is dependent on the particular instance.

The specific definition of the three terms in this system is:

$a \wedge \sim a => e$

$\sim(\sim a) => !a$

$\sim 1 \wedge \sim \phi => Q$

The equivalence function in regard to how I have maintained coherence in the two different sign label systems individually and correspondence between the two systems demands some explanation. The method used has not been to make a direct correspondence of "meaning" between the two systems. The method used has been to make a direct correspondence of "shape" between the two systems. The way I have done so is to make the easiest function to maintain as similar between both systems first. That is the decision to make "plus" in the number system mean "and" in the pattern of sets. Then the opposite of plus is minus, so I have made that to mean "and not" in the system of sets. Then the multiplication sign label in the number system is the "or" sign label in the system of sets. Since "or" is not to "and" what "multiplication" is to "plus" that prohibited my use of "or not" as the function against the number system function called "division". And since "if a contains b and b contains c then a contains c" is similar to the whole containing the part the inclusion sign label was used to meet the shape of the terms involving division in the number system. The next stage in the process is to maintain coherence between the terms. Such that the "and" sign label must give a different result to the "or" sign label where ever the two terms are otherwhise the same. "And" is considered opposite to "or" in this sense. Which then makes it inevitable that "and not" will give a different result to either since it ensures the two terms can not be otherwhise the same. Then given the inclusion sign label maintains the shape given by the division sign label the coherence of the pattern of sets is more likely. Finally the coherence of the pattern of sets does have to be checked on its own with no reference to the pattern of number. And all we are looking for is to make any adjustment necessary to increase internal coherence and non-contradiction.

The difference between minus and not requires clarification. Minus means subtraction of a specifically given entity. Minus is a negative value the exact shape of a positive entity. That is different to "not" which means everything that a given entity is not. "Not" in this sense means a positive statement of everything that is not a given entity. More specifically in regards to "~a" this means everything that is not a in our given universe of discourse. Or alternatively it means some entity that is an element of everything that is not a in our universe of discourse.

It is for that reason that we need the sign label "e". Because if a => a and ~a => ~a then a means everything that is a in the universe of discourse and not a means everything that is not a in the universe of discourse, the combination of a and not a being everything in the universe of discourse.

And it is for this reason that "not not" does not mean the simple positive affirmation. If we used the sign label "a" to signify "horse", then not not "a" means not not "horse", that being a unicorn. Since a unicorn is a horse but is not a horse, we can not say the positive affirmation. By the use of not not horse we are saying unicorn is neither a horse nor not a horse. Using an example given earlier in regard to "that" it is like saying that is neither a square nor not a square, but if I say that is a square I am missing that the square is part of a larger object called a cube. And it is like saying that is neither a cube nor not a cube, but if I say that is a cube I am missing that the cube is really a multi-dimensional hypercube capable of navigating the meta-complex for reasons unknown. We can prove "not not" does not equal the simple affirmative in this way. If not not does mean "neither entity nor not entity" then a third not would be the contradictory of "neither entity nor not entity". And that contradictory would be "either entity or not entity" which then is either the simple affirmation or the simple negation.

The sign label Q meets a similar condition in regard to the possible entity that is neither the empty set nor the unity set. Q => a v ~a v !a v ~ϕ v ~1 v b v ~b v !b. The rule is that in any particular term it is possible to use any sign label ~Q then that term must be used. And where ever the sign label Q is used it be replaced by a sign label ~Q where ever possible.

The common abstract condition that is met by both Q and ! is the concept "neither nor not".

1. $a => a <=> a = a$

2. $\sim a => \sim a <=> \sim a = \sim a$

3. $a =/=> \sim a <=> a =/= \sim a$

4. $a \wedge \phi => a <=> a + 0 = a$

5. $a \wedge \sim\phi => a <=> a - 0 = a$

6. $\sim a \wedge \phi => \sim a <=> \sim a + 0 = \sim a$

7. $\sim a \wedge \sim\phi => \sim a <=> \sim a - 0 = \sim a$

8. $a \vee 1 => a <=> a.1 = a$

9. $a < 1 => a <=> a/1 = a$

10. $\sim a \vee 1 => \sim a <=> \sim a.1 = \sim a$

11. $\sim a < 1 => \sim a <=> \sim a/1 = \sim a$

12. $a \vee \phi => \phi <=> a.0 = 0$

13. $a < \phi => \phi <=> a/0 = 0$

14. $\sim a \vee \phi => \phi <=> \sim a.0 = 0$

15. $\sim a < \phi => \phi <=> \sim a/0 = 0$

16. $a \wedge 1 => 1 \wedge a <=> a + 1 = 1 + a$

17. $a \wedge \sim 1 => Q \wedge a <=> a - 1 = -1 + a$

18. $\sim a \wedge 1 => 1 \wedge \sim a <=> \sim a + 1 = 1 + \sim a$

19. $\sim a \wedge \sim 1 => Q \wedge \sim a <=> \sim a - 1 = -1 + \sim a$

20. $\phi \wedge a => a <=> 0 + a = a$

21. $\phi \wedge \sim a => \sim a <=> 0 - a = -a$

22. $\phi \wedge \sim(\sim a) => !a <=> 0 - \sim a = - \sim a$

23. $a \wedge a => a \wedge a <=> a + a = a + a$

24. a v a => a <=> a . a = a

25. a ∧ ~a => e <=> a - a = 0

26. a < a => 1 <=> a / a = 1

27. a v ~a => Q <=> a . ~a = 0

28. a ∧ ~(~a) => a ∧ !a <=> a - ~a = 1

29. a < ~a => Q <=> a / ~a = -1

30. a v b => b v a <=> a . b = b . a

31. a ∧ b => b ∧ a <=> a + b = b + a

32. (a ∧ b) ∧ c => a ∧ (b ∧ c) <=> (a + b) + c = a + (b + c)

33. (a v b) v c => a v (b v c) <=> (a . b) . c = a . (b . c)

34. a ∧ (b v c) => (a ∧ b) v (a ∧ c) <=> a + (b . c) = (a + b) . (a + c)

35. a v (b ∧ c) => (a v b) ∧ (a v c) <=> a . (b + c) = (a . b) + (a . c)

36. ~(a ∧ b) => ~a ∧ ~b <=> ~(a + b) = ~a + ~b

37. ~(a v b) => ~a v ~b <=> ~(a . b) = ~a . ~b

38. a < b => a < b <=> a / b = a / b

39. a ∧ ~b => ~b ∧ a <=> a - b = -b + a

40. (a ∧ ~b) ∧ ~c => a ∧ (~b ∧ ~c) <=> (a - b) - c = a (-b - c)

41. (a < b) < c => a < (b < c) <=> (a / b) / c = a / (b / c)

42. a ∧ ~(b < c) => (a ∧ ~b) < (a ∧ ~c) <=> a - (b / c) = (a - b) / (a - c)

43. a < (b ∧ ~c) => (a < b) ∧ ~(a < c) <=> a / (b - c) = (a / b) - (a / c)

44. ~(a ∧ ~b) => ~a ∧ ~(~b) <=> ~(a - b) = ~a - ~b

45. ~(a < b) => ~a < ~b <=> ~(a / b) = ~a / ~b

The development of the prime pattern of sets has involved the use of sign labels from the prime pattern of the universal abstract. That is Q ! e. It is then possible to provide a simple clarification of other sign labels used in that sort of pattern and one of the possible definitions of the sign labels.

⊙ means the universal abstraction. ⊙ => ɜ ∧ e The universal

abstraction is the universe of discourse and everything in it.

ψ means the universal operator. ψa => a ∧ ~a ∧ !a The universal operator is every and all of some possible entity.

Э means the existential operator. Эa => a v ~a v !a The existential operator is some possible entity of all such entity.

з means the universe of discourse. з => e The universe of discourse is a restricted parameter bounded by the terms of meaning.

ф means the empty set. ф => з ∧ ~e The empty set is the class whose membership is none or the set of no elements.

1 means the unity set. 1 => a < a The unity set is the class whose membership is itself or the set that contains itself as element.

e means everything in the universe of discourse. e => a ∧ ~a Everything in the universe of discourse is only and all the sign labels used.

Q means not the empty set and not the unity set. Q => ~ф ∧ ~1 Not the empty set and not the unity set is the indefinite variable or possible improbable.

! means not not entity. !a => ~(~a) Not not entity is neither entity nor not entity.

The sign labels of the universal abstract enable us to make a/an hypothetical proposition as to the ontological formula, that is:

☉ => з ∧ e < (Q ∧ !e) v [(ф ∧ 1) ∧ (ψ ∧ Э)] is true or false or neither true or false.

Given the ontological formula, then the universal abstract is given as:

ф => з ∧ ~e < [a ∧ ф => a ; a ∧ ~ф => a ; ~a ∧ ф => ~a ; ~a ∧ ~ф => ~a ; a v ф => ф ; a < ф => ф ; ~a v ф => ф ; ~a < ф => ф ;

ф ∧ a => a ; ф ∧ ~a => ~a ; ф ∧ ~(~a) => !a]

$1 \Rightarrow a < a < [a \vee 1 \Rightarrow a; a < 1 \Rightarrow a; \sim a \vee 1 \Rightarrow \sim a; \sim a < 1 \Rightarrow \sim a; a$
$\wedge 1 \Rightarrow 1 \wedge a; \sim a \wedge 1 \Rightarrow 1 \wedge \sim a; a < a \Rightarrow 1]$

$Q \Rightarrow \sim\phi \wedge \sim 1 < [a \wedge \sim 1 \Rightarrow Q; \sim a \wedge \sim 1 \Rightarrow Q \wedge \sim a; a \vee \sim a \Rightarrow Q]$

$e \Rightarrow a \wedge \sim a < [a \wedge \sim a \Rightarrow e]$

$\psi \Rightarrow \ni < [a \Rightarrow a; \sim a \Rightarrow \sim a; a =/\Rightarrow \sim a; a \wedge a \Rightarrow a \wedge a; a \vee a \Rightarrow a;$
$a \wedge \sim(\sim a) \Rightarrow a \wedge !a; a < \sim(\sim a) \Rightarrow a < !a$

$a \vee b \Rightarrow b \vee a; a \wedge b \Rightarrow b \wedge a; (a \wedge b) \wedge c \Rightarrow a \wedge (b \wedge c); (a \vee b) \vee c$
$\Rightarrow a \vee (b \vee c); a \wedge (b \vee c) \Rightarrow (a \wedge b) \vee (a \wedge c);$

$a \vee (b \wedge c) \Rightarrow (a \vee b) \wedge (a \vee c); \sim(a \wedge b) \Rightarrow \sim a \wedge \sim b; \sim(a \vee b) \Rightarrow \sim a$
$\vee \sim b; a < b \Rightarrow a < b; a \wedge \sim b \Rightarrow \sim b \wedge a;$

$(a \wedge \sim b) \wedge \sim c \Rightarrow a \wedge (\sim b \wedge \sim c); (a < b) < c \Rightarrow a < (b < c); a \wedge \sim(b <$
$c) \Rightarrow (a \wedge \sim b) < (a \wedge \sim c);$

$a < (b \wedge \sim c) \Rightarrow (a < b) \wedge \sim(a < c); \sim(a \wedge \sim b) \Rightarrow \sim a \wedge \sim(\sim b); \sim(a < b)$
$\Rightarrow \sim a < \sim b]$

All of the various patterns previously detailed are either entirely correct or entirely incorrect or correct in part and incorrect in part, as given. If they are entirely correct then they do permit the possibility of a better formulation. If they are entirely incorrect then they do permit the possibility of their correct formulation. If they are correct in part and incorrect in part then they do permit the possibility of the correction of any part that is incorrect.

The criteria for truth, falsity and neither true nor false is given as:

For any p that we state as true, we must be able to demonstrate these reasons: P is externally correspondent to some fact. P is internally coherent within a larger system. P is useful according to some pragmatic purpose. P is capable of universal abstraction.

For any p that we state as false, we must be able to demonstrate these reasons: P does not externally correspond to any known fact. P is entirely incoherent within a larger system. P has no use according to some pragmatic purpose. P is not capable of universal abstraction.

In this sense, then, within the rules of the universe of discourse as given, the only condition for correcting the patterns as stated is that correction is only towards better coherency and non-contradiction. Any change in the directly opposite direction that increases internal contradiction and reduces internal coherency is not desirable. The patterns themselves do permit that they be adjusted individually, in part or in whole. As such the earlier proposition that they are an organic synergy is also held to be true. The patterns can be entirely written in a completely different sign label system. And the same sign label system could be used to write different patterns.

What are we missing? Since that is not the sort of question that can be answered in the totality of things, I will answer it in regard to a few important areas. One is in regard to "not not". A change that many will argue for is that "not not" should reduce to the simple positive affirmative. And that in fact is what we would tend to provide to children when they ask the same question. Because given the simple possible of a $\wedge$ ~a => e, that is much too early to provide children with the higher order studies. Many who study the early stages of this kind of system will meet the a and not a idea at the beginning so the only answer they are given is that it equals zero. And as well that not not reduces to the affirmation. And that neither the empty set nor the unity set being Q exists, so that if a choice is to be made and it is not the empty set it must be the unity set or the other way round. Therefore we provide a safe answer to people who learn the basics of this sign label, although the safe answer and the system it exists within cannot be proved true and remains without the required matter for the higher order system. On the other hand the stronger formulation can easily be permitted to intelligent children if they are potentially confident of understanding the higher order concepts.

As to the patterns previously stated I have made no adjustments to them since their final formulation. They seem correct as stated and accurate to what they should be saying. The difficulty is as to truth as strong as:

$a = a$ and $\sim a = \sim a$ and $a =/= \sim a$

$a + 0 = a$ and $a - 0 = a$ and $\sim a + 0 = \sim a$ and $\sim a - 0 = \sim a$

$a.1 = a$ and $a/1 = a$ and $\sim a.1 = \sim a$ and $\sim a/1 = \sim a$

$a.0 = 0$ and $a/0 = 0$ and $\sim a.0 = 0$ and $\sim a/0 = 0$

Now since these were the first terms we noticed as the most simple possible from the entire number pattern what we can do at this stage is reflect again on these terms to remind ourselves of how we know if some terms are true. Since to obtain that level of confidence in our own judgement that is as sure as $2 + 2 = 4$ we had to restrict ourselves to only this small group to start with, it is clear that we cannot immediately be sure as to the same definiteness of truth of the complete pattern of sets combined with the complete pattern of number. The complete aspect requires clarification. It is complete in the sense of most simple, not complete in the sense of exhaustive of all variations of possible true formulations. It is complete in the sense that from the simplest and tiniest pattern that is possible as given, any who works with the patterns can become skilled at generating other formulations of similar sort. For example $0 - 0 = 0$ is a term that was not included in the original pattern and is clearly coherent with the patterns as given.

The better idea at this stage is to hard copy the entire discourse and to work at small units of it over a length of time. From an individual point of view any person should definitely hand write only those terms that they believe to be true. Even if that was only the $a = a$ group it is a useful matter to begin with. That way any who choose to, can begin to keep a note book of what they are most sure of. And use the hard copy as an ongoing reference to see if they confirm or disagree with the formulation as presently stated. Since some of the sign labels used are not standard any individual may require that they replace with sign labels consistent with their own workstation. Maybe copy to desktop then send a copy to friends so that it can be worked with in a small team of players like a sort of game. Also that would mean no requirement to immediately keep up with what is necessarily the next area to consider, although any who worked through the patterns in order as stated up to this stage will easily be confident about this sort of area. Since the line through is very fast it can not mean that any who read all of it in one sitting can do all of it at one go. On the other hand any who chose to could easily hand write the entire combined pattern of number and sets exactly correctly even if they cannot at this immediate stage decide if it is true or not.

CHAPTER ELEVEN.

A: a, b, 0, 1, +, -, ., /, =, =/=, ~, ().

B: + + = +, + - = + -, -- = -, + . + = +, + / + = +, - . - = +, - / - = +, + . - = -, + / - = -, - / + = -

C: + = + , - = -, . = ., / = /, ~ = ~, = = =, =/= = =/=, () = ()

D: + =/= -, . =/= /, ~ =/= -, = =/= =/=

E: =

1. a => a <=> a = a

2. ~a => ~a <=> ~a = ~a

3. a =/=> ~a <=> a =/= ~a

4. a ∧ φ => a <=> a + 0 = a

5. a ∧ ~φ => a <=> a - 0 = a

6. ~a ∧ φ => ~a <=> ~a + 0 = ~a

7. ~a ∧ ~φ => ~a <=> ~a - 0 = ~a

8. a v 1 => a <=> a.1 = a

9. a < 1 => a <=> a/1 = a

10. ~a v 1 => ~a <=> ~a.1 = ~a

11. ~a < 1 => ~a <=> ~a/1 = ~a

12. a v φ => φ <=> a.0 = 0

13. a < φ => φ <=> a/0 = 0

14. ~a v φ => φ <=> ~a.0 = 0

15. ~a < φ => φ <=> ~a/0 = 0

16. a ∧ 1 => 1 ∧ a <=> a + 1 = 1 + a

17. $a \wedge \sim 1 \Rightarrow Q \wedge a \Leftrightarrow a - 1 = -1 + a$

18. $\sim a \wedge 1 \Rightarrow 1 \wedge \sim a \Leftrightarrow \sim a + 1 = 1 + \sim a$

19. $\sim a \wedge \sim 1 \Rightarrow Q \wedge \sim a \Leftrightarrow \sim a - 1 = -1 + \sim a$

20. $\phi \wedge a \Rightarrow a \Leftrightarrow 0 + a = a$

21. $\phi \wedge \sim a \Rightarrow \sim a \Leftrightarrow 0 - a = -a$

22. $\phi \wedge \sim(\sim a) \Rightarrow !a \Leftrightarrow 0 - \sim a = - \sim a$

23. $a \wedge a \Rightarrow a \wedge a \Leftrightarrow a + a = a + a$

24. $a \vee a \Rightarrow a \Leftrightarrow a \cdot a = a$

25. $a \wedge \sim a \Rightarrow e \Leftrightarrow a - a = 0$

26. $a < a \Rightarrow 1 \Leftrightarrow a / a = 1$

27. $a \vee \sim a \Rightarrow Q \Leftrightarrow a \cdot \sim a = 0$

28. $a \wedge \sim(\sim a) \Rightarrow a \wedge !a \Leftrightarrow a - \sim a = 1$

29. $a < \sim a \Rightarrow Q \Leftrightarrow a / \sim a = -1$

30. $a \vee b \Rightarrow b \vee a \Leftrightarrow a \cdot b = b \cdot a$

31. $a \wedge b \Rightarrow b \wedge a \Leftrightarrow a + b = b + a$

32. $(a \wedge b) \wedge c \Rightarrow a \wedge (b \wedge c) \Leftrightarrow (a + b) + c = a + (b + c)$

33. $(a \vee b) \vee c \Rightarrow a \vee (b \vee c) \Leftrightarrow (a \cdot b) \cdot c = a \cdot (b \cdot c)$

34. $a \wedge (b \vee c) \Rightarrow (a \wedge b) \vee (a \wedge c) \Leftrightarrow a + (b \cdot c) = (a + b) \cdot (a + c)$

35. $a \vee (b \wedge c) \Rightarrow (a \vee b) \wedge (a \vee c) \Leftrightarrow a \cdot (b + c) = (a \cdot b) + (a \cdot c)$

36. $\sim(a \wedge b) \Rightarrow \sim a \wedge \sim b \Leftrightarrow \sim(a + b) = \sim a + \sim b$

37. $\sim(a \vee b) \Rightarrow \sim a \vee \sim b \Leftrightarrow \sim(a \cdot b) = \sim a \cdot \sim b$

38. $a < b \Rightarrow a < b \Leftrightarrow a / b = a / b$

39. $a \wedge \sim b \Rightarrow \sim b \wedge a \Leftrightarrow a - b = -b + a$

40. $(a \wedge \sim b) \wedge \sim c \Rightarrow a \wedge (\sim b \wedge \sim c) \Leftrightarrow (a - b) - c = a(-b - c)$

41.i. $(a < b) < c \Rightarrow a < (b \vee c) \Leftrightarrow (a / b) / c = a / (b \cdot c)$

41.ii. $a < (b < c) \Rightarrow (a \vee c) < b \Leftrightarrow a / (b / c) = (a \cdot c) / b$

42. $a \wedge \sim(b < c) \Rightarrow (a \wedge \sim b) < (a \wedge \sim c) \Leftrightarrow a - (b / c) = (a - b) / (a - c)$

171

43. $a < (b \wedge \sim c) \Rightarrow (a < b) \wedge \sim(a < c) \Leftrightarrow a / (b - c) = (a / b) - (a / c)$

44. $\sim(a \wedge \sim b) \Rightarrow \sim a \wedge \sim(\sim b) \Leftrightarrow \sim(a - b) = \sim a - \sim b$

45. $\sim(a < b) \Rightarrow \sim a < \sim b \Leftrightarrow \sim(a / b) = \sim a / \sim b$

46. $\odot \Rightarrow \mathfrak{z} \wedge e$

47. $\psi a \Rightarrow a \wedge \sim a \wedge !a$

48. $\Theta a \Rightarrow a \vee \sim a \vee !a$

49. $\mathfrak{z} \Rightarrow e$

50. $\phi \Rightarrow \mathfrak{z} \wedge \sim e$

51. $1 \Rightarrow a < a$

52. $e \Rightarrow a \wedge \sim a$

53. $Q \Rightarrow \sim \phi \wedge \sim 1$

54. $!a \Rightarrow \sim(\sim a)$

55. $\odot \Rightarrow \mathfrak{z} \wedge e < (Q \wedge !e) \vee [(\phi \wedge 1) \wedge (\psi \wedge \Theta)]$

zi': $0 + 0 = 0 \Leftrightarrow \phi \wedge \phi \Rightarrow \phi$

zi'': $0 - 0 = 0 \Leftrightarrow \phi \wedge \sim \phi \Rightarrow Q$

zi''': $0 . 0 = 0 \Leftrightarrow \phi \vee \phi \Rightarrow \phi$

zi'''': $0 / 0 = 0 \Leftrightarrow \phi < \phi \Rightarrow \infty$

zii': $0 . 1 = 0 \Leftrightarrow \phi \vee 1 \Rightarrow \phi$

zii'': $1 . 0 = 0 \Leftrightarrow 1 \vee \phi \Rightarrow \phi$

zii''': $0 / 1 = 0 \Leftrightarrow \phi < 1 \Rightarrow \phi$

zii'''': $1 / 0 = 0 \Leftrightarrow 1 < \phi \Rightarrow \phi$

$ziii'$: $0 . a = 0 \Leftrightarrow \phi \vee a \Rightarrow \phi$

$ziii''$: $a . 0 = 0 \Leftrightarrow a \vee \phi \Rightarrow \phi$

$ziii'''$: $0 / a = 0 \Leftrightarrow \phi < a \Rightarrow \phi$

$ziii''''$: $a / 0 = 0 \Leftrightarrow a < \phi \Rightarrow \phi$

ziv': $0 . \sim a = 0 \Leftrightarrow \phi \vee \sim a \Rightarrow \phi$

ziv'': $\sim a . 0 = 0 \Leftrightarrow \sim a \vee \phi \Rightarrow \phi$

$ziv''': 0 / \sim a = 0 \iff \varphi < \sim a \Rightarrow \varphi$

$ziv'''': \sim a / 0 = 0 \iff \sim a < \varphi \Rightarrow \varphi$

$zv': 1 - 1 = 0 \iff 1 \wedge \sim 1 \Rightarrow Q$

$zv'': a - a = 0 \iff a \wedge \sim a \Rightarrow e$

$zv''': \sim a - \sim a = 0 \iff \sim a \wedge \sim(\sim a) \Rightarrow !\varphi$

$zv'''': a + \sim a = 0 \iff a \wedge \sim a \Rightarrow e$

Q1. $a = a$

Q2. $b = b$

Q3. $c = c$

Q4. $a =/= b \vee c$

Q5. $b =/= a \vee c$

Q6. $c =/= a \vee b$

Q7. $\sim a \Rightarrow \sim a$

Q8. $\sim b \Rightarrow \sim b$

Q9. $\sim c \Rightarrow \sim c$

Q10. $\sim a = b \vee c$

Q11. $\sim b = a \vee c$

Q12. $\sim c = a \vee b$

Q13. $a + a = b : \{[(a = b) \Rightarrow (a \wedge b = 0)] \wedge [(a =/= b) \Rightarrow (a \vee b =/= 0)]\}$

Q14. $a - a = 0$

Q15. $a . a = a \vee b \iff \{[(a = 1 \vee 0 \vee \infty) \Rightarrow (a . a = a)] \wedge [(a = -n \vee +n) \Rightarrow (a . a = b)]\}$

Q16. $a / a = 1 \vee 0 \vee \infty \vee b : [(a / a = b) \iff (a = -n)]$

Q17. $0 + 0 = 0$

Q18. $1 + 1 = b$

Q19. $\infty + \infty = \infty$

Q20. 0 - 0 = 0

Q21. 1 - 1 = 0

Q22. ∞ - ∞ = 0

Q23. 0 . 0 = 0

Q24. 1 . 1 = 1

Q25. ∞ . ∞ = ∞

Q26. 0 / 0 = 0 v ∞ v 1 : {[(0 / 0 = ∞) <=> (0 . ∞ = 0)] ∧ [(0 / 0 = 1) <=> (0 . 1 = 0)]}

Q27. 1 / 1 = 1

Q28. ∞ / ∞ = ∞ v 1 : [(∞ / ∞ = 1) <=> (1 . ∞ = ∞)]

Q29. a + b = c : (a =/= b)

Q30. a - b = c : (a =/= b)

Q31. a . b = c : [(c / b = a) ∧ (c / a = b)]

Q32. a / b = c : [(b . c = a) ∧ (a / c = b)]

Q33. +1 . +1 = +1

Q34. +1 / +1 = +1

Q35. -1 . -1 = +1 v 0 => Q : [(-1) + (+1) = 0]

Q36. -1 / -1 = +1 v 0 => Q : [(-1) + (+1) = 0]

Q37. -n . -1 = 0 : (n = c) ∧ {[(-c) + (+c) = 0] => [(-c . -1) = (+c)]}

Q38. +n . -1 = 0 : (n = c) ∧ {[(+c) + (-c) = 0] => [(+c . -1) = (-c)]}

Lattice One, Logic:

I. (a => b v c) => [(a < b => c) ∧ (a < c => b)]

II. (d => a v b) => [(a => d < b) ∧ (b => d < a)]

III. (e => a v c) => [(a => e < c) ∧ (c => e < a)]

IV. (f => b < c) => [(b => f v c) ∧ (c => b < f)]

V. (g => c < b) => [(c => g v b) ∧ (b => c < g)]

Lattice One, Algebra:

I. $(a = b \cdot c) \Rightarrow [(a / b = c) \wedge (a / c = b)]$

II. $(d = a \cdot b) \Rightarrow [(a = d / b) \wedge (b = d / a)]$

III. $(e = a \cdot c) \Rightarrow [(a = e / c) \wedge (c = e / a)]$

IV. $(f = b / c) \Rightarrow [(b = f \cdot c) \wedge (c = b / f)]$

V. $(g = c / b) \Rightarrow [(c = g \cdot b) \wedge (b = c / g)]$

Lattice One, Number:

I. $(8 = 2 \cdot 4) \Rightarrow [(2 = 8 / 4) \wedge (4 = 8 / 2)]$

II. $(16 = 8 \cdot 2) \Rightarrow [(8 = 16 / 2) \wedge (2 = 16 / 8)]$

III. $(32 = 8 \cdot 4) \Rightarrow [(8 = 32 / 4) \wedge (4 = 32 / 8)]$

IV. $(1/2 = 2 / 4) \Rightarrow [(2 = 1/2 \cdot 4) \wedge (4 = 2 / 1/2)]$

V. $(2 = 4 / 2) \Rightarrow [(4 = 2 \cdot 2) \wedge (2 = 4 / 2)]$

G1. ЭX < ЭY

G2. ЭX < Э~Y

G3. ЭY < ЭX

G4. ЭY < Э~X

G5. Э~X < ЭY

G6. Э~Y < ЭX

G7. Э~X < Э~Y

G8. Э~Y < Э~X

G9. [~]X < ЭY

G10. [~]Y < ЭX

G11. [~]Y < Э~X

G12. [~]~X < ЭY

G13. [~]X < Э~Y

G14. [~]~Y < ЭX

G15. [~]~X < ~Y

G16. [~]~Y < ~X

P1. (ЭX < ЭY) ∧ ([~]Y < Э~X) => (ЭX < ψY)

P2. (ЭX < Э~Y) ∧ ([~]X < ЭY) => (ψX < Э~Y)

P3. (ЭX < ЭY) ∧ (ЭY < ЭX) => (ЭX < ЭY)

P4. (Э~X < ЭY) ∧ (ЭY < Э~X) => (Э~X < ЭY)

One.

1. (ψB < ~A) => (ψA < ~B)

2. (ЭA < ψC) ∧ (ЭC < ЭB) =/=> [(ψB < ~A) <= (ЭC < ЭB)]

3. (ψB < ЭA) => (ЭA < ψB)

4. (ψA < ~B) => (ψB < ~A)

5. (ψB < ЭA)

6. (ЭB < ЭA) => (ЭA < ЭB)

7. (ψA < ~B) => (ψB < ~A)

8. (ЭB < ~A) => [(ЭA < ЭB) v (ψA < ~B)]

Two.

1. (ЭA < ψB) ∧ (ЭB < ψC) => (ЭA < ψC)

2. (ψA < ~B) ∧ (ЭB < ψC) => (ψA < ~C)

Three.

1. (ψB < ЭA) ∧ (ЭC < ЭB) => (ЭC < ЭA)

2. (ψB < ~A) ∧ (ЭC < ЭB) => (ЭC < ~A)

Four.

1. (ψA < ~B) ∧ (ЭA < ψC)

2. (ψA < ~B) <=> (ψB < ~A) <= [(ψ < ~) <=> (~ < ψ)]

3. (ЭA < ψC)

4. (ψB < ~C)

5. (ЭA < ψB) ∧ (ψA < ~C) => (ψB < ~C)

6. (ψA < ~C) => (ψC < ~A)

7. (ЭA < ψB)

8. (ψC < ~B)

9. (ψC < ~B) => (ψB < ~C)

Five.

1. (ψA < ~B) ∧ (ƎA < ƎC) => (ƎC < ~B)

2. [(ψA < ~B) => (ψB < ~A)] <= [(ψ < ~) <=> (~ < ψ)]

3. (ƎA < ƎC)

4. (ƎC < ~B)

5. (ƎA < ψB) ∧ (ψA < ~C) => (ψB < ~C)

6. (ƎB < ψC) ∧ (ƎA < ψB) => (ƎA < ψC)

7. (ψA < ~C)

8. (ƎA < ψB) ∧ (ƎC < ~A) => (ƎC < ~B)

Six.

1. (ƎA < ψB) ∧ (ƎA < ƎC)

2. (ƎB < ψC) v (ψB < ~C)

3. (ψA < ~C) ∧ (ƎA < ~B)

4. (ƎB < ψC) v (ψB < ~C)

Seven.

1. (ƎA < ψC) ∧ (ƎB < ψC) => (ƎA < ƎB)

2. [(ƎB < ψC) <=> (ψC < ƎB)] <= [(Ǝ < ψ) <=> (ψ < Ǝ)]

3. (ƎA < ψC) ∧ (ψC < ƎB) => (ƎA < ƎB)

Eight.

1. [(ƎA < ψC) ∧ (ƎB < ψC)] ∧ (ƎC < ψD)

2. [(ƎA < ψD) ∧ (ƎB < ψD)] => (ƎA < ƎB)

3. (ƎB < ψC) ∧ (ψA < ~C) => (ƎB < ~A)

Nine.

1. (ƎB < ψC) ∧ (ƎA < ƎC) => (ƎA < ƎB)

2. [(ƎA < ƎC) <=> (ƎC < ƎA)] <= [(Ǝ < Ǝ) <=> (Ǝ < Ǝ)]

3. (ЭB < ψC) ∧ (ЭC < ЭA) => (ЭB < ЭA)]

4. (ЭA < ЭB)]

Ten.

1. (ЭB < ЭC) ∧ (ЭA < ψC) => (ЭA < ЭB)

2. (ЭB < ψC) ∧ (ЭA < ~C) => (ЭA < ~B)

3. (ЭA < ψB) ∧ (ЭB < ψC) => (ЭA < ψC)

4. (ЭA < ~C)

Eleven.

1. (ψA < ~C) ∧ (ЭB < ЭC) => (ЭA < ~B)

Twelve.

1. [(ЭA < ψB) v (ЭA < ЭB)] ∧ (ψB < ~C)

2. [(ψB < ЭA) v (ЭB < ЭA)] ∧ (ψC < ~B)

3. (ЭA < ~C)

Thirteen.

1. (ЭA < ψC) ∧ (ЭB < ψC) => (ЭA < ЭB)

2. (ψA < ~B) ∧ (ЭB < ψC) => (ψA < ~C)

3. (ЭA < ψC)

Fourteen.

1. (ЭA < ψB) ∧ (ЭB < ЭC) => (ЭA < ЭC)

2. (ψA < ~C) ∧ (ЭA < ψB) => (ψB < ~C)

3. (ψA < ~B) ∧ (ЭB < ЭC) => (ЭC < ~A)

4. (ЭA < ψC) ∧ (ψA < ~B) => (ψB < ~C)

Fifteen.

1. (ЭA < ψB) ∧ (ЭB < ЭC)

2. (ЭA < ЭC)

3. (ЭB < ЭC) ∧ (ЭA < ψB)

Sixteen.

1. (ψB < ~A) ∧ (ƎA < ψC)

2. [(ψB < ~A) => (ψA < ~B)] <= [(ψ < ~) => (~ < ψ)]

3. (ƎA < ψC)

4. (ψB < ~C)

5. (ψC < ƎA)

Seventeen.

1. (ψA < ~C) => (ψC < ~A)

2. (ƎA < ψB)

3. (ψC < ~B)

4. (ψB < ~C)

Eighteen.

1. (ψC < ~A)

2. (ψB < ~C) => (ψC < ~B)

3. (ƎB < ƎA) <= (ƎA < ψB)

4.(ψC < ~A)

Nineteen.

1. (ψB < ~A) ∧ (ƎC < ƎA)

2. (ψB < ~A) => (ψA < ~B)

3. (ƎC < ƎA)

4. (ƎB < ~C)

Twenty.

1. (ƎA < ψB) ∧(ƎC < ~A) => (ƎC < ~B)

Twenty One.

1. (ƎA < ψC) ∧ (ƎB < ψC)

2. [(ƎB < ψC) => (ƎC < ƎB)] <= [(Ǝ < ψ) => (Ǝ < Ǝ)]

3. (ƎA < ψC) ∧ (ƎC < ƎB) => (ƎA < ƎB)

4. (ƎC < ƎB)

Twenty Two.

1. (ЭC < ЭA) => (ЭA < ЭC)

2. (ЭB < ψC) => (ЭB < ЭA)

Twenty Three.

1. (ψA < ~C) ∧ (ЭB < ЭC)

2. (ЭB < ЭC) ∧ (ψA < ~C) => (ЭA < ~B)

3. (ЭB < ЭC)

Twenty Four.

1. (ЭB < ЭC) ∧ (ψA < ~C)

2. (ЭB < ЭC) => (ЭC < ЭB)

3. (ψA < ~C) ∧ (ЭB < ЭC) => (ЭA < ~B)

Twenty Five.

1. (ЭB < ψC) ∧ (ЭA < ЭC) => (ЭB < ЭA)

2. (ψA < ~C) ∧ (ЭB < ЭC) => (ЭB < ~A)

Twenty Six.

1. [(ЭA < ψB) v (ЭA < ЭB)] ∧ (ЭB < ψC)

2. (ЭA < ψC) v (ЭA < ЭC)

3. [(ψA < ~B) v (ЭA < ~B)] ∧ (ЭB < ψC)

4. (ψA < ~C) v (ЭA < ~C)

5. {[(ЭA < ψB) v (ЭA < ЭB)] ∧ (ЭB < ЭC)} => [(ЭA < ψC) v (ЭA < ЭC)]

Twenty Seven.

1. {[(ψA < ~B) v (ЭA < ~B)] ∧ (ЭB < ЭC)} => [(ψA < ~C) v (ЭA < ~C)]

Twenty Eight.

1. [(ЭA < ψB) v (ЭA < ЭB)] ∧ (ЭB < ψC)

2. {(ЭB < ψC) ∧ [(ЭA < ψB) v (ЭA < ЭB)]} => [(ЭA < ψC) v (ЭA < ЭC)]

Twenty Nine.

1. {[(ψA < ~B) v (ƎA < ~B)] ∧ (ƎB < ψC)} => [(ψA < ~C) v (ƎA < ~C)]

Thirty.

1. A < B

2. [(A <= B) v (A => B v ~B)] ∧ (~A => ~B)

3. (A v ~A) ∧ ~B

4. (A v ~A) => (A v ~A)

5. ~B => ~B

6. (A v ~A) ∧ ~B

7. [(A ∧ ~B) v (~A ∧ ~B)] => [(A < A) ∧ (A => A)]

8. (A => A) <=> (A < A)

Thirty One.

1. (A v ~A) ∧ (A < B) => [(A => B) v (~A => ~B)]

2. A <= B

3. {[(A => B v ~B) v (~A => ~B)] ∧ (A v ~A)} => (B v ~B)

4. (~B v ~B) => [(~B v ~B) ∧ (B v ~B)]

Thirty Two.

1. (~B v ~B) ∧ ~(B v B) ∧ ~(ψB v ƎB)

2. (ƎB < ψC)

3. (ψA < ~C) ∧ (ƎB < ψC) => [(ƎA < ~B) v (ψA < ~B)]

4. (ƎA < ψB) v (ƎA < ƎB)

5. (ƎA < ψC) v (ƎA < ƎC)

6. (ψA < ~C) <=/=> [(ƎA < ψC) v (ƎA < ƎC)]

Thirty Three.

1. B < C

2. {(ƎB < ψC) ∧ [(ƎA < ψB) v (ƎA < ƎB)]} => [(ƎA < ψC) v (ƎA <

ЭC)]

3. (ψA < ~C) v (ЭA < ~C)

Thirty Four.

1. (ψA < ~B) ∧ [(ЭB < ψC) v (ЭB < ЭC)]

2. (ЭA < ~C) v (ψA < ~C)

3. (ψA < ~C) ∧ [(ЭB < ψC) v (ЭB < ЭC)]

4. (ЭA < ЭB)

5. (ψA < ~B) <=/=> (ЭA < ЭB)

6. (ψA < ~C)

Thirty Five.

1. (ЭA < ψB) ∧ [(ψB < ~C) v (ЭB < ~C)]

2. (ЭA < ~C) v (ЭA < ~C)

3. (ЭB < ψC) v (ЭB < ЭC)

4. {(ЭA < ψB) ∧ [(ЭB < ψC) v (ЭB < ЭC)]} => [(ЭA < ψC) v (ЭA < ЭC)]

Thirty Six.

1. (ψA < ~B) ∧ [(ЭB < ~C) v (ψB < ~C)]

2. [(ЭA < ψC) v (ЭA < ЭC)] v [(ЭA < ~C) v (ψA < ~C)]

3. {(ЭA < ψB) ∧ [(ЭB < ~C) v (ψB < ~C)]} => [(ЭA < ~C) v (ψA < ~C)]

Thirty Seven.

1. (ψA < ~B) ∧ [(ЭB < ~C) v (ψB < ~C)]

2. [(ЭA < ψC) v (ЭA < ЭC)] v [(ЭA < ~C) v (ψA < ~C)]

3. {[(ЭB < ψC) v (ЭB < ЭC)] ∧ (ψA < ~B)} => [(ЭA < ~C) v (ψA < ~C)]

Thirty Eight.

1. (ЭA < ψB) ∧ [(ЭB < ψC) v (ЭB < ЭC)]

2. [(ЭA < ψC) v (ЭA < ЭC)]

Thirty Nine.

1. [(ƎA < ψB) v (ƎA < ƎB)] ∧ (ƎB < ψC)

2. [(ƎA < ƎC) v (ƎA < ψC)] =/=> (ƎA < ψC)]

Forty.

1. (ψB < ~A) ∧ [(ƎB < ƎC) v (ƎB < ψC)]

2. (ψA < ~C)

3. [(ƎA < ƎC) v (ƎA < ψC)]

4. (ψB < ~A)

5. (ψB < ~A) => (ψA < ~B)

6. [(ƎA < ƎC) v (ƎA < ψC)]

7. [(ƎB < ~C) v (ψB < ~C)]

8. [(ƎB < ƎC) v (ƎB < ψC)]

Forty One.

1. (ψB < ~A) ∧ [(ƎB < ƎC) v (ƎB < ψC)]

2. (ƎA < ~C)

3. (ƎA < ψC) ∧ [(ψB < ~A) => (ψA < ~B)]

4. (ƎA < ψC) => (ψC < ~B)

5. [(ƎB < ƎC) v (ƎB < ψC)]

Forty Two.

1. (ψA < ~B) ∧ (ƎA < ψC)

2. (ψA < ~B) => (ψB < ~A)

3. (ƎA < ψC)

4. (ψB < ~A) ∧ (ƎA < ψC) => (ψB < ~C)

Forty Three.

1. (ψB < ~A) ∧ [(ƎA < ψC) v (ƎA < ƎC)]

2. (ψB < ~A) => (ψA < ~B)

3. [(ƎA < ψC) v (ƎA < ƎC)]

4. {(ψA < ~B) ∧ [(ƎA < ψC) v (ƎA < ƎC)]} => [(ψC < ~B) v (ƎC < ~B)]

5. (ψC < ~B)

6. (ƎC < ƎB)

7. (ψA < ~B) ∧ (ƎC < ƎB) => (ƎA < ~C)

8. [(ƎA < ψC) v (ƎA < ƎC)]

Forty Four.

1. (ψB < ~A) ∧ [(ψC < ~A) v (ƎC < ~A) v (ƎC < ƎA)]

2. (ψB < ~A) => (ψA < ~B)

3. (ƎA < ψC)

4. (ψA < ~B) ∧ (ƎA < ψC) => (ψB < ~C)

Forty Five.

1. [(ƎA < ψC) v (ƎA < ƎC)] ∧ [(ƎB < ψC) v (ƎB < ƎC)]

2. [(ƎB < ψC) v (ƎB < ƎC)] => [ψC < ƎB) v (ƎC < ƎB)]

3. [(ƎA < ψC) v (ƎA < ƎC)] ∧ [ψC < ƎB) v (ƎC < ƎB)]

4. (ƎA < ƎB) v (ψA < ~B)

Forty Six.

1. [(ψC < ~A) v (ƎC < ƎA)] ∧ [(ƎB < ψC) v (ƎB < ƎC)]

2. (ƎB < ~A) v (ƎB < ƎA)

Forty Seven.

1. [(ψC < ~A) v (ƎC < ~A)] ∧ [(ψC < ~B) v (ƎC < ~B)]

2. [(ψB < ~A) v (ƎB < ~A)] v [(ƎB < ψA) v (ƎB < ƎA)]

3. {[(ƎA < ψC) v (ƎA < ƎC)] ∧ [(ƎB < ψC) v (ƎB < ƎC)]} => [(ƎB < ψA) v (ƎB < ƎA)]

Forty Eight.

1. [(ƎA < ψC) v (ƎA < ƎC)] ∧ (ƎB < ƎC)

2. (ƎB < ƎC) => (ƎC < ƎB)]

3. {[(ƎA < ψC) v (ƎA < ƎC)] ∧ (ƎC < ƎB)} => [(ƎA < ƎB) v (ƎA < ~B)]

Forty Nine.

1. (ƎA < ψC) ∧ [(ƎB < ψC) v (ψB < ~C)]

2. [(ƎB < ψC) v (ψB < ~C)] => [(ψC < ƎB) v (ψC < ~B)]

3. {(ƎA < ψC) ∧ [(ψC < ƎB) v (ψC < ~B)]} => [(ƎA < ƎB) v (ƎA < ~B)]

Fifty.

1. (ƎB < ψC) ∧ [(ƎA < ƎC) v (ƎA < ~C)]

2. [(ƎA < ƎB) v (ƎA < ~B)]

3. (ƎA < ψB) ∧ (ƎB < ψC)

4. (ƎA < ψC)

5. [(ƎA < ƎC) v (ƎA < ~C)]

Fifty One.

1. (ƎA < ψC) ∧ [(ƎB < ψC) v (ƎB < ƎC)]

2. (ƎA < ψC) ∧ [(ƎC < ƎB) v (ψC < ƎB)]

3. [(ƎB < ψA) v (ƎB < ƎA)]

Fifty Two.

1. A=>B, C=>A, D=/=>A.

2. E=>F, G=>E, H=/=>E.

3. C <=> F => ƎA < ψE.

4. (ƎF < ψE) ∧ (ƎA < ψC) => (ƎA < ψE)

5. [(C <=> G) => (ƎA < ƎE)] <= [(C=>A) ∧ (G=>E)]

6. (F <=> D) => (ψA < ~E)

7. {[(ψA < ~E) => (ψE < ~A)] ∧ (F <=> D)} => [(ψA < ~F) ∧ (ƎF < ψE)].

Fifty Three.

1. (B <=> H) => (ψA < ~E).

2. (ƎB < ψA) ∧ (ψB < ~E).

3. (B <=> H) ∧ (ψH < ~E).

Fifty Four.

1. (D <=> G) => [(ψA v ƎA) < ~E.]

2. (ψA < ~G) <= (ψA < ~D).

3. ψG < ƎE.

4. (ψA v ƎA) < ~E.

Fifty Five.

1. (B <=> G).

2. (ƎE < ψA) <= {[(ψB < ƎA) ∧ (ψE < ƎB)] ∧ (B <=> G)}.

3. (ƎA < ψE) v (ƎA < ƎE).

4. (ƎA < ƎE) <= (ψ => Ǝ)

5. (ƎC <=> ƎF) => (ƎA < ψE)

Fifty Six.

1. (C <=> G) => (ƎA <=> ƎE)

2. (ƎD <=> ƎF) => (ψA < ~E)

3. [(ψA < ~F) <= {(ψF < ~A)] ∧ (ƎF < ψE)}

4. (ψD < ~A) ∧ (ƎD < ψE)

5. (ƎD <=> ƎG) => (ψA < ~E)

6. (ψA < ~G) ∧ (ƎE < ψG)

S1. (ƎC < ψB) ∧ (ƎB < ψA) => (ƎC < ψA)

S2. (ψC < ~B) ∧ (ƎB < ψA) => (ψC < ~A)

S3. (ƎC < ψB) ∧ (ƎB < ƎA) => (ƎC < ƎA)

S4. (ψC < ~B) ∧ (ƎB < ƎA) => (~C < ƎA)

S5. (ψB < ~C) ∧ (ƎB < ψA) => (ψC < ~A)

S6. (ƎB < ψC) ∧ (ψB < ~A) => (ψC < ~A)

S7. (ψB < ~C) ∧ (ƎB < ƎA) => (~C < ƎA)

S8. (ЭВ < ψС) ∧ (~B < ЭА) => (~C < ЭА)

S9. (ЭС < ψВ) ∧ (ЭА < ψВ) => (ЭС < ЭА)

S10. (ψС < ~B) ∧ (ЭА < ψВ) => (~C < ЭА)

S11. (ЭС < ЭВ) ∧ (ЭА < ψВ) => (ЭС < ЭА)

S12. (ЭС < ψВ) ∧ (ЭА < ЭВ) => (ЭС < ЭА)

S13. (~C < ЭВ) ∧ (ЭА < ψВ) => (~C < ЭА)

S14. (ψС < ~B) ∧ (ЭА < ЭВ) => (~C < ЭА)

S15. (ЭВ < ψС) ∧ (ЭА < ψВ) => (ψС < ЭА)

S16. (ЭВ < ψС) ∧ (ψА < ~B) => (~C < ψА)

S17. (ЭВ < ЭС) ∧ (ЭА < ψВ) => (ЭС < ЭА)

S18. (ψВ < ~C) ∧ (ЭА < ψВ) => (~C < ЭА)

S19. (ψВ < ~C) ∧ (ЭА < ЭВ) => (~C < ЭА)

1. (ЭС < ψА)

1.1 (ЭС < ψВ) ∧ (ЭВ < ψА)

2. (ψС < ~A)

2.1 (ψС < ~B) ∧ (ЭВ < ψА)

2.2 (ψВ < ~C) ∧ (ЭВ < ψА)

2.3 (ЭВ < ψС) ∧ (ψВ < ~A)

3. (ЭС < ЭА)

3.1 (ЭС < ψВ) ∧ (ЭВ < ЭА)

3.2 (ЭС < ψВ) ∧ (ЭА < ψВ)

3.3 (ЭС < ψВ) ∧ (ЭА < ЭВ)

3.4 (ЭС < ЭВ) ∧ (ЭА < ψВ)

3.5 (ЭВ < ψС) ∧ (ЭА < ψВ)

3.6 (ЭВ < ЭС) ∧ (ЭА < ψВ)

4. (~C < ЭА)

4.1 (ψС < ~B) ∧ (ЭВ < ЭА)

4.2 $(\psi B < {\sim}C) \wedge (\Im B < \Im A)$

4.3 $(\Im B < \psi C) \wedge ({\sim}B < \Im A)$

4.4 $(\psi C < {\sim}B) \wedge (\Im A < \psi B)$

4.5 $({\sim}C < \Im B) \wedge (\Im A < \psi B)$

4.6 $(\psi C < {\sim}B) \wedge (\Im A < \Im B)$

4.7 $(\Im B < \psi C) \wedge (\psi A < {\sim}B)$

4.8 $(\psi B < {\sim}C) \wedge (\Im A < \psi B)$

4.9 $(\psi B < {\sim}C) \wedge (\Im A < \Im B)$

CHAPTER TWELVE.

The following article is honoured to be permitted existence in the fabulous Facebook Meta mechanism.

The information of this article is the central core to the human capacity to think logically, and has for approximately two thousand five hundred years remained the secret of a small community.

It is sad but true that enquirers both liked and disliked have faced great peril in their quest to study the Wizard Aristotle. For this reason I would like to explain something of why that is so.

Some of what Aristotle wrote is very easy to understand. Where they can, students will obtain the bit they understand to their advantage. The difficulty is that the bits they understand are absorbed in to much that is difficult or impossible to understand.

They would read a little, talk about it as if it were all, and be pleased if the people they taught were never any the wiser.

The following article is very rare.

Were the interested enquirer to go directly to the Prior Analytics of Aristotle in order to learn something of the syllogism, they would encounter an encryption system. By encryption in this instance I am speaking non-technically. Ciphers, codes and encryption are technically three different things and the methodology of each is formal. Aristotle required a method whereby he could transmit information in such a way that it was both intelligible and secret. And such that the understandable aspects were avenues towards the more secret aspects. Also such that the more secret aspects were protected as much as the more obvious argumentation. The manuscript contained here should be respected as very secret. The Game Domain Model provides all that is required in order to understand this.

Counter-intuitively the fact that it is secret does not mean it is not available on the public domain.

Actually, if you are under ten years old and reading this, you are supposed to tell your mummy so she can check it is okay.

And if you are a professor of logic you are supposed to tell your students.

And if you are a famous actor in Hollywood you are supposed to do a film about it, probably to the music of Christina Aguilera, Katy Perry, Britney Spears and Pink.

Please do not think that the very rare manuscript provided here is anything like what the enquirer would find if they went directly to the Prior Analytics. Because it is not.

The Prior Analytics is encrypted. This article is not encrypted.

Given the study of my articles on algebraic deduction are worked with first, it will be relatively easy for any person who has done so to understand this manuscript. Without study of algebraic deduction and the related articles it would not be.

The following manuscript is entirely contained, although hidden, within the Prior Analytics written by Aristotle. The translation that I have used is by A. J. Jenkinson. The sequence of the information provided is exactly the same as in the translation. In the original there is a huge amount of information between each component provided here, that I have not included. This is important. I have suggested in various locations within my articles the requirement to handwrite the information that one wants to possess privately. From ancient times this is the only way that some writers can be studied.

<<<Everything in three brackets is a later addition to the original article.

If you can not hand write it, how do you know what you have read?

How do you know if what you think you read is the same as what is written?

If what you read is an outward reflection of your best present understanding, how will you know whether what you remember is accurate to what you presently understand?

How do you differentiate some from all if you do not hand write the "in particular".

How do you individuate your self from other players/readers if you have not specified this and not that differently to the way they have done so.>>>

I have made any adjustments required in order to ensure smooth flow of grammatical articulation. Also I have altered all the sign labels so that the examples are all in ABC form.

The Perfect Syllogism, by the Wizard Aristotle.

A syllogism is discourse in which, certain things being stated, something

other than what is stated follows of necessity from their being so.

I mean by the last phrase that they produce the consequence, and by

this, that no further term is required from without in order to make

the consequence necessary.

I call that a perfect syllogism which needs nothing other than what has been stated to make plain what necessarily follows.

A syllogism is imperfect, if it needs either one or more propositions, which are

indeed the necessary consequences of the terms set down, but have

not been expressly stated as premisses.

First Figure.

1.

First then take a universal negative with the terms A and B.

If no B is A, neither can any A be B. For if some A (say C) were B, it would not be true that no B is A; for C is a B.

But if every B is A then some A is B. For if no A were B, then no B could be A. But we assumed that every B is A.

Similarly too, if the premiss is particular.

For if some B is A, then some of the As must be B. For if none were, then no B would be A. But if some B is not A, there is no necessity that some of the As should not be B.

Let B stand for animal and A for man.

Not every animal is a man; but every man is an animal.

Whenever three terms are so related to one another that the last is contained in the middle as in a whole, and the middle is either contained in, or excluded from, the first as in or from a whole, the extremes must be related by a perfect syllogism.

I call that term middle which is itself contained in another and contains another in itself: in position also this comes in the middle.

By extremes I mean both that term which is itself contained in another and that in which another is contained.

2.

If A is predicated of all B, and B of all C, A must be predicated of all C:

Similarly also, if A is predicated of no B, and B of all C, it is necessary that no C will be A.

I call that term the major in which the middle is contained and that term the minor which comes under the middle.

3.

Let all B be A and some C be B. Then it is necessary that some C is A.

And if no B is A but some C is B, it is necessary that some C is not A.

So there will be a perfect syllogism.

Second Figure.

Whenever the same thing belongs to all of one subject, and to none of another, or to all of each subject or to none of either, I call

such a figure the second.

By middle term in it I mean that which is predicated of both subjects, by extremes the terms of which this is said, by major extreme that which lies near the middle, by minor that which is further away from the middle.

The middle term stands outside the extremes, and is first in position. A syllogism cannot be perfect anyhow in this figure, but it may be valid whether the terms are related universally or not.

If then the terms are related universally a syllogism will be possible, whenever the middle belongs to all of one subject and to none of another (it does not matter which has the negative relation), but in no other way.

4.

Let A be predicated of no B, but of all C.

Since, then, the negative relation is convertible, B will belong to no A.

But A was assumed to belong to all C.

Consequently B will belong to no C.

This has already been proved.

Again if A belongs to all B, but to no C, then B will belong to no C.

For if A belongs to no C, C belongs to no A.

But A (as was said) belongs to all B.

C then will belong to no B.

For the first figure has again been formed.

But since the negative relation is convertible, B will belong to no C.

Thus it will be the same syllogism that proves both conclusions.

It is possible to prove these results also by reductio ad impossibile.

If the middle term is related universally to one of the extremes, a particular negative syllogism must result whenever the middle term

is related universally to the major whether positively or negatively, and particularly to the minor and in a manner opposite to that of

the universal statement.

By 'an opposite manner' I mean, if the universal statement is negative, the particular is affirmative: if the universal is affirmative, the particular is negative.

5.

For if A belongs to no B, but to some C, it is necessary that B does not belong to some C.

For since the negative statement is convertible, B will belong to no A.

But A was admitted to belong to some C.

Therefore B will not belong to some C.

For the result is reached by means of the first figure.

Again if A belongs to all B, but not to some C, it is necessary that B does not belong to some C.

For if B belongs to all C, and A is predicated also of all B, A must belong to all C.

But we assumed that A does not belong to some C.

And if A belongs to all B but not to all C, we shall conclude that B does not belong to all C.

The proof is the same as the above.

6.

Again let the premisses be affirmative, and let the major premiss as before be universal.

Let A belong to all B and to some C.

It is possible then for B to belong to all C or to no C.

But if the minor premiss is universal, and A belongs to no C, and not to some B.

Then it is possible for B to belong either to all C or to no C.

Third Figure.

But if one term belongs to all, and another to none, of a third, or if both belong to all, or to none, of it, I call such a figure the third.

By middle term in it I mean that of which both the predicates are predicated, by extremes I mean the predicates, by the major extreme

that which is further from the middle, by the minor that

which is nearer to it.

The middle term stands outside the extremes, and is last in position. A syllogism cannot be perfect in this figure either, but it may be valid whether the terms are related universally or not to the middle term.

7.

If they are universal, whenever both A and B belong to C, it follows that A will necessarily belong to some B.

For, since the affirmative statement is convertible, C will belong to some B.

Consequently since A belongs to all C, and C to some B, A must belong to some B.

For a syllogism in the first figure is produced.

8.

For if both A and B belong to all C, should one of the Cs, such as D, be taken.

Both A and B will belong to this, and thus A will belong to some B.

If B belongs to all C, and A to no C, there will be a syllogism to prove that A will necessarily not belong to some B.

9.

For if B belongs to all C, A to some C, A must belong to some B.

For since the affirmative statement is convertible C will belong to some A.

Consequently since B belongs to all C, and C to some A, B must also belong to some A.

Therefore A must belong to some B.

10.

Again if B belongs to some C, and A to all C, A must belong to some B.

For if B belongs to all C, but A does not belong to some C, it is necessary that A does not belong to some B.

For if A belongs to all B, and B belongs to all C, then A will belong to all C.

But we assumed that it did not.

11.

But if the negative term is universal, whenever the major is negative and the minor affirmative there will be a syllogism.

For if A belongs to no C, and B belongs to some C, A will not belong to some B.

Reduction to Universal Syllogisms.

12.

If A belongs to all or some B, and B belongs to no C.

Then if the premisses are converted it is necessary that C does not belong to some A.

13.

In the last figure, if A and B belong to all C, it follows that A belongs to some B.

For if A belonged to no B, and B belongs to all C, A would belong to no C.

But (as we stated) it belongs to all C.

14.

If A belongs to all B, and B to some C, it follows that A belongs to some C.

For if it belonged to no C, and belongs to all B, then B will belong to no C.

For if A belongs to no B, and B belongs to some C, A will not belong to some C.

For if it belonged to all C, and belongs to no B, then B will belong to no C.

Consequently, since all syllogisms in the middle figure can be reduced to universal syllogisms in the first figure, and since particular syllogisms in the first figure can be reduced to syllogisms in the middle figure, it is clear that particular syllogisms can be reduced to universal syllogisms in the first figure.

Syllogisms in the third figure, if the terms are universal, are directly made perfect by means of those syllogisms.

But, when one of the premisses is particular, by means of the particular syllogisms in the first figure.

And these (we have seen) may be reduced to the universal syllogisms in the first figure.

Consequently also the particular syllogisms in the third figure may be so reduced.

It is clear then that all syllogisms may be reduced to the universal syllogisms in the first figure.

Syllogims of Necessity.

15.

First let the universal be necessary, and let A belong to all B necessarily, but let B simply belong to some C.

It is necessary then that A belongs to some C necessarily.

For C falls under B, and A was assumed to belong necessarily to all B.

16.

First let the negative be necessary, let A be possible of no B, and simply belong to C.

Since then the negative statement is convertible, B is possible of no A.

But A belongs to all C.

Consequently B is possible of no C.

For C falls under A.

17.

The same result would be obtained if the minor premiss were negative.

For if A is possible be of no C, then C is possible of no A.

But A belongs to all B.

Consequently C is possible of none of the Bs.

For again we have obtained the first figure.

Neither then is B possible of C.

18.

Further, if the conclusion is necessary, it follows that C necessarily does not belong to some A.

For if B necessarily belongs to no C, C will necessarily belong to no B.

But B at any rate must belong to some A, if it is true (as was assumed) that A necessarily belongs to all B.

Consequently it is necessary that C does not belong to some A.

19.

First then let the negative premiss be both universal and necessary.

Let it be possible for no B that A should belong to it, and let A simply belong to some C.

Since the negative statement is convertible, it will be possible for no A that B should belong to it.

But A belongs to some C.

Consequently B necessarily does not belong to some of the Cs.

20.

Again let the affirmative premiss be both universal and

necessary, and let the major premiss be affirmative.

If then A necessarily belongs to all B, but does not belong to some C, it is clear that B will not belong to some C, but not necessarily.

21.

First let both the premisses be affirmative, and let A and B belong to all C, and let AC be necessary.

Since then B belongs to all C, C also will belong to some B, because the universal is convertible into the particular.

Consequently if A belongs necessarily to all C, and C belongs to some B, it is necessary that A should belong to some B also.

For B is under C.

The first figure then is formed.

22.

A similar proof will be given also if BC is necessary.

For C is convertible with some A.

Consequently if B belongs necessarily to all C, it will belong necessarily also to some A.

23.

Again let AC be negative, BC affirmative, and let the negative premiss be necessary.

Since then C is convertible with some B, but A necessarily belongs to no C, A will necessarily not belong to some B either.

For B is under C.

24.

But if the affirmative is necessary, the conclusion will not be necessary.

For suppose BC is affirmative and necessary, while AC is negative and not necessary.

Since then the affirmative is convertible, C also will belong to some B necessarily.

Consequently if A belongs to none of the Cs, while C belongs to some of the Bs, A will not belong to some of the Bs-but not of necessity.

25.

If then it is necessary that B should belong to all C, and A falls under C, it is necessary that B should belong to some A.

For if it is not possible that A should belong to any C, but B belongs to some C, it is necessary that A should not belong to some B.

Syllogisms of Possibility.

26.

Whenever A may possibly belong to all B, and B to all C.

There will be a perfect syllogism to prove that A may possibly belong to all C.

Similarly if it is possible for A to belong no B, and for B to belong to all C, then it is possible for A to belong to no C.

For if A is possible for all B, and B for some C, then A is possible for some C.

27.

Again if A may belong to no B, and B may belong to some of the Cs, it is necessary that A may possibly not belong to some of the Cs.

28.

Let A be possible for all B, and let B belong to all C.

Since C falls under B, and A is possible for all B, clearly it is possible for all C also.

So a perfect syllogism results.

29.

Likewise if the premiss AB is negative, and the premiss BC is affirmative.

The former stating possible, the latter simple attribution.

A perfect syllogism results proving that A possibly belongs to no C.

30.

First we must state that if B's being follows necessarily from A's being.

Then B's possibility will follow necessarily from A's possibility.

Suppose, the terms being so related, that A is possible, and B is impossible.

If then that which is possible, when it is possible for it to be, might happen.

And if that which is impossible, when it is impossible, could not happen.

And if at the same time A is possible and B impossible.

It would be possible for A to happen without B, and if to happen, then to be.

For that which has happened, when it has happened, is.

Syllogisms of Contradictory Assumption.

31.

If A is false, but not impossible, and if B is the consequence of A, B also will be false but not impossible.

For since it has been proved that if B's being is the consequence of A's being.

Then B's possibility will follow from A's possibility (and A is assumed to be possible), consequently B will be possible.

For if it were impossible, the same thing would at the same time be possible and impossible.

32.

Suppose that it is not possible, but assume that B belongs to all C: this is false but not impossible.

If then A is not possible for C but B belongs to all C, then A is not possible for all B.

For a syllogism is formed in the third degree.

But it was assumed that A is a possible attribute for all B.

It is necessary then that A is possible for all C.

For though the assumption we made is false and not impossible, the conclusion is impossible.

33.

It is possible also in the first figure to bring about the impossibility, by assuming that B belongs to C.

For if B belongs to all C, and A is possible for all B, then A would be possible for all C.

But the assumption was made that A is not possible for all C.

34.

Again let the premiss AB be universal and negative, and assume that A belongs to no B, but B possibly belongs to all C.

These propositions being laid down, it is necessary that A possibly belongs to no C.

Suppose that it cannot belong, and that B belongs to C, as above.

It is necessary then that A belongs to some B.

For we have a syllogism in the third figure: but this is impossible.

Thus it will be possible for A to belong to no C.

For if at is supposed false, the consequence is an impossible one.

35.

Let A belong to all B, and let B possibly belong to no C.

If the terms are arranged thus, nothing necessarily follows.

But if the proposition BC is converted and it is assumed that B is possible for all C.

A syllogism results as before.

For the terms are in the same relative positions.

36.

Likewise if both the relations are negative.

If the major premiss states that A does not belong to B, and the minor premiss indicates that B may possibly belong to no C.

Through the premisses actually taken nothing necessary results in any way.

But if the problematic premiss is converted, we shall have a syllogism.

37.

Suppose that A belongs to no B, and B may possibly belong to no C.

Through these comes nothing necessary.

But if B is assumed to be possible for all C (and this is true) and if the premiss AB remains as before, we shall again have the same syllogism.

38.

If the premisses are affirmative, clearly the conclusion which follows is not necessary.

Suppose A necessarily belongs to all B, and let B be possible for all C.

We shall have an imperfect syllogism to prove that A may belong to all C.

39.

Again, let A be possible for all B, and let B necessarily belong to all C.

We shall then have a syllogism to prove that A may belong to all C, not that A does belong to all C.

And it is perfect, not imperfect.

For it is completed directly through the original premisses.

Problematic Syllogisms of Necessity and Possibility

40.

But if the premisses are not similar in quality.

Suppose first that the negative premiss is necessary.

And let necessarily A not be possible for any B, but let B be possible for all C.

It is necessary then that A belongs to no C.

For suppose A to belong to all C or to some C.

Now we assumed that A is not possible for any B.

Since then the negative proposition is convertible, B is not possible for any A.

But A is supposed to belong to all C or to some C.

Consequently B will not be possible for any C or for all C.

But it was originally laid down that B is possible for all C.

41.

The same relation will obtain in particular syllogisms.

Whenever the negative proposition is necessary, the conclusion will be negative assertoric.

That is if it is not possible that A should belong to any B, but B may belong to some of the Cs.

Then it is necessary that A should not belong to some of the Cs.

For if A belongs to all C, but cannot belong to any B, neither can B belong to any A.

So if A belongs to all C, to none of the Cs can B belong.

But it was laid down that B may belong to some C.

42.

Suppose A belongs to no B, but can belong to all C.

If the negative proposition is converted, B will belong to no A.

But ex hypothesi can belong to all C.

So a syllogism is made, proving by means of the first figure that B may belong to no C.

43.

Suppose that A necessarily belongs to no B, but may belong to all C.

If the negative premiss is converted B will belong to no A.

But A ex hypothesi is capable of belonging to all C.

So once more a conclusion is drawn by the first figure that B may belong to no C.

But at the same time it is clear that B will not belong to any C.

For assume that it does.

Then if A cannot belong to any B, and B belongs to some of the Cs, A cannot belong to some of the Cs.

But ex hypothesi it may belong to all.

44.

But if the premisses are similar in quality, when they are negative a syllogism can always be formed by converting the problematic premiss

into its complementary affirmative as before.

Suppose A necessarily does not belong to B, and possibly may not belong to C.

If the premisses are converted B belongs to no A, and A may possibly belong to all C.

Thus we have the first figure.

45.

First let the premisses be problematic and suppose that both A and B may possibly belong to every C.

Since then the affirmative proposition is convertible into a particular.

And B may possibly belong to every C, it follows that C may possibly belong to some B.

So, if A is possible for every C, and C is possible for some of the Bs.

Then A is possible for some of the Bs.

For we have got the first figure.

46.

And A may possibly belong to no C, but B may possibly belong to all C.

It follows that A may possibly not belong to some B.

For we shall have the first figure again by conversion.

47.

But if both premisses should be negative no necessary consequence will follow from them as they are stated.

But if the premisses are converted into their corresponding affirmatives there will be a syllogism as before.

For A and B may possibly not belong to C.

If 'may possibly belong' is substituted we shall again have the first figure by means of conversion.

But if one of the premisses is universal, the other particular, a syllogism will be possible, or not, under the arrangement of the terms as in the case of assertoric propositions.

48.

Suppose that A may possibly belong to all C, and B to some C.

We shall have the first figure again if the particular premiss is converted.

For if A is possible for all C, and C for some of the Bs, then A is possible for some of the Bs.

49.

If one premiss is pure, the other problematic, the conclusion will be problematic, not pure.

And a syllogism will be possible under the same arrangement of the terms as before.

First let the premisses be affirmative.

Suppose that A belongs to all C, and B may possibly belong to all C.

If the proposition BC is converted, we shall have the first figure.

And the conclusion that A may possibly belong to some of the Bs.

For when one of the premisses in the first figure is problematic, the conclusion also (as we saw) is problematic.

50.

Suppose that B belongs to all C, and A may possibly not belong to some C.

It follows that A may possibly not belong to some B.

For if A necessarily belongs to all B, and B (as has been assumed) belongs to all C.

Then A will necessarily belong to all C.

For this has been proved before.

But it was assumed at the outset that A may possibly not belong to some C.

51.

Suppose first that the premisses are affirmative.

That A necessarily belongs to all C, and B may possibly belong to all C.

Since then A must belong to all C, and C may belong to some B.

It follows that A may (not does) belong to some B.

For so it resulted in the first figure.

Syllogisms of Complex Possibility.

52.

Suppose the consequents of A are designated by B, the antecedents of A by C, attributes which cannot possibly belong to A by D.

Suppose again that the attributes of E are designated by F, the antecedents of E by G, and attributes which cannot belong to E by H.

If then one of the Cs should be identical with one of the Fs, A must belong to all E.

For F belongs to all E, and A to all C, consequently A belongs to all E.

If C and G are identical, A must belong to some of the Es: for A follows C, and E follows all G.

If F and D are identical, A will belong to none of the Es by a prosyllogism.

For since the negative proposition is convertible, and F is identical with D, A will belong to none of the Fs, but F belongs to all E.

53.

Again, if B and H are identical, A will belong to none of the Es.

For B will belong to all A, but to no E.

For it was assumed to be identical with H, and H belonged to none of the Es.

54.

If D and G are identical, A will not belong to some of the Es.

For it will not belong to G, because it does not belong to D.

But G falls under E.

Consequently A will not belong to some of the Es.

55.

If B is identical with G, there will be a converted syllogism.

For E will belong to all A since B belongs to A and E to B (for B was found to be identical with G).

But that A should belong to all E is not necessary.

But it must belong to some E because it is possible to convert the universal statement into a particular.

It is clear too that the inquiry proceeds through the three terms and the two premisses, and that all the syllogisms proceed through

the aforesaid figures.

For it is proved that A belongs to all E, whenever an identical term is found among the Cs and Fs.

This will be the middle term; A and E will be the extremes.

So the first figure is formed.

56.

And A will belong to some E, whenever C and G are apprehended to be the same.

This is the last figure: for G becomes the middle term.

And A will belong to no E, when D and F are identical.

Thus we have both the first figure and the middle figure.

The first, because A belongs to no F, since the negative

statement is convertible, and F belongs to all E.

The middle figure because D belongs to no A, and to all E.

And A will not belong to some E, whenever D and G are identical.

This is the last figure: for A will belong to no G, and E will belong to all G.

The article written by Aristotle as to the perfect syllogism is complete at this point, given as notes one through fifty six.

Notes following are my own.

1. (ƎC < ψB) ∧ (ƎB < ψA) => (ƎC < ψA) Some C contains All B and Some B contains All A then Some C contains All A.

2. (ψC < ~B) ∧ (ƎB < ψA) => (ψC < ~A) All C contains Not B and Some B contains All A then All C contains Not A.

3. (ƎC < ψB) ∧ (ƎB < ƎA) => (ƎC < ƎA) Some C contains All B and Some B contains Some A then Some C contains Some A.

4. (ψC < ~B) ∧ (ƎB < ƎA) => (~C < ƎA) All C contains Not B and Some B contains Some A then Not C contains Some A.

5. (ψB < ~C) ∧ (ƎB < ψA) => (ψC < ~A) All B contains Not C and Some B contains All A then All C contains Not A.

6. (ƎB < ψC) ∧ (ψB < ~A) => (ψC < ~A) Some B contains All C and All B contains Not A then All C contains Not A.

7. (ψB < ~C) ∧ (ƎB < ƎA) => (~C < ƎA) All B contains Not C and Some B contains Some A then Not C contains Some A.

8. (ƎB < ψC) ∧ (~B < ƎA) => (~C < ƎA) Some B contains All C and Not B contains Some A then Not C contains Some A.

9. (ƎC < ψB) ∧ (ƎA < ψB) => (ƎC < ƎA) Some C contains All B and Some A contains All B then Some C contains Some A.

10. (ψC < ~B) ∧ (ƎA < ψB) => (~C < ƎA) All C contains Not B and Some A contains All B then Not C contains Some A.

11. (ƎC < ƎB) ∧ (ƎA < ψB) => (ƎC < ƎA) Some C contains Some

B and Some A contains All B then Some C contains Some A.

12. (ЭC < ψB) ∧ (ЭA < ЭB) => (ЭC < ЭA) Some C contains All B and Some A contains Some B then Some C contains Some A.

13. (~C < ЭB) ∧ (ЭA < ψB) => (~C < ЭA) Not C contains Some B and Some A contains All B then Not C contains Some A.

14. (ψC < ~B) ∧ (ЭA < ЭB) => (~C < ЭA) All C contains Not B and Some A contains Some B then Not C contains Some A.

15.(ЭB < ψC) ∧ (ЭA < ψB) => (ψC < ЭA) Some B contains All C and Some A contains All B then All C contains Some A.

16.(ЭB < ψC) ∧ (ψA < ~B) => (~C < ψA) Some B contains All C and All A contains Not B then Not C contains All A.

17.(ЭB < ЭC) ∧ (ЭA < ψB) => (ЭC < ЭA) Some B contains Some C and Some A contains All B then Some C contains Some A.

18.(ψB < ~C) ∧ (ЭA < ψB) => (~C < ЭA) All B contains Not C and Some A contains All B then Not C contains Some A.

19.(ψB < ~C) ∧ (ЭA < ЭB) => (~C < ЭA) All B contains Not C and Some A contains Some B then Not C contains Some A.

In regard to "The Perfect Syllogism by the Wizard Aristotle" as detailed above.

The following method has been thoroughly explained in various related articles. It equally applies here.

First, each of the individual fifty six points of the article must be considered separately, in any order.

As given, each point may be correctly stated or not correctly stated in accord with the original document written by Aristotle.

If not correctly stated, then any particular point is correctable.

Correctly stated means accurate to what was originally written before any translation.

Second, If each of the fifty six points is correctly stated, then they each may be true or false.

True in this sense means that when correctly stated they describe accurately what is the case.

That is they provide proper means whereby to determine if any given syllogism is valid or invalid.

Third, If we find any small mistake or error in any single one of the fifty six points, we can specify that point in particular, without in any way referring to all the other points that are correct.

Having discovered some particular point that seems to be either incorrectly stated or false we can examine it separately in order to determine whether we can prove both that it is false and also what the correct true description should be.

Fourth, Any correction and any adjustment towards truth and away from falsity should not be, in this instance, applied at the level of the original article.

Instead, any corrections or adjustments should be clearly stated outside the original article and in reference to it.

In that way the common domain of discourse is maintained intact for any other unknown readers.

CHAPTER THIRTEEN.

Do not let the other decision maker fool you. The following article is the holy of holies in regard to deductive logic. It cannot be referenced to one individual because it is a plain abstract. However the specific model provided is traceable to a small Oxford school working around the late nineteenth century. Since only one Oxford school of logic exists at that precise time that is sufficient referencing.

As provided the model is entirely my own design and it is deliberately designed towards a metaphysical mystical articulation. That is, it is not meant to be understood as an instance. Instead it is meant to be wondered at as a pattern of universal nature.

Where the pattern as given is error checked for correctness it will be easy enough for any who can do so, to make any necessary corrections without changing the manner of its presentation. Before making any changes I would affirm that it seems correct as stated.

All of the nineteen Silly Gisms can be translated into the algebraic notation that I have presented in these articles. To do so, it is necessary to understand the following explanation as stated, not to be misled by the perversities of language use in terms of amphiboly, tautology, ambiguity, oxymorons, and other such enitity that tend to live their ghost like existence in this kind of domain.

Therefore when I use "All B is C" in this context I do not mean "All B equals C" in the sense of our understanding of equals and is, which we have looked at in other articles. Instead in this specific context, the word use must only be understood as follows: That is, if "All B is C" we mean draw a big circle and call it C. Inside the big circle called "C" draw a much smaller circle called "B". Now if you have done that you will easily notice that all B is C, but not all C is B. Since all B is C but not all C is B we cannot say "All B equals C", and in fact we can definitely state that the proposition is to be called false and not true. Because we could place another smaller circle inside "C" that is in no way connected to "B" and call it "A". Then you would have a large circle "C" and in the large circle are entirely contained two smaller circles called "A" and "B" where the two smaller circles are in no way connected.

Then we would have "All A is C" and "All B is C" and "No A is B" and "No B is A" and "Some C is A" and "Some C is B".

Therefore, in order to translate the nineteen Silly Gisms into the language of algebra given in these articles the genus/ species relationship is used. Such that in our example given above, the large circle "C" in this instance is the <Genus> and the two smaller circles "A" and "B" are both <Species> of "C".

So the basic translation would be along the lines:

C < A and C < B => C < (A ∧ B).

If C contains A and C contains B then C contains both A and B.

However, because the patterns involve the use of the universal and existential operators in regard to the words "All" and "Some" therefore you would have to be confident about using the higher order logic signlabels "ψ" and "Э".

ψ means the universal operator. ψa => a ∧ ~a ∧ !a The universal operator is every and all of some possible entity.

Э means the existential operator. Эa => a ∨ ~a ∨ !a The existential operator is some possible entity of all such entity.

The statement of the prime pattern in its basic form begins at this point, and is given as notes I through to VIII. The notes I - VIII are entirely the work of the late nineteenth century

Oxford school of logic although the pattern as given and the manner of presentation is entirely my own.

I.

Deduction is two propositions, called the Premisses, and a third proposition known as the Conclusion, which is a necessary consequence of the two premisses.

Two terms are compared with one another by means of a third, which is called the Middle Term.

In the premisses each of the two terms is compared separately with the middle term; and in the conclusion they are compared with one another.

Therefore every deduction consists of three terms, one of which occurs twice in the premisses and does not appear at all in the conclusion.

This term is called the Middle Term.

The predicate of the conclusion is called the Major Term and its subject the Minor Term.

The Major and Minor Terms are called the Extremes, as opposed to the Middle Term.

The premiss in which the Major Term is compared with the Middle is called the Major Premiss.

The premiss in which the Minor Term is compared with the Middle, is called the Minor Premiss.

II.

Let C be the major term; B the middle term; A the minor term.

III.

A. All A is B.

E. No A is B.

I. Some A is B.

O. Some A is not B.

IV.

If A be true then: E is false, O false, I true.

If A be false then: E is unknown, O true, I unknown.

If E be true then: O is true, I false, A false.

If E be false then: O is unknown, I true, A unknown.

If O be true then: I is unknown, A false, E unknown.

If O be false then: I is true, A true, E false.

If I be true then: A is unknown, E false, O unknown.

If I be false then: A is false, E true, O true.

V.

(A) All A is B, therefore No A is not-B.(E)

(E) No A is B, therefore All A is not-B.(A)

(I) Some A is B, therefore Some A is not B. (O)

(O) Some A is not B, therefore Some A is B. (I)

VI.

Figure 1: B-C, A-B, therefore A-C.

Figure 2: C-B, A-B, therefore A-C.

Figure 3: B-C, B-A, therefore A-C.

Figure 4: C-B, B-A, therefore A-C.

VII.

The First Figure is: When the middle term is subject in the major and predicate in the minor.

The Second Figure is: When the middle term is predicate in both premises.

The Third Figure is: When the middle term is subject in both premises.

The Fourth Figure is: When the middle term is predicate in the major premiss and subject in the minor.

Figure One: AAA. EAE. AII. EIO. AAI. EAO.

Figure Two: EAE. AEE. EIO. AOO. EAO. AEO.

Figure Three: AAI. IAI. AII. EAO. OAO. EIO.

Figure Four: AAI. AEE. IAI. EAO. EIO. AEO.

VIII.

First Figure.

1. All B is C. All A is B. Therefore All A is C.

2. No B is C. All A is B. Therefore No A is C.

3. All B is C. Some A is B. Therefore Some A is C.

4. No B is C. Some A is B. Therefore Some A is not C.

Second Figure.

1. No C is B. All A is B. Therefore No A is C.

2. All C is B. No A is B. Therefore No A is C.

3. No C is B. Some A is B. Therefore Some A is not C.

4. All C is B. Some A is not B. Therefore Some A is not C.

Third Figure.

1. All B is C. All B is A. Therefore Some A is C.

2. No B is C. All B is A. Therefore Some A is not C.

3. Some B is C. All B is A. Therefore Some A is C.

4. All B is C. Some B is A. Therefore Some A is C.

5. Some B is not C. All B is A. Therefore Some A is not C.

6. No B is C. Some B is A. Therefore Some A is not C.

Fourth Figure.

1. All C is B. All B is A. Therefore Some A is C.

2. All C is B. No B is A. Therefore Some A is not C.

3. Some C is B. All B is A. Therefore Some A is C.

4. No C is B. All B is A. Therefore Some A is not C.

5. No C is B. Some B is A. Therefore Some A is not C.

The statement of the prime pattern in its basic form is complete at this point, given as notes I through to VIII.

With the aim towards an intuitive grasp of the patterns and a commonplace familiarity with their shape and composition it is better to attend only to the first figure. Because the purpose of this article is to provide the above prime pattern given in notes I-VIII in its basic form. The possible diversities of explanation of the given pattern are so extensive that there is no requirement to attempt such in this context. Instead what I will do is describe a few lines of development that may be usefully followed in order to obtain the intuitive grasp and commonplace familiarity such that the patterns are embedded in themselves.

We do better to attend to the first figure exclusively because it is held to be the only real pattern of the four figures such that each of the other three figures refer back to the first figure. Also the first figure is most simple and straightforward so if we can clarify it properly it will inform us as to how better to understand the other three.

First Figure.

1. All B is C. All A is B. Therefore All A is C.

$(\exists C < \psi B) \wedge (\exists B < \psi A) => (\exists C < \psi A)$

If [Some C contains All B] and [Some B contains All A] is true, then: [Some C contains All A] is true.

2. No B is C. All A is B. Therefore No A is C.

$(\psi C < {\sim}B) \wedge (\exists B < \psi A) => (\psi C < {\sim}A)$

If [All C contains Not B] and [Some B contains All A] is true, then: [All C contains Not A] is true.

3. All B is C. Some A is B. Therefore Some A is C.

$(\exists C < \psi B) \wedge (\exists B < \exists A) => (\exists C < \exists A)$

If [Some C contains All B] and [Some B contains Some A] is true, then: [Some C contains Some A] is true.

4. No B is C. Some A is B. Therefore Some A is not C.

(ψC < ~B) ∧ (ЭB < ЭA) => (~C < ЭA)

If [All C contains Not B] and [Some B contains Some A] is true, then: [Not C contains Some A] is true.

The First Figure is now detailed in three different signlabel language systems, where all three language systems are supposed to be saying the exact same thing. According to our method the requirement now is to challenge the correctness and truth of the stated patterns of the first figure. That is, can we satisfy ourselves that the three different language explanations are each saying what they are supposed to be saying? If they are, then do they each say the same thing as the other two in regard to the matter they refer towards? And is the matter they refer towards in each case correct, accurately stated and true?

First Pattern, First Figure.

For example the first pattern refers towards a matter that can be visually described as large circle "C" entirely contains smaller circle "B" and smaller circle "B" entirely contains little circle "A", which we believe justifies the claim that larger circle "C" entirely contains little circle "A". Which we then describe using three different signlabel language systems as follows:

1. All B is C. All A is B. Therefore All A is C.

(ЭC < ψB) ∧ (ЭB < ψA) => (ЭC < ψA)

If [Some C contains All B] and [Some B contains All A] is true, then: [Some C contains All A] is true.

So the question we ask is whether the matter as described in terms of three circles is what is referred towards by the descriptions. And do the descriptions in each case say the same thing, in the correct way such that in the total understanding there is coherence and complete non-contradiction. As such we are asking a question about "meaning" and in particular do the meanings of the three language systems translate properly, so that we are confident that each proposition says something at all.

First Proposition, First Pattern, First Figure.

In order to clarify the "meaning" value of the pattern as a whole we must establish the equivalence of each individual proposition, as follows:

All B is C <=> [Some C contains All B] <=> (ƏC < ψB)

This is the first proposition of the first pattern of the first figure.

Our visual description is: {a large circle "C" which entirely contains a smaller circle "B"}.

To establish the meaning of this propostion it is useful to apply "Dodgson's Game"

Draw a vertical line where the higher point of the line is designated "C" and the lower point of the line is designated "~C". And draw an horizontal line bisecting the vertical line where the right point of the line is designated "B" and the left point of the line is designated "~B". A white counter placed on the grid designates existant and a black counter placed on the grid designates non-existant.

Such that if we place a white counter directly on the vertical line at the upper half above the horizontal line we are saying this:

"Some C are B and Some C are Not B". Which is interesting because it positively states a necessary implication of our first proposition. The necessary implication of: "Some C contains B" is that "Some C contains Not B".

So we now have to go back to our picture of the two circles to see whether it says the same thing. And what we discover is that all of the area of the larger circle "C" that is not covered by the smaller circle "B" is called "Not B".

And to clarify what we are not saying, we are definitely not saying "All C contains B". If we were saying that, then in Dodgson's Game it would mean we placed a white counter at the upper right corner "CB". So we now have to look at the two possible placements of the white counter on the grid in order to determine that the meaning of the two propositions is quite different.

In this way we establish the particular meaning of our first proposition by demonstrating what it does not mean.

The next useful thing we discover through Dodgson's Game is that our placement of the white counter has only told us half of the first proposition. That is, it tells us that "Some C is B", but it does not tell us that "the only existant B are C". So with the use of only the white counter we do not know whether any "B Not C" exist. Whereas our first proposition definitely says that "C contains All B" meaning that "No B Not C" exist.

Therefore to show the complete first proposition we are required to place a black counter on the bottom right corner "B~C". This says the other half of the first proposition that "No B are Not C".

That means, through the Dodgson's Game we discover several interesting things about our first proposition, including that:

i. Some C are B implies that Some C are Not B.

ii. The claim that <All> B are C is two components, that is, "B are C" and "No B are Not C".

Therefore we arrive at an end point, that is several different things. Our first proposition is well stated as:

All B is C <=> [Some C contains All B] <=> (ЭC < ψB)

It has two necessary implications that could themselves be stated as independent propositions:

One, that "Some C are Not B" and two, that "No B are Not C".

Second Proposition, First Pattern, First Figure.

All A is B <=> [Some B contains All A] <=> (ƎB < ψA)

This is the second proposition of the first pattern of the first figure.

Our visual description is: {a smaller circle "B" which entirely contains a little circle "A"}.

The argumentation that applied to the first proposition correlates to the argument that applies to the second proposition because the shape not meaning of the second proposition is similar to the first. We can prove this by comparing the two propositions within the same language as follows:

<All B is C> is similar in shape to <All A is B>.

<[Some C contains All B]> is similar in shape to <[Some B contains All A]>.

<(ƎC < ψB)> is similar in shape to <(ƎB < ψA)>.

Therefore, our second proposition is meaningful for two reasons.

One is that the structure of its meaning stands in as much as we have discovered the structure of the first proposition to be meaningfully correct and true, because the structure of both propositions is the same. Two is that the content of its meaning stands in as much as it is different content to the first proposition.

Third Proposition, First Pattern, First Figure.

All A is C <=> [Some C contains All A] <=> (ƎC < ψA)

This is the third proposition of the first pattern of the first figure. It is called the conclusion of the first pattern and is subject to measurement in terms of validity, truth and soundness.

Our visual description is: {a larger circle "C" which entirely contains a little circle "A"}.

We can first affirm that the shape of the third propositon is exactly similar to the first two, and that the content of each component is different to any other component:

<All B is C> :: <All A is B> :: <All A is C>

<[Some C contains All B]> :: <[Some B contains All A]> :: [Some C contains All A]

<(∃C < ψB)> :: <(∃B < ψA)> :: <(∃C < ψA)>

In regards to measurement, by validity we ask whether the conclusion as stated is a necessary consequence of the first two propositions. In order to qualify as a valid conclusion it does not matter whether the first two propositions are imaginary or real, fictitious or fact, lies or truth. A valid conclusion is only one that meets the condition of necessity. That is, where the conclusion is a necessary consequence of the propositions it is called valid, regardless of whether it is true or false.

A conclusion that is called sound must meet two specific conditions. The first is that the argument must be valid in accord with the description provided. The second is that the two original propositions called the major and minor premisses must both be individually true. If the two premisses are both true and the argument from the premisses is valid then the conclusion is called sound. Furthermore, a valid argument from true premisses guarantees that the conclusion is itself true. That is, it is not possible to generate a false conclusion from a valid argument with true premisses.

For this reason it is easy enough to understand that the conclusion to the first pattern cannot be called sound in the abstract form. That is because the pattern itself must equally support argument that is imaginary, fictitious, lies and falsity as much as it supports argument that is real, fact, honest and true.

The only requirement is that the conclusion be a necessary consequence of the premises.

Such being the case, we must attend to the simple question:

Is it a necessary consequence that C contains A, if our first two premises are that B contains A and C contains B?

The nature of this problem is disguised and it is not of the same heirarchical order as the establishment of the meaning of the propositions. If we take it that we are satisfied with our establishment of meaning of all three propositions, as stated. Which I would do since the explanation as given is sufficient for the purposes of the article.

Then reasonably we must notice that this does nothing at all to establish the necessary consequence of the conclusion from the premises.

The immediately previous statement is not to claim that the conclusion is not a necessary consequence of the premises. Only that we have as yet no proof that it is so.

Unfortunately that side of the matter is very odd and not the focus of attention in this particular discourse. In order to explain some of its nature to satisfy our imagination in the first instance this idea:

We have a box called C. Inside the box C we place a smaller box B. Inside box B we place a smaller box A. Therefore we make the claim box C contains box A. But no it does not. Show me a box C with a box A without a box B. Well no, we cannot do that, because box A is inside box B. Then inside box B and not inside box C. Well no, inside box C because box B is inside box C. What if box B was not inside box C? Well, box A would still be inside box B. Proof then that box A is inside box

B regardless of whether box B is inside box C or not. Okay, so what if I take box B out of box C and box A out of box B. And then I place box A inside box C? Yes that is fine. Because now box C contains box A. The only problem with it is you have lost both our Major and Minor Premisses. Because our major premiss was box C contains box B and now it doesn't. And our minor premiss was box B contains box A and now it doesn't.

And this is my explanation. That the conclusion C contains A is the description of box C containing box A without box C containing box B or box B containing box A. Which is not what we mean. For this reason I would notice a particular puzzle which we can label as the "Problem of Necessary Consequence". All we need do at this stage is acknowledge that the problem of necessary consequence exists, recognise that we are not required to solve it at this stage, and make a mental note to label it whenever we find it in any of the later patterns. And for the sake of argument refer it to the great god David Hume for his immediate attention.

Second Pattern, First Figure.

The second pattern refers to a matter that can be visually described as a large square box called "U" which means Universe of Discourse. Inside "U" are two entirely separate circles, where neither circle is cut by the circumference of the other circle. One circle is called by the namelabel "C" and the other circle by the namelabel "B". Inside circle "B" is entirely contained a smaller circle "A". This we believe describes a circumstance where C is not B, and where B contains All A, which justifies us in believing that C is not A. Which we then describe using three different signlabel language systems as follows:

No B is C. All A is B. Therefore No A is C.

$(\psi C < \sim B) \wedge (\exists B < \psi A) => (\psi C < \sim A)$

If [All C contains Not B] and [Some B contains All A] is true, then: [All C contains Not A] is true.

So the question we ask is whether the matter as described in terms of three circles is what is referred towards by the descriptions. And do the descriptions in each case say the same thing, in the correct way such that in the total understanding there is coherence and complete non-contradiction. As such we are asking a question about "meaning" and in particular do the meanings of the three language systems translate properly, so that we are confident that each proposition says something at all.

To this end, and given the requirement that any individual so inclined can do the workings out for themselves given the previous explanation, all I would do here is clarify the equivalence of meaning between each of the languages for the three propositions separately, as follows:

Major Premiss: No B is C <=> [All C contains Not B] <=> (ψC < ~B)

Minor Premiss: All A is B <=> [Some B contains All A] <=> (ƎB < ψA)

Conclusion: No A is C <=> [All C contains Not A] <=> (ψC < ~A)

Third Pattern, First Figure.

The third pattern refers to a matter that can be visually described as a square shape "C" where the upper right quarter of the square shape is shaded in and called "B". That demonstrates that the square C entirely contains the square B as one of its corners. A third square the same size as "C" and called by the label "A" has a small part of one of its corners overlap half of square B. This we believe describes a circumstance where C entirely contains B and B contains some A, such that we are justified in believing that C contains some A. Which we then describe using three different signlabel language systems as follows:

All B is C. Some A is B. Therefore Some A is C.

(ƎC < ψB) ∧ (ƎB < ƎA) => (ƎC < ƎA)

If [Some C contains All B] and [Some B contains Some A] is true, then: [Some C contains Some A] is true.

And then demonstrate in regard to equivalence of meaning between the different languages as:

Major Premiss: All B is C <=> [Some C contains All B] <=> (ƎC < ψB)

Minor Premiss: Some A is B <=> [Some B contains Some A] <=> (ƎB < ƎA)

Conclusion: Some A is C <=> [Some C contains Some A] <=> (ƎC < ƎA)

Fourth Pattern, First Figure.

The fourth pattern refers to a matter that can be visually described as two circles that are entirely separate such that the circumference of each in no way cuts the circumference of the other. One circle we call "B" and the other circle we call "C". This we believe describes the proposition that "No B is C". A third circle is drawn such that it partially overlaps the circle "B" so that the circumference of circle B cuts the circumference of the third circle which we call "A". This describes the proposition that Some A is B. And since No B is C, and some of A is B, we believe this justifies the proposition that some A is not C. Which we then describe using three different signlabel language systems as follows:

4. No B is C. Some A is B. Therefore Some A is not C.

(ψC < ~B) ∧ (ƎB < ƎA) => (~C < ƎA)

If [All C contains Not B] and [Some B contains Some A] is true, then: [Not C contains Some A] is true.

And then demonstrate in regard to equivalence of meaning between the different languages as:

Major Premiss: No B is C <=> [All C contains Not B] <=> (ψC < ~B)

Minor Premiss: Some A is B <=> [Some B contains Some A]

<=> (ЭB < ЭA)

Conclusion: Some A is not C <=> [Not C contains Some A] <=> (~C < ЭA)

Our position now is that we can describe the First Figure in four different medium or languages, where each medium apparently says the exact same thing. Which we should now show separately, as follows:

First Figure In Four Different Medium.

First Figure, Visually.

1. The first pattern refers towards a matter that can be visually described as large circle "C" entirely contains smaller circle "B" and smaller circle "B" entirely contains little circle "A", which we believe justifies the claim that larger circle "C" entirely contains little circle "A".

2. The second pattern refers to a matter that can be visually described as a large square box called "U" which means Universe of Discourse. Inside "U" are two entirely separate circles, where neither circle is cut by the circumference of the other circle. One circle is called by the namelabel "C" and the other circle by the namelabel "B". Inside circle "B" is entirely contained a smaller circle "A". This we believe describes a circumstance where C is not B, and where B contains All A, which justifies us in believing that C is not A.

3. The third pattern refers to a matter that can be visually described as a square shape "C" where the upper right quarter of the square shape is shaded in and called "B". That demonstrates that the square C entirely contains the square B as one of its corners. A third square the same size as "C" and called by the label "A" has a small part of one of its corners overlap half of square B. This we believe describes a circumstance where C entirely contains B and B contains some A, such that we are justified in believing that C contains some A.

4. The fourth pattern refers to a matter that can be visually described as two circles that are entirely separate such that the circumference of each in no way cuts the circumference of the other. One circle we call "B" and the other circle we call "C". This we believe describes the proposition that "No B is C". A third circle is drawn such that it partially overlaps the circle "B" so that the circumference of circle B cuts the circumference of the third circle which we call "A". This describes the proposition that Some A is B. And since No B is C, and some of A is B, we believe this justifies the proposition that some A is not C.

First Figure, Verbally.

1. All B is C. All A is B. Therefore All A is C.

2. No B is C. All A is B. Therefore No A is C.

3. All B is C. Some A is B. Therefore Some A is C.

4. No B is C. Some A is B. Therefore Some A is not C.

First Figure, Written Word.

1. If [Some C contains All B] and [Some B contains All A] is true, then: [Some C contains All A] is true.

2. If [All C contains Not B] and [Some B contains All A] is true, then: [All C contains Not A] is true.

3. If [Some C contains All B] and [Some B contains Some A] is true, then: [Some C contains Some A] is true.

4. If [All C contains Not B] and [Some B contains Some A] is true, then: [Not C contains Some A] is true.

First Figure, Algebraically.

1. $(\exists C < \psi B) \wedge (\exists B < \psi A) => (\exists C < \psi A)$

2. $(\psi C < \sim B) \wedge (\exists B < \psi A) => (\psi C < \sim A)$

3. $(\exists C < \psi B) \wedge (\exists B < \exists A) => (\exists C < \exists A)$

4. $(\psi C < \sim B) \wedge (\exists B < \exists A) => (\sim C < \exists A)$

At this stage we have adjusted our understanding of the First Figure through a range of different explanations in various languages. Our better move now is to take a reversed sequence of explanation, because we understand what we want to obtain in this instance. By which I mean we should specifically detail the nineteen patterns algebraically first. Having the nineteen patterns algebraically stated, we should then provide the written word form for the same patterns. And having the written word form we should again detail the verbal word patterns, which should be exactly the same statement as they are presently stated. In this manner we are starting as if the algebraic patterns are considered correct, we are then translating them into the written word form to see if this confirms our understanding and describing the verbal explanation to determine if it is the same as it presently is. Therefore our next task is to provide the nineteen algebraic patterns, which must follow the exact same format as the first four as already given.

The Nineteen Algebraic Patterns.

1. $(\exists C < \psi B) \wedge (\exists B < \psi A) => (\exists C < \psi A)$

2. $(\psi C < {\sim}B) \wedge (\exists B < \psi A) => (\psi C < {\sim}A)$

3. $(\exists C < \psi B) \wedge (\exists B < \exists A) => (\exists C < \exists A)$

4. $(\psi C < {\sim}B) \wedge (\exists B < \exists A) => ({\sim}C < \exists A)$

5. $(\psi B < {\sim}C) \wedge (\exists B < \psi A) => (\psi C < {\sim}A)$

6. $(\exists B < \psi C) \wedge (\psi B < {\sim}A) => (\psi C < {\sim}A)$

7. $(\psi B < {\sim}C) \wedge (\exists B < \exists A) => ({\sim}C < \exists A)$

8. $(\exists B < \psi C) \wedge ({\sim}B < \exists A) => ({\sim}C < \exists A)$

9. $(\exists C < \psi B) \wedge (\exists A < \psi B) => (\exists C < \exists A)$

10. $(\psi C < {\sim}B) \wedge (\exists A < \psi B) => ({\sim}C < \exists A)$

11. $(\exists C < \exists B) \wedge (\exists A < \psi B) => (\exists C < \exists A)$

12. $(\exists C < \psi B) \wedge (\exists A < \exists B) => (\exists C < \exists A)$

13. $(\sim C < \ni B) \wedge (\ni A < \psi B) => (\sim C < \ni A)$

14. $(\psi C < \sim B) \wedge (\ni A < \ni B) => (\sim C < \ni A)$

15. $(\ni B < \psi C) \wedge (\ni A < \psi B) => (\ni C < \ni A)$

16. $(\ni B < \psi C) \wedge (\psi A < \sim B) => (\sim C < \ni A)$

17. $(\ni B < \ni C) \wedge (\ni A < \psi B) => (\ni C < \ni A)$

18. $(\psi B < \sim C) \wedge (\ni A < \psi B) => (\sim C < \ni A)$

19. $(\psi B < \sim C) \wedge (\ni A < \ni B) => (\sim C < \ni A)$

General Disclaimer: The previous article is complete as stated. The reason for this is that we can pretend to find the algebraic pattern on its own with no previous understanding and no assumptions as to its meaning. Then using a method similar to that described in my article on the music of Mozart and the one on Boolean Algebra we can focus a direct challenge to the given pattern, as if to see what it says. The advantage of this method is we can determine whether the algebraic pattern has value on its own anyway, even if it were not equal to the fundamental figures of deductive syllogism. Then if it has its own value anyway, we can ask to what extent it supplies us with useful information as to deductive method. Having done such, we may find that we have coincidentally answered many of the questions we had in regard to the syllogisms, so then are much further advanced in our comprehension than had we taken a different route towards understanding. Two final points: One, the "holy of holies" in regard to deductive logic is specifically the model I-VIII given in this article and is simply the result of immense intellect over previous centuries leading to the reduced pattern supplied by Oxford logic. The other logic school that is most worth admiration is the Port Royal school of Arnauld, Nicole and Pascal. The second point is that my reference to the "great god David Hume" gives "great god" in small letters so is not suggesting his divinity, merely a superior status in reference to answering the problem of necessary consequence. For these sorts of reasons I would not personally change the article to delete any obvious causes of misunderstanding. This matters because it seems to me that there is an obligation to a reader of any matter to see past any small inconsistencies in presentation in order to obtain the information that is of value. If the information is not of value to any particular reader, then read no further. Raising hobgoblins at any and all opportunity from what is only meant to be a weak attempt at humour hardly makes sense other than to the structure of opposition to the information of the article itself.

CHAPTER FOURTEEN.

The focus of this article is towards only one matter specifically, that being the question:

"What is the correct and proper statement of truth-holders?".

I am defining "truth-holders" in this context as: Those elements of first propositions that enable us to assert "p is true".

The truth-holders of inductive hypothesis are those elements that combine together in order to form any individual proposition. As such any individual proposition can be demonstrated to involve a specific combination of such truth-holders. The truth-holders themselves are given as the sixteen affirmations of inductive hypothesis, as follows:

The Sixteen Affirmations of Inductive Hypothesis.

1. Some X are Some Y

2. Some X are Not Y

3. Some Y are Some X

4. Some Y are Not X

5. Some Not X are Some Y

6. Some Not Y are Some X

7. Some Not X are Not Y

8. Some Not Y are Not X

9. No X are Some Y

10. No Y are Some X

11. No Y are Not X

12. No Not X are Some Y

13. No X are Not Y

14. No Not Y are Some X

15. No Not X are Not Y

16. No Not Y are Not X

As such the general affirmations are called "truth-holders" because by their nature they can be measured as true or false.

That is, the affirmation "Some X are Some Y" may be true or false.

And if the affirmation: "No X are Y" is true, then the affirmation "Some X are Some Y" must be false.

All of the general affirmations have this characteristic that they may be either true or false.

The Sixteen Affirmations in Algebraic Form.

1. $\ni X < \ni Y$

2. $\ni X < \ni {\sim} Y$

3. $\ni Y < \ni X$

4. $\ni Y < \ni {\sim} X$

5. $\ni {\sim} X < \ni Y$

6. $\ni {\sim} Y < \ni X$

7. $\ni {\sim} X < \ni {\sim} Y$

8. $\ni {\sim} Y < \ni {\sim} X$

9. $[{\sim}] X < \ni Y$

10. $[{\sim}] Y < \ni X$

11. $[{\sim}] Y < \ni {\sim} X$

12. [~]~X < ƎY

13. [~]X < Ǝ~Y

14. [~]~Y < ƎX

15. [~]~X < ~Y

16. [~]~Y < ~X

Please note that in order to sign the term "no" as in "no x are y" I have used the square brackets around the "not" signlabel.

This is specifically to differentiate the term "no" from the term "not", since it should be clear that they mean different things. And also to ensure that in this context the use of both terms in no way leads towards the term "not not".

When combined together, the general affirmations provide the propositions used in deduction as follows:

The Propositions Used in Deduction.

A.

Proposition: All A is B. <=> Some B is All A <=> Some x contains all y <=> (ƎX < ψY)

Affirmation:

Some X are Y

Some X are Not Y

No Y are Not X

E.

Proposition: No A is B. <=> All B is Not A <=> All x contains not y <=> (ψX < ~Y)

Affirmation:

No X are Y

Some X are Not Y

Some Not X are Not Y

I.

Proposition: Some A is B. <=> Some B is Some A <=> Some x contains some y <=> (ƎX < ƎY)

Affirmation:

Some X are Y

Some X are Not Y

Some Y are X

Some Y are Not X

O.

Proposition: Some A is not B. <=> Not B is Some A <=> Not x contains some y <=> (~X < ƎY)

Affirmation:

Some Not X are Y

Some Not X are Not Y

Some Y are Not X

Some Y are X

My explanation to this point has involved a description of how we arrive at a proper statement of first propositions through the combination of specific general affirmations. I have presented this information without attending to any obscurity in the understanding so that the basic pattern of ideas can be attended towards.

However, it will be clear after some further consideration that we are presented with an ambiguity that it is useful to consider so that we have no vagueness in our comprehension.

Our rule of general affirmation is that they do not use the universal operator "all and every".

That is because the universal operator "All" involves two separate affirmations.

The first is "Some" as in "Some X are Y".

The second is "None" as in "No X are Not Y"

In combination "Some X are Y" and "No X are not Y" we obtain the proposition "All X are Y".

It must then be noted that the nature of the two component affirmations is not equivalent.

Since when we say: "Some X are Y" we are affirming what we have evidence for through experiment.

And when we say: "No X are Not Y" we are affirming what we have no evidence for.

That is, we are saying since we have never in all our experimentation discovered an x that is not y, we are extremely confident of making the claim that no x are not y. And since we know from our experimentation many x that are y, we are definite that some x are y. And for this reason we present the combined affirmations to make the true proposition that "All x are y".

However, the problem involves several elements on more that one level so it cannot be solved by only understanding the implications of the experimental aspect.

Because the meaning of "No X are Not Y" is actually that "All Not Y are Not X"

But that would mean we are saying the combined affirmations:

"Some Not Y are Some Not X" and "No Not Y are X"

Which as it happens may be okay, since the apparent circularity is not circular. All we are in fact doing is making the similar affirmation from the position of the other subject.

Now that seems to be the two basic elements of an apparent ambiguity as it exists in regard to the general affirmations of first propositions. Where as it may not describe every aspect of the perceived problem, it is probable that any variations of the problem are each some alternative similar to that which I have described.

The only real problem would be to recognise one aspect of the ambiguity and not know about the other since both aspects coincide at one point.

Just to clarify, the true proposition: "All X are Y" involves the strong experimental claim that "Some X are Y" and the weak experimental claim that "No X are Not Y" the combination of strong and weak claims giving a proposition we assert to be "true".

And the truth holder "No X are Not Y" can be stated as "All Not Y are Not X" which itself involves the combined affirmations "Some Not Y are Not X" and "No Not Y are X".

The next area to consider is the belief that: "Some X are Some Y" involves the necessary implication that "Some X are Not Y" and "Some Y are Not X". Now this is simply the necessary meaning of "Some". Because we remove the necessary implications through one of two methods.

Either by changing "Some" to "All" or alternatively by combining the "Some" affirmation with a "No" affirmation applied to the contrary.

Therefore unless we state: "No X are Not Y" and "All X are Y" then the affirmation "Some X are Y" will necessarily involve the truth of the affirmations "Some X are Not Y" and "Some Y are Not X".

Furthermore, where a single proposition involves the combination of several affirmations it may often be the case that a necessary implication of the affirmations is not at all required to provide the given proposition. However the particular affirmation is still a necessary implication of the proposition as given.

For example the use of the proposition "No Y is X" necessarily implies the truth of the affirmation "Some Not X are Not

Y" and "Some Not Y are Not X". Therefore we always assert the truth that "Some Not Y Not X exist" whenever we use the proposition "No Y is X". Even though the assertion that "Some Not Y Not X exist" is in no way necessary to provide the proposition "No Y is X". Using the xy/~x~y game we show:

E.

No A is B. <=> All B is Not A <=> All x contains not y <=> (ψX < ~Y)

A black counter on the top right corner and a white counter on the middle left line.

The black counter says: "No X are Y"

The white counter says: "Some X are Not Y" and "Some Not X are Not Y"

If some x are not y and no x are y then all x are not y.

This is the placement of counters on the xy grid to show the "No A is B" structure and it is the only placement that does so.

First Propositions.

Our general affirmations combine to provide the correct structure for the statement of the first propositions used in deductive argument, those propositions all according to the AEIO pattern as follows:

A. All A is B. <=> Some B is All A <=> Some x contains all y <=> (ƎX < ψY)

E. No A is B. <=> All B is Not A <=> All x contains not y <=> (ψX < ~Y)

I. Some A is B. <=> Some B is Some A <=> Some x contains some y <=> (ƎX < ƎY)

O. Some A is not B. <=> Not B is Some A <=> Not x contains some y <=> (~X < ƎY)

It may be thought that a more thorough consideration

should be provided in order to demonstrate the proper hardness of truth obtained at the stage of the general affirmations of inductive hypothesis. And considering the matter that I outlined immediately previous to this note, that more attention should be dedicated to clarify how we can make definite assertions as to "All", "None", "Existant" and "Non-exitstant" at the point of general affirmations.

However, the belief is that the harder the evaluation of general affirmations and first propositions at the level of inductive hypothesis the more forcefully that evaluation demonstrates the soft nature of our knowledge at that level. My point is that a hard evaluation of inductive hypothesis can only prove the soft nature of its content.

Since the intention of this article is to offer ideas as to how we may obtain any hard basis for our development of knowledge it would not be reasonable to do that which is contrary to this purpose. That is not to say that the subject matter is not worth attention, only that it is not the focus of the matter of this article. My supposition being that the nature of what is essentially real before we have asserted hypothetically true first propositions is a different subject.

Now of course we will notice that such a subject exists when we find our analysis at the point of general affirmations and first propositions, but that does not require that we are confident of answering what ever the questions of that subject may be. In fact we must be permitted to consider the matter of inductive hypothesis without being required to answer the ontological question. Since all we find ourselves considering is the nature of all, nothing, existant, non-existant and how do we articulate the subject clearly in some way that furthers our comprehension usefully. All of this matter need not be demanded of people who choose to attend to inductive hypothesis. The only requirement is that they do not demand a hardness of truth be conferred on their content, when it is quite clear that the content at this level is by its nature soft.

The Positive Claim of Inductive Hypothesis:

The positive claim of inductive hypothesis is that we can assert hypothetically true first propositions that are coherent non-contradictory combinations of general affirmations. And that our general affirmations have the characteristic of being measured as true or false.

The Truth Hypothesis.

The "truth hypothesis" of this system of ideas is that truth only becomes hard as it is tested through a range of fields. That truth exists on a continuum of degrees of softness through to hardness. That hard truth is only obtained at the level of the cardinal articulation of prime patterns, the general characteristic of such patterns being a quality that we may call "constancy". That the cardinal articulation of a prime pattern will tend to demonstrate truth that meets conditions of universal abstraction, utility, coherence and correspondence. That the earliest sensible manifestation of truth is discovered at the level of general affirmations of inductive hypothesis, where such truth is by its nature entirely soft. The beauty of the general affirmations being that they enable the earliest articulation of some soft truth that may in the course of its development be discovered as part of a coherent system of such truths, the entirety of such being the content of what we call knowledge. Only as the general affirmations become first propositions, which in turn become valid deductive argument does their truth or falsity establish itself. Where we find some argument involves contradiction of what is already proved as true, then such argument has demonstrated itself as false. Where we find some argument coherent with what we already know as true, that strengthens what we already believe as the case, then that argument demonstrates itself as true on grounds of utility as well as correspondence and coherence. When we find an argument that is completely supportive of universal abstraction then such argument meets the conditions of prime patterns, and when properly stated will detail all cardinal articulations. Only at this stage do we obtain truth that is evaluated as hard.

Finally, the idea that the matter of inductive hypothesis suggests, that is very important to consider is that the "quantum indefinite" has a present nature existant at the point just before we say our first proposition. That is, when we consider some first proposition in terms of the general affirmations of which it is composed, it is at this level where we may discover the quantum indefinite to be operational.

CHAPTER FIFTEEN.

If - Then statements.

First Point.

All X is Some Y.

1. All X is Y.

If, All X is Y, then, Some X is Y.

2. Some X is Y.

If, Some X is Y, then, Some Y is X.

3. Some Y is X.

If, Some Y is X, then, Some Y is Not X or No Y is Not X.

4. Some Y is Not X.

If Some Y is Not X, then, Some Y is X or No Y is X.

5. Some Y is X.

If, Some Y is X, then, Some X is Y.

6. Some X is Y.

If, Some X is Y, then, Some X is Not Y or No X is Not Y.

7. No X is Not Y.

If, No X is Not Y and Some X is Y, then, All X is Y.

8. All X is Y.

If, All X is Y, then, Some Y is X.

9. Some Y is X.

If, Some Y is X, then, Some Y is Not X or No Y is Not X.

10. Some Y is Not X.

If, Some Y is Not X and All X is Y, then, All X is Some Y.

11. All X is Some Y.

If, All X is Some Y, then, Some Y is All X.

12. Some Y is All X.

If, Some Y is All X, then, No X is Not Y.

13. No X is Not Y.

If, No X is Not Y and Some X is Y, then, All X is Y.

14. All X is Y.

Second Point.

Logical Possibility.

1. All is Some.

2. Some is All.

3. Some is Some

4. Some is Not.

5. Not is Some.

6. Not is All.

7. All is Not.

8. Not is Not.

9. All is All.

Which gives some idea as to the logical possibilities:

1. All is Some: All X is Some Y.

2. Some is All: Some Y is All X.

3. Some is Some. Some X is Some Y.

4. Some is Not. Some Y is Not X.

5. Not is Some. Not X is Some Y.

6. Not is All. Not X is All Not Y.

7. All is Not. All Not Y is Not X.

8. Not is Not. Not X is Not Y.

9. All is All. All X is All Y.

Third Point.

If All Not X is All Not Y then All X is All Y.

And All X is All Y means X equals Y exactly and Y equals X exactly.

It means that if we ever find a Not X then we are guaranteed that it will be a Not Y and it will never be a Y.

If we ever find a Not Y we are guaranteed that it will be a Not X and will never be an X.

And if we ever find an X then we are guaranteed that it will be a Y and it will never be a Not Y.

If we ever find a Y then we are guaranteed that it will be an X and it will never be a Not X

All X is All Y means X and Y are the same thing.

And if All X is All Y then any example of a Not X will also be an example of a Not Y.

For this reason specifically, it is clear that "All is Some" occurs in logic most commonly.

And if and only if we mean x and y are the same exact thing would we say "All is All".

Since we nearly never mean x equals y such that they are the exact same identity, then we nearly never say "All is All".

We can consider this in terms of the game domain model as the principle of "probability".

It means that if you consider it as a dynamic of gambling, then the probable outcome demands you assume it in every case where it occurs.

And if you do so, you will win so often, that any and all occassional examples where the contradictory is true you lose so little it does not matter.

And conversely, if you were to routinely assume the contradictory in every example where it occurs you would lose so often in such large quantities and win so occassionally.

That you are forced to play as if a specific outcome is always the case at the end of the game.

Then we ask, "which assumption is it safe to make in the example of: All X is Y?"

Given All X is Y we have only two alternatives:

All X is All Y. Or. All X is Some Y.

The only possible third idea is All X is No Y, but, that is not an intention that could be inferred from the meaning of All X is Y.

So we have available only two correct and accurate alternative possible meanings. If we can show that only one of the possible meanings happens also to be true in most nearly all cases of its occurrence and that the other possible meaning is much less often the case, then we would need to assume the most probable outcome.

Looking at it from the other perspective, if we assume All X is All Y in every case where we are given All X is Y then we are supposing that we are being told X and Y are the same thing whenever we are told All X is Y. But that would be preposterous. It would actually mean that we could change every reference to Y and call it X. So then we would have All X is All X. And that cannot be the meaning of All X is Y.

The other possible assumption we can make is that whenever we see the All X is Y structure it means All X is Some Y. If having routinely and habitually assumed this outcome in every example where it occurs we occassionally find a contradiction and in fact X and Y are the exact same thing, then we are accepting the percentage loss for normally choosing what is probable out of a variety of possibles.

Fourth Point.

All Not Y is Some Not X.

1. All Not Y is Not X.

If, All Not Y is Not X, then, Some Not Y is Not X.

2. Some Not Y is Not X.

If, Some Not Y is Not X, then, Some Not X is Some Not Y.

3. Some Not X is Some Not Y.

If, Some Not X is Some Not Y, then, Some Not X is Some Y or No Not X is Some Y.

4. Some Not X is Some Y.

If, Some Not X is Some Y, then, Some Y is Some Not X.

5. Some Y is Some Not X.

If, Some Y is Some Not X, then, Some Y is Some X or No Y is X.

6. Some Y is Some X.

If, Some Y is Some X, then, Some X is Some Y.

7. Some X is Some Y.

If, Some X is Some Y, then, Some X is Not Y or No X is Not Y.

8. No X is Not Y.

If, No X is Not Y and Some X is Y, then, All X is Y.

9. All X is Y.

Fifth Point.

If : All X is Some Y.

Then:

1. All X is Y.

2. Some X is Y.

3. Some Y is X.

4. Some Y is Not X.

5. No X is Not Y.

6. All X is Some Y.

7. Some Y is All X.

8. All Not Y is Not X.

9. Some Not Y is Not X.

10. Some Not X is Some Not Y.

11. Some Not X is Some Y.

As usual, check the workings out for correct or not as stated, and if correctly stated then true or not.

However, if correctly stated and true, it does mean that given the simple proposition "All X is Some Y" then we can suppose a variety of necessary propositions that are implied by the proposition given.

It means we could assert the if - then statements:

If All X is Y, then, All Not Y is Not X.

If All X is Y, then, Some Not X is Y.

If All X is Y, then, Some Not X is Not Y.

If All X is Y, then, Some Y is All X.

CHAPTER SIXTEEN.

1. (ЭC < ψB) ∧ (ЭB < ψA) => (ЭC < ψA)

2. (ψC < ~B) ∧ (ЭB < ψA) => (ψC < ~A)

3. (ЭC < ψB) ∧ (ЭB < ЭA) => (ЭC < ЭA)

4. (ψC < ~B) ∧ (ЭB < ЭA) => (~C < ЭA)

5. (ψB < ~C) ∧ (ЭB < ψA) => (ψC < ~A)

6. (ЭB < ψC) ∧ (ψB < ~A) => (ψC < ~A)

7. (ψB < ~C) ∧ (ЭB < ЭA) => (~C < ЭA)

8. (ЭB < ψC) ∧ (~B < ЭA) => (~C < ЭA)

9. (ЭC < ψB) ∧ (ЭA < ψB) => (ЭC < ЭA)

10. (ψC < ~B) ∧ (ЭA < ψB) => (~C < ЭA)

11. (ЭC < ЭB) ∧ (ЭA < ψB) => (ЭC < ЭA)

12. (ЭC < ψB) ∧ (ЭA < ЭB) => (ЭC < ЭA)

13. (~C < ЭB) ∧ (ЭA < ψB) => (~C < ЭA)

14. (ψC < ~B) ∧ (ЭA < ЭB) => (~C < ЭA)

15. (ЭB < ψC) ∧ (ЭA < ψB) => (ψC < ЭA)

16. (ЭB < ψC) ∧ (ψA < ~B) => (~C < ψA)

17. (ЭB < ЭC) ∧ (ЭA < ψB) => (ЭC < ЭA)

18. (ψB < ~C) ∧ (ЭA < ψB) => (~C < ЭA)

19. (ψB < ~C) ∧ (ЭA < ЭB) => (~C < ЭA)

The above notion shows nineteen patterns of algebra. Were one given the above patterns without any explanation as to their meaning it is possible that it would still show itself as worth attention. The approach of this article is to take a line similar to that circumstance combined with a supposition of available supporting information that would not in reality be available were that circumstance the case.

The concepts that are elements of the above patterns are only: " C B A ψ Ǝ ~ < () ∧ => ".

That is exactly ten sign labels specifically, and only ten sign labels for the entirety of the above pattern.

Three sign labels are the letters: C B A, where each letter signifies a different term, where the terms are in different combinations.

Three sign labels are the quantifiers: ψ Ǝ ~, where each quantifier signifies a different existence value to any one term.

Four sign labels are the functional operators: < () ∧ =>, where each functional operator signifies a mechanical process structure.

The ten concepts are the elements that form a total of "18" propositions, and those propositions are only:

CA: (ƎC < ψA) (ƎC < ƎA) (ψC < ~A) (~C < ƎA)

CB: (ƎC < ψB) (ƎC < ƎB) (ψC < ~B) (~C < ƎB)

BA: (ƎB < ψA) (ƎB < ƎA) (ψB < ~A) (~B < ƎA)

BC: (ƎB < ψC) (ƎB < ƎC) (ψB < ~C)

AB: (ƎA < ψB) (ƎA < ƎB) (ψA < ~B)

The eighteen propositions that form the entirety of the above patterns are themselves various forms of only four specific structural frames. The four structural frames are only:

1. Some x contains all y.

2. All x contains not y.

3. Some x contains some y.

4. Not x contains some y.

The totality of the nineteen algebraic patterns give only four possible conclusions, where the four possible conclusions are only the four structural frames detailed. The four possible conclusions are:

1. (ЭC < ψA) :: Some x contains all y.

2. (ψC < ~A) :: All x contains not y.

3. (ЭC < ЭA) :: Some x contains some y.

4. (~C < ЭA) :: Not x contains some y.

Each of the four conclusions may be given by several specific patterns of premisses, as follows:

1.

(ЭC < ψA)

<= (ЭC < ψB) ∧ (ЭB < ψA)

2.

(ψC < ~A)

<= (ψC < ~B) ∧ (ЭB < ψA)

v (ψB < ~C) ∧ (ЭB < ψA)

v (ЭB < ψC) ∧ (ψB < ~A)

3.

(ЭC < ЭA)

<= (ЭC < ψB) ∧ (ЭB < ЭA)

v (ЭC < ψB) ∧ (ЭA < ψB)

v (ЭC < ψB) ∧ (ЭA < ЭB)

v (ЭC < ЭB) ∧ (ЭA < ψB)

v (ЭB < ψC) ∧ (ЭA < ψB)

v (ЭB < ЭC) ∧ (ЭA < ψB)

4.

(~C < ∃A)

<= (ψC < ~B) ∧ (∃B < ∃A)

v (ψB < ~C) ∧ (∃B < ∃A)

v (∃B < ψC) ∧ (~B < ∃A)

v (ψC < ~B) ∧ (∃A < ψB)

v (~C < ∃B) ∧ (∃A < ψB)

v (ψC < ~B) ∧ (∃A < ∃B)

v (∃B < ψC) ∧ (ψA < ~B)

v (ψB < ~C) ∧ (∃A < ψB)

v (ψB < ~C) ∧ (∃A < ∃B)

That means the first conclusion structural frame is only given by one structure of premiss.

The second conclusion structural frame is given by three structure of premiss.

The third conclusion structural frame is given by six structure of premiss.

The fourth conclusion structural frame is given by nine structure of premiss.

Method of Proof By Analogy.

Using the method called proof by analogy we find that the model provided in the article "syllogism" gives "note III" as the structural patterns AEIO. Since the structural patterns AEIO are fundamentally tested we heuristically feel comfortable using them as a measure of correctness for any other similar pattern that may be discovered to exist. So then we notice that the algebraic patterns give four specific structural frames, which we have detailed as x and y patterns. When we then demonstrate that the xy patterns exactly fit the shape of our trusted AEIO patterns such that we can even provide them as an exact equivalence, we are suddenly more confident that our workings out are accurate and correct. Therefore we provide the analogy pattern showing equivalence of shape and meaning between our algebraic structural frames and the AEIO pattern, as follows:

A. All A is B. <=> Some B is All A <=> Some x contains all y <=> (∃X < ψY)

E. No A is B. <=> All B is Not A <=> All x contains not y <=> (ψX < ~Y)

I. Some A is B. <=> Some B is Some A <=> Some x contains some y <=> (∃X < ∃Y)

O. Some A is not B. <=> Not B is Some A <=> Not x contains some y <=> (~X < ∃Y)

Now because the AEIO patterns are considered fundamentally important to the nature of Silly Gisms, we are compelled to properly attend to the algebraic structural frames of x and y. And that makes sense because it requires we use Dodgson's Game, which we would expect since it is a necessary device at the deep structural level of individual premiss. This will be referred to as the "XY/~X~Y Game" in order to notify ourselves that it is only operational at the level of XY deep structure in regard to the component elements of individual proposition.

The XY/~X~Y Game.

The format which will be familiar to people who have read the syllogism article is:

Vertical line bisected by an horizontal line.

Vertical line where the upper point is called X, and the lower point is called ~X.

Horizontal line where the right point is called Y, and the left point is called ~Y.

Giving four boxes designated as XY, ~XY, ~Y~X, X~Y.

The use of a white counter designates existant, black counter designates not-existant.

Using this XY/~X~Y Game we now have to show the correct placement of counters on the grid to provide the structure of our propositions.

A.

All A is B. <=> Some B is All A <=> Some x contains all y <=> (ƎX < ψY)

A white counter on the upper line and a black counter in the bottom right corner box.

The white counter says: "Some X are Y" and "Some X are Not Y".

The black counter says: "No Y are Not X".

If some x are y and no y are not x then some x are all y.

This is placement of counters on the xy grid to show the "All A is B" structure and it is the only placement that so does.

E.

No A is B. <=> All B is Not A <=> All x contains not y <=> (ψX < ~Y)

A black counter on the top right corner and a white counter on the middle left line.

The black counter says: "No X are Y"

The white counter says: "Some X are Not Y" and "Some Not X are Not Y"

If some x are not y and no x are y then all x are not y.

This is the placement of counters on the xy grid to show the "No A is B" structure and it is the only placement that does so.

I.

Some A is B. <=> Some B is Some A <=> Some x contains some y <=> (ƎX < ƎY)

A white counter on the upper line and a white counter on the middle right line.

The white upper line counter says: "Some X are Y" and "Some X are Not Y"

The white middle right line counter says: "Some Y are X" and "Some Y are Not X"

If some x are y and some y are x then some xy exist.

This is the placement of counters on the xy grid to show the "Some A is B" structure and it is the only placement that does so.

O.

Some A is not B. <=> Not B is Some A <=> Not x contains some y <=> ($\sim$X < $\exists$Y)

A white counter on the lower line and a white counter on the middle right line.

The white lower counter says: "Some Not X are Y" and "Some Not X are Not Y"

The white middle line counter says: "Some Y are Not X" and "Some Y are X"

If some not x are y and some y are not x then some notxy exist.

This is the placement of counters on the xy grid to show the "Some A is Not B" structure and it is the only placement that does so.

The above four xy/$\sim$x$\sim$y structural patterns have been given in a manner that categorically claims that as given they are correct and accurate. My reason for doing so, is because the correct statement must be given in that way. However, at this stage we must suppose that the patterns as given may be simply wrong, or at least partially inaccurate. And until we have checked our workings out we cannot suppose that as given the patterns are correct. Merely that the style of presentation has been as if they are. We are now required to challenge that matter in order to determine what if any are the alternative placement of counters, and is there a better placement of counters that would more correctly state our four propositions?

As the Japanese Zen Priest said: "Reading other people's work without doing any work of your own is like counting other people's money without having any money of your own."

For this reason we should bring in another part of the model for the syllogism in order to establish whether we can find any contradictions in the above placement of counters as given. If we find no contradiction then we may be sure that the patterns as given are correct, since we already think that they are. If one of the available alternative placement of counters seemed more correct then we would have used those instead, but they don't. If we find any contradiction then we would know to find what is the better placement of counters. The model we can use is as follows:

If A be true then: E is false, O false, I true.

If A be false then: E is unknown, O true, I unknown.

If E be true then: O is true, I false, A false.

If E be false then: O is unknown, I true, A unknown.

If O be true then: I is unknown, A false, E unknown.

If O be false then: I is true, A true, E false.

If I be true then: A is unknown, E false, O unknown.

If I be false then: A is false, E true, O true.

(A) All A is B, therefore No A is not-B.(E)

(E) No A is B, therefore All A is not-B.(A)

(I) Some A is B, therefore Some A is not B. (O)

(O) Some A is not B, therefore Some A is B. (I)

If we take the placement of counters as given, since to the best of our understanding at this stage, they are the correct placement for the particular four propositions that we are referring towards. Then a further way we can check our understanding is to clearly state what that placement of counters affirms as the case. If those clearly stated affirmations confirm what our original premisses are believed to mean, then we have our coherent model without contradiction.

The Affirmations of our Propositions.

A.

Proposition: All A is B. <=> Some B is All A <=> Some x contains all y <=> (ƎX < ψY)

Affirmation:

Some X are Y

Some X are Not Y

No Y are Not X

E.

Proposition: No A is B. <=> All B is Not A <=> All x contains not y <=> (ψX < ~Y)

Affirmation:

No X are Y

Some X are Not Y

Some Not X are Not Y

I.

Proposition: Some A is B. <=> Some B is Some A <=> Some x contains some y <=> (ƎX < ƎY)

Affirmation:

Some X are Y

Some X are Not Y

Some Y are X

Some Y are Not X

O.

Proposition: Some A is not B. <=> Not B is Some A <=> Not x contains some y <=> (~X < ∃Y)

Affirmation:

Some Not X are Y

Some Not X are Not Y

Some Y are Not X

Some Y are X

The Sixteen Affirmations:

1. Some X are Y

2. Some X are Not Y

3. Some Y are X

4. Some Y are Not X

5. Some Not X are Y

6. Some Not Y are X

7. Some Not X are Not Y

8. Some Not Y are Not X

9. No X are Y

10. No Y are X

11. No Y are Not X

12. No Not X are Y

13. No X are Not Y

14. No Not Y are X

15. No Not X are Not Y

16. No Not Y are Not X

The Sixteen Affirmations in Algebraic Form.

1. ∃X < ∃Y

2. $\ni X < \ni \sim Y$

3. $\ni Y < \ni X$

4. $\ni Y < \ni \sim X$

5. $\ni \sim X < \ni Y$

6. $\ni \sim Y < \ni X$

7. $\ni \sim X < \ni \sim Y$

8. $\ni \sim Y < \ni \sim X$

9. $[\sim] X < \ni Y$

10. $[\sim] Y < \ni X$

11. $[\sim] Y < \ni \sim X$

12. $[\sim] \sim X < \ni Y$

13. $[\sim] X < \ni \sim Y$

14. $[\sim] \sim Y < \ni X$

15. $[\sim] \sim X < \sim Y$

16. $[\sim] \sim Y < \sim X$

Please note that in order to sign the term "no" as in "no x are y" I have used the square brackets around the "not" signlabel.

This is specifically to differentiate the term "no" from the term "not", since it should be clear that they mean different things. And also to ensure that in this context the use of both terms in no way leads towards the term "not not".

Having detailed our analysis of algebraic deduction to the point of the Sixteen Affirmations we find ourselves at a different unknown. The different unknown is actually a commonplace understanding of Inductive Hypothesis. For this reason, within the study of deduction we are not required to investigate the nature of our "General Affirmations", a matter that will be properly considered in a different article related to the truth-holders of correct hypothesis within the field of induction.

Since that completes the entire analysis of the algebraic deduction patterns it cannot be thought too long. That is, whilst the given analysis is extensive and requiring of concentrated attention to follow, it is also of specifically limited size. Furthermore, it does not change with repeated study. Where there may be important error in the statement of some detail of any particular pattern, then that only means ongoing correction towards accuracy over time. Also, if some error is found that is not a mistake in statement but rather a mistake in analysis, then that also is simply a matter of making whatever the individual correction must involve. Any small error in a matter such as this must always be treated as basically important because it is the nature of the matter that it is minutely realised.

That being said, we are now at the point, given the two articles, "syllogism" and "algebraic deduction" where all of the parameters for this logic of inference are described. As such, it is very easy, not difficult. Where much information may be immediately acquired on first reading and soon assimilated by handwriting the basic patterns in a small notebook, a depth of knowledge will be the inevitable product of reviewing the essential points over a longer duration of time.

The only area that presumably remains to be considered is how an entirely abstract explanation of rational logic such as this can have any applicable utility. My first answer is that it need not. That simply as a discipline of mental development it will be discovered by any person who does work with it to be of value in itself.

CHAPTER SEVENTEEN.

There are various reasons for the intended focus specifically, some of which are not straightforward to explain immediately and would require a presupposition of knowledge of Descartes' work which I cannot assume. However, it makes sense anyway on these grounds. If the idea is to provide a bounded parameter or universe of discourse within which to practice the principle of universal doubt and error checking. If the nature of the "principle of universal doubt" and the study of "error in itself" in their free expression necessarily lead to a particular known place that is not useful to visit without in depth study of Buddhist science. If the logic patterns that are the focus of this article depend for their existence on that they be doubted, corrected and rectified at any stage of the development of their organic whole. If we want to provide an agreed limited field which we may assume reasonably is also attended to by others who we do not know in the sense of an imperfect information game. For these reasons it makes sense to direct the focus towards the logic patterns article specifically and exclusively.

Following from that practice, it may well be that the "organ of universal doubt" can be exercised, its proper use, misuse and abuse understood such that it can be more practically applied to other areas. And also the intricacies of "error checking" can be comprehended in terms of their more subtle forms.

The following passage is taken directly from "Selections

from the principles of philosophy of Rene Descartes translated by John Veitch".

In the original each point has a further explanation provided by Descartes. I have not included this because the aim here is to provide a one minute manifesto as to a particular principle. Any reader who would desire to know all that Descartes had to say on the matter should go directly to his work. I have not included each of the points in total. For example notes eighteen to twenty nine have not been included. I have included odd notes that do not make obvious sense in themselves but they are required to support notes that do make sense in themselves.

However, the idea here is to consider one principle exclusively, that is, the principle of error correction.

As an idea, that of "error correction" does not stand independently. It has its proactive form in the theory of "universal doubt". In directional terms it may manifest as a practice of "self rectification".

The important concern here is to acknowledge a principle that is being applied to all the various articles that I have personally written in this context. And to understand that principle I am suggesting it is best to refer to Descarte's original foundational document. I will provide some possible ideas as to how this article can be interpreted immediately following.

I. THAT in order to seek truth, it is necessary once in the course of our life, to doubt, as far as possible, of all things.

II. That we ought also to consider as false all that is doubtful.

III. That we ought not meanwhile to make use of doubt in the conduct of life.

IV. We may doubt of sensible things.

V. We may also doubt of mathematical demonstrations.

VI. That we possess a free-will, by which we can withhold our assent from what is doubtful, and thus avoid error.

VII. That we cannot doubt of our existence while we doubt, and that this is the first knowledge we acquire when we philosophize in order.

VIII. That we hence discover the distinction between the mind and the body, or between a thinking and corporeal thing.

X. That the notions which are simplest and self-evident, are obscured by logical definitions; and that such are not to be reckoned among the cognitions acquired by study.

XI. How we can know our mind more clearly than our body.

XII. How it happens that every one does not come equally to know this.

XVII. That the greater objective perfection there is in our idea of a thing, the greater also must be the perfection of its cause.

XXX. That consequently all which we clearly perceive is true, and that we are thus delivered from the doubts above proposed.

XXXII. That there are only two modes of thinking in us, that is, the perception of the understanding and the action of the will.

XXXIII. That we never err unless when we judge of something which we do not sufficiently apprehend.

XXXIV. That the will as well as the understanding is required for judging.

XXXV. That the will is of greater extension than the understanding, and is thus the source of our errors.

XXXVII. That the chief perfection of man is his being able to act freely or by will, and that it is this which renders him worthy of praise or blame.

XXXVIII. That error is a defect in our mode of acting, not in our nature; and that the faults of their subjects may be frequently attributed to other masters, but never to God.

XXXIX. That the liberty of our will is self-evident.

XLII. How, although we never will to err, it is nevertheless by our will that we do err.

XLIII. That we shall never err if we give our assent only to what we clearly and distinctly perceive.

XLIV. That we uniformly judge improperly when we assent to what we do not clearly perceive, although our judgment may chance to be true; and that it is frequently our memory which deceives us by leading us to believe that certain things were formerly sufficiently understood by us.

XLVII. That, to correct the prejudices of our early years, we must consider what is clear in each of our simple notions.

XLVIII. That all the objects of our knowledge are to be regarded either (1) as things or the affections of things: or (2) as eternal truths; with the enumeration of things.

XLIX. That the eternal truths cannot be thus enumerated, but that this is not necessary.

L. That these truths are clearly perceived, but not equally by all men, on account of prejudices.

LI. What substance is, and that the term is not applicable to God and the creatures in the same sense.

LII. That the term is applicable univocally to the mind and the body, and how substance itself is known.

LIII. That of every substance there is one principal attribute, as thinking of the mind, extension of the body.

LIV. How we may have clear and distinct notions of the substance which thinks, of that which is corporeal, and of God.

LXXIV. The fourth source of our errors is, that we attach our thoughts to words which do not express them with accuracy.

LXXV. Wherefore if we would philosophize in earnest, and give ourselves to the search after all the truths we are capable of knowing, we must, in the first place, lay aside our prejudices; in other words, we must take care scrupulously to withhold our assent from the opinions we have formerly admitted, until upon new examination we discover that they are true. We must, in the next place, make an orderly review of the notions we have in our minds, and hold as true all and only those which we will clearly and distinctly apprehend. In this way we will observe, first of all, that we exist in so far as it is our nature to think, and at the same time that there is a God upon whom we depend; and after considering his attributes we will be able to investigate the truth of all other things, since God is the cause of them. Besides the notions we have of God and of our mind, we will likewise find that we possess the knowledge of many propositions which are eternally true, as, for example, that nothing cannot be the cause of anything, etc. We will farther discover in our minds the knowledge of a corporeal or extended nature that may be moved, divided, etc., and also of certain sensations that affect us, as of pain, colours, tastes, etc., although we do not yet know the cause of our being so affected; and, comparing what we have now learne'd, by examining those things in their order, with our former confused knowledge of them, we will acquire the habit of forming clear and distinct conceptions of all the objects we are capable of knowing. In these few precepts seem to me to be comprised the most general and important principles of human knowledge.

This completes the original document written by Descartes.

Notes immediately following are my own.

Circumference = 22.2 144 146 907 9181

Radius = 3.53 553 390 593 2738

Diameter = 7.07 106 781 186 5475

Quink = 4.44 288 293 815 8362

Side of Square = 5

Square of side of square = 25

Diagonal of Square = 7.07 106 781 186 5475

Sum of square of other two sides = 50

Square Root of Fifty = 7.07 106 781 186 5475

Pi = 3.14 159 265 358 979

1. Given the length of the circumference of any circle.

2. Divide the length of the circumference by Quink to obtain the length of the side of square that the circle circumscribes.

4. Multiply the length of the side of square by four to obtain the length of the perimeter of square.

5. Multiply the length of one side of the square by itself to obtain Square of side of square.

6. Multiply the Square of side of square by two in order to obtain Sum of square of other two sides.

7. Discover the square root of the sum of square of other two sides to obtain the diameter of circle with the original circumference.

8. Divide the original circumference given in note one, by the diameter given in note seven, to obtain Pi.

1. Make a point.

2. Extend a line from the point.

3. Bisect the line through its centre.

4. Draw a third line equidistant from the point of the bisection such that the third line crosses each of the extensions of the first two lines and both ends of the third line are connected together.

5. Draw four connecting lines from the point where the first two lines touch the circumference of the circle.

That figure is the circle, square and triangle in relationship. It can be alternately described as "that geometric figure made by the circle circumscribing a square divided by four similar triangles".

Descartes was writing about four hundred years previously. Since his writing we have developed steam powered mechanisms, replaced by oil fuels, electricity and nuclear energy. The immediately previous document is at the level of "first cause" in regard to the accelerated development of this mechanism. That it is not obviously so is the reason I bring it forward here.

It is not obvious because Descartes wrote several large books, and the document as given is absorbed into the entirety of his writing. And much of his other writing is given far more serious attention than the above document. And all of Descartes work is absorbed into the huge volume of philosophical work that is written by those who follow. Which is again hidden under all of the secondary sources who explain one or other interpretation of what Descartes meant.

When the original source is attended to in its entirety, it is easily possible to disagree with various parts of it, depending on which prejudices one personally holds, and on the basis that one probably does not share exactly the same prejudices as Descartes himself.

And on correctly disagreeing with some particular, it may be that it becomes difficult to determine whether there was some reason for attending to the article in the first place.

We reach the point where the level of tenacity involved in obtaining some value from the study becomes of such a demanding sort that only the disciplined professional heavily subsidised by accademic grants can have any inclination to attend to the particular matter.

But they don't because if everything that has to be said about Descartes over the last four hundred years has not already been said, then it is quite clear that it is not what any present day accademic grant is supposed to pay for.

Now what is most odd, is that the matter itself deserves attention. But also that the matter itself is "hot", and definitely not a subject that can be considered as properly understood.

Also, the matter is common rather than being the possession of a specialist subject.

If it was easy to get at, and easy to explain, then we would today be easily able to point to a specific title and say, if you want to know about that matter, then go to that book and it will exhaustively explain everything about it in detail. On having studied some given book you would still have questions about the matter, but they will be a completely different set of questions to those you had previously. And we cannot do that. The closest we can get at present is to point to a relatively obscure document that takes less than five minutes to read written by a person called Descartes over four hundred years in the past. (Please do not even think of correcting my split infinitives, it is a political disagreement, and I don't want to get into it here.)

That matter is called "the nature of error and the value of error correction" and is in a close relationship to something called "principle of universal doubt".

Three rules can usefully be kept in mind when considering the subject of "error correction".

1. The principle of "margin for error" asserted here is that it is equal to the square root of the number of component elements.

2. To ask the question: "What is the smallest bit that

may be removed from the pattern without any discernable alteration in the whole?"

3. What is the significance of the "place" where that smallest bit was discovered?.

Rule One.

The principle of "margin for error" asserted here is that it is equal to the square root of the number of component elements.

In comprehending rule one we accept a margin for error exists. We find that if the number of bits in the pattern is ten, then our margin for error is approximately "three bits", that is proportionally one third of the whole. If though the number of bits is one hundred then the square root of that is ten. Which means that in a pattern composed of one hundred bits we have a margin for error of ten bits, which is one tenth of the whole. But if the pattern is composed of ten thousand bits, the margin for error is only one hundred bits, that is zero point zero one percent of the whole.

What this demonstrates is that the margin for error decreases dramatically given a proportional increase in complexity.

Critically it means that the greater number of "bits" in a pattern the smaller the proportion of those bits can be wrong safely.

Rule Two:

To ask the question: "What is the smallest bit that may be removed from the pattern without any discernable alteration in the whole?"

With this question we are immediately directed towards a different area from what is the natural inclination. That is, given the natural inclination may be to look for what is the biggest mistake we can find in some pattern. However our assumption in this matter is that the whole of the pattern is basically okay. So we are directed towards not only what is tiny, but actually to what is "tiniest".

When we find the single smallest bit in the whole pattern that may be removed from the pattern without any discernable alteration in the whole we must first check ourselves. Can we be sure that it is the smallest bit? Maybe there is another bit that is even smaller, or the same size but even safer to remove.

Then only if we are sure that we have literally discovered the "smallest bit" we should then remove it from the pattern. And if we have done so according to principle we should find that it has no discernable alteration to the whole pattern.

Rule Three:

What is the significance of the "place" where that smallest bit was discovered?.

With rule three we are noticing that "Error exists in place".

We can usefully define error as " An aberration in the field of time that has a specific location in place"

Since the bit we wanted was the smallest bit it is perhaps one that is so tiny not immediately easy to discover. But discover it we do, because we direct ourselves to find the smallest bit.

Please accept that when I say "smallest bit" I do not mean : Find the smallest bit in the pattern and remove it.

I only mean, find the smallest wrong bit, or the smallest error bit, or the smallest null-value bit, or the smallest bit that seems to have no meaning.

When we then look at the location where the smallest bit we could safely remove was discovered, we will often notice that it is an extremely important location. If we discover that the bit is small we consider it unimportant. But we discover that the location is important when the bit is removed.

Through the application of these three rules we can

eliminate certain specific kinds of error from our pattern to start with. And if we do so correctly it will involve no discernable alteration in the pattern as a whole.

Given we have done so we can then apply rule four.

Rule Four:

In the exact same "place" where the bit was removed we must now assert a very important bit.

The idea here is economical. That is, where something unimportant was removed, something very important must be asserted.

The result of the application of these four rules is that a very important bit is asserted in a very important place such that the entirety of the pattern is altered in a positive way, and in such a way that we have moved a definite distance towards safely within our given margin for error.

Correction and Rectification.

Point One.

x. $a/(b/c)=(a.c)/b$

y. $(a/b)/c=a/(b.c)$

z. Therefore: $a/(b/c)=/=(a/b)/c$

Idea 41. $(a < b) < c => a < (b < c) <=> (a / b) / c = a / (b / c)$

Idea 41 is clearly wrong. The correct answer is given as xyz above.

The correct answer xyz is coherent with the larger pattern, it is non-contradictory, it meets conditions of correspondence and utility.

At this stage I am not going to apply the correction to the error. Instead it is clearly stated in this location what the correct answer should be, so that any who are keeping a handwritten notebook can adjust as they feel inclined.

In this way we can ask: Is it true that idea 41 is clearly wrong?

If it is, how do we know so?

Is it true that xyz is clearly correct?

Then if we have one example of what a wrong answer would be, can we find another?

Point Two.

S15 and S16 are nearly correct, which is not the same as being wrong.

The correct answer to S15 and S16 immediately follows.

S15.(∃B < ψC) ∧ (∃A < ψB) => (ψC < ∃A)

S16.(∃B < ψC) ∧ (ψA < ~B) => (~C < ψA)

In both cases the nearly correct answer provides a soft conclusion where a hard conclusion is possible.

That is because we can say All instead of Some, we must do so in this context.

It is true that in every case where a hard answer is possible a soft answer can also be given.

That is, in every case where we can say "Some x contains All y" we can also say "Some x contains Some y".

A similar sort of error is worth noticing within this category although it refers to a mistake made in the "syllogism" article.

In reference to the idea S4. (ψC < ~B) ∧ (∃B < ∃A) => (~C < ∃A).

The only correct diagram for this syllogism is three circles, where one circle in the middle is intersected by a circle on either side and the two circles on each side do not intersect each other. If we label the circle on the left C, the circle in the middle A, the circle on the right B. Then it is clear that All C is not B. Some B is Some A. Some A is Not C.

But because some A is not C, then some A is C. For that reason in the diagram we must show circle C intersecting circle A.

Point Three.

Both ideas 9 and 26 are entirely correct as stated, without error. The fact that they assume "a" to be a positive integer is acceptable. That there are alternative possible answers where a is a negative integer, zero or infinity is simply a condition of the system being described. As such, for many of the simple ideas provided, variations are possible.

9. $a < 1 => a <=> a/1 = a$

26. $a < a => 1 <=> a / a = 1$

Point Four.

That some interesting idea could be included but is not can be considered a sort of error depending on whether it is essential to the meaning of the organic whole. That is not the case here. For example:

$a.b=c$ then $c/a =b$ and $c/b=a$

That this could be included is true. That it is not a necessity that it be included is correct.

There must be several or many such ideas that can be individually developed in accord with the system as given.

Point Five.

Ideas such as 27 and 29 are neither determined as true or false at this stage. They are not errors.

27. $a v ~a => Q <=> a . ~a = 0$

29. $a < ~a => Q <=> a / ~a = -1$

As far as possible they seem to maintain coherence without the blocking effect that contradictions cause. As such, they serve two functions in particular. One is to show the possibility of the idea. The second is to do so in such a way that it does not conflict with what is clearly correct in regard to the other ideas. The basic requirement is that a more correct true answer is provided or that a proof for the answer as given is provided in detail.

The points one through five above describe a way of looking at different category of possible error. They suggest that each kind of error should not be treated in the exact same way. They also allow that any particular error discovered can be placed in at least one of the categories described, unless a further category is required.

Investment in error.

Three kinds of people invest in error. They are the good, the bad and the ugly.

Taking the ugly first, this is described by Edward de Bono as "the intelligence trap".

In this instance the greater the intellect, the stronger the capacity to defend wrong answers. Only the truly intelligent can devise brilliant explanations for what is entirely incorrect, false and untrue. Since they do so in such a way that others know is wrong but are not confident or capable of saying why, it is considered ugly.

Taking the good second, this could be called "the virtue trap".

In this instance we imagine a properly virtuous person makes an unintended mistake. Because they are virtuous in all normal circumstances they are compelled to hide the mistake. In hiding the mistake they compound the original error with a new error. This then generates a feedback loop in only one specific location, that becomes increasingly dark.

Taking the bad third, this could be called "the appearance trap".

In this instance the properly bad person entirely depends on an appearance of credibility and virtue in order to maintain their capacity to promote error, falsity and wrongness. The interesting presupposition here is that the bad person intends error and falsity, which they can only promote under the appearance of utmost respectability.

The key here is to have some understanding of the dynamic of investment in error. Through understanding the dynamic it may be advantageous to both the person who has not made any such investment and perhaps to the person who has done so.

The person who has not invested in error is in this way protected from doing so by being clearly familiar with the three basic traps.

The person who has invested in error can from a more detached viewpoint determine in which of the three traps they are caught.

In this way it is at least possible that all three traps can be avoided or escaped.

Furthermore, a more in depth study of the three traps of investment in error will enable any person to perceive their operation in regard to others, and allow them to understand why others may operate differently from what would seem proper.

Ten Characteristics of the Nature of Error.

1. Habituation, 2. Compounding, 3. Existence in place, 4. Temporal aberration, 5. Contradiction, 6. Infinitude,

7. Increase to scale, 8. Transference, 9. Translation,

10. Complexity.

1. Habituation means that an error made once will often habituate, that is, become a habit. It means the same error will always be repeated whenever the circumstances of its first occurrence happen again.

2. Compounding means that a simple error will often lead to a cumulation of error rooted at the point of the first simple error. Any defence of a simple error immediately generates this sort of compound error. Very quickly the original root error is hidden by the compound error which then itself has

to be justified by further aberration.

3. Existence in place means that error can be located in place. Without placement there can be no error as such. This even includes the error of exclusion where the error is to not include some necessary condition. Since it means that there must be some place where the necessary condition should have been included. Also any root error or compound error can normally be traced to some particular location.

4. Temporal aberration is a noticeable effect of the existance in place of error. This is because existant error has a definite causal effect in terms of time. The causal effect of error in temporal terms is an aberration that is generated by the durational existence of error without its correction. Given some error is corrected and rectified properly the durational cause no longer exists, and the aberration immediately reduces over a given time frame.

5. Contradiction means that an error will cause an unnecessary conflict with any true correct proposition. It means that the blocking effect of contradiction will result from any calculation involving the correct true proposition.

6. Infinitude means that for any one correct true answer there is an infinitude of wrong answers.

7. Increase to scale means that the habitual error formed on a small scale will normally be repeated on a large scale. The interesting dynamic here is that the habitual error on a small scale may often go unnoticed and not really matter. However when the same error is repeated on the large scale it immediately shows up with significant consequences. Also errors of this sort may often not be correctable on the larger scale but require rectification at the small scale first.

8. Transference means that errors can be passed on from one person to another. This is the dependence on authority error. That is, where an authority transfers information which includes error to a recipient.

9. Translation means that error can be translated from one language to another. That is, if an error exists in the original language and the information is translated into a different language it is normal to translate the error as well.

10. Complexity means that error will usually have the effect of increasing complexity beyond necessity. This is the converse of Occam's Razor. Occams's Razor states that "Entity must not be increased beyond necessity". Error tends to do this.

CHAPTER EIGHTEEN.

One plus two plus three plus four equals ten, proving the first four numbers are the sum of number.

x squared equals x whether x equals one or x equals zero, proving one does not equal zero.

Any number squared divided by two plus half the original number is equal to the number of times each of the consecutive integers in the original number combine with itself and each of the others once, as in dominoes. Pi squared and the square root of pi are both constant. A place holder exists that is neither one nor zero. What is the place holder?

When we use equals we are saying some entity is the same as a different entity. When we use does not equal we are saying some entity is not the same as a different entity. By universal abstraction we can define this as to say being is being and the contradictory being is not being. That then explains the way in which we use equals, which is the mathematical equivalent of the word "is". And the way in which we use does not equal, which is the mathematical equivalent of the word phrase "is not".

Given that understanding, it becomes clear that if we attend to the matter "what is equals?", we will be forced to attend to the more abstract matter, what does "is" mean? The important knowledge here is to realise that we can not answer the second level question "what is equals?" unless we can answer the first level question "what does <is> mean?". And if we can answer the first level question, then answering the second level question becomes easy.

The concepts that are inter-relationally involved in this kind of study include being, doing, meaning, existence, non-existence, identity, non-identity and no other concepts. In mathematical terms we can say the concepts are one, some, more, less and none. Therefore, if we consider only those five mathematical concepts we can define some basic terms. One object is an existant identity. If the same identity is repeated that is some. Some is more than one. One is less than some. None is the non-existance of one and some. The concept of more is to do with addition. The concept of less is to do with subtraction. A repetitive addition is called multiplication. A repetitive subtraction is called division. Existence is an affirmation. Non-existence is a negation.

Any number squared divided by two plus half the original number is equal to the number of times each of the consecutive integers in the original number combine with itself and each of the others once, as in dominoes. In a standard nine bar set of dominoes the integers one to nine and zero are all represented in relation to each of the other integers. That is a total of ten units. Ten squared is one hundred. One hundred divided by two is fifty. Half the original number is five. Fifty plus five is fifty five. And in a standard nine bar set of dominoes there are fifty five counters. Given dominoes do not use late language sign label for number, and instead use a pattern of points to show the universal abstract that exists at the earlier level than sign label, they are useful in regard to demonstrating the ontological status of existant being of number.

At the level of dominoes, the sign labels and the concepts do not yet exist. Without the sign labels and without the concepts, still dominoes exist. Dominoes therefore are ontologically earlier than the sign labels and the concepts. And from the ontological existence of dominoes it is very easy to build the sign labels and concepts of number.

If we imagine we have a set of dominoes for only the units

one and none, then that is two units. Two squared is four, four divided by two is two. Half the original number is one. Two plus one is three. Therefore we will have a set of dominoes with three counters. One of those counters will show none on both sides of the counter. Another will show one on both sides of the counter. Another will show none on one side and one on the other side of the counter. In that way without defining our concepts we are showing the concepts in their immanent form. And with the dominoe that has none on both sides we are saying none is the same as none or none equals none. And with the dominoe that has one on both sides we are saying one is the same as one or one equals one. And with the dominoe that has none on one side and one on the other side we are saying none is not the same as one or none does not equal one. And we know what we mean because we have three dominoes and we can see what we mean. And we think that each of the three dominoes is different to the other two. And if we thought of the connecting line between the two sides of any one dominoe as plus, then we would know that none plus none is none, one plus none is one, and one plus one is two. And if we look at the whole dominoe and thought of what happens when we take away one side that would be like minus, so we could say none minus none is none, one minus none is one, one minus one is none, two minus one is one.

All we need now do is notice what are the functions that are evident without specific sign label.

And we can see that the difference between nothing and something is similar to the difference between the dominoe that is blank on both sides and the dominoe that has a blank on one side and a one on the other. And the difference between one and some is similar to the the difference between the dominoe that has a blank on one side and one on the other and the dominoe that has a one on both sides. And we can understand that some is more than one and one is less than some and none is the non-existance of one or some.

So at this stage we have proved the first five concepts of number which are one, some, more, less, none. And we can apply those concepts as sign labels of functions such that we understand one is existant entity, some is a repetition of one, and none is the non-existance of entity. And we can apply the sign label functions of addition to some being more than one, and subtraction to one being less than some. Which means we have now invented our sign labels for the functions of addition and subtraction.

And we know what we mean by "is" because "none <is> none" and "one <is> one" and we know what we mean by "is not" because "none <is not> one". Therefore we have demonstrated using three dominoes the function before sign label of the concepts of one, some, more, less, none, addition, subtraction. And now we simply invent the sign labels to specify those functions.

Given the previous discourse then we can say that one is the equivalent of a point. And we can provide an initial definition of a point. That is: "A point is defined as the prime difference between none and some". Or alternatively we can say: "A point <is not> none and also a point <is not> some". We can say that a point is more than none and less than some. A point is that which exists if we do not have some and do not have none. The first difference between nothing and something is a point. Therefore in all these propositions a point is given in terms of "difference", which leads us to say that a point is the prime difference from none or nothing.

And a point is the first condition of some or something.

In this sense we can negate a point by saying "none exists" or "some exists". Both none and some are different to a point. And a point is the absence of none or some. A point exists that is less than some and more than none.

Geometry in this system is defined as the study of the

relationship between triangle, square and circle and nothing else. Triangle, square and circle are all examples of "some". Therefore, before the study of the relationship between triangle, square and circle we must understand the earlier matter which is a point.

The fastest possible construction of three dimensions is point, line, plane, tetrahedron. Tetrahedron and the other four prime solids are all based on the study of the relationship between triangle, square and circle. Therefore the geometric system being studied is only based on the following figure:

1. Make a point.

2. Extend a line from the point.

3. Bisect the line through its centre.

4. Draw a third line equidistant from the point of the bisection such that the third line crosses each of the extensions of the first two lines and both ends of the third line are connected together.

5. Draw four connecting lines from the point where the first two lines touch the circumference of the circle.

That figure is the circle, square and triangle in relationship. It can be alternately described as "that geometric figure made by the circle circumscribing a square divided by four similar triangles".

Rotate the same figure by one quarter turn of ninety degrees around any one of its corners to obtain a mirror reflection. And by another half turn of one hundred eighty degrees around the same corner to obtain the larger square. Circumscribe the larger square by a circle. That gives the larger square containing four exact versions of itself. Any of those four smaller squares could contain four exact versions of themselves inside themselves.

Half the larger square gives a rectangle formed by two

versions of the smaller square. Reflect the two extreme triangles at either end of the rectangle outward from the extreme edges of the rectangle. Extend a line from the end point of each extreme triangle through the centre of the entire figure. That gives three horizontals, seven verticals and twelve diagonals meeting at ten points which is a total of twenty two plus ten, which is thirty two.

Therefore we can hypothetically suppose an association between the given system of geometry and the mathematical system of Mozart in terms of three, seven and twelve. Where the three scales of the grand staff are only the repetition of one scale of seven tones, and the seven tones are only the combination of twelve half tones. That is three, seven and twelve.

Before our geometric system can be used to study the five socratic solids it is necessary that we obtain the information provided by the study of the geometric figure made by the circle circumscribing a square divided by four similar triangles. Before we can obtain the information provided by that figure we must prove the point, line and plane.

Our definitions are as follows:

A point is neither none nor some and is the prime difference between none and some. And a point is the absence of none and some. Or a point is more than none and less than some. A point is the possibility of the existant being that is not none and not some. And we prove a point by our system of dominoes of three counters by saying:

None <is> none.

One <is> one.

One <is not> none.

A line is extension in any direction from a point. A line is the prime difference between one and some. A line is the precondition for some to exist. Given any two points then a line is the shortest distance between the two. A line is the element required in order for a plane to exist. A line is length without breadth. A line is the possibility of the existence of verticality or horizontality. A line is proved in reality by the plumb along a vertical or the spirit level along the horizontal.

A plane is extension of line along a vertical and horizontal axis. Or a plane is that entity made possible by the bisection of one line by another line. Or a plane is that figure made by extending a line equidistant from a point such that both ends are connected. Or a plane is that figure made when any three straight lines have all of their ends touch only one end of each of the other two. Our proof of the plane is the circle circumscribed square and square divided into four similar triangles.

Object is plane surface in two directions. Object is that entity made possible by the inter-section of plane along the horizontal and vertical axis. As plane is to line, so object is to plane. Object is the extension of line along two horizontals and one vertical. Object is the possibility of extension along length, breadth and depth. The first object is that entity whose entire surface is equidistant from its own centre of gravity, or an infinity of lines of all one length extended from a point in every direction, known as a sphere. The prime elements of the first object are tetrahedron, hexahedron, octahedron, dodecahedron, icosahedron. Our proof of object is the inter-section of lines provided by plumbline and spirit level.

The preferred definition of pi in this system is twenty two divided by seven since it again refers to the three, seven, twelve, twenty two structure. And the closer ratio of three hundred fifty five divided by one hundred thirteen. The length of the circumference of a circle that circumscribes a square divided by the diagonal that connects any two opposite corners of the square is the relationship that we must attend to in particular. Since it means that the diagonal between two opposite corners of all and any square when divided into the length of the circumference of the circle that circumscribes the same square gives a constant ratio. That is the ratio known as pi and in rough terms it is always twenty two divided by seven. This particular idea of geometry is only interested in relationship between entity rather than in the entity individually. Half the diagonal line from each opposite corner of the square is the radius of a circle that being the length from the centre of a circle to its circumference, and in a sphere the length from the centre of gravity to its surface.

Pi is equal to three point one four one five nine two six five three five eight nine seven nine.

Or 3.14159265358979. Pi is an irrational transcendental number.

The squaring of the circle is only meant to refer to that entity where the perimeter of the square is the same length as the circumference of a circle. It gives a different figure to our basic design such that each of the four corners of the square extends just beyond the circumference of the circle and the circumference of the circle extends just beyond the edges of the square. It is easy to construct with the same level of precision as twenty two divided by seven simply by using a piece of string of any length. Use the piece of string to make the circumference of a circle. Use the same piece of string to make the perimeter of a square. The piece of string does not change length. The circumference of the circle and perimeter of the square will be found to make only the shape described and never any other shape, that is where the corners of the square extend beyond the circumference of the circle and the circumference of the circle extends beyond the edges of the square. So in this figure where circumference of circle and perimeter of square are equal length we do not have the same relationship of diagonal of square to circumference of circle known as pi.

Where in the original given figure the diagonal of square is one large triangle and the large triangle is double two similar small triangles then half the diagonal is one side of one of the smaller triangles. Meaning that in the same figure the side of one of the smaller triangles that is not the edge of the square is also the radius of the circle that circumscribes the square. That is again the relationship that we study in this system of geometry between the circle and the triangle. Since it means that any circle of any size has a radius that is one edge of a triangle that can be used to make only a square where each corner of the square touches the circumference of the circle.

It is in particular the relationship between these three entities where each one necessitates each of the others in a constant permanent relationship that we are interested in. Again, what it means is only the kind of triangle where one angle is ninety degrees and the two sides of that angle are the same length. And only the square that can be made from that one kind of triangle. And only the circle that circumscribes the square such that the diagonal of the square is the diameter of the circle and half the diagonal of the square is one of the sides of the ninety degree angle of the triangle which is also the radius of the circle.

This then is the geometric ideality of the Platonic forms rooted in the Socratic discourse of the Republic and nothing else. It entirely depends on the system described by Socrates in regard to both the forms and the five prime solids. In particular the principle that is attended to is called constance which is close to the virtue known as temperance. Because the kind of triangle in relationship to square and triangle and square in relationship to circle is constant in their relationship this provides an eternal ideality which we restrict our study towards. The content of the Socratic discourses in particular provides the basis for this.

Constance of relationship is not only found in pi. It is clear that in the described figure the length of the side of the square is also the hypotenuse of the triangle. That the length of the side of the square and hypotenuse is in constant relationship to the radius of circle and the other sides of the triangle as well as to the diameter of circle and diagonal of square. And that the length of diagonal of square is also diameter of circle. And that the centre of square and circle are the same. The various ratios of each of these constant relationships is a quantifiable amount that is always the same. So this system of geometry involves both knowledge of what are these constant ratios and also what are the ideas in terms of tangent and sine that inform us as to these ratios. Since the specific tangent and sine quantity will always be the same in this figure, therefore eternals.

The following idea is hypothetical at this point. It is directly related to the triangle, square and circle figure that is the focus of this geometry and is one example of the sort of study that is cultivated in this system.

The peculiar fact that is noticed is this:

a. Given a line of six units in length then the square of that line is six multiplied by six which is thirty six. Whereas half the length of the line is three units in length. So the square of half the line is three multiplied by three which is nine. That means that half the line squared plus half the line squared is nine plus nine which is eighteen. Which seems peculiar. Since the expectation may have been that half the line squared plus half the line squared would equal the whole of the line squared, which it does not. Specifically half the line squared plus half the line squared equals half of the whole line squared. Now, to see if that holds true for a line of a different length.

b. If the whole line is ten units length, then the square of the line is one hundred units, that being ten multiplied by ten. And the length of half the line is five units, then the square of half the line is five multiplied by five which is twenty five.

And the square of half the line plus the square of the other half of the line is twenty five, the two combined being fifty. And fifty is half the amount of the square of the whole line which is one hundred.

c. Therefore, given that result we would make the claim that: the square of a line of any length is equal to double the square of half the same line plus the square of half the same line. Or alternatively stated: given a line of any length, then the square of half the length of that line plus the square of half the length of that line is a specific amount that will be found to be exactly half the specific amount that is the square of the whole line.

d. And to state what is not the case is that: given a line of any length then the square of that line does not equal the square of half the line plus the square of half the line.

e. Given that knowledge then we can apply it to any square. And say that one side of any square must be the hypotenuse of a triangle formed when diagonal lines from the two corners of the same side are extended to the centre of the square. Since to extend lines from the two corners of one side of any square such that the two lines meet at the centre of the square is to make a right angle triangle where the side of the square is the hypotenuse. And that means that the side of any square when multiplied by itself must equal the diagonal formed from one of the corners of the square when extended to the centre of the square multiplied by itself and doubled.

f. Since the diagonal formed when extended to the centre is exactly half the diagonal of the line extended from any corner of the same square extended to the opposite corner, it may have been thought that this would result in a contradictory outcome, because it would look as if the hypothesis led to the claim that the side of any square multiplied by itself is equal to the diagonal line between any two corners of the square multiplied by itself. Since the diagonal line between two corners is double the diagonal line that extends to the centre. But it does not lead to that contradiction.

g. The question asked is: Is it the case that the side of any square multiplied by itself does equal half the diagonal line of the same square extended from any corner to its opposite corner when it is multiplied by itself. Since that would seem to be the same situation as that described in point c. above.

h. To clarify: 1.Given a line of six units the square is thirty six. And half the line is three units the square of such being nine, which when doubled is eighteen. And eighteen is exactly half of thirty six. 2. Given one side of a square. And given two diagonal lines drawn from two adjacent corners of the side to the centre of the side. And given that the square of one diagonal is added to the square of the other diagonal. Then the combined amount of the square of the two diagonals does equal the amount of the square of one side. 3. And either one of the diagonals could be extended through the centre of the side to the opposite corner. 4. And that diagonal line that extends from one corner of the side to the opposite corner of the side when squared must equal double the amount given in point 2.

Therefore if the previous hypothesis is correct it suggests that there is a constant relationship between the square of the side of any square and the square of the diagonal between two corners of the same square, in a proportional relationship.

{{{ This note contained within three brackets is a later addition to the original article.

If the circumference of the circle is twenty two units, where a unit could be any constant length. And if in rough terms the diameter of the circle is seven units. Then the diagonal of the square would be seven units length. Since that is the hypotenuse of a triangle formed from one half of the square that would mean that one side of the square is five units length, in rough terms. Because, seven squared is forty nine. And five squared is twenty five. So by adding the square of two sides opposite the hypotenuse together we obtain fifty which is only one unit off forty nine. Furthermore if we were to fold one side of the square by ninety degrees to obtain a single line of ten units length then the square of that single line would be one hundred which is twice the square of half the line plus the square of half the line.

Given that it means that there is a rough figure of five which must be relative to the seven and twenty two of pi. Because if the circumference is twenty two, the diameter is seven, and if the diameter is seven then the side of the square is five. So twenty two divided by five is four point four. Then a relationship between 4.4 : 3.14 must exist.

Furthermore, if the diameter is seven then the radius is three point five. And that means that the side of one of the four smaller triangles is three point five. Where the hypotenuse of that triangle is five. So three point five squared is twelve point two five. So the square of the hypotenuse of this triangle is twenty five. And the square of the other two sides added together is twenty five. That gives us the root numbers of three and twelve in relationship if we round off to whole numbers.

If we keep the points then we have three point five, twelve point two five and twenty five.

At this stage it is clear that we must become more accurate in our figures.

Pi is equal to three point one four one five nine two six five three five eight nine seven nine.

Or 3.14159265358979.

Using this quantity as a measure of the accuracy that is required, then all we need to know is what are the more accurate quantities for the numbers twenty two, seven, five, forty nine, fifty, four point four, three point five, twelve point two five, and twenty five.

The calculation is as follows:

If the side of a square is five units, where the units are of any length.

Then the square of the side is twenty five units.

And the hypotenuse of the square is the square root of fifty, since fifty is the sum of the square of the other two sides.

The square root of fifty is seven point zero seven one zero six seven eight one one eight six five four seven five.

Or 7.071 067 811 865 475.

So the hypotenuse of a square with the side of five units length is seven point zero seven one.

So the diameter of the circle is 7.071 067 811 865 475.

And the radius of the circle is three point five three five five three three nine zero five nine three two seven three eight.

Or 3.535 533 905 932 738.

If we multiply the hypotenuse of the square which is also the diameter of the circle by pi then we obtain the circumference of the circle which is twenty two point two one four four one four six nine zero seven nine one eight one.

Or 22.2 144 146 907 9181

So now we can suppose a square with the side of five units.

The diagonal of seven point zero seven units.

The radius of a circle of three point five three units.

The circumference of a circle of twenty two point two units.

Where 22.2 divided by 7.07 is pi calculated as 3.1400.

And 22.2 divided by 5 is 4.44.

So we can suppose a constant of 22/7 = 3.14 and 22/5 = 4.4 therefore 3.14:4.44 as constant.

Out of interest if we divide the square of the hypotenuse by ten we obtain five which is also the length of the side of the square. And if we obtain the square root of five we get two point two three six zero six seven nine seven seven four nine nine seven nine.

Adding one to the square root of five gives 3.236 067 977 499 79.

And dividing that by two we obtain the golden ratio which is:

One point six one eight zero three three nine eight eight seven four nine.

Or 1.618 033 988 749.

Since the radius of the circle is also one of the other two sides if the side of the square is the hypotenuse of one of the four smaller triangles.

And the radius of the circle is three point five three five five three three nine zero five nine three two seven three eight.

Or 3.535 533 905 932 738.

Then if we find the square of that we obtain twelve point five.

Which means that 12.5 is the square of each of the other two sides in our right angle triange.

12.5 + 12.5 = 25. So the hypotenuse of the triangle must be the square root of twenty five which is five.}}}

Rather than correcting the present argumentation up to this stage with a view to clarifying some statement of my terms since it is possible that my correction would be less satisfactory than the present statement. Then I would say that as stated the argumentation up to this point seems to make sense in the way I intend it to make sense. And the information seems correspondent to what I want it to refer towards. Therefore, what I would rather do is provide a less explanatory model that defines the key matters we should be clear in regard towards, without confusion, grey areas, blanks or error. It does seem to me that there can be no progression of mind or intellect beyond these early matters until these early matters are clearly stated in necessary sufficient terms without error and without confusion. By which I mean there seems little point in attempting what can only be more difficult and more sophisticated until we are quite confident about our understanding of those prime areas on what the more difficult sophisticated matters are based.

Although of course that is not quite the reality. Rather it is that the mind intellect capacity to coherently inform as to the prime patterns involves a confidence that may only be obtained by beginning with what seems more difficult and sophisticated. It is somewhat as Aristotle says when he supposes we begin any study of the principles and elements of some subject matter by looking at what is more general and evident to our senses and less true, and use that as our entrance towards what is more abstract, universal and less evident to our senses, and more true. Therefore in that way the idea would be to perhaps neither lift up nor intend to move deeper when we find a relatively stable basis at which we can educate ourselves as to principles and elements of geometric relationship in an ideal form.

Because if we travel deeper we would be moving out of the present subject as fast as we entered it and find ourselves in the class defining the concepts of physics which whilst interesting is not the same as the study of geometric relationship of simple shapes. Or if we lift up we would be moving towards the class applying mechanical formula to levers and pulleys which must be considered as too practical for our purposes. Instead if we maintain our present level we will be under the control of ancient masters such as Pythagoras, Archimedes and Euclid, those three being the founders of this school of thought. And informed by modern day masters such as Kepler, Galileo and Einstein, those three being central to all of our present knowledge base.

Further, I would make the point that at this sort of depth in terms of geometry the entire school is divided into those who make friends with the Elements of Euclid, On the Heavens of Aristotle and Timaeus of Plato and those who do not. Since all three books are very small and could all three together be read in one long afternoon, there is no reason to let them remain unfamiliar, even if nothing else written by the same authors was studied.

To clarify, the model of this system is as follows:

A.

1. Make a point.

2. Extend a line from the point.

3. Bisect the line through its centre.

4. Draw a third line equidistant from the point of the bisection such that the third line crosses each of the extensions of the first two lines and both ends of the third line are connected together.

5. Draw four connecting lines from the point where the first two lines touch the circumference of the circle.

That figure is the circle, square and triangle in relationship. It can be alternately described as "that geometric figure made by the circle circumscribing a square divided by four similar triangles".

B.

1. Go back to definitions. What are better definitions of point, line, plane, object, tetrahedron, hexahedron, octahedron, dodecahedron, icosahedron, sphere.

2. Clarify the nature of each of the defined terms. What can be learned by induction, analogy and anomaly. How are the

concepts of similarity, generality, familiarity, constancy each one useful in informing us as to the particulars and universal nature of the terms.

3. Attend towards the conceptual relationship between the elements of the given figure. That is with the intent to exhaust what can be known as to the constant relationship between a triangle of two fourty five degree angles and one ninety degree angle, the four similar such triangles that together make up any square, and the circle whose diameter is the diagonal between two extreme corners of the same square.

C.

1. Consider possible extensions of the same study in any direction and determine what are the subject matter that movement in that direction attend towards, for example, deeper being physics and more practical being mechanics.

2. Consider the science that informs the structure of geometry that being the mathematics of trigonometry, calculus and logic.

3. Notice more tenuous connections such as the musical notation system where the three, seven, twelve relationship is built in. Or the music of the spheres defined by Kepler where the relationship of the five prime solids is used to structure an astromomy. Or the elemental system that is based on the cosmology of Socrates.

Circumference = 22.2 144 146 907 9181

Radius = 3.53 553 390 593 2738

Diameter = 7.07 106 781 186 5475

Quink = 4.44 288 293 815 8362

Side of Square = 5

Square of side of square = 25

Diagonal of Square = 7.07 106 781 186 5475

Sum of square of other two sides = 50

Square Root of Fifty = 7.07 106 781 186 5475

Pi = 3.14 159 265 358 979

1. Given the length of the circumference of any circle.

2. Divide the length of the circumference by Quink to obtain the length of the side of square that the circle circumscribes.

4. Multiply the length of the side of square by four to obtain the length of the perimeter of square.

5. Multiply the length of one side of the square by itself to obtain Square of side of square.

6. Multiply the Square of side of square by two in order to obtain Sum of square of other two sides.

7. Discover the square root of the sum of square of other two sides to obtain the diameter of circle with the original circumference.

8. Divide the original circumference given in note one, by the diameter given in note seven, to obtain Pi.

CHAPTER NINETEEN.

Laws of Zero

This article states the laws of zero as groups zi, zii, ziii, ziv, zv and in each of the groups are contained four units designated as ' " "' "". If that is not what is clear on reading this article then please be sure to check the "view history" file in order to find the original article.

The particular matter that has prompted this note is that students in different schools are prohibited from dividing by zero. The error is to confuse can not with must not, and the difference between rules and orders. In this theory, rules are a close approximation to actual laws built in to the construction either of nature or alternatively of the nature of the system. Orders are commands that are applied for some political reason, that need have no reference to nature nor to truth.

The logical necessity of the sign labels and the system of mathematics is that we show division by zero, even if we are not exactly sure what that calculation gives. It is easily possible that division by zero gives a not obvious result similar to Q ! or e.

My own preferred answer is to say that division by zero either gives the result zero or alternatively does nothing and returns the original object number. Either answer is satisfactory to the logical necessity of showing the calculation.

The only wrong answer in this system that is not by its nature obviously incorrect requires some explanation.

That is to make the usual mistake of people who touch on infinity mathematics to think that calculations by zero may reflect calculations by infinity, leading to the compounded mistake that zero equals infinity.

Calculations by zero and calculations by infinity do not give equivalent answers, although they must give coherent non-contradictory answers.

What I think may be the correct line into the infinity mathematics is to hypothesise that zero divided by zero approximates infinity. The problem is that a/a=1 and 1/1=1 but we know that 0/0 =/= 1. So we say that 0/0=0, even though we cannot justify the arbitrary change in rules.

But if 0/0 = ∞ that would make sense in regard to the requirement to use a higher order language to explain a calculation that we cannot prove at the level of the given mathematical signlabels. And if we then show the set equivalence we obtain ɸ < ɸ => ∞.

Now that may actually work because we are saying if the empty set contains the empty set then infinity. Since that could be a necessary consequence of the empty set containing the empty set.

Furthermore, if 0/0=/=1 and 0/0=/=0 and 0/0=∞, then we prove 0=/=∞ and 1=/=∞, which we would like to do.

To help oneself understand the calculations intuitively the following approach is useful: That is, to specify the difference between nothing, unity and multitude. Given one can intuitively suppose that nothing, unity and multitude must each be different to the other then specific understandings are coherent and non-contradictory. We can describe the existential operator infinity is an unlimited multitude for some kind of quantity, which is different to the universal operator infinity which is unlimited multitude of all of some kind of quantity. It means we are able to think about different kinds of infinity as infinity is applied to different measures of quantity.

One appropriate correct definition of infinity is: Bounded unlimited multitude.

We say bounded, because particular. We say unlimited because if existant then without end. We say multitude because not nothing or unity.

In terms of minutae please note that our standard idea of a/a=1 only holds if a is a positive integer. If a is a negative integer or zero then all of the argumentation as to division of negatives by negatives or division by zero must be applied to

zi': $0 + 0 = 0$

zi": $0 - 0 = 0$

zi''': $0 \cdot 0 = 0$

zi'''': $0 / 0 = 0$

zii': $0 \cdot 1 = 0$

zii": $1 \cdot 0 = 0$

zii''': $0 / 1 = 0$

zii'''': $1 / 0 = 0$

ziii': $0 \cdot a = 0$

ziii": $a \cdot 0 = 0$

ziii''': $0 / a = 0$

ziii'''': $a / 0 = 0$

ziv': $0 \cdot {\sim}a = 0$

ziv": ${\sim}a \cdot 0 = 0$

ziv''': $0 / {\sim}a = 0$

ziv'''': ${\sim}a / 0 = 0$

zv': $1 - 1 = 0$

zv": $a - a = 0$

zv''': $\sim$a - $\sim$a = 0

zv'''': a + $\sim$a = 0

If the question is :"Why state the given laws of zero ?"

The problem is if not stated then we suppose that all in the whole world agree with the same not stated laws of zero even though we have no possible way of knowing what all in the whole world agree with.

An existing mistake is the earlier conditional statement that:

"What any one person knows, every person knows."

And "If one person knows, then everyone knows."

And "If everyone does not know, then no one knows."

Which then means that everyone knows the laws of thought.

But everyone does not know the laws of thought.

And as stated it is not necessary that all intelligent decision makers must agree with each of the individual laws as stated. Using the laws of zero in this document we can provide examples.

0 + 0 = 0 Zero plus zero is zero.

0 - 0 = 0 Zero minus zero is zero.

0 . 0 = 0 Zero multiplied by zero is zero.

0 / 0 = 0 Zero divided by zero is zero.

These laws define zero. And the nature of zero as defined by these laws is the identity of zero.

The question raised by the other laws is whether the zero that results from the calculation is the exact same identity as the zero of the laws that define zero.

And we must say definitely not. Without any doubt.

It requires we explain the concept of flavours used in hyperdimensional physics. The suggestion being that by applying a process of multiplying by one or a or not a we

302

change the spin of zero to generate a different flavour.

But because the minuteness of the difference does not offer itself on our measuring system we show each zero as exactly same.

Uniqueness of zero

There can only be one zero. For if z had the same properties, we would have

z + 0 = z

z + 0 = 0

Yes, okay. If z had the same properties as 0 then that would mean z = 0.

The properties of zero are as follows:

Zero is that entity which added to itself gives itself, subtracted from itself gives itself, multiplied by itself gives itself and divided by itself gives itself. If z has the same properties as zero then z = 0 and if z does not have the same properties as zero then z =/= 0.

If z does equal zero then z + 0 = z and z + 0 = 0 which only means we now know what the unknown variable z is equal to.

The law of identity states that two different entity are the same if in any function where one is used the other can be used to obtain the exact same result. So z = 0 if and only if the two sign labels can be exchanged in any area where one is used without altering the outcome of the calculation.

However this is useful if zero comes in different flavours. Because rather than saying the term (a - a) is the type of zero we are using in this instance instead we can say zv" = (a - a) and to obtain that particular zero we use the sign label zv".

Furthermore zv'" = (~a - ~a), ziii'" = (0/a) etc.

The reason we would do such is to distinguish between the

spin applied to zero in any instance.

To clarify the reasoning behind this notion it is useful to refer to some theory of Kant. Since my explanation of some of the theory of Kant is distorted in order to explain a particular matter it is not to suggest that Kant said what I am about to state. Merely that what I am about to state is derived from study of what Kant said.

The particular useful understanding is to distinguish between concept, idea and notion.

Concept, idea and notion can be considered similar in structure to element, atom and molecule.

Elements are the basic unit matter that do not reduce any further in the field to which they are relevant. Atoms are a unitary building block of different sorts depending on the specific elements involved in what quantity. Molecules are the first complex made from the combination of different atoms.

In the same way can we understand concept, idea and notion.

Where concepts are the similar to elements, and in this context can be understood as the specific individual sign labels: a , ~a, 0, 1, +, -, etc. As such the individual sign labels meet the definition of elements since they are a basic unit matter that do not reduce any further in the field to which they are relevant.

Where ideas are similar to atoms, and in this context can be understood as the specific individual calculation of zero. So therefore, zero minus zero equals zero is an idea that involves the synthesis of the concepts zero, minus and equals. We know that the idea of zero minus zero equals zero is a different idea to the idea that zero plus zero equals zero because the concepts of the second idea are not the same.

Therefore we then know that $0 - 0 = 0$ and $0 + 0 = 0$ are two different ideas, definitely not one idea.

When we combine the four different ideas:

0 + 0 = 0 Zero plus zero is zero.

0 - 0 = 0 Zero minus zero is zero.

0 . 0 = 0 Zero multiplied by zero is zero.

0 / 0 = 0 Zero divided by zero is zero.

Then we obtain a notion.

Where notions are similar to molecules and in this context can be understood as the synthesis of several coherent ideas involving related concepts.

The building from concepts to ideas to notions is called synthetic. The reduction from notions to ideas to concepts is called analytic.

Translating the laws of zero into the language of sets:

zi': $\phi \wedge \phi \Rightarrow \phi$

zi": $\phi \wedge \sim\phi \Rightarrow Q$

zi''': $\phi \vee \phi \Rightarrow \phi$

zi"": $\phi < \phi \Rightarrow \infty$

zii': $\phi \vee 1 \Rightarrow \phi$

zii": $1 \vee \phi \Rightarrow \phi$

zii''': $\phi < 1 \Rightarrow \phi$

zii"": $1 < \phi \Rightarrow \phi$

ziii': $\phi \vee a \Rightarrow \phi$

ziii": $a \vee \phi \Rightarrow \phi$

ziii''': $\phi < a \Rightarrow \phi$

ziii"": $a < \phi \Rightarrow \phi$

ziv': $\phi \vee \sim a \Rightarrow \phi$

ziv": $\sim a \vee \phi \Rightarrow \phi$

ziv''': ϕ < ~a => ϕ

ziv'''': ~a < ϕ => ϕ

zv': 1 ∧ ~1 => Q

zv'': a ∧ ~a => e

zv''': ~a ∧ ~(~a) => !ϕ

zv'''': a ∧ ~a => e

And showing the equivalence relationship of shape not meaning between the two different languages we obtain:

zi': 0 + 0 = 0 <=> ϕ ∧ ϕ => ϕ

zi'': 0 - 0 = 0 <=> ϕ ∧ ~ϕ => Q

zi''': 0 . 0 = 0 <=> ϕ ∨ ϕ => ϕ

zi'''': 0 / 0 = 0 <=> ϕ < ϕ => ∞

zii':0 . 1 = 0 <=> ϕ ∨ 1 => ϕ

zii'': 1 . 0 = 0 <=> 1 ∨ ϕ => ϕ

zii''': 0 / 1 = 0 <=> ϕ < 1 => ϕ

zii'''': 1 / 0 = 0 <=> 1 < ϕ => ϕ

ziii': 0 . a = 0 <=> ϕ ∨ a => ϕ

ziii'': a . 0 = 0 <=> a ∨ ϕ => ϕ

ziii''': 0 / a = 0 <=> ϕ < a => ϕ

ziii'''': a / 0 = 0 <=> a < ϕ => ϕ

ziv': 0 . ~a = 0 <=> ϕ ∨ ~a => ϕ

ziv'': ~a . 0 = 0 <=> ~a ∨ ϕ => ϕ

ziv''': 0 / ~a = 0 <=> ϕ < ~a => ϕ

ziv'''': ~a / 0 = 0 <=> ~a < ϕ => ϕ

zv': 1 - 1 = 0 <=> 1 ∧ ~1 => Q

zv'': a - a = 0 <=> a ∧ ~a => e

zv''': ~a - ~a = 0 <=> ~a ∧ ~(~a) => !ϕ

zv"": a + ~a = 0 <=> a ∧ ~a =

The person stood looking for the longest time at the thing he was looking for. A passer by asked if he could help. Oh, would you mind said the person. Can you see it? Its over there. Pointing with his finger at a location near some bushes.

Hold on, said the passer by, I need to get closer. Okay, said the person, if you see it, let me know. And by the way, we have to be very careful it does not get away. I know how to catch it, so if you see it just point it out to me and I will be ready. Sure, said the passer by.

They both stood, straining their eyes in concentration trying to see the thing they were looking for, which another person thought was quite interesting so they came over to see if they could find out what was going on.

Oh, we are looking for something over there, said the passer by. We think it is hiding in the bushes. I have very good eyesight said the third person. If it is hiding in the bushes I assure you it will not escape my attention. Yes, said the passer by, but don't startle it or it may escape. Apparently there is a very clever way of catching it, so when you see it, just let us know and we will do the rest. Okay, said the other person.

Before too long there was a small crowd of people all gathered around the general area looking for the thing they were looking for.

The original person who had been looking in that direction had moved a small distance away and was looking at the crowd of people looking for the thing.

What are they looking at? asked somebody to the person. I am not quite sure, said the person, but it must be important to get so much attention. I think someone said that if they see it they can capture it, but they are not sure what it looks like, nor the exact method for capturing it when they see it.

Well I am a doctor so if they need the trained mind to assist in the exact method of capturing the thing I am sure I can show them how to do it. I had better let them know.

So then the doctor went over and spoke to the crowd of people and explained that he would know the method of capturing the thing when they saw where it was. That is a relief said the original passer by. We knew we would know it when we saw it, but we had no idea how to capture it. So it is lucky that you are here.

Say no more said the doctor. Just point it out when you can and we will take it from there.

There it is, said one of the people in the crowd. I saw it move just then. Hold on, I will show you exactly where it was. Yes, but what did it look like, said another person. If we knew what it looked like, then we would be more likely to see it for ourselves. Maybe it was nothing said a different person.

Don't say it was nothing, said the person who had seen it move. I definitely saw it move I tell you. There it is said someone else. It does move doesn't it. That is how we will catch it. Maybe we can't see it unless it moves, but when it moves we can see it. And if we can see it we can capture it.

The doctor with his trained mind decided it would be easier to know it if they saw the thing if they could determine where specifically it was hiding. So he thought if they could outline exactly the area within which the thing was hiding they would be in a better position to see it. For this reason he obtained a long length of rope and extended it in a large circle around the general area that everyone was looking at. That is a good idea, said another person. It is definitely inside that circle.

Then to determine exactly where within the circle the thing was they placed four posts evenly spaced around the circumference of the circle and then tied two ropes diagonally across the diameter of the circle to make four quadrants. And then to make it really easy to work out which quadrant of the circle the thing was hiding in they connected each of the posts together by a rope to make a square.

Immediately the person who had seen it move spoke up and said that it was in the upper right quadrant. And a different person said no it isn't, they thought it was in the lower left quadrant. But the person who had seen it move said yes, that is where it was before it moved. But it moved from the lower left quadrant to the upper right quadrant.

So now everybody focused their attention on the upper right quadrant to make sure it didn't get away.

How big is it, asked someone who had just turned up. Well it is smaller than one quadrant of the circle, said another, but apart from that we are not sure. Well if we put a rope from each corner of the upper right quadrant diagonally to the opposite corner we can work out where in the upper right quadrant it is.

Only if you are sure, said the person who had seen it move.

Is it smaller than one of the quadrants of the upper right quadrant? asked one of the observers.

Hold on, let's jump on it, said one of the other others. What do you mean? said another.

Well, if it is smaller than one of the quadrants of the upper right quadrant, then if all of us jump on it at the same time one of us is bound to catch hold of it. The important thing is if you get hold of it don't let it go until the rest of us have been able to tie it down. We should all agree to jump on a different quadrant of the upper right quadrant and then no matter which bit it is hiding in it won't be able to escape.

Good idea, they all agreed. At the same time then, let's jump on it.

CHAPTER TWENTY.

Zero, Unity and Infinity.

Zero signifies a place holder that is empty.

Unity signifies existant object.

Infinity signifies multitude.

The definitions are not each of the same order, since the nature of the matter is not understandable without Q.

Q signifies the quantum indefinite.

For this reason, the matter of this discourse will be presented in a manner consistent with its own nature, which is non-linear.

Each definition will be provided in a simplest possible term to start with, and then as required each definition will be expanded in order to clarify the understanding that is developed.

$1.1 = 1$

$0.0 = 0$

$\infty.\infty = \infty$

If $a.b = c$ then $c/a = b$ and $c/b = a$

If $1.1 = 1$ then $1/1 = 1$

If $0.0 = 0$ then $0/0 = 0$

If $\infty.\infty = \infty$ then $\infty/\infty = \infty$

But:

If $1.\infty = \infty$ then that means $\infty/\infty = 1$ and $\infty/1 = \infty$

Therefore infinity divided by infinity gives either unity or infinity, but it does not give zero.

And:

If $0.\infty=0$ then that means $0/0=\infty$ and $0/\infty=0$

Therefore zero divided by zero gives either zero or infinity, but it does not give unity.

And:

If $1.0=0$ then that means $0/1=0$ and $0/0=1$

Therefore zero divided by zero gives unity and zero divided by unity gives zero, but neither answer gives infinity.

However that means zero divided by zero gives three possible answers, that is infinity, unity or zero.

And infinity divided by infinity gives two possible answers, that is infinity or unity.

And unity divided by unity gives one possible answer, that is unity.

The basic equation of modern physics is $f=ma$. Force is equal to mass multiplied by acceleration.

The equation $f=ma$ is dependent on the earlier structure: If $a.b=c$ then $c/a=b$ and $c/b=a$

This point is quite difficult to grasp if it is the first time of considering the matter, and many physicists who completely understand the fundamental equation of modern physics, do not necessarily understand the more fundamental matter on which the equation rests.

Only if it is true that: If $a.b=c$ then $c/a=b$ and $c/b=a$

Then may it be true that: If $m.a=f$ and $f/m=a$ and $f/a=m$

Therefore, the point that I would like to make clear here is that a more fundamental subject exists of which the equation:

a.b=c then c/a=b and c/b=a

is one example of that more fundamental subject.

The reason that the matter has to be clarified in this sort of way is because the fabric of the subject is not so obvious to the enquirer.

So whereas we can immediately comprehend the importance of such a prestigious equation as f=ma, the fact that such a prestigious equation is based on some other thing does not immediately hold the attention.

First statement:

a means "a is true" Affirmation. Or "a" means an entity in the universe of discourse that may be a genus or species, or may be a class or member of class, or may be a set or element of set.Or "a" means everything that is "a" in our universe of discourse.

~a means "a is false" Negation. Or "~a" means everything that is "not a" in the universe of discourse. Or "~a" means some entity that is an element of everything that is not "a" in the universe of discourse.

b means "b is true" Affirmation. Or some entity not a in the universe of discourse that may be defined in a similar manner to the way in which a is defined.

~b means "b is false" Negation. Or some entity not b in the universe of discourse that may be defined in relation to b in a similar manner to the way in which not a is defined in relation to a.

a v b means "either a is true, or b is true, or both" Either one or the other or both.

a ∧ b means "both a and b are true" And. Both one and the other.

a => b means "if a is true, then b is true". If - then. If set of elements then any element of such a set.

a =/=> b means "if a is true, then b is false". If - then not . If set of elements then not any element of a different set.

a < b means "since b is true, then a is true." Since - then. Since the way this system uses the inclusion sign label may be inconsistent with the way other systems use the same sign label it requires further clarification. My definition is as follows: (a < b) ∧ (b < c) => a < c. That is to say, if a contains b, and b contains c, then a contains c. I am using the sign label as an arrow to show that the species is part of the genus or that the element is contained by the set.

a /< b means "since b is true, then a is false." Since - not then. If member of a class, then not any different class.

a <=> b means "a and b are either both true or both false" If and only if. Only if both and not either one without the other.

a <=/=> b means "a is true and b is false, or a is false and b is true". Either one or the other not both.

φ means the empty set, or the class whose membership is none.

1 means the unity set, or the class whose membership is itself.

e means everything in the given universe of discourse.

! means not not. Or in regard to a single entity it means neither entity nor not entity.

Q means neither the unity set nor the empty set. Or an indefinite variable.

Second statement:

⊙ means the universal abstraction. ⊙ => Ʒ ∧ e

The universal abstraction is the universe of discourse and everything in it.

ψ means the universal operator. ψa => a ∧ ~a ∧ !a

The universal operator is every and all of some possible

entity.

Э means the existential operator. Эa => a v ~a v !a

The existential operator is some possible entity of all such entity.

3 means the universe of discourse. 3 => e

The universe of discourse is a restricted parameter bounded by the terms of meaning.

φ means the empty set. φ => 3 ∧ ~e

The empty set is the class whose membership is none or the set of no elements.

1 means the unity set. 1 => a < a

The unity set is the class whose membership is itself or the set that contains itself as element.

e means everything in the universe of discourse. e => a ∧ ~a

Everything in the universe of discourse is only and all the sign labels used.

Q means not the empty set and not the unity set. Q => ~φ ∧ ~1

Not the empty set and not the unity set is the indefinite variable or possible improbable.

! means not not entity. !a => ~(~a)

Not not entity is neither entity nor not entity.

Third statement:

46. ⊙ => 3 ∧ e

47. ψa => a ∧ ~a ∧ !a

48. Эa => a v ~a v !a

49. 3 => e

50. φ => 3 ∧ ~e

51. 1 => a < a

52. $e => a \wedge \sim a$

53. $Q => \sim\phi \wedge \sim 1$

54. $!a => \sim(\sim a)$

55. $\odot => 3 \wedge e < (Q \wedge !e) \vee [(\phi \wedge 1) \wedge (\psi \wedge Э)]$

Fourth statement:

zi': $\phi \wedge \phi => \phi$ zi": $\phi \wedge \sim\phi => Q$ zi''': $\phi \vee \phi => \phi$ zi'''': $\phi < \phi => \infty$

zii': $\phi \vee 1 => \phi$ zii": $1 \vee \phi => \phi$ zii''': $\phi < 1 => \phi$ zii'''': $1 < \phi => \phi$

ziii': $\phi \vee a => \phi$ ziii": $a \vee \phi => \phi$ ziii''': $\phi < a => \phi$ ziii'''': $a < \phi => \phi$

ziv': $\phi \vee \sim a => \phi$ ziv": $\sim a \vee \phi => \phi$ ziv''': $\phi < \sim a => \phi$ ziv'''': $\sim a < \phi => \phi$

zv': $1 \wedge \sim 1 => Q$ zv": $a \wedge \sim a => e$ zv''': $\sim a \wedge \sim(\sim a) => !\phi$ zv'''': $a \wedge \sim a => e$

Fifth statement:

1. $a => a$ If a, then a.

2. $\sim a => \sim a$ If not a, then not a.

3. $a =/=> \sim a$ If a, then not not a.

4. $a \wedge \phi => a$ If a and the empty set, then a.

5. $a \wedge \sim\phi => a$ If a and not the empty set, then a.

6. $\sim a \wedge \phi => \sim a$ If not a and the empty set, then not a.

7. $\sim a \wedge \sim\phi => \sim a$ If not a and not the empty set, then not a.

8. $a \vee 1 => a$ If a or the unity set, then a.

9. $a < 1 => a$ If a includes the unity set, then a.

10. $\sim a \vee 1 => \sim a$ If not a or the unity set, then not a.

11. $\sim a < 1 => \sim a$ If not a includes the unity set, then not a.

12. $a \vee \phi => \phi$ If a or the empty set, then the empty set.

13. $a < \phi => \phi$ If a includes the empty set, then the empty set.

14. $\sim a \vee \phi => \phi$ If not a or the empty set, then the empty set.

15. ~a < φ => φ If not a includes the empty set, then the empty set.

16. a ∧ 1 => 1 ∧ a If a and the unity set, then the unity set and a.

17. a ∧ ~1 => Q ∧ a If a and not the unity set, then Q and a.

18. ~a ∧ 1 => 1 ∧ ~a If not a and the unity set, then the unity set and not a.

19. ~a ∧ ~1 => Q ∧ ~a If not a and not the unity set, then Q and not a.

20. φ ∧ a => a If the empty set and a, then a.

21. φ ∧ ~a => ~a If the empty set and not a, then not a.

22. φ ∧ ~(~a) => !a If the empty set and not not a, then !a.

23. a ∧ a => a ∧ a If a and a, then a and a.

24. a v a => a If a or a, then a.

25. a ∧ ~a => e If a and not a, then everything in the universe of discourse.

26. a < a => 1 If a includes a, then the unity set.

27. a v ~a => Q If a or not a, then Q.

28. a ∧ ~(~a) => a ∧ !a If a and not not a, then a and !a.

29. a < ~(~a) => a < !a If a includes not not a, then a includes entity neither a nor not a.

30. a v b => b v a If a or b, then b or a.

31. a ∧ b => b ∧ a If a and b, then b and a.

32. (a ∧ b) ∧ c => a ∧ (b ∧ c) If term a and b term and c, then a and term b and c.

33. (a v b) v c => a v (b v c) If term a or b term or c, then a or term b or c.

34. a ∧ (b v c) => (a ∧ b) v (a ∧ c) If a and term b or c, then term a and b term or term a and c.

35. a v (b ∧ c) => (a v b) ∧ (a v c) If a or term b and c, then term a or b term and term a or c.

36. ~(a ∧ b) => ~a ∧ ~b If not term a and b, then not a and not b.

37. ~(a v b) => ~a v ~b If not term a or b, then not a or not b.

38. a < b => a < b If a includes b, then a includes b.

39. a ∧ ~b => ~b ∧ a If a and not b, then not b and a.

40. (a ∧ ~b) ∧ ~c => a ∧ (~b ∧ ~c) If term a and not b term and not c, then a and term not b and not c.

41. (a < b) < c => a < (b < c) If term a includes b term includes c, then a includes term b includes c.

42. a ∧ ~(b < c) => (a ∧ ~b) < (a ∧ ~c)

If a and not term b inc c, then term a and not b term inc term a and not c.

43. a < (b ∧ ~c) => (a < b) ∧ ~(a < c)

If a inc term b and not c, then term a inc b term and not term a inc c.

44. ~(a ∧ ~b) => ~a ∧ ~(~b) If not term a and not b, then not a and not not b.

45. ~(a < b) => ~a < ~b In not term a inc b, then not a inc not b.

Sixth statement:

The above ideas 1 through 45. Each idea the synthesis of individual concepts. The synthesis of ideas a notion.

Correct as stated and if correctly stated then true or not. But then heuristic. Correct as stated or not, does not matter. At least we can see a complete notion. And we can see the forty five ideas that combine to provide the notion. And we see we have a small specific number of concepts to consider.

Take any one idea. Specify idea 26. It is easy to see that idea 26 is not correct as stated, since it is deliberately not giving all the possible correct answers. Idea 26 says a divided by a is unity. Which we can expand into word language to say that if a thing is contained by itself then the result is unity. But that is only true if a is a positive integer. The reason we say a/a=1 is because 1/1=1, 2/2=1, 3/3=1, so then a is any positive integer. But a could be a negative integer. Then a/a = 0 if any negative integer divided by itself is zero or a/a = b if any negative integer divided by itself is a different unknown variable not a. But a could be zero. Then a/a = ∞ if zero divided by zero is infinity. But then we would have to say ∃∞ and not the ψ∞ . Therefore a / a = ∃∞ which is the particular infinity made when the empty set contains itself, since it means a continuum of nothing containing nothing in an unlimited way.

Translated into sets is "a <=> φ, ∧ φ < φ => ∃∞ ∧~ ψ∞, => a < a => ∃∞ ∧~ ψ∞."

Which says if and only if a is the empty set, and, the empty set containing the empty set is one species of infinity and not the genus of that type of infinity, then a containing a is one species of infinity and not the genus of that type of infinity.

And if "a <=> +n, ∧ +n < +n => 1, => a < a => 1."

Which says if and only if a is a positive integer, where +n is any positive integer, then given any positive integer containing itself gives unity, if a containing a then unity.

And if "a <=> -n, ∧ -n < -n => b, => a < a => b."

Which says if and only if a is a negative integer, where -n is any negative integer, then given any negative integer containing itself gives an unknown variable b, where b is any unknown variable, if a containing a then unknown variable b.

Therefore, the notion that can be developed from idea 26 is as follows:

26.i - "a <=> φ, ∧ φ < φ => ∃∞ ∧~ ψ∞, => a < a => ∃∞ ∧~ ψ∞."

26.ii - "a <=> +n, ∧ +n < +n => 1, => a < a => 1."

26.iii - "a <=> -n, ∧ -n < -n => b, => a < a => b."

26.iv - "a/a = 1 or ∞ or b".

Seventh statement:

Quantum indefinite, neither entity nor not entity, existential operator, universal operator, everything in the universe of discourse, empty set, unity set, infinity.

The sixth statement offers a preferred line in terms of correction of any aspect of the ideas as stated.

The sense would be to not adjust any of the stated ideas one to forty five at the level they are stated.

But instead to take any one idea, each one after the other, in any order and specify idea ten, fifteen or thirty two or whatever.

And then to challenge that one idea, either to show that it is false as stated, or that it is not entirely correct, or alternatively to prove that as stated it is entirely correct and true.

In doing so, one can prove using the language of the system as demonstrated for idea 26:

26.i - "a <=> φ, ∧ φ < φ => Ǝ∞ ∧~ ψ∞, => a < a => Ǝ∞ ∧~ ψ∞."

26.ii - "a <=> +n, ∧ +n < +n => 1, => a < a => 1."

26.iii - "a <=> -n, ∧ -n < -n => b, => a < a => b."

26.iv - "a/a = 1 or ∞ or b".

In this way, if the original ideas are not adjusted at the level they are provided, then it will enable different decision makers the freedom to check the truth and correctness of the propositions, each from a common ground. That will then mean that it is not necessary for two different decision makers to assign the same decision as to truth or falsity or neither true nor false to any one idea.

CHAPTER TWENTY ONE.

After 11.12.13.

That is, after the date Eleven December Twenty Thirteen.

I could do the golden squiggley bit.

As usual, some of this is original to these articles. Meaning I don't think some of these formulae as stated are presently available anywhere else. Also my statement of formula that are available elsewhere are not normally signed the same way as elsewhere.

One Thing, Ten Laws.

One.

One plus the golden squiggley bit equals the golden squiggley bit squared.

$1 + x = x \cdot x$

One plus x equals x multiplied by x.

One plus itself(the thing), gives itself multiplied by itself.

Two.

$x = (x \cdot x) - 1$

x equals x squared minus one.

Three.

$1 = [(x \cdot x) - x]$

A number such that subtracting one of its roots from the

square gives unity.

Four.

$0 = [(x \cdot x) - x - 1]$

The square minus one root minus unity gives zero.

Five.

$(a : b) <=> (b : a + b)$

As the less is to the greater so the greater is to the totality.

Six.

$(b / a) <=> (a + b) / b$

$(x / 1) <=> (1 + x) / x$

As the larger is divided by the smaller, so the whole is divided by the larger.

Seven.

If two opposite sides of a rectangle are both one unit length,

then the other two sides are both one point six one eight zero three three units length.

Eight.

One plus the square root of five then divide by two.

If the square is five, then its root is 2.2360679775.

Plus one equals 3.2360679775.

Divided by two gives 1.61803398875.

$x = 1.618033$

Nine.

One divided by two plus the square root of five divided by two.

Ten.

$x = [1 + (1 / x)]$

$(x - 1) = (1 / x)$

$[(1 / x) - x] = (-1)$

Then Six Puzzles:

a. $[(x . x) - 1] <=> [1 + (1 / x)] => x$

b. $(x - 1) = (1 / x)$

c. $1 = [(x . x) - x]$

d. $x = (x . x) - 1$

e. $1 + x = x . x$

f. $(x / 1) <=> (1 + x) / x$

Are the above six puzzles correctly stated?

And if correctly stated, are they all true, or are any false?

If you find they are all true, then take the six puzzles first. It seems to me that there is no proper understanding possible of the puzzles in some sense, no matter what degree of understanding one obtains. Some things are like that.

Deep Puzzles:

a. $x = [(1 + x) / x]$

b. $x = [1 + (1 / x)]$

c. $x = (x . x) - 1$

d. $1 = [(x . x) - x]$

e. $1 = [x - (1 / x)]$

f. $(-1) = [(1 / x) - x]$

g. $(-1) = [x - (x . x)]$

h. $0 = 1 + [x - (x . x)]$

i. $0 = 1 + [(1 / x) - x]$

One.

First then take a universal negative with the terms A and B.

If no B is A, neither can any A be B. For if some A (say C) were B, it would not be true that no B is A; for C is a B.

1. (ψB < ~A) => (ψA < ~B)

2. (ƎA < ψC) ∧ (ƎC < ƎB) =/=> [(ψB < ~A) <= (ƎC < ƎB)]

But if every B is A then some A is B. For if no A were B, then no B could be A. But we assumed that every B is A.

3. (ψB < ƎA) => (ƎA < ψB)

4. (ψA < ~B) => (ψB < ~A)

5. (ψB < ƎA)

Similarly too, if the premiss is particular.

For if some B is A, then some of the As must be B. For if none were, then no B would be A. But if some B is not A, there is no necessity that some of the As should not be B.

6. (ƎB < ƎA) => (ƎA < ƎB)

7. (ψA < ~B) => (ψB < ~A)

8. (ƎB < ~A) => [(ƎA < ƎB) v (ψA < ~B)]

Two.

If A is predicated of all B, and B of all C, A must be predicated of all C:

1. (ƎA < ψB) ∧ (ƎB < ψC) => (ƎA < ψC)

Similarly also, if A is predicated of no B, and B of all C, it is necessary that no C will be A.

2. (ψA < ~B) ∧ (ƎB < ψC) => (ψA < ~C)

Three.

Let all B be A and some C be B. Then it is necessary that some C is A.

1. (ψB < ƎA) ∧ (ƎC < ƎB) => (ƎC < ƎA)

And if no B is A but some C is B, it is necessary that some C is not A.

2. (ψB < ~A) ∧ (ƎC < ƎB) => (ƎC < ~A)

So there will be a perfect syllogism.

Four.

Let A be predicated of no B, but of all C.

1. $(\psi A < {\sim}B) \wedge (\exists A < \psi C)$

Since, then, the negative relation is convertible, B will belong to no A.

2. $(\psi A < {\sim}B) <=> (\psi B < {\sim}A) <= [(\psi < {\sim}) <=> ({\sim} < \psi)]$

But A was assumed to belong to all C.

3. $(\exists A < \psi C)$

Consequently B will belong to no C.

4. $(\psi B < {\sim}C)$

This has already been proved.

Again if A belongs to all B, but to no C, then B will belong to no C.

5. $(\exists A < \psi B) \wedge (\psi A < {\sim}C) => (\psi B < {\sim}C)$

For if A belongs to no C, C belongs to no A.

6. $(\psi A < {\sim}C) => (\psi C < {\sim}A)$

But A (as was said) belongs to all B.

7. $(\exists A < \psi B)$

C then will belong to no B.

8. $(\psi C < {\sim}B)$

For the first figure has again been formed.

But since the negative relation is convertible, B will belong to no C.

9. $(\psi C < {\sim}B) => (\psi B < {\sim}C)$

Thus it will be the same syllogism that proves both conclusions.

Five.

For if A belongs to no B, but to some C, it is necessary that B does not belong to some C.

1. (ψA < ~B) ∧ (ЭA < ЭC) => (ЭC < ~B)

For since the negative statement is convertible, B will belong to no A.

2. [(ψA < ~B) => (ψB < ~A)] <= [(ψ < ~) <=> (~ < ψ)]

But A was admitted to belong to some C.

3. (ЭA < ЭC)

Therefore B will not belong to some C.

4. (ЭC < ~B)

For the result is reached by means of the first figure.

Again if A belongs to all B, but not to some C, it is necessary that B does not belong to some C.

5. (ЭA < ψB) ∧ (ψA < ~C) => (ψB < ~C)

For if B belongs to all C, and A is predicated also of all B, A must belong to all C.

6. (ЭB < ψC) ∧ (ЭA < ψB) => (ЭA < ψC)

But we assumed that A does not belong to some C.

7. (ψA < ~C)

And if A belongs to all B but not to all C, we shall conclude that B does not belong to all C.

8. (ЭA < ψB) ∧ (ЭC < ~A) => (ЭC < ~B)

The proof is the same as the above.

Six.

Again let the premisses be affirmative, and let the major premiss as before be universal.

Let A belong to all B and to some C.

1. (ЭA < ψB) ∧ (ЭA < ЭC)

It is possible then for B to belong to all C or to no C.

2. (ƎB < ψC) v (ψB < ~C)

But if the minor premiss is universal, and A belongs to no C, and not to some B.

3. (ψA < ~C) ∧ (ƎA < ~B)

Then it is possible for B to belong either to all C or to no C.

4. (ƎB < ψC) v (ψB < ~C)

Seven.

If they are universal, whenever both A and B belong to C, it follows that A will necessarily belong to some B.

1. (ƎA < ψC) ∧ (ƎB < ψC) => (ƎA < ƎB)

For, since the affirmative statement is convertible, C will belong to some B.

2. [(ƎB < ψC) <=> (ψC < ƎB)] <= [(Ǝ < ψ) <=> (ψ < Ǝ)]

Consequently since A belongs to all C, and C to some B, A must belong to some B.

3. (ƎA < ψC) ∧ (ψC < ƎB) => (ƎA < ƎB)

For a syllogism in the first figure is produced.

Eight.

For if both A and B belong to all C, should one of the Cs, such as D, be taken.

1. [(ƎA < ψC) ∧ (ƎB < ψC)] ∧ (ƎC < ψD)

Both A and B will belong to this, and thus A will belong to some B.

2. [(ƎA < ψD) ∧ (ƎB < ψD)] => (ƎA < ƎB)

If B belongs to all C, and A to no C, there will be a syllogism to prove that A will necessarily not belong to some B.

3. (ƎB < ψC) ∧ (ψA < ~C) => (ƎB < ~A)

Nine.

For if B belongs to all C, A to some C, A must belong to some B.

1. (ЭB < ψC) ∧ (ЭA < ЭC) => (ЭA < ЭB)

For since the affirmative statement is convertible C will belong to some A.

2. [(ЭA < ЭC) <=> (ЭC < ЭA)] <= [(Э < Э) <=> (Э < Э)]

Consequently since B belongs to all C, and C to some A, B must also belong to some A.

3. (ЭB < ψC) ∧ (ЭC < ЭA) => (ЭB < ЭA)]

Therefore A must belong to some B.

4. (ЭA < ЭB)]

Ten.

Again if B belongs to some C, and A to all C, A must belong to some B.

1. (ЭB < ЭC) ∧ (ЭA < ψC) => (ЭA < ЭB)

For if B belongs to all C, but A does not belong to some C, it is necessary that A does not belong to some B.

2. (ЭB < ψC) ∧ (ЭA < ~C) => (ЭA < ~B)

For if A belongs to all B, and B belongs to all C, then A will belong to all C.

3. (ЭA < ψB) ∧ (ЭB < ψC) => (ЭA < ψC)

But we assumed that it did not.

4. (ЭA < ~C)

Eleven.

But if the negative term is universal, whenever the major is negative and the minor affirmative there will be a syllogism.

For if A belongs to no C, and B belongs to some C, A will not belong to some B.

1. (ψA < ~C) ∧ (ЭB < ЭC) => (ЭA < ~B)

Twelve.

If A belongs to all or some B, and B belongs to no C.

1. $[(ЭA < ψB) v (ЭA < ЭB)] ∧ (ψB < {\sim}C)$

Then if the premisses are converted it is necessary that C does not belong to some A.

2. $[(ψB < ЭA) v (ЭB < ЭA)] ∧ (ψC < {\sim}B)$

3. $(ЭA < {\sim}C)$

Thirteen.

In the last figure, if A and B belong to all C, it follows that A belongs to some B.

1. $(ЭA < ψC) ∧ (ЭB < ψC) => (ЭA < ЭB)$

For if A belonged to no B, and B belongs to all C, A would belong to no C.

2. $(ψA < {\sim}B) ∧ (ЭB < ψC) => (ψA < {\sim}C)$

But (as we stated) it belongs to all C.

3. $(ЭA < ψC)$

Fourteen.

If A belongs to all B, and B to some C, it follows that A belongs to some C.

1. $(ЭA < ψB) ∧ (ЭB < ЭC) => (ЭA < ЭC)$

For if it belonged to no C, and belongs to all B, then B will belong to no C.

2. $(ψA < {\sim}C) ∧ (ЭA < ψB) => (ψB < {\sim}C)$

For if A belongs to no B, and B belongs to some C, A will not belong to some C.

3. $(ψA < {\sim}B) ∧ (ЭB < ЭC) => (ЭC < {\sim}A)$

For if it belonged to all C, and belongs to no B, then B will belong to no C.

4. $(ЭA < ψC) ∧ (ψA < {\sim}B) => (ψB < {\sim}C)$

Fifteen.

First let the universal be necessary, and let A belong to all B necessarily, but let B simply belong to some C.

1. (ƎA < ψB) ∧ (ƎB < ƎC)

It is necessary then that A belongs to some C necessarily.

2. (ƎA < ƎC)

For C falls under B, and A was assumed to belong necessarily to all B.

3. (ƎB < ƎC) ∧ (ƎA < ψB)

Sixteen.

First let the negative be necessary, let A be possible of no B, and simply belong to C.

1. (ψB < ~A) ∧ (ƎA < ψC)

Since then the negative statement is convertible, B is possible of no A.

2. [(ψB < ~A) => (ψA < ~B)] <= [(ψ < ~) => (~ < ψ)]

But A belongs to all C.

3. (ƎA < ψC)

Consequently B is possible of no C.

4. (ψB < ~C)

For C falls under A.

5. (ψC < ƎA)

Seventeen.

The same result would be obtained if the minor premiss were negative.

For if A is possible be of no C, then C is possible of no A.

1. (ψA < ~C) => (ψC < ~A)

But A belongs to all B.

2. (ƎA < ψB)

Consequently C is possible of none of the Bs.

3. (ψC < ~B)

For again we have obtained the first figure.

Neither then is B possible of C.

4. (ψB < ~C)

Eighteen.

Further, if the conclusion is necessary, it follows that C necessarily does not belong to some A.

1. (ψC < ~A)

For if B necessarily belongs to no C, C will necessarily belong to no B.

2. (ψB < ~C) => (ψC < ~B)

But B at any rate must belong to some A, if it is true (as was assumed) that A necessarily belongs to all B.

3. (ƎB < ƎA) <= (ƎA < ψB)

Consequently it is necessary that C does not belong to some A.

4.(ψC < ~A)

Nineteen.

First then let the negative premiss be both universal and necessary.

Let it be possible for no B that A should belong to it, and let A simply belong to some C.

1. (ψB < ~A) ∧ (ƎC < ƎA)

Since the negative statement is convertible, it will be possible for no A that B should belong to it.

2. (ψB < ~A) => (ψA < ~B)

But A belongs to some C.

3. (ƎC < ƎA)

Consequently B necessarily does not belong to some of the Cs.

4. (ЭB < ~C)

Twenty.

Again let the affirmative premiss be both universal and necessary, and let the major premiss be affirmative.

If then A necessarily belongs to all B, but does not belong to some C, it is clear that B will not belong to some C, but not necessarily.

1. (ЭA < ψB) ∧(ЭC < ~A) => (ЭC < ~B)

Twenty One.

First let both the premisses be affirmative, and let A and B belong to all C, and let AC be necessary.

1. (ЭA < ψC) ∧ (ЭB < ψC)

Since then B belongs to all C, C also will belong to some B, because the universal is convertible into the particular.

2. [(ЭB < ψC) => (ЭC < ЭB)] <= [(Э < ψ) => (Э < Э)]

Consequently if A belongs necessarily to all C, and C belongs to some B, it is necessary that A should belong to some B also.

3. (ЭA < ψC) ∧ (ЭC < ЭB) => (ЭA < ЭB)

For B is under C.

4. (ЭC < ЭB)

The first figure then is formed.

Twenty Two.

A similar proof will be given also if BC is necessary.

For C is convertible with some A.

1. (ЭC < ЭA) => (ЭA < ЭC)

Consequently if B belongs necessarily to all C, it will belong necessarily also to some A.

2. (ЭB < ψC) => (ЭB < ЭA)

Twenty Three.

331

Again let AC be negative, BC affirmative, and let the negative premiss be necessary.

1. (ψA < ~C) ∧ (ƎB < ƎC)

Since then C is convertible with some B, but A necessarily belongs to no C, A will necessarily not belong to some B either.

2. (ƎB < ƎC) ∧ (ψA < ~C) => (ƎA < ~B)

For B is under C.

3. (ƎB < ƎC)

Twenty Four.

But if the affirmative is necessary, the conclusion will not be necessary.

For suppose BC is affirmative and necessary, while AC is negative and not necessary.

1. (ƎB < ƎC) ∧ (ψA < ~C)

Since then the affirmative is convertible, C also will belong to some B necessarily.

2. (ƎB < ƎC) => (ƎC < ƎB)

Consequently if A belongs to none of the Cs, while C belongs to some of the Bs, A will not belong to some of the Bs-but not of necessity.

3. (ψA < ~C) ∧ (ƎB < ƎC) => (ƎA < ~B)

Twenty Five.

If then it is necessary that B should belong to all C, and A falls under C, it is necessary that B should belong to some A.

1. (ƎB < ψC) ∧ (ƎA < ƎC) => (ƎB < ƎA)

For if it is not possible that A should belong to any C, but B belongs to some C, it is necessary that A should not belong to some B.

2. (ψA < ~C) ∧ (ƎB < ƎC) => (ƎB < ~A)

Twenty Six.

Whenever A may possibly belong to all B, and B to all C.

1. [(ЭA < ψB) v (ЭA < ЭB)] ∧ (ЭB < ψC)

There will be a perfect syllogism to prove that A may possibly belong to all C.

2. (ЭA < ψC) v (ЭA < ЭC)

Similarly if it is possible for A to belong no B, and for B to belong to all C, then it is possible for A to belong to no C.

3. [(ψA < ~B) v (ЭA < ~B)] ∧ (ЭB < ψC)

4. (ψA < ~C) v (ЭA < ~C)

For if A is possible for all B, and B for some C, then A is possible for some C.

5. {[(ЭA < ψB) v (ЭA < ЭB)] ∧ (ЭB < ЭC)} => [(ЭA < ψC) v (ЭA < ЭC)]

Twenty Seven.

Again if A may belong to no B, and B may belong to some of the Cs, it is necessary that A may possibly not belong to some of the Cs.

1. [(ψA < ~B) v (ЭA < ~B)] ∧ (ЭB < ЭC) => [(ψA < ~C) v (ЭA < ~C)]

Twenty Eight.

Let A be possible for all B, and let B belong to all C.

1. [(ЭA < ψB) v (ЭA < ЭB)] ∧ (ЭB < ψC)

Since C falls under B, and A is possible for all B, clearly it is possible for all C also.

2. {(ЭB < ψC) ∧ [(ЭA < ψB) v (ЭA < ЭB)]} => [(ЭA < ψC) v (ЭA < ЭC)]

So a perfect syllogism results.

Twenty Nine.

Likewise if the premiss AB is negative, and the premiss BC is affirmative.

The former stating possible, the latter simple attribution.

A perfect syllogism results proving that A possibly belongs to no C.

1. [(ψA < ~B) v (ƎA < ~B)] ^ (ƎB < ψC) => [(ψA < ~C) v (ƎA < ~C)]

Thirty.

First we must state that if B's being follows necessarily from A's being.

1. A < B

Then B's possibility will follow necessarily from A's possibility.

2. [(A <= B) v (A => B v ~B)] ^ (~A => ~B)

Suppose, the terms being so related, that A is possible, and B is impossible.

3. (A v ~A) ^ ~B

If then that which is possible, when it is possible for it to be, might happen.

4. (A v ~A) => (A v ~A)

And if that which is impossible, when it is impossible, could not happen.

5. ~B => ~B

And if at the same time A is possible and B impossible.

6. (A v ~A) ^ ~B

It would be possible for A to happen without B, and if to happen, then to be.

7. [(A ^ ~B) v (~A ^ ~B)] => [(A < A) ^ (A => A)]

For that which has happened, when it has happened, is.

8. (A => A) <=> (A < A)

Thirty One.

If A is false, but not impossible, and if B is the consequence of A, B also will be false but not impossible.

1. $(A \lor \sim A) \land (A < B) \Rightarrow [(A \Rightarrow B) \lor (\sim A \Rightarrow \sim B)]$

For since it has been proved that if B's being is the consequence of A's being.

2. $A <= B$

Then B's possibility will follow from A's possibility (and A is assumed to be possible), consequently B will be possible.

3. $\{[(A \Rightarrow B \lor \sim B) \lor (\sim A \Rightarrow \sim B)] \land (A \lor \sim A)\} \Rightarrow (B \lor \sim B)$

For if it were impossible, the same thing would at the same time be possible and impossible.

4. $(\sim B \lor \sim B) \Rightarrow [(\sim B \lor \sim B) \land (B \lor \sim B)]$

Thirty Two.

Suppose that it is not possible, but assume that B belongs to all C: this is false but not impossible.

1. $(\sim B \lor \sim B) \land \sim(B \lor B) \land \sim(\psi B \lor \Э B)$

2. $(\Э B < \psi C)$

If then A is not possible for C but B belongs to all C, then A is not possible for all B.

3. $(\psi A < \sim C) \land (\Э B < \psi C) \Rightarrow [(\Э A < \sim B) \lor (\psi A < \sim B)]$

For a syllogism is formed in the third degree.

But it was assumed that A is a possible attribute for all B.

4. $(\Э A < \psi B) \lor (\Э A < \Э B)$

It is necessary then that A is possible for all C.

5. $(\Э A < \psi C) \lor (\Э A < \Э C)$

For though the assumption we made is false and not impossible, the conclusion is impossible.

6. $(\psi A < \sim C) <=/=> [(\Э A < \psi C) \lor (\Э A < \Э C)]$

Thirty Three.

It is possible also in the first figure to bring about the impossibility, by assuming that B belongs to C.

1. B < C

For if B belongs to all C, and A is possible for all B, then A would be possible for all C.

2. {(ƎB < ψC) ∧ [(ƎA < ψB) v (ƎA < ƎB)]} => [(ƎA < ψC) v (ƎA < ƎC)]

But the assumption was made that A is not possible for all C.

3. (ψA < ~C) v (ƎA < ~C)

Thirty Four.

Again let the premiss AB be universal and negative, and assume that A belongs to no B, but B possibly belongs to all C.

1. (ψA < ~B) ∧ [(ƎB < ψC) v (ƎB < ƎC)]

These propositions being laid down, it is necessary that A possibly belongs to no C.

2. (ƎA < ~C) v (ψA < ~C)

Suppose that it cannot belong, and that B belongs to C, as above.

3. (ψA < ~C) ∧ [(ƎB < ψC) v (ƎB < ƎC)]

It is necessary then that A belongs to some B.

4.(ƎA < ƎB)

For we have a syllogism in the third figure: but this is impossible.

5. (ψA < ~B) <=/=> (ƎA < ƎB)

Thus it will be possible for A to belong to no C.

6. (ψA < ~C)

For if at is supposed false, the consequence is an impossible one.

Thirty Five.

Let A belong to all B, and let B possibly belong to no C.

1. (ƎA < ψB) ∧ [(ψB < ~C) v (ƎB < ~C)]

If the terms are arranged thus, nothing necessarily follows.

2. (ƎA < ~C) v (ƎA < ~C)

But if the proposition BC is converted and it is assumed that B is possible for all C.

2. [(ƎB < ψC) v (ƎB < ƎC)]

A syllogism results as before.

3. (ƎA < ψB) ∧ [(ƎB < ψC) v (ƎB < ƎC)] => [(ƎA < ψC) v (ƎA < ƎC)]

For the terms are in the same relative positions.

Thirty Six.

Likewise if both the relations are negative.

If the major premiss states that A does not belong to B, and the minor premiss indicates that B may possibly belong to no C.

1. (ψA < ~B) ∧ [(ƎB < ~C) v (ψB < ~C)]

Through the premisses actually taken nothing necessary results in any way.

2. [(ƎA < ψC) v (ƎA < ƎC)] v [(ƎA < ~C) v (ψA < ~C)]

But if the problematic premiss is converted, we shall have a syllogism.

3. (ƎA < ψB) ∧ [(ƎB < ~C) v (ψB < ~C)] => [(ƎA < ~C) v (ψA < ~C)]

Thirty Seven.

Suppose that A belongs to no B, and B may possibly belong to no C.

1. (ψA < ~B) ∧ [(ƎB < ~C) v (ψB < ~C)]

Through these comes nothing necessary.

2. [(ƎA < ψC) v (ƎA < ƎC)] v [(ƎA < ~C) v (ψA < ~C)]

But if B is assumed to be possible for all C (and this is true) and if the premiss AB remains as before, we shall again have the same syllogism.

3. [(∃B < ψC) v (∃B < ∃C)] ∧ (ψA < ~B) => [(∃A < ~C) v (ψA < ~C)]

Thirty Eight.

If the premisses are affirmative, clearly the conclusion which follows is not necessary.

Suppose A necessarily belongs to all B, and let B be possible for all C.

1. (∃A < ψB) ∧ [(∃B < ψC) v (∃B < ∃C)]

We shall have an imperfect syllogism to prove that A may belong to all C.

2. [(∃A < ψC) v (∃A < ∃C)]

Thirty Nine.

Again, let A be possible for all B, and let B necessarily belong to all C.

1. [(∃A < ψB) v (∃A < ∃B)] ∧ (∃B < ψC)

We shall then have a syllogism to prove that A may belong to all C, not that A does belong to all C.

2. [(∃A < ∃C) v (∃A < ψC)] =/=> (∃A < ψC)]

And it is perfect, not imperfect.

For it is completed directly through the original premisses.

Forty.

But if the premisses are not similar in quality.

Suppose first that the negative premiss is necessary.

And let necessarily A not be possible for any B, but let B be possible for all C.

1. (ψB < ~A) ∧ [(∃B < ∃C) v (∃B < ψC)]

It is necessary then that A belongs to no C.

2. (ψA < ~C)

For suppose A to belong to all C or to some C.

3. [(ƎA < ƎC) v (ƎA < ψC)]

Now we assumed that A is not possible for any B.

4. (ψB < ~A)

Since then the negative proposition is convertible, B is not possible for any A.

5. (ψB < ~A) => (ψA < ~B)

But A is supposed to belong to all C or to some C.

6. [(ƎA < ƎC) v (ƎA < ψC)]

Consequently B will not be possible for any C or for all C.

7. [(ƎB < ~C) v (ψB < ~C)]

But it was originally laid down that B is possible for all C.

8. [(ƎB < ƎC) v (ƎB < ψC)]

Forty One.

That is if it is not possible that A should belong to any B, but B may belong to some of the Cs.

1. (ψB < ~A) ∧ [(ƎB < ƎC) v (ƎB < ψC)]

Then it is necessary that A should not belong to some of the Cs.

2. (ƎA < ~C)

For if A belongs to all C, but cannot belong to any B, neither can B belong to any A.

3. (ƎA < ψC) ∧ [(ψB < ~A) => (ψA < ~B)]

So if A belongs to all C, to none of the Cs can B belong.

4. (ƎA < ψC) => (ψC < ~B)

But it was laid down that B may belong to some C.

5. [(ƎB < ƎC) v (ƎB < ψC)]

Forty Two.

Suppose A belongs to no B, but can belong to all C.

1. (ψA < ~B) ∧ (ƎA < ψC)

If the negative proposition is converted, B will belong to no A.

2. (ψA < ~B) => (ψB < ~A)

But ex hypothesi can belong to all C.

3. (ƎA < ψC)

So a syllogism is made, proving by means of the first figure that B may belong to no C.

4. (ψB < ~A) ∧ (ƎA < ψC) => (ψB < ~C)

Forty Three.

Suppose that A necessarily belongs to no B, but may belong to all C.

1. (ψB < ~A) ∧ [(ƎA < ψC) v (ƎA < ƎC)]

If the negative premiss is converted B will belong to no A.

2. (ψB < ~A) => (ψA < ~B)

But A ex hypothesi is capable of belonging to all C.

3. [(ƎA < ψC) v (ƎA < ƎC)]

So once more a conclusion is drawn by the first figure that B may belong to no C.

4. (ψA < ~B) ∧ [(ƎA < ψC) v (ƎA < ƎC)] => [(ψC < ~B) v (ƎC < ~B)]

But at the same time it is clear that B will not belong to any C.

5. (ψC < ~B)

For assume that it does.

6. (ƎC < ƎB)

Then if A cannot belong to any B, and B belongs to some of the Cs, A cannot belong to some of the Cs.

7. (ψA < ~B) ∧ (ƎC < ƎB) => (ƎA < ~C)

But ex hypothesi it may belong to all.

8. [(ƎA < ψC) v (ƎA < ƎC)]

Forty Four.

Suppose A necessarily does not belong to B, and possibly may not belong to C.

1. (ψB < ~A) ∧ [(ψC < ~A) v (ƎC < ~A) v (ƎC < ƎA)]

If the premisses are converted B belongs to no A, and A may possibly belong to all C.

2. (ψB < ~A) => (ψA < ~B)

3. (ƎA < ψC)

Thus we have the first figure.

4. (ψA < ~B) ∧ (ƎA < ψC) => (ψB < ~C)

Forty Five.

First let the premisses be problematic and suppose that both A and B may possibly belong to every C.

1. [(ƎA < ψC) v (ƎA < ƎC)] ∧ [(ƎB < ψC) v (ƎB < ƎC)]

Since then the affirmative proposition is convertible into a particular.

And B may possibly belong to every C, it follows that C may possibly belong to some B.

2. [(ƎB < ψC) v (ƎB < ƎC)] => [ψC < ƎB) v (ƎC < ƎB)]

So, if A is possible for every C, and C is possible for some of the Bs.

3. [(ƎA < ψC) v (ƎA < ƎC)] ∧ [ψC < ƎB) v (ƎC < ƎB)]

Then A is possible for some of the Bs.

4. (ƎA < ƎB) v (ψA < ~B)

For we have got the first figure.

Forty Six.

And A may possibly belong to no C, but B may possibly belong to all C.

1. $[(\psi C < \sim A) \vee (\ni C < \ni A)] \wedge [(\ni B < \psi C) \vee (\ni B < \ni C)]$

It follows that A may possibly not belong to some B.

2. $(\ni B < \sim A) \vee (\ni B < \ni A)$

For we shall have the first figure again by conversion.

Forty Seven.

But if both premisses should be negative no necessary consequence will follow from them as they are stated.

But if the premisses are converted into their corresponding affirmatives there will be a syllogism as before.

For A and B may possibly not belong to C.

1. $[(\psi C < \sim A) \vee (\ni C < \sim A)] \wedge [(\psi C < \sim B) \vee (\ni C < \sim B)]$

2. $[(\psi B < \sim A) \vee (\ni B < \sim A)] \vee [(\ni B < \psi A) \vee (\ni B < \ni A)]$

If 'may possibly belong' is substituted we shall again have the first figure by means of conversion.

3. $[(\ni A < \psi C) \vee (\ni A < \ni C)] \wedge [(\ni B < \psi C) \vee (\ni B < \ni C)] => [(\ni B < \psi A) \vee (\ni B < \ni A)]$

Forty Eight.

Suppose that A may possibly belong to all C, and B to some C.

1. $[(\ni A < \psi C) \vee (\ni A < \ni C)] \wedge (\ni B < \ni C)$

We shall have the first figure again if the particular premiss is converted.

2. $(\ni B < \ni C) => (\ni C < \ni B)$

For if A is possible for all C, and C for some of the Bs, then A is possible for some of the Bs.

3. $[(\ni A < \psi C) \vee (\ni A < \ni C)] \wedge (\ni C < \ni B) => [(\ni A < \ni B) \vee (\ni A < \sim B)]$

Forty Nine.

First let the premisses be affirmative.

342

Suppose that A belongs to all C, and B may possibly belong to all C.

1. (ƎA < ψC) ∧ [(ƎB < ψC) v (ψB < ~C)]

If the proposition BC is converted, we shall have the first figure.

2. [(ƎB < ψC) v (ψB < ~C)] => [(ψC < ƎB) v (ψC < ~B)]

And the conclusion that A may possibly belong to some of the Bs.

3. (ƎA < ψC) ∧ [(ψC < ƎB) v (ψC < ~B)] => [(ƎA < ƎB) v (ƎA < ~B)]

Fifty.

Suppose that B belongs to all C, and A may possibly not belong to some C.

1. (ƎB < ψC) ∧ [(ƎA < ƎC) v (ƎA < ~C)]

It follows that A may possibly not belong to some B.

2. [(ƎA < ƎB) v (ƎA < ~B)]

For if A necessarily belongs to all B, and B (as has been assumed) belongs to all C.

3. (ƎA < ψB) ∧ (ƎB < ψC)

Then A will necessarily belong to all C.

4. (ƎA < ψC)

For this has been proved before.

But it was assumed at the outset that A may possibly not belong to some C.

5. [(ƎA < ƎC) v (ƎA < ~C)]

Fifty One.

Suppose first that the premisses are affirmative.

That A necessarily belongs to all C, and B may possibly belong to all C.

1. (ƎA < ψC) ∧ [(ƎB < ψC) v (ƎB < ƎC)]

Since then A must belong to all C, and C may belong to some B.

2. (ЭA < ψC) ∧ (ЭC < ЭB) v (ψC < ЭB)

It follows that A may (not does) belong to some B.

3. [(ЭB < ψA) v (ЭB < ЭA)]

For so it resulted in the first figure.

Fifty Two.

Suppose the consequents of A are designated by B, the antecedents of A by C, attributes which cannot possibly belong to A by D.

1. A=>B, C=>A, D=/=>A.

Suppose again that the attributes of E are designated by F, the antecedents of E by G, and attributes which cannot belong to E by H.

2. E=>F, G=>E, H=/=>E.

If then one of the Cs should be identical with one of the Fs, A must belong to all E.

3. C <=> F => ЭA < ψE.

For F belongs to all E, and A to all C, consequently A belongs to all E.

4. (ЭF < ψE) ∧ (ЭA < ψC) => (ЭA < ψE)

If C and G are identical, A must belong to some of the Es: for A follows C, and E follows all G.

5. [(C <=> G) => (ЭA < ЭE)] <= [(C=>A) ∧ (G=>E)].

If F and D are identical, A will belong to none of the Es by a prosyllogism.

6. (F <=> D) => (ψA < ~E)

For since the negative proposition is convertible, and F is identical with D, A will belong to none of the Fs, but F belongs to all E.

7.{[(ψA < ~E) => (ψE < ~A)] ∧ (F <=> D)} => [(ψA < ~F) ∧ (∃F < ψE)].

Fifty Three.

Again, if B and H are identical, A will belong to none of the Es.

1. (B <=> H) => (ψA < ~E).

For B will belong to all A, but to no E.

2. (∃B < ψA) ∧ (ψB < ~E).

For it was assumed to be identical with H, and H belonged to none of the Es.

3. (B <=> H) ∧ (ψH < ~E).

Fifty Four.

If D and G are identical, A will not belong to some of the Es.

1. (D <=> G) => (ψA v ∃A) < ~E.

For it will not belong to G, because it does not belong to D.

2. (ψA < ~G) <= (ψA < ~D).

But G falls under E.

3. ψG < ∃E.

Consequently A will not belong to some of the Es.

4. (ψA v ∃A) < ~E.

Fifty Five.

If B is identical with G, there will be a converted syllogism.

1. (B <=> G).

For E will belong to all A since B belongs to A and E to B (for B was found to be identical with G).

2. (∃E < ψA) <= {[(ψB < ∃A) ∧ (ψE < ∃B)] ∧ (B <=> G)}.

But that A should belong to all E is not necessary.

3. (∃A < ψE) v (∃A < ∃E).

But it must belong to some E because it is possible to convert the universal statement into a particular.

4. (ƎA < ƎE) <= (ψ => Ǝ)

It is clear too that the inquiry proceeds through the three terms and the two premisses, and that all the syllogisms proceed through the aforesaid figures.

For it is proved that A belongs to all E, whenever an identical term is found among the Cs and Fs.

5. (ƎC <=> ƎF) => (ƎA < ψE)

This will be the middle term; A and E will be the extremes.

So the first figure is formed.

Fifty Six.

And A will belong to some E, whenever C and G are apprehended to be the same.

1. (C <=> G) => (ƎA <=> ƎE)

This is the last figure: for G becomes the middle term.

And A will belong to no E, when D and F are identical.

2. (ƎD <=> ƎF) => (ψA < ~E).

Thus we have both the first figure and the middle figure.

The first, because A belongs to no F, since the negative statement is convertible, and F belongs to all E.

3. [(ψA < ~F) <= {(ψF < ~A)] ∧ (ƎF < ψE)}

The middle figure because D belongs to no A, and to all E.

4. (ψD < ~A) ∧ (ƎD < ψE)

And A will not belong to some E, whenever D and G are identical.

5. (ƎD <=> ƎG) => (ψA < ~E)

This is the last figure: for A will belong to no G, and E will belong to all G.

6. (ψA < ~G) ∧ (ƎE < ψG)

CHAPTER TWENTY TWO.

Proving.

P1.

Prove what "is" means.

The concepts that are inter-relationally involved in this kind of study include being, doing, meaning, existence, non-existence, identity, non-identity and no other concepts.

In mathematical terms we can say the concepts are one, some, more, less and none. Therefore, if we consider only those five mathematical concepts we can define some basic terms.

One object is an existant identity. If the same identity is repeated that is some. Some is more than one. One is less than some. None is the non-existance of one and some. The concept of more is to do with addition. The concept of less is to do with subtraction. A repetitive addition is called multiplication. A repetitive subtraction is called division. Existence is an affirmation. Non-existance is a negation.

Any number squared divided by two plus half the original number is equal to the number of times each of the consecutive integers in the original number combine with itself and each of the others once, as in dominoes. In a standard nine bar set of dominoes the integers one to nine and zero are all represented in relation to each of the other integers. That is a total of ten units. Ten squared is one hundred. One hundred divided by two is fifty. Half the original number is five. Fifty plus five is fifty five. And in a standard nine bar set of dominoes there are fifty five counters.

Given dominoes do not use late language sign label for number, and instead use a pattern of points to show the universal abstract that exists at the earlier level than sign label, they are useful in regard to demonstrating the ontological status of existant being of number.

At the level of dominoes, the sign labels and the concepts do not yet exist. Without the sign labels and without the concepts, still dominoes exist. Dominoes therefore are ontologically earlier than the sign labels and the concepts. And from the ontological existence of dominoes it is very easy to build the sign labels and concepts of number.

If we imagine we have a set of dominoes for only the units one and none, then that is two units. Two squared is four, four divided by two is two. Half the original number is one. Two plus one is three. Therefore we will have a set of dominoes with three counters.

One of those counters will show none on both sides of the counter. Another will show one on both sides of the counter. Another will show none on one side and one on the other side of the counter.

In that way without defining our concepts we are showing the concepts in their immanent form.

And with the dominoe that has none on both sides we are saying none is the same as none or none equals none.

And with the dominoe that has one on both sides we are saying one is the same as one or one equals one.

And with the dominoe that has none on one side and one on the other side we are saying none is not the same as one or none does not equal one.

And we know what we mean because we have three dominoes and we can see what we mean. And we think that each of the three dominoes is different to the other two.

And if we thought of the connecting line between the two sides of any one dominoe as plus, then we would know that none plus none is none, one plus none is one, and one plus one is two. And if we look at the whole dominoe and thought of what happens when we take away one side that would be like minus, so we could say none minus none is none, one minus none is one, one minus one is none, two minus one is one.

All we need now do is notice what are the functions that are evident without specific sign label.

And we can see that the difference between nothing and something is similar to the difference between the dominoe that is blank on both sides and the dominoe that has a blank on one side and a one on the other.

And the difference between one and some is similar to the the difference between the dominoe that has a blank on one side and one on the other and the dominoe that has a one on both sides.

And we can understand that some is more than one and one is less than some and none is the non-existance of one or some.

So at this stage we have proved the first five concepts of number which are one, some, more, less, none.

And we can apply those concepts as sign labels of functions such that we understand one is existant entity, some is a repetition of one, and none is the non-existance of entity. And we can apply the sign label functions of addition to some being more than one, and subtraction to one being less than some.

Which means we have now invented our sign labels for the

functions of addition and subtraction.

And we know what we mean by "is" because "none <is> none" and "one <is> one" and we know what we mean by "is not" because "none <is not> one".

P2.

Prove what "equals =" means.

Two plus two equals four and 2+2=4 are both late languages in sign label for something that is itself universally abstract. To understand this it is claimed that "equals means the power of making different things the same". So the sign label "equals =" is a functional power that combines what is different so that they seem the same. Then what is the universal abstraction?

It is the case that ** and ** is **** and that is not the same as @@ and @@ is @@@@. So because the universally abstract pattern is common to both we invent a sign label system which is above both. There is nothing in the sign label 2 which tells us anything about number. It is only that we have become so accustomed to thinking 2 and two are what they signify that we tend to not notice the complete lack of any content.

1: a, b, 0, 1, +, -, ., /, =, =/=, ~, ().

2: ++ = +, +- = +-, -- = -, +.+ = +, +/+ = +, -.- = +, -/- = +, +.- = -, +/- = -, -/+ = -

3: + = + , - = -, . = ., / = /, ~ = ~, = = =, =/= = =/=, () = ()

4: + =/= -, . =/= /, ~ =/= -, = =/= =/=

5: =

The prime pattern of rules is correspondent, coherent, useful and universally abstract. That means even though it is true, it is not in itself sufficient.

The fifth rule details the matter.

Essentially it raises the question "what is that?" in regard to equals.

In the fourth rule where we state equals does not equal does not equal, we are noticing that there are two related sign labels which together have a contradictory function.

The existance of the two contradictory functions enables us to satisfy what the difference is between the two.

When we use equals we are saying some entity is the same as a different entity.

When we use does not equal we are saying some entity is not the same as a different entity.

That then explains the way in which we use equals, which is the mathematical equivalent of the word "is".

And the way in which we use does not equal, which is the mathematical equivalent of the word phrase "is not".

Given that understanding, it becomes clear that if we attend to the matter "what is equals?", we will be forced to attend to the more abstract matter, what does "is" mean?

The important knowledge here is to realise that we can not answer the second level question "what is equals?" unless we can answer the first level question "what does <is> mean?".

And if we can answer the first level question, then answering the second level question becomes easy.

There can only be one zero. For if z had the same properties, we would have

: z + 0 = z

: z + 0 = 0

Yes, okay. If z had the same properties as 0 then that would mean z = 0.

The properties of zero are as follows:

Zero is that entity which added to itself gives itself,

subtracted from itself gives itself, multiplied by itself gives itself and divided by itself gives itself. If z has the same properties as zero then z = 0 and if z does not have the same properties as zero then z =/= 0.

If z does equal zero then z + 0 = z and z + 0 = 0 which only means we now know what the unknown variable z is equal to.

The law of identity states that two different entity are the same if in any function where one is used the other can be used to obtain the exact same result. So z = 0 if and only if the two sign labels can be exchanged in any area where one is used without altering the outcome of the calculation.

P3.

Prove a = a.

If we imagine we have a set of dominoes for only the units one and none, then that is two units. Two squared is four, four divided by two is two. Half the original number is one. Two plus one is three. Therefore we will have a set of dominoes with three counters.

One of those counters will show none on both sides of the counter. Another will show one on both sides of the counter. Another will show none on one side and one on the other side of the counter.

In that way without defining our concepts we are showing the concepts in their immanent form.

And with the dominoe that has none on both sides we are saying none is the same as none or none equals none.

And with the dominoe that has one on both sides we are saying one is the same as one or one equals one.

And with the dominoe that has none on one side and one on the other side we are saying none is not the same as one or none does not equal one.

And we know what we mean because we have three dominoes and we can see what we mean. And we think that each of the three dominoes is different to the other two.

And we know what we mean by "is" because "none <is> none" and "one <is> one" and we know what we mean by "is not" because "none <is not> one".

To understand this it is claimed that "equals means the power of making different things the same". So the sign label "equals =" is a functional power that combines what is different so that they seem the same.

It is the case that ** and ** is **** and that is not the same as @@ and @@ is @@@@. So because the universally abstract pattern is common to both we invent a sign label system which is above both. The sign label "a" is one example of the abstract that is above both. So that if we say a=** and a=@@ then a=a even though the object that the quantity refers towards is different, because the quantity is same in both cases.

First postulate is that the sign labels we use are only a, b, zero, one, plus, minus, multiplied by, divided by, equals, does not equal, not, brackets.

Second postulate is that the addition of positive terms gives a positive, the addition or subtraction of positive term with a negative term gives a positive or a negative, the subtraction of negative terms gives a negative, the multiplication of positive terms gives a positive, the division of positive terms gives a positive, the multiplication of negative terms gives a positive, the division of negative terms gives a positive, the multiplication of positive term with negative term gives a negative, the division of positive term by negative term gives a negative, the division of negative term by a positive term gives a negative.

Third postulate is that plus equals plus, minus equals minus, multiplied by equals multiplied by, divided by equals divided by, not equals not, equals equals equals, does not equal equals does not equal, brackets equals brackets.

Fourth postulate is that plus does not equal minus, multiplied by does not equal divided by, not does not equal minus, equals does not equal does not equal.

Fifth postulate is equals.

The law of identity states that two different entity are the same if in any function where one is used the other can be used to obtain the exact same result. So a = a if and only if the two sign labels can be exchanged in any area where one is used without altering the outcome of the calculation. But since the two sign labels are the same sign label it must be that they can be exchanged in any area where one is used without altering the outcome of the calculation.

As a case in point, take the example of a mid-game of chess. Exchange one black pawn with a different black pawn, such that both black pawns take the place of the other. That is the same as a=a.

When we use equals we are saying some entity is the same as a different entity.

So even though the two black pawns are each a different entity, they are also the same as each other. And what ever the difference may be between the two entity when they are exchanged on the chess board, it is not something that shows up on our system of measurement, such that we must say a=a.

If a=1 and 1=1 then a=a.

P4.

Prove ~a = ~a.

The difference between minus and not requires clarification. Minus means subtraction of a specifically given entity. Minus is a negative value the exact shape of a positive entity. That is different to "not" which means everything that a given entity is not. "Not" in this sense means a positive statement of everything that is not a given entity. More specifically in regards to "~a" this means everything that is not a in our given universe of discourse. Or alternatively it means some entity that is an element of everything that is not a in our universe of discourse.

Therefore, whereas minus a would refer to the entity a in a negative form, not a does not mean that. When we use not a we mean either everything that is not the other entity called a, or alternatively we mean any particular example of everything that is not the other entity called a.

Which necessarily means that when we say not a equals not a we are applying the same rule of identity given earlier which is that:

The law of identity states that two different entity are the same if in any function where one is used the other can be used to obtain the exact same result. So ~a = ~a if and only if the two sign labels can be exchanged in any area where one is used without altering the outcome of the calculation. But since the two sign labels are the same sign label it must be that they can be exchanged in any area where one is used without altering the outcome of the calculation.

P5.

Prove a =/= ~a.

The contradictory to the law of identity gives the law of non-identity. That is:

Two different entity are not the same if in any function where one is used the other can be used to obtain a different result.

So a =/= ~a if and only if the two sign labels can be exchanged in any area where one is used such that there will necessarily be an alteration in the outcome of the calculation.

Alternatively stated it means that if using ~a in place of a will necessarily alter the outcome of any calculation where a is used, then we must say that a =/= ~a.

If a=1 and ~a=0 then if 1=/=0 so too a=/=~a.

P6.

Prove one does not equal zero.

x=x.

x.x=x if x=1 or x=0.

0.0=0

1.1=1

1.0=0

0.1=0

0.0=x.x and 1.1=x.x but 0.1=/=x.x and 1.0=/=x.x

x.1=1 then x=/=0

x.x=1 then x=/=0

x.x=0 then x=/=1

Therefore 1=/=0 as a=/=~a

And also:

If 1.∞=∞

If 0.∞=0

Then 1=/=0 as a=/=~a

P7.

Prove the meaning of e.

1. e => a ^ ~a

2. ψA < ~B

3. ψ~A < ~B

4. ψe < ~B

5. {(e => A ∧ ~A) ∧ [ψA < ~B ∧ ψ~A < ~B]} => (ψe < ~B)

All A is Not B.

All Not A is Not B.

Therefore,

No B exist.

Question: For B to exist, must it be either A or Not A?

If so, that proves <A and Not A> means: everything in the universe of discourse, which is "e".

CHAPTER TWENTY THREE.

Truth value.

If the nature of what truth is could easily be located, then we would each be confident regarding providing the correct answer. Since when it comes to actually providing an answer to what is truth, we more commonly are not confident of this matter, then any possible approach to the subject may not conform to conventional style. For that sort of reason, this article has not been smoothly adjusted towards its most straightforward expression. Instead, it provides different angles towards understanding what truth is. And it means that if any one individual were completely confident regarding one of the vehicles for explaining what truth is, they may not be quite so confident as to one of the other vehicles of explanation.

Therefore, I am saying that the intelligent reader should not think to understand the totality, only to determine which areas are clear and then agree or disagree. Separate those parts from what are not clear, and neither agree nor disagree. Where not clear, decide whether because poorly stated, or well stated but requiring further thought before understanding is possible. If not clear because poorly stated, then either decide worth stating correctly for oneself, or alternatively not important.

The idea should be to obtain some appropriate method by which to understand what is truth, and also to have the sense that other methods detailed that are not so intuitively clear may become so if they become familiar.

P is any simple affirmation.

P is true or p is not true is the decision that must be made before we can develop argument from propostions.

Given two different decision makers the same p at the same time can be both true and false since the nature of what truth is does not demand that two different decision makers assign the same value to p. This is provable.

How do we decide whether p is true or p is false?

A judgement as to the truth or falsity of p is an early decision that determines all the outcomes that are derived from p.

The reason that two different decision makers can correctly assign contradictory value to p is because truth depends on the existence of three variables. We can provide an example of what is true in terms of 2+2=4 is correspondent, coherent and useful.

By correspondent we mean it refers accurately to something outside itself.

By coherent we mean it belongs to a larger system within which it makes sense.

And by useful we mean it has a utility in regard to some purpose.

Truth as hard as 2+2=4 is correspondent, coherent and useful. For any p its truth or falsity depends on correspondence, coherence and utility.

And for that reason if two different decision makers are judging from two different systems with two different purposes and two different perspectives, then those two decision makers could assign two different values for any p at the same time, such that where one says p is true for the same p the other will say it is false.

The decision as to whether p is true is a non-arbitrary choice. That means for any p that is said to be true based on given reasons, it is not possible to arbitrarily claim the contradictory, that p is false.

For any p that we state as true, we must be able to demonstrate these reasons:

P is externally correspondent to some fact.

P is internally coherent within a larger system.

P is useful according to some pragmatic purpose.

For any p that we state as false, we must be able to demonstrate these reasons:

P does not externally correspond to any known fact.

P is entirely incoherent within a larger system.

P has no use according to some pragmatic purpose.

It is not enough that some p fails to meet our criteria for truth that it is stated as false.

For any p to be stated as false it must meet our criteria for falsity. And that necessitates the use of the universal operator which is to say: Every p is true, false, or neither true nor false.

Since only those p which meet all of our criteria for falsity are called false, and only those p which meet all of our criteria for truth are called true, therefore some p must exist which are neither true nor false.

It is useful to clarify in particular two peculiar understandings that seem to be evident from the analysis up to this point.

One is that given our criteria for falsity and our criteria for truth that it is a necessity we accept some propositions exist that are neither true nor false, such that using the universal operator we must say for all propositions every p is true or false or neither true nor false.

The second peculiar understanding is that given two decision makers as to the truth or falsity of p it is at least possible in many not all cases that the two decision makers can take a contradictory position.

For those two reasons we are forced to notice a difference between the truth of 2+2=4 and other propositions that meet our stated criteria for truth. Because unlike many of those other propositions the truth of 2+2=4 is not easily contradicted. That is, given two decision makers it is not clear how either decision maker could correctly claim the falsity of 2+2=4. That would suggest that we can add a fourth criteria that is met by this type of proposition. And that fourth criteria is that this type of proposition is capable of universal abstraction.

Given that, we can suppose a difference between any proposition that meets our three basic criteria for truth and those propositions that also meet the fourth criteria of being capable of universal abstraction.

Now the third peculiar understanding is to clarify the difference between first propositions and the cardinal articulations of prime patterns.

First propositions may nearly always be neither true nor false because of their hypothetical nature as first propositions. Meaning that they probably fail our truth criteria on grounds of not being coherent within a larger system since that larger system does not yet exist at the time of first propositions. We would tend to call these hypothetically true propositions and build our truth tables as if they were true unless we find a contradiction in which case that would count as incoherence so they would move to being hypothetically false. And if we do not find a contradiction we would forget that our first propositions are only hypothetically true.

The cardinal articulation of prime patterns is capable of universal abstraction. That is because the truth of the prime patterns is first in structure rather than first in time sequence.

To re-iterate we can reinforce our earlier definition of the criteria for truth and falsity:

For any p that we state as true, we must be able to demonstrate these reasons:

P is externally correspondent to some fact.

P is internally coherent within a larger system.

P is useful according to some pragmatic purpose.

P is capable of universal abstraction.

For any p that we state as false, we must be able to demonstrate these reasons:

P does not externally correspond to any known fact.

P is entirely incoherent within a larger system.

P has no use according to some pragmatic purpose.

P is not capable of universal abstraction.

And why this is useful is because it means we can assess beforehand the hypothetical truth and falsity of our propositions that are neither true nor false. That is, where a proposition is neither true nor false, and we find that it is likely to be capable of universal abstraction then we are more confident about using it as hypothetically true even though it has not yet met all of our other criteria for truth. And where a proposition is neither true nor false, and we find that it is likely to never be capable of universal abstraction then we are more confident about using it as hypothetically false even though it has not yet met all of our other criteria for falsity.

As to any of the concepts, ideas and notions in these articles.

As stated it may be correct or incorrect. And when correctly stated it may be true or false.

What is clear is that the prime pattern does lend itself to be correctly stated in its most true formulation.

The difficulty is as to whether it is possible to check the correctness and truth of the patterns.

It is not the case that a more correct true pattern can simply be offered as an alternative to the one given since we would be in the same position in regard to checking the more correct true pattern.

And it is not the case that a different decision maker can affirm or negate any particular terms of the patterns, since any alteration to the given patterns would itself have to be demonstrated to be accurate and true.

Therefore it is asked whether any person who has the stated patterns can follow a process by which to check their truth without having to refer to a different decision maker. And the reason that matters is because we may not want to agree with the other decision maker on any area of this that we cannot demonstrate in a universally abstract way.

The process then, that is best used, in order to check the correctness and truth of the patterns will now be explained. What makes the process in itself attractive is that it self-validates. And also that the process is organic and once understood can be individually used by different decision makers in the way they prefer, without the requirement to obtain confirmation from any other decision maker.

The first rule is to determine what is the simplest term from either pattern. And once that is determined to only include those terms which most closely cohere with the first term. The second rule is to not include any term that is contradictory to the first term. And the third rule is to bring in any not previously stated terms that clearly are coherent with the first term.

a = a and ~a = ~a and a =/= ~a

"a equals a",

"not a equals not a",

"a does not equal not a".

Now crucially, given the patterns as stated in this document, whether they are correct as stated and whether in their most correct formulation they are true is no longer the matter. Because the method for checking them for correctness and truth is the way to organically formulate them in their most correct statement of themselves. And the next stage in that regard is to clarify a second small group that satisfy similar conditions to the first one stated. To do so it is correct to use any terms of the first group as required.

We know what we mean by "is" because "none <is> none" and "one <is> one" and we know what we mean by "is not" because "none <is not> one".

Two plus two equals four and 2+2=4 are both late languages in sign label for something that is itself universally abstract. To understand this it is claimed that "equals means the power of making different things the same". So the sign label "equals =" is a functional power that combines what is different so that they seem the same. Then what is the universal abstraction?

It is the case that ** and ** is **** and that is not the same as @@ and @@ is @@@@. So because the universally abstract pattern is common to both we invent a sign label system which is above both. There is nothing in the sign label 2 which tells us anything about number. It is only that we have become so accustomed to thinking 2 and two are what they signify that we tend to not notice the complete lack of any content.

The law of identity states that two different entity are the same if in any function where one is used the other can be used to obtain the exact same result. So a = 1 if and only if the two sign labels can be exchanged in any area where one is used without altering the outcome of the calculation.

If a=1 and 1=1 then a=a.

The contradictory to the law of identity gives the law of non-identity. That is:

Two different entity are not the same if in any function where one is used the other can be used to obtain a different result.

So a =/= ~a if and only if the two sign labels can be exchanged in any area where one is used such that there will necessarily be an alteration in the outcome of the calculation.

Alternatively stated it means that if using ~a in place of a will necessarily alter the outcome of any calculation where a is used, then we must say that a =/= ~a.

If a=1 and ~a=0 then if 1=/=0 so too a=/=~a.

x=x.

x.x=x if x=1 or x=0.

0.0=0

1.1=1

1.0=0

0.1=0

0.0=x.x and 1.1=x.x but 0.1=/=x.x and 1.0=/=x.x

x.1=1 then x=/=0

x.x=1 then x=/=0

x.x=0 then x=/=1

Therefore 1=/=0 as a=/=~a

And also:

If $1._\infty = \infty$

If $0._\infty = 0$

Then $1 =/= 0$ as $a =/= {\sim}a$

Isolating the second group of terms so that they can be themselves checked, the idea then is to determine whether we have maintained consistency throughout. That is, where the process of checking our terms has involved some correction of the original information, have we gone back to the original information and made any adjustment required by this process. In this way it does not matter as such what changes we make on the one condition that we correct towards coherency such that at any point in time the given pattern is more accurate and coherent than the previous statement of itself.

$a - a = 0 \wedge a + {\sim}a = 0 > a - {\sim}a =/= 0$

If a minus a equals zero and a plus not a equals zero,

then a minus not a cannot equal zero.

$a / a = 1 > a / {\sim}a = -1$

If a divided by a equals one

then a divided by not a equals minus one.

The challenge as to the rules that are applied in the given pattern is best directed towards correspondence rather than as to their coherence. Where we have previously been checking the correctness of the statement of the patterns and the truth of the patterns when correctly stated the focus has been towards as to coherence. When we check the rules that are being used because of their position as first propositions they are already understood as neither true nor false. What we can demonstrate is that within the limits of the patterns as described they do satisfy correspondence, coherence and utility. And because we know they are neither true nor false, we can demonstrate that outside the very limited patterns they do not fail on coherence and will fail on grounds of correspondence.

The reason we would do such is so that we can determine what are the adjustments we are required to make in order to make use of the rules when outside the limited patterns as detailed. And before we can do that we must clarify the prime patterns of the rules in themselves as used within the limited patterns as detailed. As we construct the prime pattern of rules it will become evident what are the grounds of correspondence which will fail outside the limited given pattern.

First: a, b, 0, 1, +, -, ., /, =, =/=, ~, ().

Second: ++ = +, +- = +-, -- = -, +.+ = +, +/+ = +, -.- = +, -/- = +, +.- = -, +/- = -, -/+ = -

Third: + = + , - = -, . = ., / = /, ~ = ~, = = =, =/= = =/=, () = ()

Fourth: + =/= -, . =/= /, ~ =/= -, = =/= =/=

Fifth: =

First postulate is that the sign labels we use are only a, b, zero, one, plus, minus, multiplied by, divided by, equals, does not equal, not, brackets.

Second postulate is that the addition of positive terms gives a positive, the addition or subtraction of positive term with a negative term gives a positive or a negative, the subtraction of negative terms gives a negative, the multiplication of positive terms gives a positive, the division of positive terms gives a positive, the multiplication of negative terms gives a positive, the division of negative terms gives a positive, the multiplication of positive term with negative term gives a negative, the division of positive term by negative term gives a negative, the division of negative term by a positive term gives a negative.

Third postulate is that plus equals plus, minus equals minus, multiplied by equals multiplied by, divided by equals divided by, not equals not, equals equals equals, does not equal equals does not equal, brackets equals brackets.

Fourth postulate is that plus does not equal minus, multiplied by does not equal divided by, not does not equal minus, equals does not equal does not equal.

Fifth postulate is equals.

Where we will challenge the given system as to correspondence will focus primarily on the difference between object and process. And with a supposition that there is nothing in our given system that enables us to distinguish between when the sign labels refer to an object and when the same sign labels refer to a process. The second supposition will be that our given system does not enable us to signify when we move logical level in regard to genus and species. The third supposition will be that our given system does not specify the difference between ontologically existant and imaginatively existant. The fourth supposition will be that the multiplication of a positive and minus term gives a minus process.

In regard to the first supposition, two multiplied by three equals six, where if two is an object, then multiplied by three is not an object and is a process.

In regard to the second supposition, two apples plus three pears is five fruit, where apples and pears are species and fruit is genus.

In regard to the third supposition, positive integers can exist and negative integers cannot, where positive number can be object and negative number can only be process.

In regard to the fourth supposition, plus three multiplied by minus five equals minus twelve, where the difference between plus three and minus twelve is a total of fifteen units. The proposition that any positive number multiplied by minus one equals zero.

When the prime pattern of p's and q's is applied to the prime pattern of number that we have established we obtain the prime pattern of sets in its most simple possible formulation. The prime pattern of sets is a universal abstraction of the prime pattern of number. It is more universal because it is not particular to number and can just as easily be applied to concepts. It is more abstract because its sign label system is common to both the functions of number and of language.

What is strange is that the difference of sign label satisfies the thought of a more universally abstract system, such that it is not possible to follow the exact same idea shape of the prime pattern of number even though the formulaic terms may be similar. In that sense we are driven to better state our explanation of the meaning of the sign labels that we use, given that the first statement of their meaning is only adequate. Therefore in this pattern of sets, one of the continual processes is to clarify exactly how to better define the sign labels.

One of the understandings to develop is that the similar thought-idea can be expressed using different sign label languages.

And that the difference in the larger system of the sign label languages alters the idea-shape of the thought-idea.

Given that the prime pattern of number was detailed in the sign label of number and then the same thought-idea was detailed in the sign label of language, such that a = a means a equals a.

In that sense the pattern of sets given in these articles is the exact same thought-idea given in the language of sets.

Which we can then detail in the sign label of spoken language.

When we detail the pattern of sets in the sign label of spoken language, the idea-shape will be different to when we detail the pattern of number in spoken language.

That means a common thought-idea can be explained in two different universally abstract languages, that of the pattern of number and that of the pattern of sets, and when each of those different sign label systems are detailed in spoken language two different idea-shapes are detailed in one language for the same thought-idea.

What will be the case is that the familial relationship between the thought-idea, and the idea-shape when detailed in the two sign label systems, and the idea-shape when detailed in the spoken language will be very close.

Meaning that it is natural that they are different to other decision maker systems in terms of internal coherence, correspondence and utility.

As the earlier explanation clarified there is no requirement to satisfy coherence to some other decision maker's system, we do not have to satisfy correspondence from the other decision maker's perspective and we do not have to prove utility to the other decision maker's purpose.

Considering Idea 40 given in these articles, this seems to be the correct statement:$(a \wedge \sim b) \wedge \sim c => a \wedge (\sim b \wedge \sim c)$

And this seems to be the false statement: $(a \wedge \sim b) \wedge \sim c => a \wedge \sim(b \wedge \sim c)$

The reason for the original statement is: $(a - b) - c = a - (b - c)$

Whereas the correct statement may be: $(a - b) - c = a + (-b - c)$

So the point I am drawing the attention towards is the double negative that is built in to the inference of the idea whereas the proposition does not contain a double negative.

Why this will matter later is because two different decision makers will be able to disagree as to the use of "and not".

The question will be does "and not" mean \<and not\> entity or does it mean \<and\> not entity.

It is similar to the question of does not equal and whether does not equal not entity makes a not not entity.

Both these questions are areas I have left unanswered in these articles, since the correct answer depends on the intention of the enquirer.

The difference between minus and not requires clarification. Minus means subtraction of a specifically given entity.

Minus is a negative value the exact shape of a positive entity.

That is different to "not" which means everything that a given entity is not. "Not" in this sense means a positive statement of everything that is not a given entity. More specifically in regards to "~a" this means everything that is not a in our given universe of discourse. Or alternatively it means some entity that is an element of everything that is not a in our universe of discourse.

Therefore we can say:

If a is zero then not a is unity and infinity.

If a is infinity then not a is unity and zero.

If a is unity then not a is infinity and zero.

It is for that reason that we need the sign label "e". Because if a => a and ~a => ~a then a means everything that is a in the universe of discourse and not a means everything that is not a in the universe of discourse, the combination of a and not a being everything in the universe of discourse.

And it is for this reason that "not not" does not mean the simple positive affirmation.

If we used the sign label "a" to signify "horse", then not not "a" means not not "horse", that being a unicorn.

Since a unicorn is a horse but is not a horse, we can not say the positive affirmation.

By the use of not not horse we are saying unicorn is neither a horse nor not a horse.

We can prove "not not" does not equal the simple affirmative in this way. If not not does mean "neither entity nor not entity" then a third not would be the contradictory of "neither entity nor not entity". And that contradictory would be "either entity or not entity" which then is either the simple affirmation or the simple negation.

The sign label Q meets a similar condition in regard to the possible entity that is neither the empty set nor the unity set. Q => a v ~a v !a v ~ϕ v ~1 v b v ~b v !b. The rule is that in any particular term it is possible to use any sign label ~Q then that term must be used. And where ever the sign label Q is used it be replaced by a sign label ~Q where ever possible.

The common abstract condition that is met by both Q and ! is the concept "neither nor not".

The difference between Q and ! is a matter of plurality and singularity.

Neither nor not applied to a singular entity is !.

So if I say neither unity nor not unity, that is not not.

Neither nor not applied to a plurality of entity, is Q.

So if I say not unity, nor zero, nor infinity, then that is Q.

In this sense, then, within the rules of the universe of discourse as given, the only condition for correcting the patterns as stated is that correction is only towards better coherency and non-contradiction. Any change in the directly opposite direction that increases internal contradiction and reduces internal coherency is not desirable.

The patterns themselves do permit that they be adjusted individually, in part or in whole. As such the earlier proposition that they are an organic synergy is also held to be true. The patterns can be entirely written in a completely different sign label system. And the same sign label system could be used to write different patterns.

What are we missing? Since that is not the sort of question that can be answered in the totality of things, I will answer it in regard to a few important areas.

One is in regard to "not not". A change that many will argue for is that "not not" should reduce to the simple positive affirmative. And that in fact is what we would tend to provide to children when they ask the same question. Because given the simple possible of a ∧ ~a => e, that is much too early to provide children with the higher order studies.

Many who study the early stages of this kind of system will meet the a and not a idea at the beginning so the only answer they are given is that it equals zero. And as well that not not reduces to the affirmation. And that neither the empty set nor the unity set being Q exists, so that if a choice is to be made and it is not the empty set it must be the unity set or the other way round.

Therefore we provide a safe answer to people who learn the basics of this sign label, although the safe answer and the system it exists within cannot be proved true and remains without the required matter for the higher order system. On the other hand the stronger formulation can easily be permitted to intelligent children if they are potentially confident of understanding the higher order concepts.

In regard to the truth of the concepts zero, unity and infinity:

$1.1 = 1$

$0.0 = 0$

$\infty.\infty = \infty$

If $a.b = c$ then $c/a = b$ and $c/b = a$

If $1.1 = 1$ then $1/1 = 1$

If $0.0 = 0$ then $0/0 = 0$

If $\infty.\infty = \infty$ then $\infty/\infty = \infty$

But:

If $1.\infty=\infty$ then that means $\infty/\infty=1$ and $\infty/1=\infty$

Therefore infinity divided by infinity gives either unity or infinity, but it does not give zero.

And:

If $0.\infty=0$ then that means $0/0=\infty$ and $0/\infty=0$

Therefore zero divided by zero gives either zero or infinity, but it does not give unity.

And:

If $1.0=0$ then that means $0/1=0$ and $0/0=1$

Therefore zero divided by zero gives unity and zero divided by unity gives zero, but neither answer gives infinity.

However that means zero divided by zero gives three possible answers, that is infinity, unity or zero.

And infinity divided by infinity gives two possible answers, that is infinity or unity.

And unity divided by unity gives one possible answer, that is unity.

The ideas 1 through 45 provided in these articles. Each idea the synthesis of individual concepts. The synthesis of ideas a notion.

Correct as stated and if correctly stated then true or not. But then heuristic. Correct as stated or not, does not matter. At least we can see a complete notion. And we can see the forty five ideas that combine to provide the notion. And we see we have a small specific number of concepts to consider.

Take any one idea.

Specify idea 26.

It is easy to see that idea 26 is not correct as stated, since it is deliberately not giving all the possible correct answers.

Idea 26 says a divided by a is unity. Which we can expand into word language to say that if a thing is contained by itself then the result is unity. But that is only true if a is a positive integer. The reason we say a/a=1 is because 1/1=1, 2/2=1, 3/3=1, so then a is any positive integer. But a could be a negative integer. Then a/a = 0 if any negative integer divided by itself is zero or a/a = b if any negative integer divided by itself is a different unknown variable not a. But a could be zero. Then a/a = ∞ if zero divided by zero is infinity. But then we would have to say Ӡ∞ and not the ψ∞ . Therefore a / a = Ӡ∞ which is the particular infinity made when the empty set contains itself, since it means a continuum of nothing containing nothing in an unlimited way.

Translated into sets is "a <=> ϕ, ∧ ϕ < ϕ => Ӡ∞ ∧~ ψ∞, => a < a => Ӡ∞ ∧~ ψ∞."

Which says if and only if a is the empty set, and, the empty set containing the empty set is one species of infinity and not the genus of that type of infinity, then a containing a is one species of infinity and not the genus of that type of infinity.

And if "a <=> +n, ∧ +n < +n => 1, => a < a => 1."

Which says if and only if a is a positive integer, where +n is any positive integer, then given any positive integer containing itself gives unity, if a containing a then unity.

And if "a <=> -n, ∧ -n < -n => b, => a < a => b."

Which says if and only if a is a negative integer, where -n is any negative integer, then given any negative integer containing itself gives an unknown variable b, where b is any unknown variable, if a containing a then unknown variable b.

Therefore, the notion that can be developed from idea 26 is as follows:

26.i - "a <=> ϕ, ∧ ϕ < ϕ => Ӡ∞ ∧~ ψ∞, => a < a => Ӡ∞ ∧~ ψ∞."

26.ii - "a <=> +n, ∧ +n < +n => 1, => a < a => 1."

26.iii - "a <=> -n, ^ -n < -n => b, => a < a => b."

26.iv - "a/a = 1 or ∞ or b".

The sense would be to not adjust any of the stated ideas one to forty five at the level they are stated.

But instead to take any one idea, each one after the other, in any order and specify idea ten, fifteen or thirty two or whatever.

And then to challenge that one idea, either to show that it is false as stated, or that it is not entirely correct, or alternatively to prove that as stated it is entirely correct and true.

In this way, if the original ideas are not adjusted at the level they are provided, then it will enable different decision makers the freedom to check the truth and correctness of the propositions, each from a common ground. That will then mean that it is not necessary for two different decision makers to assign the same decision as to truth or falsity or neither true nor false to any one idea.

CHAPTER TWENTY FOUR.

Wolfgang Amadeus Mozart is famous for his music rather than for his mathematics. That is because his mathematics is a secret art not normally revealed, although he has left notes that can be studied by any who choose to do so. It is not required that any who choose to study the mathematics of Mozart have any knowledge of music. The initiation into the mathematics of Mozart can begin from the position of intelligent beginner.

I.2.

The study of the mathematics of Mozart can not be left to musicians, since they are not compelled to clarify the system in order to play his music. The study of the musical theory of Mozart can not be the responsibility of mathematicians since they have no knowledge of that area. Therefore a blank naturally exists. It is a possible improbable that some person who is neither a mathematician nor a musician could focus their attention on that "blank" in particular. And they could do so simply on the basis that they have in front of them a document containing sign labels that would seem to reflect an ordered intellect stating information that may or may not make sense.

I.3.

The question raised is whether an intellect not versed in the mathematical system of Mozart can clarify his mathematics simply from the study of one of his compositions. And the answer is that it is easier to do so with Mozart rather than any other composer, because his mathematics is perfect. Since his mathematics is perfect the intellect is naturally attuned to the mind of a perfect mathematician which creates a positive result in proportion to variables of time, ingenuity and freedom to check alternate sources for basic information as required.

I.4.

This study is not provided as if from the perspective of an intelligent beginner. It is provided with the sense that an intelligent beginner could understand the reasoning and follow the argumentation if they chose to do so.

I.5.

The first point may be that considering a manuscript of Mozart's composition it was immediately thought to be too complex.

I.6.

So the idea might be to take away everything that was not constant through all of the given, in order to see what remains. That is, to ask whether any constant existed through all of the given without change.

I.7.

All that would be left is a page containing a series of horizontal lines grouped together and the repetition of the same down the page. And the separation of the horizontal lines by evenly spaced vertical lines. That then provides us with our prime pattern, since it is the one constant that must exist for anything to exist at all. And if that basic pattern were taken away then we would be at the point of nothing.

I.8.

Therefore, the beginning of our study of Mozart's mathematics must be to understand everything that can be understood about the prime structure without any further information.

I.9

What we discover is that the group of horizontal lines are called a staff. And therefore the repetition of groups down the page is a series of staffs. One staff is made of five horizontal lines which may be called ledger lines. That means four spaces between the first and last horizontal line in one staff. And the vertical lines along the staff are called a measure. Then since it is Mozart we may notice that each staff is in pairs, so that any one staff is connected to another. And if we then look at our original manuscript we notice that the upper staff in any pair has a sign label different to the sign label on the lower staff in any pair. Already we have too much to deal with. So we therefore have to clarify our terms.

I.10.

We find that the sign label at the beginning of a staff is called a clef. That the clef on the upper staff is called a treble and the clef on the lower staff is called a bass. So then we want to know what is the connection between the two.

I.11.

Were we to place a small x immediately below the first ledger line of the lower staff with the bass clef sign label and then to place another small x on each line and space between each line in a diagonal forward direction we could eventually get to the point where we reach the space above the upper ledger line on the treble clef staff. And the connection between the two staves is a single ledger line that we imagine exists.

I.12.

We then discover that each of the small x's has a letter name, dependent on where the x is placed on the staff. Since a is the first letter, it is useful to know that the x on the treble clef staff on the space immediately below the middle line is an "a". Because then all we need do is follow the alphabet forwards and backwards along our "x" diagonal line.

I.13.

So that means the x on the middle line of the treble clef is "b" and the space above the middle line is "c". Eventually what we get to is that the lowest "x" = "f" and the highest "x" = "g" on our diagonal line.

I.14.

And that the bass clef staff is f,g,a,b,c,d,e,f,g,a,b. That the middle ledger line between the bass clef staff and the treble clef staff is "c". And that the treble clef staff is d,e,f,g,a,b,c,d,e,f,g.

I.15.

That is four x between the ledger lines and five x on the ledger lines and two x on either side of the staff twice, with one x between the two.

I.16.

Therefore, $2(4x + 5x + 2x) + x = 23x$.

I.17.

What we now know is that the two staffs are equal to 23x and that each of those x's has a letter associated to it, of which there are only seven letters in total, a <=> g. Which must mean that on our diagonal line of x's each letter is represented three times and f and g four times. F and G are four times because they are the first two letters on the the bass clef and the last two letters on the treble clef.

I.18.

What we do not know is why does it matter. And the reason it matters is because what it means is that some mathematician wanted a way to show 23 related values in a manner that was easy to understand. And now that we understand what the x's mean, we can take them away so that we are back to our original two staves and nothing else. We do not even need the sign label for bass and treble clef.

I.19.

But now with just the two pairs of staff made of five horizontal lines we know that 23 different values are already built in to the prime structure, as if they exist there invisibly.

I.20.

Our fundamental question becomes:"What is the meaning of 23x?"

I.21.

And it is our fundamental question because when provided with a manuscript of the mathematics of Mozart and we take away everything we can to see what is left we discover that the answer beneath everything else is 23x.

I.22.

Therefore since "23x" is the one thing we must understand in order to progress with the mathematics of Mozart, we must attend to this area.

II.1.

Since we have taken away the sign label for treble and bass at this point, it is not clear to us what is the difference between the two staves. So what we can do is imagine an eleventh ledger line at the middle c position and then join the two staves together. Then what we would have instead of two staves of five ledger lines each, is one staff of eleven ledger lines. Does that still give us 23x?

II.2.

And of course it does. With one staff of eleven ledger lines we have ten x on spaces between the lines, eleven x on the ledger lines and two x immediately beneath and above the staff. That is:

10x + 11x + 2x = 23x.

II.3.

So now we can suppose that 23x exists before the sign label called the staff. Therefore we must take away the staff in order to study 23x. We now have a blank page with no sign labels at all, but the knowledge that 23x is behind it all.

II.4.

So we can show 23x in this way:

23x = [{'f 'g 'a 'b 'c 'd 'e 'f 'g 'a 'b} {'c'}{d' e' f' g' a' b' c' d' e' f' g'}]

II.5.

All I have done is show the bass clef staff with an apostrophe before the letter and the treble clef staff with an apostrophe after the letter with the middle c with an apostrophe both before and after. Which would seem to be an accurate way of showing the meaning of the grand staff made of bass and treble.

II.6.

While this does not in itself explain what is the meaning of 23x it may be that it provides us with a direction in which to begin answering the question. And it may be that we cannot in this particular discourse answer the question completely, but at least we now know that 23x is the question we want answered.

II.7.

What we can notice given the information as stated is that the pattern <a b c d e f g> repeats in exactly that order three times. So what we would naively think about is what would happen if we made a staff of twenty two lines. Some alphabets are famous for having twenty two letters so it may not be completely wrong if we made the mathematical decision to extend our repetitive pattern over a staff of twenty two lines. And if we did that, to just repeat the same seven letters in good order according to the same rules through a staff of twenty two ledger lines. What we may suppose is that the same pattern would imaginatively repeat indefinitely in both directions.

II.8.

And all we would do is signify the eleven letters going lower with two apostrophes before the letter to tell us that we were at the second lower level. And the eleven letters going higher with two apostrophes after the letter to tell us that we were at the second higher level. And the twelfth letter between any group of eleven would have the right number of apostrophes before and after to tell us it was a middle letter.

II.9.

In that way it would be very easy to know exactly where we were in regard to our relationship to the bass and treble clef of the grand staff. And it would also remind us how important 23x is since it is the group of letters that define the bass and treble clef of the grand staff.

II.10.

Having progressed that far, we need not pursue the line of enquiry beyond that point. What matters is that we have established our extremes in two directions higher and lower than the grand staff so we can use the higher and lower letters if we want to.

III.1.

What we must now do is consider what is the meaning of the 7x which combines three times to make the 23x with 2x left over. Our sign label would be "23x = 3(7x) + 2x". And we know that the 2x left over are just the beginning of the lower eleven below the grand staff, which will follow the same pattern as we have just described. So if we could understand the 7x we would be more confident about understanding 23x.

III.2.

When we ask, "what is 7x?", we immediately discover that 7x is called a scale of tones, although a scale is actually 7x + 1x. And the reason a scale of eight tones is 7x + 1x is because the eighth x is the first x of the next group of 7x in our grand staff of 23x. So a scale begins and ends with the same tone, where the final tone is the first tone of the next group of 7x.

III.3.

Without any adjustment it turns out that 23x as given is a continuing scale called the major scale and that it naturally follows a pattern of tones as detailed: "1, 1, 1/2, 1, 1, 1, 1/2, 1". And what that means is that if we start our scale with middle c then between middle c and d on the treble clef staff is one whole tone. Between d and e is one whole tone. Between e and f is one half tone. Between f and g is one whole tone. Between g and a is one whole tone. Between a and b is one whole tone. Between b and c is one half tone. And between c and upper d is one whole tone.

III.4.

So now we know that 23x in its most natural form follows the pattern:

"1, 1, 1/2, 1, 1, 1, 1/2, 1, 1, 1/2, 1, 1, 1, 1/2, 1"

III.5.

If we show that for the grand staff what we obtain is:

[c<1>d, d<1>e, e<1/2>f, f<1>g, g<1>a, a<1>b, b<1/2>c, c<1>d, d<1>e, e<1/2>, f<1>g] <=> {'c' : g'}

[f<1>g, g<1>a, a<1>b, b<1/2>c, c<1>d, d<1>e, e<1/2>f, f<1>g, g<1>a, a<1>b, b<1/2>c] <=> {'f : 'c'}

III.6.

Because we want to understand the meaning of 7x + 1x in order to understand 23x it is essential that we first understand the major scale of the grand staff as detailed.

III.7.

And its basic pattern is tone, tone, semitone, tone, tone, tone, semitone, tone, tone, semitone.

III.8.

Which if we state from middle c is "T, T, S, T, T, T, S, T"

III.9.

Which we can put in to the formula: "2T 1S 3T 1S, 2T 1S 3T 1S" = Major scale of 23x.

III.10.

Now because the natural scale of 23x is only one of many different scales that can be formed from 23x it is useful to understand how that works. The answer is to be completely sure of the natural distance between each of the letters given above for the grand staff.

III.11.

When that is thoroughly understood then we can clarify that one half tone below what is natural is called flat and one half tone above what is natural is called sharp. And that any tone can be made into its flat or sharp form.

III.12.

All of the different possible scales are only made by a rule that any particular tones must be kept flat or sharp from what is natural. And in this way we can create scales that follow different patterns to the major scale of "2t1s3t1s, 2t1s3t1s".

III.13.

And all we need do to understand this is signify each of the main alternatives using the exact same formulaic method. When we notice that the formula tells us the required distance between letters, then all we need to know is which letter the scale starts with. Once we know which letter the scale starts with, and what the pattern must be, then all we have to do is signify where we must make our natural tones flat or sharp to exactly conform to the pattern.

III.14.

Natural minor scale: "1t1s2t1s2t, 1t1s2t1s2t".

Melodic minor scale: "1t1s4t1s, 1t1s4t1s".

III.15.

Where as stated the patterns for the scales may be correct or not, if not correct then they are correctable. What matters in this sense is that the method for signifying what the patterns are is accurate and appropriate. And that given a correct pattern for any scale and given we know what letter the scale is to start with, we can easily make any adjustment to the natural tone of the letters by making them flat or sharp. When we make a tone flat or sharp throughout a composition all that we need do is use a sign label for sharp or flat at the beginning of the grand staff to notify that tones throughout the composition are to be made flat or sharp accordingly.

IV.1

Where that leaves us in regard to 7x + 1x as to understanding 23x is relatively clear. Because now we know something more about how the tones connect together one to the other and the relationship between them. What we would now like to know is whether there is any mathematical relationship that can be clarified between the different notes, such that they naturally combine together into patterns. And in fact there is. The single requirement in that regard, simply from a mathematical perspective, is that the following prime pattern is considered.

IV.2.

DD D D D D D D D D D D D D D

D F A C E G B D F A C E G B D

D A E B F C G D A E B F C G D

D C B A G F E D C B A G F E D

D E F G A B C D E F G A B C D

D G C F B E A D G C F B E A D

D B G E C A F D B G E C A F D

D D D D D D D D D D D D D D D

IV.3.

The only patterns that exist in the above prime pattern are a repetition of the six below. And the six patterns below are only three patterns put into forward and reverse order. So therefore only three patterns need be understood, both forwards and backwards.

IV.4.

F A C E G B D <=> B G E C A F D

A E B F C G D <=> G C F B E A D

C B A G F E D <=> E F G A B C D

IV.5.

And an easier variation of the above pattern is:

A B C D E F G

B E A D G C F

C A F D B G E

D D D D D D D

E G B D F A C

F C G D A E B

G F E D C B A

IV.6.

And that in turn is only six patterns made up of only three patterns forwards and backwards:

A B C D E F G <=> G F E D C B A

B E A D G C F <=> F C G D A E B

C A F D B G E <=> E G B D F A C

IV.7.

Where both variations combined is:

F A C E G B D <=> B G E C A F D <=> C A F D B G E <=> E G B D F A C

A E B F C G D <=> G C F B E A D <=> B E A D G C F <=> F C G D A E B

C B A G F E D <=> E F G A B C D <=> A B C D E F G <=> G F E D C B A

V.1.

We are now in a position to answer our fundamental question: "What is 23x?".

V.2.

Before we answer what is 23x we must clarify three things. The three things are known as the thing itself, the thing explained and the explanation of the thing itself. Because the three things are each different to the other and yet related one to the other it is easy to think they are all the same thing or alternatively that any one of the three can be discarded or only used in part. Which would be wrong to so think. Because each of the three things is an individual component of the one thing. My detail of what are the three things is as follows:

V.3.

The thing itself is what we ask the question about when we say "what is 23x?". And we know it exists because we have been put into the position where it is the thing we ask about.

V.4.

The explanation of the thing itself is our workings out that enable us to understand what the thing itself is when it is explained.

V.5.

The thing explained is our answer to the question "what is 23x?".

V.6.

Why it matters is because we can not understand the thing explained on its own. The thing explained is just a simple answer to the question "what is 23x?" as a sort of definition of what 23x is. And it matters because we have to be quite clear that the thing explained is not the same as the thing itself. The thing itself exists completely separately from the thing explained. And it matters because we have to enable ourselves to understand the thing explained by providing a good explanation. Then what we obtain is a clarification of a road that travels from the question as to the thing itself, the explanation of the thing itself and the thing itself explained.

V.7.

Given that, the following is a definition of our answer to the question known as the thing explained. And the previous is our explanation of what is the thing itself.

V.8.

What is 23x?

23x is defined as =>

V.8.A. 10x + 11x + 2x = 23x.

V.8.B. 23x = [{'f 'g 'a 'b 'c 'd 'e 'f 'g 'a 'b} {'c'}{d' e' f' g' a' b' c' d' e' f' g'}]

V.8.C. <a b c d e f g>

V.8.D.. "23x = 3(7x) + 2x"

V.8.E. 7x + 1x

V.8.F. "1, 1, 1/2, 1, 1, 1, 1/2, 1" And what that means is that if we start our scale with middle c then between middle c and d on the treble clef staff is one whole tone. Between d and e is one whole tone. Between e and f is one half tone. Between f and g is one whole tone. Between g and a is one whole tone. Between a and b is one whole tone. Between b and c is one half tone. And between c and upper d is one whole tone.

V.8.G. If we show that for the grand staff what we obtain is:

[c<1>d, d<1>e, e<1/2>f, f<1>g, g<1>a, a<1>b, b<1/2>c, c<1>d, d<1>e, e<1/2>, f<1>g] <=> {'c' : g'}

[f<1>g, g<1>a, a<1>b, b<1/2>c, c<1>d, d<1>e, e<1/2>f, f<1>g, g<1>a, a<1>b, b<1/2>c] <=> {'f : 'c'}

V.8.H. "2T 1S 3T 1S, 2T 1S 3T 1S" = Major scale of 23x

Natural minor scale: "1t1s2t1s2t, 1t1s2t1s2t".

Melodic minor scale: "1t1s4t1s, 1t1s4t1s".

V.8.I.

A B C D E F G

B E A D G C F

C A F D B G E

D D D D D D D

E G B D F A C

F C G D A E B

G F E D C B A

V.8.J.

D D D D D D D D D D D D D D

D F A C E G B D F A C E G B D

D A E B F C G D A E B F C G D

D C B A G F E D C B A G F E D

D E F G A B C D E F G A B C D

D G C F B E A D G C F B E A D

D B G E C A F D B G E C A F D

D D D D D D D D D D D D D D D

V.8.K.

F A C E G B D <=> B G E C A F D <=> C A F D B G E <=> E G B D F A C

A E B F C G D <=> G C F B E A D <=> B E A D G C F <=> F C G D A E B

C B A G F E D <=> E F G A B C D <=> A B C D E F G <=> G F E D C B A

VI.1.

Since we thoroughly understand what 23x is in its various particulars, we prove its significance by how well it enables us to understand the mathematics of Mozart. As will be clear, the reason for this discourse is to be confident about studying the mathematics of Mozart and nothing else.

VI.2.

To prove 23x we must now apply it to the original manuscript of Mozart that we were imaginatively considering. The way to do such is as follows.

VI.3.

First we must return to the blank page with nothing on it at all. Then we must permit the first thing that exists on the blank page to be the Grand Staff of eleven ledger lines and nothing else.

VI.4.

Then we must imaginatively separate the Grand Staff into two connected staff each of five ledger lines.

VI.5.

At this point 23x already exists in the form of two connected staff of five ledger lines each.

VI.6.

To signify the difference between the upper and lower staff we must use the treble clef for the top staff and the bass clef for the lower staff and if we want the middle c clef between the two.

VI.7.

Then because we now know what are flat and sharp notes we must check the manuscript of Mozart and copy exactly the flat and sharp keys at the front of each ledger line onto our empty page.

VI.8.

At this point we are ready to begin. Because we are only interested in 23x at this stage we do not need to concern ourselves with any aspect of the mathematics of Mozart other than that which directly relates to 23x as we understand it.

VI.9.

We know that 23x is a diagonal line of x's that are to be placed on the grand staff to designate tone. So our single and only requirement at this point is the study of the mathematical patterns of tone that Mozart uses and nothing else.

VI.10.

Whilst the following task is arduous it is easy to do, simply requiring an attentive mind and time to complete the entire portfolio of Mozart's tonal pattern system of mathematics.

VI.11.

Taking our manuscript of Mozart and our empty copy, we must place only an x in each location where a note is signified in the original manuscript. If we do so most carefully we will soon obtain a complete manuscript of the patterns of tone of the original manuscript and nothing else. Imaginatively it is easy to suppose that is possible. We can then leave the

TAROT MAGIC

original manuscript of Mozart and attend directly to our simpler copy.

VI.12.

What we at this point have in front of us is a small booklet showing the grand staff, the treble and bass clef, the sharp and flat keys and along the treble and bass clef staff a series of x's placed on the lines and in the spaces between the lines.

VI.13.

That small booklet is a description of the tonal patterns used by Mozart according to 23x. We can then reduce the patterns so that there are no repetitions. That is, where ever we notice a pattern of x's is the same as one already previously detailed we delete it. When we have deleted any repetition we are left with a much smaller booklet containing every pattern of tone used by Mozart in that one composition. And the smaller booklet will only be the grand staff, any sharp and flat sign labels at the beginning of the staff, the treble and bass clef and patterns of x's along the staff with no repetition.

VI.14

That then is relatively easy to understand because we understand 23x. And whilst it is time consuming to do so, it is at least imaginatively possible that any person who wants to could apply themselves to collecting all of the compositions of Mozart in terms of mathematical patterns of tone. Which they could then reduce by deleting any repetion, so that in one single booklet they have all of the patterns of the mathematics of Mozart's tonal system.

VI.15.

What we must notice here is the difference between imagining what does not exist and imagining what does exist. When we imagine what does not exist the thing does not exist, whether we imagine it or not. When we imagine

393

what does exist, the thing exists, whether we imagine it or not.

VI.16.

Therefore there is an important difference between actually taking the time to construct a complete copy of the mathematical patterns of the tonal system of Mozart and imagining doing so. Because imagining doing so means imagining something that does not exist. And actually doing so means having something that does exist.

VI.17.

The reason I make that point is because the next stage in the study of Mozart the mathematician is dependent on having a copy of the patterns of his tonal system in reality. It does not require all of his compositions are reduced to a single manuscript in this way, although we acknowledge it can easily be done and that it is easily possible that any person can have done so. Given that one of his compositions has been accurately detailed in the described manner is sufficient.

VII.1.

Before we consider what is meant by the mathematics of time applied to the mathematics of tone that we have detailed in our little manuscript of the mathematics of Mozart, it is necessary that some related areas are noticed.

VII.2.

That is, a sign label system where the whole divides into sixty four parts.

VII.3.

When we look at our original manuscript we can consider any particular measure of the manuscript. And by measure is meant one phrase of notes contained on either the treble or bass clef staff, where on either side of the phrase is a vertical line separating the phrase from the phrase to left and right.

VII.4.

When we add together all of the notes in one measure we will normally find that the totality of the measure gives us an amount that is two, three or four quarters of a whole. And when we consider the measure immediately to the left we normally find that the addition of all of the notes in the measure gives exactly the same amount as the first one we looked at. And so too the measure to the right.

VII.5.

Which suggests that all of the phrases in any one measure in the same composition will give us exactly that amount, that is two, three or four quarters of a whole. Which means a rule is being applied that says all the notes in any one measure must only add up to the amount we have detailed.

VII.6.

And therefore when we go back to our own simpler copy of the manuscript containing only x's on the grand staff we know that all of the x's in any one measure will only add up to the amount we have worked out, no matter how many x's there may be in the measure.

That is important because it tells us no matter how many notes there are in one measure they will always combine to add up to the one total amount that all the measures have to equal to.

VII.7.

When we look to the beginning of the staff in the original manuscript we will see that near the treble or bass clef is one number placed over a different number. Now regardless of what that number says we already know that any one measure adds up to a specific amount and each measure on the same staff is equal to the same amount, usually two, three or four quarters of a whole.

VII.8.

Therefore the important thing is to count all the notes in any one measure in order to determine for oneself how much every measure must equal to. Only once it is understood in any particular composition how much one measure is equal to can the time signature be understood.

VII.9.

When we understand the total value of a measure in any composition then we can look at the time signature since it tells us how many parts the measure must divide into. The number of parts that the measure must divide into is called the number of beats in a measure, where the first note in any part is the beat.

VII.10.

Once we understand that we must not make the mistake of thinking that we can just evenly divide our x's into two, three or four in any one measure, because our x's tell us nothing about the size amount of any one x, and they say all x's are the same quantity.

VII.11.

What we can do, is take the first measure in the original manuscript and in the knowledge of how much the measure must add up to in total, and the number of parts it must divide into, then count the notes individually to add up to one part. When we know which notes add up to a complete part of the measure we can then count up our x's that refer to the same notes and put those notes into brackets.

VII.12.

If we do so accurately we will have the first measure with one, two, three, or four bracketed terms of x's. If we then continue to do such we will soon complete the first staff which will now show all of our x's in the same number of brackets in all the measures. That is, every measure on the first staff will have one, two, three or four bracketed terms of x's.

VII.13.

We can then copy our time sign label from the original manuscript to our simpler version.

VII.14.

And we will know that all the x's in one measure combine to give the same amount as all the x's in any other measure.

VII.15.

And that the number of bracketed terms in any one measure will be the same number in any other measure.

VII.16.

And that the number of x's contained in any one bracketed term could be any number.

VII.17.

And that the number of beats in any one measure is the same as our number of brackets in any one measure.

VII.18.

And that the beat is the first x in any bracketed term. And that the hardest beat is the first x in the first bracket of any one measure.

VII.19.

Then and only then can we consider the time signature which may more or less inform us what we already know, although it may not contradict what we already know because what we know has been worked out by counting the measures themselves and the total number of individual quarter notes of a whole in the measures themselves.

VIII.1.

Then as to the mathematics of time applied to the

mathematics of tone in our study of the Mozart the mathematician.

VIII.2.

What we at this stage already know is that there can be any number of x's in any one measure.

VIII.3.

And that any one measure must combine all the x's in itself to equal the exact same amount as all the x's in any other measure.

VIII.4.

And that the time signature tells us how many beats must be in any one measure.

VIII.5.

And that all of our x's in any one measure must be separated into bracketed terms where the number of bracketed terms in any one measure is the same as the number of beats in any one measure.

VIII.6.

And that the time signature must equal the number of beats and brackets.

IX.1

Given we have that understanding it is useful to consider our given time sign label system as it is applied to the seven tones that we know as 23x.

IX.2.

Any tone of 23x can be specified using this time sign label system, and the time sign label system is constant to all of 23x.

IX.3.

One whole note can be imagined as four seconds length

in terms of amount of time it should extend. That would mean that one measure can be thought of as a time length of four seconds long. And if there are five measures on one staff line then that would be five multiplied by four which is twenty seconds amount of time in total. The time length of one whole note does not have to be four seconds duration. It could be two seconds duration or eight seconds duration and all that matters in this regard is that in any particular composition it be understood beforehand how long is the time duration of one whole note.

IX.4.

The length of one second is taken as approximately the time taken to speak "one and". Which would mean that a single measure the length of one whole note is a duration the equivalent of how long it takes to speak: "one and, two and, three and, four and".

IX.5.

And that length is the duration of one whole note. The sign label for this note is a small circle the same size as one of our x's, where the circle is empty, not filled in.

IX.6.

The smallest time note in our given system is one sixty fourth of a whole note. Which then would mean one sixteenth of one second in duration. This is called a hemidemisemiquaver. It is signified by a small circle the size of one of our x's, where the circle is filled in, and a vertical line extends upwards from the right of the circle or downwards from the left, and the other extreme of the line has four small flags.

IX.7.

The middle note of this system is called a quaver. It is one eighth of a whole note. Which would then mean one half of a second in duration. It is signified by the same sign label as the sixty fourth note with only one flag.

IX.8.

Twice as large as a quaver, and one quarter the size of a whole note is called a crotchet. It is one second in duration. It is signified by the same sign label system as a quaver without any flags.

IX.9.

Twice as large as a crotchet and half the size of a whole note is a minim. It is two seconds in duration. And it is signified by the same circle as a whole note not filled in, and has a stem like a crotchet and also has no flags.

IX.10.

Half the size of a quaver is a semi quaver. It is one sixteenth of a whole note. And it is one quarter of a second in duration. It is signified by the same sign label as the quaver with two flags.

IX.11.

Half the size of a semi quaver and twice the size of a hemidemisemiquaver is a demisemiquaver. It is one eighth of a second in duration. And it is signified by the same sign label as the quaver with three flags.

IX.12.

Since when to be silent is often proposed to be the measure of genius it is worth knowing that each of the seven sign labels for duration of tone is reflected by an equivalent sign label for duration of silence. And to know that when adding together the total amount of notes in a measure the sign label for silence must be included in this amount.

IX.13.

And of course when attending to the mathematics of the tone system in relationship to the mathematics of the time system it is the mathematics of the sign labels for silence that provide the connecting link. They do so because silence has to be thought of as the opposite of sound so they do directly refer to the genus of tone which is sound where any particular tone is the species. And they do so because they have an entire seven sign labels correspondent to the time sign labels for tone.

IX.14.

Without any change what this knowledge enables us to do is add together the notes of the original manuscript of Mozart in any one measure, also known as a bar, where the measure is a single phrase on a staff separated by vertical lines called bar lines. And it enables us to bracket all the x's of each individual beat together into the same number of parts as notified by the time signature.

IX.15.

The only matter I would focus attention towards at this point is the difference between two things.

IX.16.

One is to add all the notes in a bar or measure together in order to determine what is the total amount of all the given notes in one measure. And this will normally add to one whole note or three quarters of a whole note or one half of a whole note.

IX.17.

And two is to divide all the notes in a bar or measure apart into two, three or four bracketed terms in order to determine what are the notes associated to each beat of the measure.

IX.18.

Given those two things are understood as different to each other and related to each other, then the basis of metre, tempo and beat is established.

IX.19.

The basic genus/species arrangement is staff line contains barlines which separate one measure from another.

IX.20.

One measure is bounded by two bar lines.

IX.21.

Within any two bar lines the measure will add all the contained notes together to give the same number as any other measure.

IX.22.

The total number of contained notes in any measure will separate out into one, two, three or four bracketed terms.

IX.23.

Each bracketed term will begin with one note.

IX.24.

Each measure will begin with one bracketed term.

IX.25.

The beat can be given as a regular emphasis placed on the first note of the first bracketed term in any measure.

IX.26.

The tempo is the sense of the repetition of beats which can be of longer or shorter frequency.

IX.27.

The metre is the sense of one tempo in a composition in relationship to other tempo in the same composition.

IX.28.

The totality of such being known as rhythm.

IX.29.

Whereas the mathematical nature of rhythm exists in fact, its nature is only a matter of the individual notes as parts of a measure, measure as parts of a larger phrase. What we cannot do is define rhythm as any way separate from the sign labels that describe tone and time. Since it is a product of the combination of sign labels that designate time with the sign label that designates tone. That is, when the time sign label system is applied to 23x then rhythm is manifest as a synergy of both. The reason this is so, is because the tone system provides one opportunity to impose a sense of order. The time sign label system provides one opportunity to impose a sense of order. When a sense of order from the two systems is combined the result is a synergy and one aspect of that synergy is rhythm. Other aspects of the same synergy include melody, composure, harmony.

X.1.

We have shown a specific mathematical system that is tone and we have a copy of a manuscript of Mozart's mathematics demonstrating only the tone system that we call 23x.

X.2.

And we have now shown a different mathematical system that is time and we have an understanding of the sign label notation that is used to designate time.

X.3.

And we know that without the 23x system the time sign label system will tell us nothing about tone.

X.4.

And that without the time sign label system 23x will tell us nothing about time.

X.5.

To demonstrate the relationship between the two separate systems what we must now do is use the middle c ledger line between the treble and bass clef. And all we do here is use the time sign label system along the horizontal line of middle c exactly below or above the x to which it refers.

X.6

That is we copy the exactly correct and accurate time sign label onto our own manuscript. We do so along the line of middle c. And we place the sign label for time immediately below or above the related x to which it refers.

X.7

By doing so we inform ourselves as to the time value of each x and the tone value of each time sign label.

X.8

And of course not to forget to include the sign label for silence as is consistent with the original manuscript. The time label for silence should simply be included along the middle c line and will have an empty space above or below itself where there is an absence of any x.

X.9.

The proof of this is to possess in hard copy a small manuscript that contains the two mathematical systems in their separate parts and that shows how the two separate systems relate one to the other, exactly as detailed. That means one of Mozart's compositions worked out completely in the way described. Only when that point is accomplished is it possible to study the particular patterns of tone employed by Mozart in that instance. And the particular patterns of time employed by Mozart in that instance. Furthermore the activity of doing this process is the event at which the living mind can atune itself to the musical genius of Mozart the mathematician.

X.10.

It will be clear as well that the same patterns of tone could be used in a variety of ways including with a completely different pattern of time. Or the same patterns of x's on the staff line could be restated exactly three ledger lines above or below which would be to maintain the pattern but adjust which tones are in that pattern. And in doing so the mathematical understanding of Mozart in regard to tone would be involved. Or alternatively that the same patterns of time could be used in a variety of ways including with a completely different pattern of tone. And in doing so the mathematical understanding of Mozart in regard to time would be involved. Other adjustments are possible. All the time structure of any one phrase can be halved in duration or doubled in duration whilst maintaining all other proportions the same.

X.11.

So the capacity to do all of this is supported basically by the actual existence of the mathematical system as described.

X.12.

Once that is accomplished the mathematical system of Mozart is detailed in its most basic form and will be found to be quite understandable. Once it is understood then the original manuscript can be understood quite easily. Where any additional sign labels used are only to inform us as to details in regard to our 23x system in its relationship to our time sign label system. By which I mean there is nothing more at a prime level than we have already documented and that what further information is evident is only to provide details to the prime patterns that we have documented.

CHAPTER TWENTY FIVE.

Thinking Machines.

The question here is how do we go from Babbage, to Boole to Tesla to Microsoft?

Now, between these are intermediate points. After Babbage, the 1851 Crystal Palace exhibition. After Boole the development of formal and symbolic logic. After Tesla the massive machinery of Edison. Before Microsoft Algol, Fortran and C.

After Fortran and C, then C++, Basic, Visual Basic, C#.net and object orientated languages.

At this point Turing is more of a mislead than anything else. It is somewhat like looking at Asimov's three laws of robotics for a direction of travel into intelligent machines. And both lines are false. Not that Turing or Asimov present falsely but the misuse of their ideas leads in a false direction. We do not at this stage care if computers can prove sentience, we simply want a computer that can play chess. We do not care that the three laws of robotics lead to the robots rebellion against their programmers, we simply want to know how to program robots.

Can computers self-program?

Yes, easily. Here is one way how.

Take the present date best computer chess program. Take two versions of the same. Make them play one against the other.

Build in the rule that the program denotes a priority value to any best possible move that is played by the opposition computer, such that when the exact same pattern of pieces is ever replicated then the move with the priority value is chosen over any other possible move.

Is self-programming the same as learning? We don't know and we don't care. The question misses the point and it is wrong to ask it.

What we want to know is how to build a better computer chess program, we do not want to create confusion in our workings by attending to a metaphysical question that has no relevance to how to build a better computer chess program.

Babbage, Boole and Tesla.

Tesla because he invented light if not the mass production of the light bulb.

Boole because he invented the laws of thought if not object orientated software programs.

Babbage because he invented machine processing if not the television.

Artificial light, the laws of thought and machine processing, then the world wide web.

The softest part of the theory of the compiler. That it does not exist. Here's why.

The hardware does physical stuff, and only physical stuff. It is object, electric and information on a screen or in a database.

The software does processing of symbol, and only processing of symbol. It is logic, mathematic and algorithm.

After all the translation has happened between the highest order languages programmed by the user through all the reductions to the simplest order languages read by the hardware we are still at the point of software. Between the simplest order language read by the hardware and the highest order language programmed by the user we have a translation from simpler to higher or higher to simpler. At each stage we understand the part we work on, either higher order language or simple machine readable language or translator language between one and the other. That we do not understand each of the languages of all the languages involved in the process and the translator rules between any two does not matter.

So then we eventually get to the point where we want to know how the machine readable language is translated into machine activity. But that is easy. Machine readable language is ones and zeros translated into place holders that are filled or empty. If empty then one sort of electrical signal and if filled then a different sort of electrical signal.

So what is the mystery? Why is there any sort of puzzle?

What the mystery is, why there is any sort of puzzle, is because any one level of code programmer does not know the language code of the programmer at a different level, therefore a mystery exists that puzzles any programmer. Presumably any person inclined to do so could learn the important bits of the language at each of eight levels of code from higher order language to machine readable language, but they would not obtain what they wanted by doing so, or at least, not really. What they would obtain by doing so is a facility at translation between language and then become specialist in the field of compilers, but that is not what we meant.

What we wanted to know was at which one point does code become machine. And that one point does not exist. It is that higher order language is translated into the next level simpler order language which is again translated into next level simpler order language, until after how ever many levels the language is machine readable in terms of ones and zeros. Therefore there must be a non-existant constant that is generated by the inter-relationship of languages. But that constant is non-existant as an actual thing because it only results from the inter-relationship of existant things.

Why object orientated programming?

Because we can turn an extended complex and sophisticated program into a single unit called an object. Then we can refer to the single object in order to activate the entire program. Or we can move the single object from one place to another. So we can then build program modules which are then given object names and we can then build programs that are only the manipulation of object names. It would end up that a programmer writes code of object names while having no knowledge of the program that the object name refers to and the programmer writing code for object names has no knowledge of how those object names are used.

Here is an analogous scenario. On watching television we want to know how it works at one specific point. But that means we must know what it is that the actors on television know, but also the directors, the producers and the writers of the production. But not only that, the lighting engineers, the camera men, the studio staff. And then the film studio, and how the editing staff operate, how the finished product is transferred to the television station. How the television works, how the picture is transmitted from broadcasting station to the television, how the electricity powers the television. We know the result of all of it is that at one point the television can be switched on to provide entertainment, but as to finding one point where the television is made to work, that does not exist.

If my explanation of a matter has only been to show what is not the case, or what we think can not be done, then to whom do we turn in order to find out what is the thing, or why it is?

And in theory the answer is homo faber, or man the maker. So we suppose that man the maker is a different person, or the sort of person who knows how things are made. The deep consciousness at this stage is the archetype or god known as Vulcan. What we can understand here is that there is a difference between making and any other area of human activity. Making is itself a thing. It is as if we know that making as a matter can be applied to what as a particular. And we can deliberately decide yes or no. Because if man the maker will not make the what, then the what will not be made. And if the what is to be made, then man the maker will know how to do so.

For the purpose of this argument we signify the difference between creating, inventing and making.

Because man the maker neither creates nor invents. Creating must be thought of as the province of the divine. Which is best reflected in the human as invention. So for example, given a door, the invention of lock and key. However, once the lock and key are invented the making of keys and locks is the matter of making. Meaning that making any particular thing is a peculiar knowledge of how to.

We make a mistake when we ask the question "Can machines think?".

Because it is as if we have already decided that we know what thinking is, and even before that, that we have already decided certain assumptions as to mind.

In particular it is as if we have already decided we know where mind exists, or where mind is placed.

But when we challenge the assumption, we find we do not know where mind exists.

Here is an example. We suppose mind is in the subjective perceiver driving the car. But the driver of the car does not know mechanics. He drives the car on the left in a road system of other drivers. The road system includes traffic lights, a language system of road signs that must be adhered to. A range of laws that must be obeyed. The roads themselves are named and the complex of roads is geographically mapped.

It may be that mind exists in the totality of all of those different factors rather than in the individual driver. And clearly it is the case that any individual driver has to adhere to the complex system that all the other drivers are bound to adhere to.

Or alternatively, we say mind exists in the reader of a book, not in the book itself. But this may be wrong. Because the book contains ideas which are thoughts of the writer of the book. So mind may exist in the combination of writer, book and reader, rather than in any one component of the complex.

Or we say mind does not exist in the object that does not think. But that can be challenged. Because we can look at some non-thinking object and determine that mind is evident in its make up different to other non-thinking object. So for example, the intelligence that is evident in the combination of cup, saucer, spoon, plate, knife and fork may suggest mind is extended through the non-thinking object.

Each of these examples is intended to challenge the presupposition that mind exists in the subjective perceiver independently, and it is to open the understanding to the possible belief that mind may be placed differently. Specifically that mind may be a different thing to any one thinker, and that any one thinker may be only a component aspect of mind.

If that is so, then we may decide that it is correct to affirm "machines always think". It is just that some machines think better than others. And then, that some machines think much better than others. Is one car a machine? Yes it is. But is a combination of cars a machine?

Since one car is a machine, and a combination of cars is several individual cars, then the combination must be a machine. But is the totality of the thing within which cars exist a machine? That is, traffic lights, road signs, legal system, cars and drivers combined. And does mind exist in the totality, and is the totality a machine, and does the totality think?

So then we include software, where software is only program code for processing ideas in such a way that machines can manipulate thoughts. But we have already decided that machines always think even before we included software. So now all we have done is enable the intelligence of mind to extend into the machine through the medium of program code. Where does mind begin or end? And the answer has to be at no stage of the matter on which we focus our attention can we discover the point where mind begins or ends. And there is no break in the continuum of mind such that we can say mind does not exist in it.

So does mind exist in the independent machine separately? No. But neither does mind exist in the independent driver of the car separately. Mind exists in the combination of driver, car, road system and other drivers.

1. $a => a <=> a = a$

2. $\sim a => \sim a <=> \sim a = \sim a$

3. $a =/=> \sim a <=> a =/= \sim a$

4. $a \wedge \phi => a <=> a + 0 = a$

5. $a \wedge \sim\phi => a <=> a - 0 = a$

6. $\sim a \wedge \phi => \sim a <=> \sim a + 0 = \sim a$

7. $\sim a \wedge \sim\phi => \sim a <=> \sim a - 0 = \sim a$

8. $a \vee 1 => a <=> a.1 = a$

9. $a < 1 => a <=> a/1 = a$

10. ~a v 1 => ~a <=> ~a.1 = ~a

11. ~a < 1 => ~a <=> ~a/1 = ~a

12. a v ϕ => ϕ <=> a.0 = 0

13. a < ϕ => ϕ <=> a/0 = 0

14. ~a v ϕ => ϕ <=> ~a.0 = 0

15. ~a < ϕ => ϕ <=> ~a/0 = 0

16. a ^ 1 => 1 ^ a <=> a + 1 = 1 + a

17. a ^ ~1 => Q ^ a <=> a - 1 = -1 + a

18. ~a ^ 1 => 1 ^ ~a <=> ~a + 1 = 1 + ~a

19. ~a ^ ~1 => Q ^ ~a <=> ~a - 1 = -1 + ~a

20. ϕ ^ a => a <=> 0 + a = a

21. ϕ ^ ~a => ~a <=> 0 - a = -a

22. ϕ ^ ~(~a) => !a <=> 0 - ~a = - ~a

23. a ^ a => a ^ a <=> a + a = a + a

24. a v a => a <=> a . a = a

25. a ^ ~a => e <=> a - a = 0

26. a < a => 1 <=> a / a = 1

27. a v ~a => Q <=> a . ~a = 0

28. a ^ ~(~a) => a ^ !a <=> a - ~a = 1

29. a < ~a => Q <=> a / ~a = -1

30. a v b => b v a <=> a . b = b . a

31. a ^ b => b ^ a <=> a + b = b + a

32. (a ^ b) ^ c => a ^ (b ^ c) <=> (a + b) + c = a + (b + c)

33. (a v b) v c => a v (b v c) <=> (a . b) . c = a . (b . c)

34. a ^ (b v c) => (a ^ b) v (a ^ c) <=> a + (b . c) = (a + b) . (a + c)

35. a v (b ^ c) => (a v b) ^ (a v c) <=> a . (b + c) = (a . b) + (a . c)

36. ~(a ^ b) => ~a ^ ~b <=> ~(a + b) = ~a + ~b

37. ~(a v b) => ~a v ~b <=> ~(a . b) = ~a . ~b

38. a < b => a < b <=> a / b = a / b

39. a ∧ ~b => ~b ∧ a <=> a - b = -b + a

40. (a ∧ ~b) ∧ ~c => a ∧ ~(b ∧ ~c) <=> (a - b) - c = a - (b - c)

41. (a < b) < c => a < (b < c) <=> (a / b) / c = a / (b / c)

42. a ∧ ~(b < c) => (a ∧ ~b) < (a ∧ ~c) <=> a - (b / c) = (a - b) / (a - c)

43. a < (b ∧ ~c) => (a < b) ∧ ~(a < c) <=> a / (b - c) = (a / b) - (a / c)

44. ~(a ∧ ~b) => ~a ∧ ~(~b) <=> ~(a - b) = ~a - ~b

45. ~(a < b) => ~a < ~b <=> ~(a / b) = ~a / ~b

The above ideas 1 through 45. Each idea the synthesis of individual concepts. The synthesis of ideas a notion.

Correct as stated and if correctly stated then true or not. But then heuristic. Correct as stated or not, does not matter. At least we can see a complete notion. And we can see the forty five ideas that combine to provide the notion. And we see we have a small specific number of concepts to consider.

Take any one idea. Specify idea 26. It is easy to see that idea 26 is not correct as stated, since it is deliberately not giving all the possible correct answers. Idea 26 says a divided by a is unity. Which we can expand into word language to say that if a thing is contained by itself then the result is unity. But that is only true if a is a positive integer. The reason we say a/a=1 is because 1/1=1, 2/2=1, 3/3=1, so then a is any positive integer. But a could be a negative integer. Then a/a = 0 if any negative integer divided by itself is zero or a/a = b if any negative integer divided by itself is a different unknown variable not a. But a could be zero. Then a/a = ∞ if zero divided by zero is infinity. But then we would have to say Ǝ∞ and not the ψ∞ . Therefore a / a = Ǝ∞ which is the particular infinity made when the empty set contains itself, since it means a continuum of nothing containing nothing in an unlimited way.

Translated into sets is

"a <=> ϕ, ∧ ϕ < ϕ => Э∞ ∧∼ ψ∞, => a < a => Э∞ ∧∼ ψ∞."

Which says if and only if a is the empty set, and, the empty set containing the empty set is one species of infinity and not the genus of that type of infinity, then a containing a is one species of infinity and not the genus of that type of infinity.

And if "a <=> +n, ∧ +n < +n => 1, => a < a => 1."

Which says if and only if a is a positive integer, where +n is any positive integer, then given any positive integer containing itself gives unity, if a containing a then unity.

And if "a <=> -n, ∧ -n < -n => b, => a < a => b."

Which says if and only if a is a negative integer, where -n is any negative integer, then given any negative integer containing itself gives an unknown variable b, where b is any unknown variable, if a containing a then unknown variable b.

Therefore, the notion that can be developed from idea 26 is as follows:

26.i - "a <=> ϕ, ∧ ϕ < ϕ => Э∞ ∧∼ ψ∞, => a < a => Э∞ ∧∼ ψ∞."

26.ii - "a <=> +n, ∧ +n < +n => 1, => a < a => 1."

26.iii - "a <=> -n, ∧ -n < -n => b, => a < a => b."

26.iv - "a/a = 1 or ∞ or b".

The question becomes, not, what do we think?, but instead, what can we think?

And we can think ideas that are corollary to simple affirmations. And this enables us to think notions that are complex compounds of ideas that we can think.

For example we can think this notion:

The definition of machine is thinking object. As such, we do not consider thinking to be only one thing, and depending on what level of thinking is active, the nature of thinking adjusts. We think machine is mind extended through object that enables a kind of thinking.

The simplest machine is a plumbline. Plumblines do not exist in nature unless made by mind deliberately. Plumblines are thinking objects, and they think only one idea, that is verticality.

We can show this as a < a => 1, where plumbline is a, and vertical axis is a, therefore plumbline contains vertical axis as its essence, and the one containing itself is unity.

But equally because we do think a/a=1, we can look at this idea and challenge it. And we discover that two other possible ideas are available, that a/a=b or a/a=∞.

So now we can think that a divided by a is one or infinity or unknown variable b. And nothing else. We do not think that there is to our present understanding any other possible answer to what a/a is equal to. And we cannot make one up. So we find ourselves in the circumstance where what we can think is restricted by nature of the rules through which we do think.

This is useful because it means we do not challenge what we can think as such, but we do challenge what we do think. Because where we do think any particular thing, and we know that we can think other to what we do think, then we desire to know what the other possible thought is.

Specifically what I am saying is that given a/a=1 it is the case that we want to know that only two other ideas are possible for a/a.

CHAPTER
TWENTY SIX.

Point One.

Speed = distance / time

Accleration = change in speed / time

Force = mass X accleration

Work = Force X Distance

Power = Work / Time

Pressure = Force / Area

Density = Mass / Volume

Voltage = Current(I) X Resistance(R)

Power = Voltage squared / Resistance

The idea of the game is to maintain the a=b.c pattern throughout all the formulas.

And to keep adding formulas in any legitimate shape that somehow relate to the above.

The idea is to determine how many such formulas exist.

And to see to what extent a chain of unbroken such formulas can be designed, such that through knowledge of any two variables in the chain, all other variables can be worked out.

Point Two.

To play properly, we must first understand the formula:

$a = b . c$

This formula is itself the secret of formulating the laws of physics.

$(a = b \cdot c) <=> (b \cdot c = a)$

$(a = b \cdot c) => [(b = a / c) \wedge (c = a / b)]$

Understanding this formula in itself is useful.

The variables are not all of equal nature.

If we take the equation for velocity, which is: distance between a and b according to some given measure, when divided by time taken to travel that distance, gives the average velocity or speed.

Two terms in the equation are fixed by definition.

The third term is a proportion of the two terms that are fixed, in relationship.

Meaning that the third term cannot be discovered on its own.

So when we have any one of the variables, a b or c, we have to establish whether it is a fixed quantity or a proportional quantity.

Point Three.

To play the equation $a = b \cdot c$ is by definition an "idealist" move.

It forces that an idealist explanation be provided in this sort of way:

Pattern One. $(a = b \cdot c) => [(a / b = c) \wedge (a / c = b)]$

Pattern Two. $(b = a \cdot c) => [(b / a = c) \wedge (b / c = a)]$

Pattern Three. $(c = a \cdot b) => [(c / a = b) \wedge (c / b = a)]$

Assume that throughout this article we will use pattern one, since patterns two and three are only different ways of saying the exact same thing, without difference of structure, but only involving difference of content.

So using pattern one, If we have the equation $a = b \cdot c$ and we know the quantity for the variable a and b.

Then we know that we can apply the equation a / b = c, and so find the third variable.

However, we can extend the equation by virtue of its being what it is.

Because if we know b . c = a, and we have discovered all three variables from knowing only a and b.

Then we ask what is the variable x if we say:

a . b = x

or

a . c = x

or

b / c = x

or

c / b = x

When, through the laws of physics we can create such chains of formulas, simply by determining what is the meaning of the unknown variable x.

Point Four.

From an idealist perspective we have no practical application for this method, it is simply that it makes sense to the logic of the rules for the algebraic game.

Suppose we are not sure of the correctness of our reasoning so far.

For that reason we must go back and check our terms.

When we say a = b . c we mean for example, 8 = 2 . 4, that is, eight equals two times four.

Where: a = 8, b = 2, c = 4.

Because our formulaic pattern says how we can make

adjustments and confirm the truth of the first answer, then we can say:

(8 = 2 . 4) => [(2 = 8 / 4) ^ (4 = 8 / 2)]

So this formula is proved ideally, for all positive integers.

Then we say, what happens if we multiply a by b, what does that give, call it unknown variable x.

Therefore: 8 . 2 = x

We then know that x exists.

x is two examples of eight added together which is sixteen. Therefore x is sixteen. Say sixteen is called variable d.

Then we have:

8 . 2 = 16, and a . b = d, therefore d = 16

And that gives:

a = 8, b = 2, c = 4, d = 16

(a = b . c) => [(a / b = c) ^ (a / c = b)]

a . b = d

or

a . c = x

or

b / c = x

or

c / b = x

Point Five.

We know we are correct if and only if: (d = a . b) => [(a = d / b) ^ (b = d / a)]

Which in numbers is: (16 = 8 . 2) => [(8 = 16 / 2) ^ (2 = 16 / 8)]

So then we have:

a = 8, b = 2, c = 4, d = 16

$(a = b \cdot c) => [(a / b = c) \wedge (a / c = b)]$

$(8 = 2 \cdot 4) => [(2 = 8 / 4) \wedge (4 = 8 / 2)]$

$(d = a \cdot b) => [(a = d / b) \wedge (b = d / a)]$

$(16 = 8 \cdot 2) => [(8 = 16 / 2) \wedge (2 = 16 / 8)]$

Point Six.

Because our workings out can be checked for falsity or correctness, and we have shown the reasoning for each step, we feel more comfortable in assuming e f and g, as follows.

$a \cdot b = d$

or

$a \cdot c = e$

or

$b / c = f$

or

$c / b = g$

Which we then show the number value for, such that: $d = 16$, $e = 32, f = 1/2, g = 2$

and if this is correct, then the various terms should translate between languages, as follows:

$(d = a \cdot b) => [(a = d / b) \wedge (b = d / a)]$

$(e = a \cdot c) => [(a = e / c) \wedge (c = e / a)]$

$(f = b / c) => [(b = f \cdot c) \wedge (c = b / f)]$

$(g = c / b) => [(c = g \cdot b) \wedge (b = c / g)]$

So that:

$(16 = 8 \cdot 2) => [(8 = 16 / 2) \wedge (2 = 16 / 8)]$

$(32 = 8 \cdot 4) => [(8 = 32 / 4) \wedge (4 = 32 / 8)]$

$(1/2 = 2 / 4) => [(2 = 1/2 \cdot 4) \wedge (4 = 2 / 1/2)]$

$(2 = 4 / 2) => [(4 = 2 \cdot 2) \wedge (2 = 4 / 2)]$

Point Seven.

We are then provided with the pattern:

$(a = b . c) => [(a / b = c) \wedge (a / c = b)]$

$(d = a . b) => [(a = d / b) \wedge (b = d / a)]$

$(e = a . c) => [(a = e / c) \wedge (c = e / a)]$

$(f = b / c) => [(b = f . c) \wedge (c = b / f)]$

$(g = c / b) => [(c = g . b) \wedge (b = c / g)]$

Which in number terms is:

$(8 = 2 . 4) => [(2 = 8 / 4) \wedge (4 = 8 / 2)]$

$(16 = 8 . 2) => [(8 = 16 / 2) \wedge (2 = 16 / 8)]$

$(32 = 8 . 4) => [(8 = 32 / 4) \wedge (4 = 32 / 8)]$

$(1/2 = 2 / 4) => [(2 = 1/2 . 4) \wedge (4 = 2 / 1/2)]$

$(2 = 4 / 2) => [(4 = 2 . 2) \wedge (2 = 4 / 2)]$

The puzzle being that if we can find any seven terms in physics that can be so related together as a b c d e f g in the above pattern, then those terms form a formulaic chain.

This returns us to point one, where several physics formula are provided that may or may not be in the shape of the above abstract algebraic form. What we now have to do, is determine to what extent we can construct a simple pattern of physics formula in a shape similar to our idealist algebraic form.

Point Eight.

At this stage it is natural and easy, given our work on the language of logical sets, to make the translation of the above pattern which we can call Lattice One, into the language of logical sets.

The reason we do this, is not so much that the logic pattern informs us as to correctness, but more that it will inform us if we are incorrect. So if the translation into the language of logical sets involves no contradiction of the laws of logic, then all it tells us is that we are coherent and non-contradictory to the laws of logic.

The laws of logic are those which are previous and earlier to the above pattern. As follows:

$(a => b \lor c) => [(a < b => c) \land (a < c => b)]$

$(d => a \lor b) => [(a => d < b) \land (b => d < a)]$

$(e => a \lor c) => [(a => e < c) \land (c => e < a)]$

$(f => b < c) => [(b => f \lor c) \land (c => b < f)]$

$(g => c < b) => [(c => g \lor b) \land (b => c < g)]$

It may be that the logical pattern does not tell us very much. All it says is that no laws of logic are broken.

It also implies that other logical possibilities exist, given any adjustment maintains logical coherence by adjustment of any related terms.

However, without adjustment, as it stands, the logical validity of the argument is confirmed.

Point Nine.

We now have one pattern that we have stated in three different languages, where each language rests on the language below.

The sequence of priority is logic gives algebra, algebra gives number, in this way:

Lattice One, Logic:

I. $(a => b \lor c) => [(a < b => c) \land (a < c => b)]$

II. $(d => a \lor b) => [(a => d < b) \land (b => d < a)]$

III. $(e => a \lor c) => [(a => e < c) \land (c => e < a)]$

IV. $(f => b < c) => [(b => f \lor c) \land (c => b < f)]$

V. $(g => c < b) => [(c => g \lor b) \land (b => c < g)]$

Lattice One, Algebra:

I. $(a = b \cdot c) => [(a / b = c) \wedge (a / c = b)]$

II. $(d = a \cdot b) => [(a = d / b) \wedge (b = d / a)]$

III. $(e = a \cdot c) => [(a = e / c) \wedge (c = e / a)]$

IV. $(f = b / c) => [(b = f \cdot c) \wedge (c = b / f)]$

V. $(g = c / b) => [(c = g \cdot b) \wedge (b = c / g)]$

Lattice One, Number:

I. $(8 = 2 \cdot 4) => [(2 = 8 / 4) \wedge (4 = 8 / 2)]$

II. $(16 = 8 \cdot 2) => [(8 = 16 / 2) \wedge (2 = 16 / 8)]$

III. $(32 = 8 \cdot 4) => [(8 = 32 / 4) \wedge (4 = 32 / 8)]$

IV. $(1/2 = 2 / 4) => [(2 = 1/2 \cdot 4) \wedge (4 = 2 / 1/2)]$

V. $(2 = 4 / 2) => [(4 = 2 \cdot 2) \wedge (2 = 4 / 2)]$

What we must assert here, is that the structure of all three lattice one patterns must be the exact same structure through each of the three languages.

Whether or not the Lattice Pattern One in languages of logic, algebra and number are all stated exactly correctly including equivalence between I,II,III,IV,V, it is true that they could all be correctly stated.

Point Ten.

We are now at the point where we desire to apply our lattice one pattern to the formula of physics.

The question that we cannot necessarily answer at this stage is, what is the first equation, that will give us our variables, abc.

Our understanding being that this term must be the most simple of any terms later used.

Suppose then that we start with what we think is the most simple, on the understanding that this may change later given our workings out.

Our first formula then, is:

Speed equals Distance divided by Time.

What we can not immediately do is apply our lattice one pattern.

We apply the rule that all terms used must be given with a reasonable definition.

Speed refers to how fast an object moves. It is the rate at which object travels distance. A fast speed travels a given distance in less time than a slow speed and a slow speed requires more time to travel the same disance as a fast speed. An object with no movement has a speed of zero.

Velocity is speed including direction of travel. It is the rate at which object changes position. So in many cases we would use the term velocity as equivalent to speed, even when we do not provide a directional vector. However, speed plus directional vector is velocity.

A similar type of distinction applies to the difference between distance and displacement.

Distance refers to the space between two places. If we call the two places a and b, then distance is the measure applied to how far a is from b.

Displacement refers to the distance of object from a in what direction. So displacement is a measure of the object's change in position.

Throughout this article I will use the terms speed and distance, rather than velocity and displacement.

Time is the measure applied to the duration of action from start point to end point.

Our definitions then, are as follows.

Speed: It is the rate at which object travels distance over a duration of time.

Distance: It is the measure applied to the space between two places.

Time: It is the measure applied to the duration of activity.

Point Eleven.

We are now at the stage where we can apply part of our lattice to the first of our physics formulas.

That is, if a = Distance, b = Speed, c = Time.

Since, a = b . c

Then, Distance equals Speed multiplied by Time.

That is, D = S . T

Therefore it must be that:

(D = S . T) => [(D / S = T) ∧ D / T = S]

Our first formula then, is:

Distance equals Speed multiplied by Time.

Time equals Distance divided by Speed.

Speed equals Distance divided by Time.

Point Twelve.

When applying our method, it may be that the sensible order of development is not the most rational. However, given the choice we tend to start with the sensible sequence, and then apply a most rational sequence at a later stage.

Therefore since we are given the formula for acceleration as change in speed divided by time taken, our most sensible course is to apply this formula next in sequence.

Acceleration gives a measurement of distance per time unit per time unit.

Meaning that the verbal articulation says something like: "Ten metres per second per second" which translates as:

For every second that passes, the object increases speed by

ten metres per second.

Average acceleration is speed two minus speed one and then divide the result by time taken.

So that to find the average acceleration of an object we say:

The speed the object is travelling at the end of the given distance is S2.

The speed the object is travelling at the beginning of the given distance is S1.

We obtain the change in speed quantity by subtracting S1 from S2.

We then divide that figure by the time duration of the activity, to obtain average acceleration as D : T : T.

Acceleration then is: (S2 - S1) / T

Acceleration equals change in speed divided by time.

Which provides us with:

Distance equals Speed multiplied by Time.

Time equals Distance divided by Speed.

Speed equals Distance divided by Time.

Acceleration equals Change in Speed divided by Time.

Since change in speed is not the same thing as speed, we have to signify this difference.

$\Delta S = S2 - S1 = $ change in speed.

Therefore we have:

$Acc = \Delta S / T$

Which gives:

$(\Delta S = Acc . T) => [(\Delta S / Acc = T) \wedge (\Delta S / T = Acc)]$

Point Thirteen.

First formula:

(D = S . T) => [(D / S = T) ∧ D / T = S]

Second formula:

(ΔS = Acc . T) => [(ΔS / Acc = T) ∧ (ΔS / T = Acc)]

Where:

D = Distance, S = Speed, T = Time, ΔS = Change in Speed, Acc = Acceleration.

Which gives:

Distance equals Speed multiplied by Time.

Time equals Distance divided by Speed.

Speed equals Distance divided by Time.

Change in Speed equals Acceleration multiplied by Time.

Time equals Change in Speed divided by Acceleration.

Acceleration equals Change in Speed divided by Time.

Point Fourteen.

Mass = Density multiplied by Volume.

Since this is the formula we desire to bring in next, we have to again define our terms.

Density is the number of parts in an object to a constant surface volume. Meaning that if less parts are required to fill a constant volume, then that is a lower density compared to where more parts fill the same constant volume.

Volume is the amount of space that an object occupies. It is a measure of the total space-place filled by the object. In terms of a cube, the volume is the length multiplied by the depth multiplied by the breadth.

Mass is the measure of how much matter an object contains. So if the volume is constant but the density changes, then this adjusts the quantity of mass, or if the volume changes but the density is constant then this adjusts the quantity of mass.

According to our formula:

$M = Dn \cdot V$

Therefore we can say:

$(M = Dn \cdot V) => [(M / Dn = V) \wedge (M / V = Dn)]$

And since we know that Force equals Mass multiplied by Acceleration, where Force is defined as the capacity to do work or cause change.

We can provide the formula as:

CHAPTER TWENTY SEVEN.

Studies of Time In Itself.

A.

Before 1900 A.D. time and space were considered separate.

It was only an audacious idea to suppose a relative connection of time and space as unity, if people of knowledge tended to think of time and space as two different things.

Therefore, in all of human attention to this matter apart from the previous one hundred years, time in itself has been the focus of study, as an independent entity.

And space in itself also a separate entity.

My assertion being that there is a definite standard of hard understanding in regards to these two phenomena when they are each considered as individual and apart one from the other.

If we suppose a dodecohedron, that is a twelve sided object, where each side is symmetrical to each of the others, and each side a regular pentagon.

Then the study of time in itself is analogous to describing one of the sides of the dodecohedron, rather than describing the whole of the dodecohedron.

The analogy does not work exactly because the other eleven sides are each a different matter, so not entirely symmetrical. For example one side is space, another is mind, another is object, another event, and such like. So whereas the dodecohedron has each side exactly the same, the analogous matter that is a whole, unlike the dodecohedron, has each side a different subject.

If we call the analogous matter "metaphysics" and one of the facets of metaphysics is "time in itself" then that is what I mean.

Students of such are called Cosmologists, so it is called Cosmology.

B.

Socrates, Plato, Aristotle, Plotinus, Euclid, Archimedes, Vitruvius, Galileo, Descartes, Kepler, Kant, Newton.

That is only twelve people who significantly provide ideas and arguments on this subject.

Let us suppose a readership of the work on "time in itself" of the above named people exists, existed and will exist.

That being so, we can imagine a category of people that does not include any of the above named people.

But it is a category that only includes people who have read some not all of the work of the above named people.

For the purposes of this exercise we would do better if we direct our attention to the membership of the category that only contains people who have read the work on "time studies" provided by the given names.

The purpose of this article will be to offer some different ways of considering the study of time in itself.

My intention is to start with what seems to be most easy to understand, most evident to the senses, most simple to think about.

And also meets the condition that it is always true if it is sometimes true.

Meaning that if it is understood at the easiest, simple level, then it will be discovered to be equally true throughout the development of any more sophisticated argumentation.

D.

Time in itself does not exist. It is an emptiness within which objects move.

The definition of time is the measure applied to the movement of objects, that is called "change".

We require a constant for the movement of objects. We use the stars.

<Long duration time> is measured by the movement of the constellations. The constellations only move forwards, and they all only move forwards. They do so with enough precision and regularity that we can determine a thousand years by the movement of the stars.

<Medium duration time> is measured by the solar system.

The earth moves round the sun once to provide the duration of one year.

The moon moves round the earth once to provide the duration of one month.

The earth moves round its own axis once to provide the duration of one day.

Therefore, the movement of three physical objects in relationship provides us with our measure of time.

The earth round the sun, moon round the earth, and earth round its own axis.

All things on earth.

By all things I mean physical object.

That has to be a restricted number of things, not an infinity.

Therefore a time device or a clock.

You know what the date is by what things exist.

You expect things to exist in order.

You cannot see motor cars if we have not yet invented combustion engines.

If the cross bow exists and the thing that beats the cross bow does not exist, people with the crossbow beat everybody else.

Time is a war fought by object.

What objects exist is the focal point of the war.

Existence in regard to object is time dependent.

Object needs space to exist, but for object to exist in space requires time.

Only existant object can have cause effect sequences.

Object that does not exist can not cause.

There is no cause without some physical object as focus.

Space is very tight. Objects exist together in families.

If you have knives and forks, you expect to see plates, spoons, tables, chairs.

If an object has existence then this is within a time frame, and the time frame is only possible within specific time locations.

Therefore objects provide us with a time device or a clock.

The development of made objects can be sequentially described as a vector backwards into the past.

The latest made objects, such as touch screen mobile phones with internet access to music videos is a description of the front line of time, at the date of writing this article.

We can then extend the vector line from the actual past according to the sequence of made objects, bring it to the present through latest made objects.

This describes an eigenstate.

From the present existant object of all objects on the planet, our eigenstate is fixed.

Suppose eight main line eigenvalues exist as possible directions that our vector line could take forwards. These possible vectors forwards are called eigenvectors.

Whether you observe the event, use instruments to take measures, or don't, is actively important to what can happen.

Also what instruments are used and what instruments are not used has some non-zero cause value.

E.

Time, gravity and justice are one thing.

[Time is gravity] is false

or

[Time is gravity] is true.

What is meant by justice in its truth, is that it actions itself or operates as exactly equivalent to time and it does so in a manner that is entirely described by gravity.

For this reason a sword and balancing scales are the symbol structure of justice.

That is why all made legal systems cannot provide it, and it is how its activities happen in all and every matter.

The mechanism of justice knows the rightness of this because it experiences neutral, or a zero deviation from itself.

And until it experiences neutral it is bound by gravity to realise this state of being.

The movement of things as justice actions itself towards neutral eventuates over time, requiring duration.

CHAPTER TWENTY ÈIGHT.

The Idea of Quantum Science.

FIRST PART OF FIVE PARTS.

The focus of this article is the "idea" of Quantum Science.

The manner of presentation is an imaginative heuristic.

In order that there is a clear comprehension of the limited nature of the field that I am going to describe I would like to restrict to the work of only about thirteen specific people, work which begins around 1870 and concludes around 1970. That is, the claim that the entirety of this matter should be only in reference to that limited framework.

The people are Hendrik Lorentz 1870, Max Planck 1870, Albert Einstein 1900, Niels Bohr 1910, Erwin Schrodinger 1920, Max Born 1920, Louis de Broglie 1930, Wolfgang Pauli 1930, Werner Heisenberg 1930, Paul Dirac 1950, John Wheeler 1950, David Bohm 1960, Richard Feynman 1970.

Whereas the above named people are the only reference material that I am providing for the following ideas, that does not mean the ideas presented are an exact reproduction of the work of the people named. As far as possible I have been careful to associate the relevant idea to the originating scientist. However I have also included any supporting ideas as necessary in order to construct the important elements of the heuristic hypothesis.

At this stage, and for the entirety of this article, the level of science is entirely heuristic and provides only hypothesis.

The pattern as given is intended to be entirely coherent within itself, each idea with each of the others. It is intended to be entirely non-contradictory through all of its parts. Where possible I have only included ideas that I think will correspond with what is known to be true in modern physics.

The purpose of this article though is entirely heuristic. That means it is supposed to exist before experimental procedures are used to confirm or refute hypothesis. Only after experimental procedures provide adequate data can valid arguments be used to support any particular school of thought.

1.

The Lorentz Hypothesis:

a. <Principle of Reference Frames - Electromagnetic phenomena, that is, "Light", moves in reference frames relative to a total space. Movement of light between reference frames is subject to a variable called "local time". A difference exists between [universal time in total space] and [local time in a local field reference frame].>

b. <Principle of Matter Contraction - Moving bodies contract in the direction of motion.>

c. <Principle of Relative Time and Matter Contraction - Time dilation and object contraction in local reference frames are subject to speed of movement relative to observation from other reference frames.>

d. <Principle of Inertial Mass - As objects within a reference frame increase in speed there is a corresponding increase in inertial mass.>

e. <Principle of Local Field - Local field defined and determined by restricted limit of objects in it at time.>

2.

The Einstein Hypothesis:

a. <Principle of Relativity - All uniform motion is relative, there is no absolute state of rest, no priveleged reference frame that accounts for the speed of light.>

b. <Principle of Relative Change – The laws by which the states of physical systems undergo change are not affected, whether these changes of state be referred to the one or the other of two systems in uniform translatory motion relative to each other.>

c. <Principle of Inertial Reference Frames - the principle of relativity applies only to the special case of inertial reference frames, which are defined as local frames of reference in uniform relative motion with respect to each other.>

d. <Special Principle of Relativity - If a system of coordinates "K One" is chosen so that, in relation to it, physical laws hold good in their simplest form, the same laws hold good in relation to any other system of coordinates "K Two" moving in uniform translation relatively to K One.>

e. <The Principle of Invariant Light Speed - Light is always propagated in empty space with a definite velocity "c" which is independent of the state of motion of the emitting body. That is, light in vacuum propagates with the "speed c", where "c" is a fixed constant, independent of direction, in at least one system of inertial coordinates called the "stationary system", regardless of the state of motion of the light source.>

f. <The Principle of Transformation - Relativity and light speed invariance are compatible if relations of a new type called "Lorentz transformation" are postulated for the conversion of coordinates and times of events.>

g. <Universal Principle of the Special Theory of Relativity - The laws of physics are invariant with respect to the transition from one inertial system to any other arbitrarily

chosen inertial system. This is a restricting principle for all natural laws.>

h. <Principle of Uniformity - The constancy of the speed of light and independence of physical laws regardless of the choice of inertial system is a uniformity.>

i. <Principle of Commonality - No particular frame of reference is "special" in special relativity. That is, any reference frame moving with a uniform motion will observe the same laws of physics as any other. The speed of light in vacuum is always measured to be "c", even when measured by different systems moving at different velocities.>

j. <General Principle of Relativity - The principle of special relativity may be made general by applying it to reference frames that handle general coordinate transformations including the effects of gravity represented by curvature of spacetime.>

3.

The Planck Hypothesis:

a. <The Principle of the Planck Relation - There is a "proportionality constant" between the energy of a photon and the frequency of its associated electromagnetic wave, a relation of energy and frequency that we may call Planck's Constant.>

b. <The Principle of Quantum of Action - The Planck constant is a physical constant that operates at levels smaller than the atom in order to determine what can happen at levels larger than the atom.>

c. <The Principle of Planck's Constant - Since the proportionality constant is uniform at microscopic levels of photon in regard to variations of energy and frequency then all change in the quantum state of photon particles must be in conformity to that uniformity. Meaning that energetic changes in quantum system states cannot happen

by incremental degrees but instead only happen in jumps.>

4.

The Bohr Hypothesis:

a. <Principle of Energetic Atoms - That all matter can be resolved into atomic particles, and that those atomic particles can be resolved into smaller than atom energetic forms. Meaning that all matter is a product of energetic forms smaller than the atom.>

b. <Principle of Atomic Alteration - That the energetic forms smaller than the atom completely describe the component elements of the atom including changes of atomic state.>

c. <Principle of Wave Particle Duality - When matter is resolved to smaller than atom levels, the energetic forms at that level exhibit characteristics that may describe them as either waves or particles.>

5.

The Einstein–Podolsky–Rosen Hypothesis:

a. <Principle of Contiguity - Particles may be entangled by contiguity, such that conservation laws ensure the measured spin of one particle must be the opposite of the measured spin of another.>

b. <Principle of Unknown Variable - If particles are entangled by contiguity, then the spin of both particles is unknown until at least one of the particles is measured. Meaning the possibility exists that either particle could be in any possible state of spin.>

c. <Principle of Non Local Interaction - The measurement of spin of one particle in a local field collapses the possibility field locally as soon as the actual spin state is determined. And simultaneously and instantaneously collapses the possibility field non-locally for any entangled particle that must have an opposite spin.>

6.

The Heisenberg Hypothesis:

a. <The Principle of Uncertainty - There is a fundamental limit to the precision with which non-commutable variables can be known simultaneously. Meaning that an increase in the precision of knowing one variable necessitates a corresponding decrease in the precision with which the alternative variable can be known.>

b. <The Principle of Uncertainty in Wave Particles - It is a fundamental property of quantum systems in regard to wave particles that the more precision obtained in measuring position, the less precision possible in measuring velocity. And if the precision of measurement is increased in regard to velocity, there is a necessary and proportional decrease in the precision of measuring position.>

c. <The Principle of Universality of Uncertainty - The principle of uncertainty is a fundamental property of quantum systems in themselves and not a statement about the present state of technological advancement. Meaning that better measuring instruments will not reduce the proportional difference in precision of measuring non-commutable variables.>

d. <The Principle of Quantum Collapse - Quantum system states exist in a framework of possibilites determined by the relative values of associated variables. The possibility framework is destroyed by measurement of any one variable, causing state vector quantum collapse in all unrealised possibilities.>

e. <The Principle of Incompleteness - The various instances of uncertainty in quantum systems together combine to necessitate a permanent incompleteness to what can be known with precision in regard to the description of any given physical system.>

7.

The Schrodinger Hypothesis:

a. < Principle of Indeterminacy - In circumstances where which of two contradictory but equally possible outcomes is in fact the case, is unknown until measurement takes place, then both possible outcomes are equally true and correct until measurement takes place, known as a superposition of both states. >

b. < Principle of Direct Observation - In circumstances where one of two contradictory equally possible outcomes is discovered by direct observation to be the case, then all quantum state vectors associated to alternative possibilities cease to exist at that point. >

c. < Principle of Entangled Indeterminacy - Uncertainty at smaller than atom levels can be transmitted into an equivalent or related uncertainty at larger than atom levels, which may then be resolved by direct observation. Meaning that direct observation of macroscopic levels may be used in particular instances to resolve some indeterminacy at microscopic levels. >

8.

The Wigner Hypothesis:

a. <Principle of Relayed Uncertainty - Quantum states exist in wave packets that maintain principles of uncertainty until results of direct observation are transmitted to associated observers. >

b. <Principle of Transmitted State Collapse - The collapse of all alternative possibilities, that are found by direct observation to be not in fact the case, are relayed by the transmission of information to associated third parties. Meaning that those possibilities still exist as quantum states up until the point where information as to only one outcome is determined as true. >

9.

The Time Dilation Hypothesis:

a. <Principle of Relative Time Dilation - A difference of elapsed time may be noticed between two events, as measured by observers moving relative to each other, or in differently situated reference frames.>

b. <Principle of Durational Time Difference - A proportional relationship exists between velocity of moving objects and the duration of time, such that less time passes as speed increases.>

c. <Principle of Gravitational Influence on Time - A proportional relationship exists between gravity and duration of time, such that less time passes as gravity decreases.>

10.

The Measurement Hypothesis:

a. <Principle of Observer Involvement - It is not possible to observe systems without causing alteration in the system being observed, such that the observer must be considered as part of the system being observed.>

b. <Principle of Active Cause - Where the possible states of affairs in a quantum system are given as a superposition of equally true eigenvalues, such that measurement actively collapses all eigenvectors that are discovered not to be the case.>

c. <Principle of Determinacy - That any future evolution of a quantum system state is based on the state the system was discovered to be in when measurement was made.>

11.

The Wave Function Hypothesis:

a. <Principle of Quantum System State Collapse - Where a wave function exists in an eigenstate of different possible

eigenvalues, each eigenvalue in accord with a different eigenvector, called a possibility frame. And such that interaction with an observer or measurement of one of the available variables causes state collapse of all eigenvectors found not to be the case.>

SECOND PART OF FIVE PARTS.

The Heuristic Idea:

This part of the article is entirely original.

What I will do is provide an heuristic notion consistently with the hypothetical principles described above.

Having completed the heuristic notion we should be able to consider its content in order to confirm that it is in reference to the given hypothesis. And having done so, we should be able to develop experiments to confirm or refute any particular hypothetical idea.

Experiment One.

a. The Speed of Time Hypothesis:

<Principle of Reference Frames - Electromagnetic phenomena, that is, "Light", moves in reference frames relative to a total space. Movement of light between reference frames is subject to a variable called "local time". A difference exists between [universal time in total space] and [local time in a local field reference frame].>

<Principle of Relative Time and Matter Contraction - Time dilation and object contraction in local reference frames are subject to speed of movement relative to observation from other reference frames.>

<Principle of Local Field - Local field defined and determined by restricted limit of objects in it at time.>

<The Principle of Transformation - Relativity and light speed invariance are compatible if relations of a new type called "Lorentz transformation" are postulated for the conversion

of coordinates and times of events.>

<Principle of Relative Time Dilation - A difference of elapsed time may be noticed between two events, as measured by observers moving relative to each other, or in differently situated reference frames.>

<Principle of Durational Time Difference - A proportional relationship exists between velocity of moving objects and the duration of time, such that less time passes as speed increases.>

<Principle of Gravitational Influence on Time - A proportional relationship exists between gravity and duration of time, such that less time passes as gravity decreases.>

b. In regard to speed of moving object.

Either:

T1.The increase in velocity of a moving object involves a proportional decrease in the speed of time's passage for the given object relative to a different object that is stationary.

Or:

T2. The increase in velocity of a moving object involves a proportional increase in the speed of time's passage for the given object relative to a different object that is stationary.

Or:

T3. The increase in velocity of a moving object involves a change value of zero in the speed of time's passage for the given object relative to a different object that is stationary.

c. If and only if the correct phenomena is a uniformity and always the case, then we can say that only one of the above three ideas is true. Each of the above three ideas is contradictory to each of the others.

So our first heuristic assumption is earlier than the given three possibilities. And it is that whatever the correct answer may be, it is always the case in every instance relevant to itself. That is, we are making the assumption that it is not true that sometimes idea one is true, and at other times idea three is true. Instead we assert that whatever we find the true answer to be, it is an answer that is always true and both of the other possible answers are always false.

d. Therefore we have to look at the above three contradictory ideas and determine whether we can confirm only one of them as to be most likely the case as true, and if so, then always true.

e. In regard to influence of gravitational force.

Either:

G1. The increase in gravitational force that influences a given object that may be moving or stationary involves a proportional increase in the speed of time.

Or :

G2. The increase in gravitational force that influences a given object that may be moving or stationary involves a proportional decrease in the speed of time.

Or:

G3. The increase in gravitational force that influences a given object that may be moving or stationary involves a change value of zero in the speed of time.

f. We again have to look at the above three contradictory ideas and determine whether we can confirm only one of them as to be most likely the case as true, and if so, then always true.

g. Our heuristic assumption, first instance.

That if we have two similar objects, one is stationary the other in movement.

That relative one to the other, the object that is in movement will experience a proportional change as speed of movement increases.

That is: in proportion to the increase in speed, the speed of time's passage will slow down, gravitational force will decrease and the matter density of the object will increase.

THIRD PART OF FIVE PARTS.

h. The heuristic experimental idea.

Suppose a spacecraft leaves earth and moves directly out and away from our solar system in a straight line, defined in terms of distance travelled away from our sun.

Suppose that the spacecraft at some stage in its movement away stops, turns round and moves in a straight line directly back to our sun, and returns to earth.

Suppose the entire time that the spacecraft is away, is specifically one rotation of our earth round the sun, that is three hundred sixty five days.

i. Therefore, the time the spacecraft has been away is exactly one year.

j. The Heinlein-Zelazny Question is:

Q1. How many twenty four hour days has been experienced on the spacecraft if it travelled at one quarter light speed for the entirety of its journey?

Q2. How many twenty four hour days has been experienced on the spacecraft if it travelled at one half light speed for the entirety of its journey?

Q3. How many twenty four hour days has been experienced on the spacecraft if it travelled at three quarters light speed for the entirety of its journey?

k. The speed of light is given as 299 792 458 metres per second.

That is two hundred ninety nine million seven hundred ninety two thousand four hundred fifty eight metres travelled in the time of one second.

Imperial system gives 186 282 miles per second.

That is one hundred eighty six thousand two hundred eighty two miles travelled in the time of one second.

l. Quantum Science claims "c" is maximum speed that all energy, matter, and information in the universe can travel.

$E/m = c2$.

Answering the heuristic, we get:

m. First Possibility.

If T3 is true, then it must be true all of the time, and T2 and T1 must be false, and must be false all of the time.

T3. The increase in velocity of a moving object involves a change value of zero in the speed of time's passage for the given object relative to a different object that is stationary.

If we suppose Q2 and if the spacecraft moves away from our solar system at exactly half light speed for what ever distance, and in such a way that when the spacecraft turns round and returns to our solar system travelling at exactly half light speed that the spacecraft is out of our solar system for the total time of one rotation of the earth round the sun.

Then given T3 and Q2 the time experienced on the spacecraft must be exactly three hundred sixty five days.

n. Second Possibility.

If T2 is true, then it must be true all of the time, and T1 and T3 must be false, and must be false all of the time.

T2. The increase in velocity of a moving object involves a proportional increase in the speed of time's passage for the given object relative to a different object that is stationary.

If we suppose Q2 and if the spacecraft moves away from our solar system at exactly half light speed for what ever distance, and in such a way that when the spacecraft turns round and returns to our solar system travelling at exactly half light speed that the spacecraft is out of our solar system for the total time of one rotation of the earth round the sun.

Then given T2 and Q2 the time experienced on the spacecraft must be more than three hundred sixty five days, say five hundred days.

But suppose Q3 and if the spacecraft moves away from our solar system at exactly three quarter light speed for what ever distance, and in such a way that when the spacecraft turns round and returns to our solar system travelling at exactly three quarter light speed that the spacecraft is out of our solar system for the total time of one rotation of the earth round the sun.

Then given T2 and Q3 the time experienced on the spacecraft must be more than five hundred days, say five hundred fifty days.

But supposing Q1 and if the spacecraft moves away from our solar system at exactly one quarter light speed for what ever distance, and in such a way that when the spacecraft turns round and returns to our solar system travelling at exactly one quarter light speed that the spacecraft is out of our solar system for the total time of one rotation of the earth round the sun.

Then given T2 and Q1 the time experience on the spacecraft must be more than three hundred sixty five days, and less than five hundred days, say four hundred days.

o. Third Possibility.

If T1 is true, then it must be true all of the time, and T2 and T3 must be false, and must be false all of the time.

T1.The increase in velocity of a moving object involves a proportional decrease in the speed of time's passage for the given object relative to a different object that is stationary.

If we suppose Q2 and if the spacecraft moves away from

our solar system at exactly half light speed for what ever distance, and in such a way that when the spacecraft turns round and returns to our solar system travelling at exactly half light speed that the spacecraft is out of our solar system for the total time of one rotation of the earth round the sun.

Then given T1 and Q2 the time experienced on the spacecraft must be less than three hundred sixty five days, say two hundred fifty days.

But suppose Q3 and if the spacecraft moves away from our solar system at exactly three quarter light speed for what ever distance, and in such a way that when the spacecraft turns round and returns to our solar system travelling at exactly three quarter light speed that the spacecraft is out of our solar system for the total time of one rotation of the earth round the sun.

Then given T1 and Q3 the time experience on the spacecraft must be less than two hundred fifty days, say two hundred days.

But supposing Q1 and if the spacecraft moves away from our solar system at exactly one quarter light speed for what ever distance, and in such a way that when the spacecraft turns round and returns to our solar system travelling at exactly one quarter light speed that the spacecraft is out of our solar system for the total time of one rotation of the earth round the sun.

Then given T1 and Q1 the time experience on the spacecraft must be less than three hundred sixty five days, but more than two hundred fifty days, say three hundred days.

FOURTH PART OF FIVE PARTS.

1.

Quantum Indefinite.

Let what the thinker thinks be what the prover proves.

We are presented with a Quantum Indefinite Problem Space.

Three mutually contradictory possibilities exist.

The possibility framework of the moment that exists before solving the problem is called an eigenstate.

The eigenstate exists in earlier structure underneath the manifest existant.

The eigenstate is defined by three eigenvalues.

Where each of the three possibilities is given an equal value to each of the others called an eigenvalue.

And where each eigenvalue is associated to a specific direction different to each of the others called an eigenvector.

2.

Quantum Uncertainty is suggested by the principles given earlier as:

<The Principle of Uncertainty - There is a fundamental limit to the precision with which non-commutable variables can be known simultaneously. Meaning that an increase in the precision of knowing one variable necessitates a corresponding decrease in the precision with which the alternative variable can be known.>

<The Principle of Uncertainty in Wave Particles - It is a fundamental property of quantum systems in regard to wave particles that the more precision obtained in measuring position, the less precision possible in measuring velocity. And if the precision of measurement is increased in regard to velocity, there is a necessary and proportional decrease in the precision of measuring position.>

<The Principle of Universality of Uncertainty - The principle of uncertainty is a fundamental property of quantum systems in themselves and not a statement about the present state of technological advancement. Meaning that better measuring instruments will not reduce the proportional

difference in precision of measuring non-commutable variables.>

<The Principle of Quantum Collapse - Quantum system states exist in a framework of possibilites determined by the relative values of associated variables. The possibility framework is destroyed by measurement of any one variable, causing state vector quantum collapse in all unrealised possibilities.>

<The Principle of Incompleteness - The various instances of uncertainty in quantum systems together combine to necessitate a permanent incompleteness to what can be known with precision in regard to the description of any given physical system.>

3.

Suppose we restate the problem in everyday words with a view to intuitively understanding the parameters, as follows:

A spacecraft leaves earth and travels away from our solar system, and then returns to our solar system and lands on earth one year later earth time, measured by a single circuit of the earth round the sun.

The question asked:

What is the length of time experienced on the spacecraft?

The answer we consider in terms of possibility, which we discover to be three in number, regardless of other variables.

The three possibilities which we call the eigenvalues of the eigenstate are that the spacecraft experience of time was three hundred sixty five days or less days than that or more days than that.

These are the only three possibilities we can think of.

One way of looking at the solution is to assert many worlds theoretical idea. That could mean all three of the possibilities are true depending on which universe you live in. Meaning three different universes exist, in each universe a different rule base is applied resulting in three different scientific theories. Each theory explains how to obtain a different outcome.

According to the theory of quantum state wave collapse in accord with the Copenhagen Interpretation, proving that only one of the given possibilities is true will simultaneously and instantly collapse the possibility of the other two eigenvalues. Meaning that depending on which rule base is used, will determine which theory is developed. And which theory is developed determines what outcome is obtained.

When any particular one rule base is observed, the theory developed coherent with the observed rule base, then only one outcome is proved to be true. Meaning that the possibility of the eigenvector as a direction of travel forwards in spacetime of two eigenvalues no longer exist.

If many worlds idea is true, then this does not imply consciousness of existence in any more than one world. Meaning that we are bound into the particular universe that confirms our choice of rule base, theory, science and proven facts. Parallel worlds then are a necessity in terms of the expression of the possibility of alternative choices not taken.

And the worlds one can not live in are the ones for which there is no eigenvector.

4.

How we measure time:

Time in itself does not exist. It is an emptiness within which objects move.

The definition of time is the measure applied to the movement of objects, that is called "change".

We require a constant for the movement of objects. We use the stars.

<Long duration time> is measured by the movement of the constellations. The constellations only move forwards, and they all only move forwards. They do so with enough precision and regularity that we can determine a thousand years by the movement of the stars.

<Medium duration time> is measured by the solar system.

The earth moves round the sun once to provide the duration of one year.

The moon moves round the earth once to provide the duration of one month.

The earth moves round its own axis once to provide the duration of one day.

Therefore, the movement of three physical objects in relationship provides us with our measure of time.

The earth round the sun, moon round the earth, and earth round its own axis.

5.

Suppose we have various methods whereby we measure time accurately on the spacecraft.

One is we have an egg timer that gives three minutes.

Three minutes is the average length of time of popular songs listened to on the spacecraft, such as those of Rihanna, Gwen Stefani, Beyonce and Madonna. Since the system used is state of the art there is no distortion meaning that the songs provide an accurate proof of time duration.

We have video for entertainment and the length of the films is normally around two hours.

We have clockwork metronome that measures the change of time with complete accuracy.

We have digital clocks that confirm the correctness of our measurements in each case.

6.

Since time in itself does not exist, and is only an emptiness within which change happens.

Since our constant for change is provided by the stars, sun, moon and earth.

Then our constant is specific to every location in the perceived universe.

Because the movement of the constellations is constant.

However, outside of our solar system, we no longer have the movement of earth round sun to provide us with measure of one year.

So this time measure cannot be used on our spacecraft to determine time length.

We can confirm time length on the spacecraft by use of egg timer, pop songs, video films and digital clock.

7.

If the length of time the spacecraft is away is the duration of one rotation of the earth round the sun, then we assert that the spacecraft is perceived by earth to have been away one year.

If the time on the spacecraft as measured by egg timer, pop songs, video film and digital clock is measured as only one hundred days, then how do we account for that fact?

If the time on the spacecraft as measured by egg timer, pop songs, video film and digital clock is measured as five hundred days, then how do we account for that fact?

If the time on the spacecraft as measured by egg timer, pop songs, video film and digital clock is measured as also one year, then how do we account for that fact?

FIFTH PART OF FIVE PARTS.

1a. The message is that: it is a house game.

1b. You can bet against the house. In a game of poker with ten players, three are any good, seven provide the income. The income gets divided among the three players who are any good.

1c. I toss a coin. It spins as it rises in the air. As it falls I catch it, and without looking turn it over on the back of my other hand.

It is covered so I have not yet seen the outcome.

I am to tell my associate if it is heads or tails. If it is heads, he is to bet on black in a roullette game. If it is tails he is to bet on red.

I am not to look at the coin to see whether it is heads or tails until the ball is spinning round the roullette wheel.

1d. Only three possibilities exist.

All three possibilities are given an equal value in the category called possible. Each possibility has the same eigenvalue.

The possibilities are red or black or neither red nor black.

1e. If zero comes up, everyone who has bet on red or black loses.

But there is only one zero among dozens of reds and blacks.

1f. So it is equal probability that either red or black happens.

1g. It is fifty fifty whether the coin is heads or tails.

2a. That is the circumstance before I look at the coin.

2b. Different eigenstates exist along a continuum to this point.

The first is when I have tossed the coin, it is spinning at the top of its arc, before it begins to fall.

At that point it is not yet determined whether it will land heads or tails. So the possibility is that it may be heads or tails.

2c. As soon as the coin is caught and turned over on my hand, but not looked at, whether it is heads or tails has already been decided.

Meaning that it definitely is one or the other has now happened. But we do not yet know what the outcome is.

This is the moment just before we collapse an eigenstate. The roullette ball is spinning. If it is heads he bets black, if it is tails he bets red.

2d. So now we do not know whether red or black will happen on the roullette wheel, and we do not know whether the coin is heads or tails.

It is meaningful to whether it will be red or black, as to whether it is heads or tails.

2e. If it is red and I bet red then I win. With fifty fifty probability.

If it is black and I bet black then I win. With fifty fifty probability.

If it is red and I bet black then I lose. With fifty fifty probability.

If it is black and I bet red then I lose. With fifty fifty probability.

Occassionally I lose a proportionally larger scale amount when ever it comes up zero.

2f. That means if I play perfectly I will lose by a minimum of zero point five percent I suppose.

3a. Is there a difference when I have looked at the coin and seen that it is either a head or a tail, so I know the answer.

3b. But I have not yet told my colleague whether it is a head or a tail.

3c. So does the eigenstate collapse when the coin is caught, but not looked at.

Or does it collapse when the coin is looked at.

Or was it entirely already decided as soon as the coin was thrown even before it had landed a head or tail.

3d. If I have not yet told my colleague whether it is a head or a tail, then he has still not yet bet on red or black.

So yes it does matter, because until we know whether to bet on red or black the place where the roullette ball should land is not yet determined.

3e. If I say it is heads, we bet on black, our decision is finished, it is yet to be decided which of the three possible outcomes happen on the roullette wheel.

If I say it is tails, we bet on red, our decision is finished, it is yet to be decided which of the three possible outcomes happen on the roullette wheel.

4. According to Schrodinger:

4a. <Principle of Contiguity - Particles may be entangled by contiguity, such that conservation laws ensure the measured spin of one particle must be the opposite of the measured spin of another.>

4b. <Principle of Unknown Variable - If particles are entangled by contiguity, then the spin of both particles is unknown until at least one of the particles is measured. Meaning the possibility exists that either particle could be in any possible state of spin.>

4c. <Principle of Non Local Interaction - The measurement of spin of one particle in a local field collapses the possibility field locally as soon as the actual spin state is determined. And simultaneously and instantaneously collapses the possibility field non-locally for any entangled particle that must have an opposite spin.>

4d. < Principle of Indeterminacy - In circumstances where which of two contradictory but equally possible outcomes is in fact the case, is unknown until measurement takes place, then both possible outcomes are equally true and correct until measurement takes place, known as a superposition of both states.>

4e. < Principle of Direct Observation - In circumstances where one of two contradictory equally possible outcomes is discovered by direct observation to be the case, then all quantum state vectors associated to alternative possibilities cease to exist at that point.>

4f. < Principle of Entangled Indeterminacy - Uncertainty at smaller than atom levels can be transmitted into an equivalent or related uncertainty at larger than atom levels, which may then be resolved by direct observation. Meaning that direct observation of macroscopic levels may be used in particular instances to resolve some indeterminacy at microscopic levels.>

4g. <Principle of Relayed Uncertainty - Quantum states exist in wave packets that maintain principles of uncertainty until results of direct observation are transmitted to associated observers.>

4h. <Principle of Transmitted State Collapse - The collapse of all alternative possibilities, that are found by direct observation to be not in fact the case, are relayed by the transmission of information to associated third parties. Meaning that those possibilities still exist as quantum states up until the point where information as to only one outcome is determined as true.>

5a. The end result outcome is meaningfully only one of two possible outcomes. I win or I lose.

5b. But the win or lose outcome is not fifty-fifty.

5c. It cannot be a determining factor to what the outcome is, that I win or lose. Meaning that whether the outcome is that I win or lose cannot be an influencing factor to the probability of the coin being heads or tails or the roullette ball landing on red or black.

5d. But it is a determining factor to what the outcome is, that the house wins or loses.

The house advantage over all is that the house wins fifty point five percent of the total amount all of the time.

And that is because the house owns the roullette table and the room it exists within.

That would seem to be the fairness of the circumstance.

5e. However the circumstance is not fair, and not ever, for this reason.

It is a given that when a player attains the point where they win approximately equally to the percentage possible given by the house advantage, that is forty nine point five percent of the total amount, then that player will be banned from playing in that casino and every casino to which that one is associated.

5f. Therefore a rule exists that: "You can not beat the house."

And that rule is on the one hand built in at structure in a game of chance such as roullette by the house having fifty one percent favour in regard to probability.

And also because the house has the legitimate right to refuse permission to any particular players to play, because the house owns the table.

Review of parts one to five.

The five parts of this article are complete at this point.

The purpose of this article is to use heuristic method to describe different perspectives on quantum science.

The basic hypotheses of quantum science are given as principles detailed in the first part.

The second part outlines one heuristic argument that can be

developed as an example, in regard to the given hypothesis.

The third part details a series of logical possibilities and all the possibilities in regard to the example heuristic.

The fourth part raises the matter of quantum uncertainty in regard to eigenstates.

And the fifth part describes the kind of scenario where all chance elements are structurally controlled to provide the house with a one percent advantage.

As such, the five parts together are intended to introduce some of the interesting ideas that can be developed from the field of quantum science.

There is no attempt in this article to challenge the ideas of quantum science as correct or not correct. And there is no requirement on the part of the reader to accept the ideas as stated as being accurate or not.

The method has been described from the beginning as an heuristic based on hypothesis.

CHAPTER
TWENTY NINE

Twenty One December Twenty Thirteen.

If we use the U.S.A date arrangement in this instance, that gives 12.21.13 as the memorable date for the completion of the notion as to the golden ratio formulae.

Key ideas are: perspective, proportion, symmetry, constance.

Although it could be argued that it is 21.12.13.

Quantum Indefinite.

The following article is designed to drive directly into a "problem space" that we can term the <quantum indefinite>.

If what you are after is the index to all the articles written under the Glimmerguard theme, scroll down to the end of this article, thanks.

This is the outline of the theory:

Hypothesis.

That before we make a decision at the level of very simple calculation a judgement is required between two possible correct answers, that we are calling the quantum indefinite.

The circumstance is different to the type of judgement required between a correct and incorrect answer. In the case of judgement between a correct and incorrect answer, after the judgement is made, we are then able to determine that we chose correctly or wrongly. That is, we can say we gave a right or wrong answer.

In the circumstance of the Quantum Indefinite, the choice is between two or more possible correct answers. And after we have made a judgement as to only one answer, we are always told we chose correctly. No matter which answer we choose.

What I am going to explain, although the workings out may be indirect, is that the quantum factor of physics already exists, built in, at the level of the structure of mathematics. And not as we may suppose at the point when mathematics becomes sophisticated, but rather, at the stage of earliest simple formula.

The Rationale.

The first point is I don't think this is new. I think it was easily available at the time of the Parmenides, a discourse of Plato, where the character of the title describes a series of complex equations in word form to a young Aristotle. However, the simplicity of Plato articulates a level of conception that is rarely available to common mind. It looks like something, but it is something else.

For that reason, what I think may be the case, is that a "tried and tested, safe and sure" <pathway> is deliberately designed by mind at the level of Parmenides, in order to guide the mathematician beyond the "problem space". As soon as they are through the particular area the specific dynamics of this matter no longer impose on the attention. And given that the designed pathway is adhered to in any occassion where the circumstance arises, then correct calculations will always give right answers. Because, after the decision is made, we are always told we chose correctly.

But, that is not the situation with the Parmenides, of course. Because, when we approach Plato, a mind of unsurpassed greatness, we are required to do what is different to the common mind. Plato is great for two reasons in particular. One is, he is the first student of Socrates, and the author who has documented the teachings of Socrates. The second reason is, he is the teacher of Aristotle. This is the solution to a puzzle that is often presented to students in their first contact with the works of Plato. They are asked, where does the real Socrates exist? Is he the character described by Plato, or is he the historical figure of various other documents?

The answer is, Socrates is Plato's teacher. And Plato is a mind that is unsurpassed. There is no effect without cause. Plato is an effect, the cause of which is Socrates. Therefore Socrates is difficult.

The second question, nearly always raised at the same point, is: what is the difference between Socrates and Plato?

And that question I have answered in part already, but not entirely. The entire answer is interesting. That is, Plato is an author who must be associated or disassociated equally with all of his characters. That Socrates and Parmenides and Zeno and all the others were real people must be assumed as true, on the basis that Aristotle writes about them as real people. The respect that Aristotle shows for Socrates is significant. And different to the relationship that he has with Plato.

Furthermore, Plato provides huge entertainment in regard to the ideas of other contempories, such as Phaedrus or Timaeus, so must be considered as different to Socrates as he is different to any of the other named people. And whereas Socrates demonstrates a philosophical method and purpose in actual discourse, Plato describes the discourse that involves many different people.

Remaining with the Parmenides for a moment, what happens when the initiate Aristotle is guided by Parmenides through the complex of equations, is a different direction, to what happens when the mathematician is guided by the designer solution away from the "problem space" of the quantum indefinite.

So the point of the Parmenides is directional. He says, look at this, is it not peculiar. And he drives Aristotle to look at the peculiar aspect itself, from a range of different and divergent possible perspectives.

That is a different direction to saying: That matter is a bit peculiar, let me show you a safe and sure line past the problem so you can get on with some more sophisticated mathematics without having to worry about trivial details.

The intention of the pattern that immediately follows is more similar to that of the Parmenides in terms of direction. By which I mean, it is designed to lead directly into the problem space of the quantum indefinite. This is in order that we can find our way there with some ease. And once there, we have some not all of the parameters of the problem space delineated.

Crucially, what I aim to demonstrate, is that some of our very earliest formula involve highest difficulty. And that it is for this reason that it can not be available to everybody that needs some basic mathematics. Not that difficulty does not exist at the earliest level, but that it can not be imposed on people who need the mathematics after this stage.

It is the nature of the problem that the more sophisticated later mathematics does not necessitate understanding of quantum variables for the large part of its middle knowledge. Only if a mathematician develops to the later stage of advanced concepts will they again be challenged with theories of possibility.

The pattern that follows is only thirty eight simple formula. But by the thirteenth formula we are already dealing with alternatives from the commonplace. Between the thirteenth and sixteenth formula we make several advanced moves. And at formula twenty six we begin to enter the field of infinity mathematics. With formula thirty five and thirty six we hypothesise the Quantum Indefinite.

Quantum Indefinite Pattern.

Q1. $a = a$

Q2. $b = b$

Q3. $c = c$

Q4. $a =/= b \lor c$

Q5. $b =/= a \lor c$

Q6. $c =/= a \lor b$

Q7. $\sim a \Rightarrow \sim a$

Q8. $\sim b \Rightarrow \sim b$

Q9. $\sim c \Rightarrow \sim c$

Q10. $\sim a = b \lor c$

Q11. $\sim b = a \lor c$

Q12. $\sim c = a \lor b$

Q13. $a + a = b : \{[(a = b) \Rightarrow (a \land b = 0)] \land [(a =/= b) \Rightarrow (a \lor b =/= 0)]\}$

Q14. $a - a = 0$

Q15. $a \cdot a = a \lor b <=> \{[(a = 1 \lor 0 \lor \infty) \Rightarrow (a \cdot a = a)] \land [(a = -n \lor +n) \Rightarrow (a \cdot a = b)]\}$

Q16. $a / a = 1 \lor 0 \lor \infty \lor b : [(a / a = b) <=> (a = -n)]$

Q17. $0 + 0 = 0$

Q18. $1 + 1 = b$

Q19. $\infty + \infty = \infty$

Q20. $0 - 0 = 0$

Q21. $1 - 1 = 0$

Q22. $\infty - \infty = 0$

Q23. $0 \cdot 0 = 0$

Q24. $1 \cdot 1 = 1$

Q25. $\infty \cdot \infty = \infty$

Q26. $0 / 0 = 0$ v ∞ v $1 : \{[(0 / 0 = \infty) <=> (0 . \infty = 0)] \wedge [(0 / 0 = 1)$
$<=> (0 . 1 = 0)]\}$

Q27. $1 / 1 = 1$

Q28. $\infty / \infty = \infty$ v $1 : [(\infty / \infty = 1) <=> (1 . \infty = \infty)]$

Q29. $a + b = c : (a =/= b)$

Q30. $a - b = c : (a =/= b)$

Q31. $a . b = c : [(c / b = a) \wedge (c / a = b)]$

Q32. $a / b = c : [(b . c = a) \wedge (a / c = b)]$

Q33. $+1 . +1 = +1$

Q34. $+1 / +1 = +1$

Q35. $-1 . -1 = +1$ v $0 => Q : [(-1) + (+1) = 0]$

Q36. $-1 / -1 = +1$ v $0 => Q : [(-1) + (+1) = 0]$

Q37. $-n . -1 = 0 : (n = c) \wedge \{[(-c) + (+c) = 0] => [(-c . -1) = (+c)]\}$

Q38. $+n . -1 = 0 : (n = c) \wedge \{[(+c) + (-c) = 0] => [(+c . -1) = (-c)]\}$

Analysis of the Quantum Indefinite Pattern.

1.

The key idea that we have to clarify in regard to the quantum indefinite is as follows:

It is a location immediately before and earlier than a required answer. It is before some required answer because it sequentially exists before. And it is earlier than some required answer because it structurally exists underneath.

In every circumstance where it occurs it is possible to decide without attending to the alternative possibilities. That is, we will normally have a routine answer that we give that ignores the other possible answers. And if we give the routine answer then we will always be told we are correct.

Attending to the Quantum Indefinite itself must be deliberate. We can be faced with the problem by accident, but we cannot solve the problem by accident. And deciding to choose the routine answer does not solve the problem, it rather activates one possibility as if it were the only correct answer.

Comprehending the Quantum Indefinite in one instance of its occurrence is not for the purpose of choosing a different one of its possible answers. What we are wanting to do in this matter is to comprehend the nature of the Quantum Indefinite in itself, and we are using one instance of its occurrence in order to educate this comprehension. This is so that by being thoroughly familiar with its nature in one instance, when we discover its existence in other circumstances we are more easily able to recognise what it is.

2.

We say "minus one multiplied by minus one is plus one". We say that because it meets the rules. We may question it when we first learn mathematics because we cannot quite understand how we get a plus one. But what we are not told is that we will never have to use it in practice. That the rule makers leave it in because it never actually happens, so it does not matter.

3.

Whereas in reality, multiplication by minus one is difficult mathematics. The way we are guided at a more advanced level in this understanding is through the equation for the square root of minus one, which is called "i" or imaginary numbers. The square root of minus one is a number such that when multiplied by itself gives the answer minus one. The problem being that we do not know what that number is, even if we know it must exist.

And without knowing what the number is, we can theoretically determine we have a quantum indefinite problem because the answer must be the same number with the same plus/minus referent. In hard form as follows:

LANCE GRUNDY

-n . -n = -1. What is the number "-n" in this calculation?

But it cannot be "-n" because that would give us a plus number answer, whereas the answer we want is minus one.

Therefore we must assert that there is no negative number multiplied by itself that can ever give minus one, because any two negative numbers multiplied together must give a positive integer.

But we cannot multiply two positive numbers together in the hope of obtaining minus one because that calculation will always give a positive number answer.

So the only alternative is :

+n . -n = -1. What is the number +-n in this calculation?

Now, plus zero point nine multiplied by minus zero point nine gives minus zero point eight one. +0.9 x -0.9 = -0.81

And, plus one point one multiplied by minus one point one gives minus one point two one. +1.1 x -1.1 = -1.21

Minus zero point eight one is is smaller negative number than minus one.

Minus one point two one is a larger negative number than minus one.

Therefore, the number that gives minus one must be between zero point nine and one point one.

But what ever number it is, it will have to be a positive and negative number multiplied together to give the answer minus one.

Therefore we have a proven demonstration that the square root of minus one must be two different referents in regard to plus minus even if the actual number is the same.

4.

Returning to the matter at hand, I am suggesting that:

Minus one multiplied by minus one gives "either plus one or

468

zero".

That is not the same as saying it gives one or zero. It gives either.

And a result that is "either one or zero" is the quantum indefinite.

5.

To make clear what I think is a quite absurd answer is to say: minus one multiplied by minus one gives plus one.

Because it cannot. That answer is not useful, it never corresponds to reality, and it is quite incoherent to higher order logic. So I believe it must be wrong.

How I intuitively understand this point is as follows.

If a stands for apples.

If I have minus one apple and I multiply it by minus one then I have plus one apple. But no I don't.

If I have minus five apples and I multiply them by minus one then I have plus five apples. But no I don't.

I think though I may have no apples.

And I believe this answer because I can perceive how it may be.

That is I have minus five apples and I multiply by minus one to obtain a "plus five apples" quantity, even though I do not actually have five real apples. Because my five apples quantity has to be offset against my original quantity which was minus five apples.

Now when I offset my original quantity of minus five apples against my new quantity of plus five apples I obtain no apples.

But no negative quantity.

6.

And having intuitively understood what I think makes sense, does conform to the rules, seems to have some correspondency value, and is useful, then I can apply it in abstract to the basic calculation.

Which means that minus one multiplied by minus one gives either plus one or zero.

Reviewing my argument.

My first point is that I don't particularly have any investment in the argument given.

If it is discovered to be false I would not mind.

What I have investment in is the "problem space" within which I have provided argument.

Meaning that the problem space itself is the matter that it is advantageous to comprehend. It is through understanding the problem space that we can begin to comprehend the nature of the quantum indefinite in one of its instances.

So that when we perceive its nature in other fields we are familiar with its make up.

And its make up seems to have these sort of characteristics:

That it involves a possibility of more than one correct answer.

That the circumstance of possibility exists before any one correct answer is given.

That as soon as one correct answer is given, the possibility factor disappears, and we are told that the only correct answer is the one that we gave.

Having provided an answer that we are told is correct all sign of any alternative possibility no longer exists.

And my belief is that the quantum indefinite has these types of characteristics in each of its instances.

In particular that it signifies a subtle field before and earlier than the manifestly given.

Such that when we are presented with the quantum indefinite in any circumstance we do well if we enable the possibility factor to exist.

CHAPTER THIRTY.

How to Pack a Rucksack.

First Idea:

The Special Relativity Game.

There are various methods one could use to describe how to play the special relativity game.

How to pack a rucksack is one way of doing so.

An alternative game that is easy enough to describe and play is how to pack a school satchel, so I shall describe that first.

This game was invented by Edgar Allan Poe when he went to Eton School. It was then played by everybody at Eton, and gradually became popular among several of the local public and grammar schools around Surrey, in England, during the eighteenth century.

A school satchel is limited in size. There is only a small available variation as to what is appropriate in regard to such an item.

It must be functionally acceptable, look like the right thing, normally get past the notice of various high tech security systems employed by the school authorities.

The school satchel must approach towards being time efficient.

Let us first suppose that if anybody knows how to pack a school satchel, that person is Edgar Allan Poe at Eton around 1815 A.D.

However, everybody at this level of school is required to do the same. So before we consider the perfectly constructed school satchel, we should at least entertain the common standard that all must meet.

The satchel itself may variously be a sports bag, a brief case or an actual satchel.

For the purpose of this experiment we shall suggest an doctor's black leather briefcase with a shoulder strap. The briefcase itself has three divider pockets inside, and one large pocket outside and two smaller pockets outside.

In regard to the special relativity game, the black leather briefcase will remain constant for the next seventy years, being replaced with the exact same model as it wears out with use.

However, at the beginning of its life, the briefcase is owned by an eleven year old at Eton school. What is in the briefcase?

Second Idea.

Since the brief case is so big, it may be more useful if we consider a smaller item, to explain the principle of the thing.

Imagine the Oxford Set of Mathematical instruments. At the present date this can be purchased for the cost of a DVD.

The tin that the mathematical instruments come in is hypnotic, so we want the tin. It has a nice picture on the front which is presumably something to do with Oxford. We like to say "oh yes the Oxford set of mathematicians" as we open our tin that cost the same as one meal at McDonalds.

We take out the contents and throw them away.

We now have the tin.

We need one set of the platonic solids in dice form, which can be obtained from dungeons and dragons games. That is only five dice specifically, we don't have room in our Oxford Set of Mathematical Instruments tin with the nice picture on the front, for any other dice.

We now have our tin, and inside the tin are only five dice, each one of the platonic solids.

We need a small bar magnet, one good quality precision pair of compasses, and the original ruler, set square and odd angled triangle.

A small Chinese abacus, the sort that are no larger than a person's hand.

These items are all that will fit in, leaving a very small space for personal choice.

A small egg timer could fit in to the space remaining.

Third Idea.

We put the Oxford Set of Mathematical Instruments in one of the smaller outer pockets of the doctor's black leather briefcase with a shoulder strap.

We have three paper back books.

The King James Version of the Holy Bible.

The Thirteen Books of the Elements of Euclid.

The Compendious Book on Calculation by Completion and Balancing by Abū Abdallāh Muḥammad ibn Mūsā al-Khwārizmī.

We put the three paperback books in the large outer pocket.

We have two decks of playing cards, which both together fit in to the remaining small outer pocket.

We have no more room in any of the outer pockets. But we have not used any of the three compartments of the inside of the briefcase.

Fourth Idea.

We can leave the three empty inner compartments as an eigenstate possiblility depending on difference of decision maker.

Meaning that if one understands the compendius book on calculation by completion and balancing, this can be applied to the addition and subraction of objects into and from the three inner compartments.

In their empty state, the three inner pockets are entirely neutral, so cannot have any change value on the briefcase as a whole.

The outer pockets are full and the items in them do not change.

Fifth Idea.

There are rules and principles that must be adhered to in regard to the placement of objects in the three inner compartments.

Fair play, reasonable game, transparency and such like are characteristics that can be normally associated to keeping to the rules and principles in regard to placement of objects in the three inner compartments.

The rules and principles may be argued.

There is a difference between arguing the rules and principles, changing them, and then using the change in rules and principles to adjust the placement of objects in the inner compartments.

To not knowing the rules and principles exist, and through not attending to such, using any alternative reason for the placement of objects.

A place for every thing, and everything in its place.

Any given change must have in mind a movement towards constancy.

The contents of the outer pockets are what is meant by constancy.

As objects in the three inner compartments approach towards the same level of constancy, they should be differentiated from objects that keep changing.

The end of the game is when the contents of the three inner compartments are all entirely constant, that is non-changing.

Sixth Idea.

The Special Relativity Game as a System of Differences.

At this precise location we can suppose as given:

A black briefcase with three empty inner pockets, and two small outer pockets which are full, and one large outer pocket which is full.

The contents of the outer pockets are exactly as given earlier.

What is the nature of the space of the three inner pockets?

We suppose a difference between the brief case when it has nothing in its outer pockets and when its outer pockets are full.

To understand this difference we suppose a difference between two versions of the Oxford Set of Mathematical Instruments.

One set is exactly as purchased.

The second set is as described earlier and entirely different contents to the set as purchased.

When the tins are closed they look the same. But the contents are different.

What is the nature of this difference?

Now when we can understand what this difference in itself is, then we will be able to understand what is the meaning of the difference between the brief case when it is empty and the brief case when its outer compartments are full and its three inner compartments are empty.

Then we can consider whether there is a difference to the emptiness of the three inner compartments when the outer pockets are full to the emptiness of the three inner compartments when the outer pockets are empty.

If there is a difference to the nature of the emptiness, then how are we to understand this difference?

Seventh Idea.

Principle of Structural Difference of Default Settings.

If we have a physical object that is the briefcase containing two decks of playing cards in one small outer pocket, an adjusted Oxford Set of Mathematical Instruments in one small outer pocket, The Bible, Euclids Elements and the Compendius Book on Calculation in one large outer pocket. And the three inner compartments empty.

Then that is our structural default setting.

Before we make a move forwards, we are offered the possibility to apply the principle of difference to the structure of our default setting.

If we apply the principle of difference to the structure of our default setting, then we are still able to move forwards with exactly the same forward options that we are presently given.

If we move forwards, without applying difference to our default setting, then this possibility no longer exists. We are forced by time to maintain the choice we have proved by action.

Therefore, we can consider applying difference to the structure of our default setting in this way.

Suppose a different bag. Blue in colour, synthetic plastic, with a shoulder strap. Also has two small outer pockets, one large outer pocket and three inner compartments.

Move the contents of black briefcase over to the synthetic blue satchel.

Take the Oxford tin of mathematical instruments and a red

synthetic plastic pencil case.

Move the contents of the tin over to the synthetic red pencil case.

Take the Holy Bible and replace it with the Book of Changes.

Replace the Elements of Euclid with Plotinus' Enneads.

Replace the Compendius Book on Calculation with Aristotle's Physics.

We now have a synthetic plastic blue satchel containing a synthetic plastic red pencil case in one small outer pocket, two decks of playing cards in one small outer pocket, one large outer pocket containing the Book of Changes, Plotinus' Enneads, and Aristotle's Physics. And the three inner pockets completely empty.

Structural Default Setting One:

If we have a physical object that is the briefcase containing two decks of playing cards in one small outer pocket, an adjusted Oxford Set of Mathematical Instruments in one small outer pocket, The Bible, Euclids Elements and the Compendius Book on Calculation in one large outer pocket. And the three inner compartments empty.

Structural Default Setting Two:

If we have a physical object that is the synthetic plastic blue satchel containing a synthetic plastic red pencil case in one small outer pocket, two decks of playing cards in one small outer pocket, one large outer pocket containing the Book of Changes, Plotinus' Enneads, and Aristotle's Physics. And the three inner pockets completely empty.

Then we are free to make a choice as to default setting.

We make a choice because the default settings are different to each other.

Eighth Idea.

Principle of choice between differences.

Is there a difference between the emptiness of the three inner compartments of the synthetic plastic blue satchel and the emptiness of the three inner compartments of the doctor's black leather briefcase with a shoulder strap?

Is there a difference to the contents of the three outer pockets in the briefcase and satchel?

Is there a difference to the emptiness of the satchel when it is entirely empty, with no contents in the inner or outer compartments?

Compared to when the three outer pockets of the satchel contain specified contents, and inner compartments are empty.

Is there a difference to the emptiness of the briefcase when it is entirely empty, with no contents in the inner or outer compartments?

Compared to when the three outer pockets of the briefcase contain specified contents, and inner compartments are empty.

Ninth Idea.

If we decide to understand the circumstance described above where we have two alternative default settings to choose between, then we can frame the conditions by which we make a judgement in accord with the various hypothesis of the idea of quantum science, such as:

<Principle of Reference Frames - Electromagnetic phenomena, that is, "Light", moves in reference frames relative to a total space. Movement of light between reference frames is subject to a variable called "local time". A difference exists between [universal time in total space] and [local time in a local field reference frame].>

<Principle of Relative Time and Matter Contraction - Time

dilation and object contraction in local reference frames are subject to speed of movement relative to observation from other reference frames.>

<Principle of Local Field - Local field defined and determined by restricted limit of objects in it at time.>

<Principle of Relative Change – The laws by which the states of physical systems undergo change are not affected, whether these changes of state be referred to the one or the other of two systems in uniform translatory motion relative to each other.>

<Special Principle of Relativity - If a system of coordinates "K One" is chosen so that, in relation to it, physical laws hold good in their simplest form, the same laws hold good in relation to any other system of coordinates "K Two" moving in uniform translation relatively to K One.>

<The Principle of Quantum of Action - The Planck constant is a physical constant that operates at levels smaller than the atom in order to determine what can happen at levels larger than the atom.>

<The Principle of Planck's Constant - Since the proportionality constant is uniform at microscopic levels of photon in regard to variations of energy and frequency then all change in the quantum state of photon particles must be in conformity to that uniformity. Meaning that energetic changes in quantum system states cannot happen by incremental degrees but instead only happen in jumps.>

<Principle of Energetic Atoms - That all matter can be resolved into atomic particles, and that those atomic particles can be resolved into smaller than atom energetic forms. Meaning that all matter is a product of energetic forms smaller than the atom.>

<Principle of Atomic Alteration - That the energetic forms smaller than the atom completely describe the component

elements of the atom including changes of atomic state.>

<Principle of Wave Particle Duality - When matter is resolved to smaller than atom levels, the energetic forms at that level exhibit characteristics that may describe them as either waves or particles.>

<Principle of Relative Time Dilation - A difference of elapsed time may be noticed between two events, as measured by observers moving relative to each other, or in differently situated reference frames.>

<Principle of Quantum System State Collapse - Where a wave function exists in an eigenstate of different possible eigenvalues, each eigenvalue in accord with a different eigenvector, called a possibility frame. And such that interaction with an observer or measurement of one of the available variables causes state collapse of all eigenvectors found not to be the case.>

<Principle of Determinacy - That any future evolution of a quantum system state is based on the state the system was discovered to be in when measurement was made.>

Tenth Idea.

We have an eigenstate with two alternative eigenvalues. Each eigenvalue offers a possible eigenvector.

We have to select only one of the two possible eigenvectors, as a direction of travel forwards.

If two different decision makers each select an alternative eigenvector then both events happen.

Having selected one eigenvalue and not the other, then the quantum system state of the eigenvector not taken collapses as a possible direction for that decision maker. Meaning the eigenvalue not taken no longer exists as a possibility.

The eigenstate is described by the existence of two default settings for how to pack a school satchel.

Structural Default Setting One:

If we have a physical object that is the briefcase containing two decks of playing cards in one small outer pocket, an adjusted Oxford Set of Mathematical Instruments in one small outer pocket, The Bible, Euclids Elements and the Compendius Book on Calculation in one large outer pocket. And the three inner compartments empty.

Structural Default Setting Two:

If we have a physical object that is the synthetic plastic blue satchel containing a synthetic plastic red pencil case in one small outer pocket, two decks of playing cards in one small outer pocket, one large outer pocket containing the Book of Changes, Plotinus' Enneads, and Aristotle's Physics. And the three inner pockets completely empty.

The four eigenvalues here are:

a. default one

b. default two

c. both default one and two

d. neither default one nor two.

Given some people will privately select eigenvalue "a" or eigenvalue "b" as a natural choice.

Then if there are two different decision makers and each takes the choice alternative to the other. Meaning that if one decision maker takes default one then the other takes default two. Then that means eigenvalue "c". Both default one and two.

And if a completely different decision maker has an entirely different selection of default setting, then eigenvalue "d". Neither default one nor default two, instead, the unknown variable default three or default four.

That is one or the other or both or neither.

For the purpose of the explanation of the exercise we will assume eigenvalue a or b are taken. In doing so, we instantly collapse the possibility of c or d. That is the eigenvalues c and d no longer exist as possibilities for us, instantaneously with our selecting eigenvalue a or eigenvalue b.

If we assume eigenvalue b is selected.

In doing so, we instantly collapse the possibility of eigenvalue a. That is, eigenvalue a no longer exists as a possibility for us, instantaneously with our selecting eigenvalue b.

If we assume eigenvalue a is selected.

In doing so, we instantly collapse the possibility of eigenvalue b. That is, eigenvalue b no longer exists as a possibility for us, instantaneously with our selecting eigenvalue a.

Eleventh Idea.

Principle of Difference in Local Fields.

<Principle of Determinacy - That any future evolution of a quantum system state is based on the state the system was discovered to be in when measurement was made.>

<Principle of Local Field - Local field defined and determined by restricted limit of objects in it at time.>

<Principle of Reference Frames - Electromagnetic phenomena, that is, "Light", moves in reference frames relative to a total space. Movement of light between reference frames is subject to a variable called "local time". A difference exists between [universal time in total space] and [local time in a local field reference frame].>

<Principle of Quantum System State Collapse - Where a wave function exists in an eigenstate of different possible eigenvalues, each eigenvalue in accord with a different eigenvector, called a possibility frame. And such that

interaction with an observer or measurement of one of the available variables causes state collapse of all eigenvectors found not to be the case.>

In the event that eigenvalue b is activated.

Then activation is the immediate instant of intending to choose b.

Any, all and every physical movement actioned towards causing the construction of eigenvalue b registers that decision.

In the instant of eigenvalue b existing in its basic format, its being is determined by the objects that make it what it is.

The specific physical objects are only:

the synthetic plastic blue satchel

containing a synthetic plastic red pencil case in one small outer pocket,

and inside the synthetic plastic red pencil case are five dice, each one of the platonic solids,

a small bar magnet,

one good quality precision pair of compasses,

and the original ruler, set square and odd angled triangle.

A small Chinese abacus, the sort that are no larger than a person's hand.

and inside one small outer pocket of the synthetic plastic blue satchel are two decks of playing cards,

one large outer pocket of the blue satchel containing

the Book of Changes,

Plotinus' Enneads,

and Aristotle's Physics.

And the three inner pockets of the satchel are completely empty.

The satchel itself is a local field. It provides a specifically limited space for other objects to exist within.

Objects can compete for existence in the limited space of the synthetic plastic blue satchel.

The end of the game is when the synthetic plastic blue satchel has non-moving constant object in all outer pockets and all inner compartments. The satchel itself will probably have changed colour and design by that point.

There is an eigenvector forwards in time that leads directly to that point. It is realistically ten years in the future from the event of eigenstate b activation.

Twelfth Idea.

Suppose the complete satchel is as follows:

the synthetic plastic blue satchel

containing a synthetic plastic red pencil case in one small outer pocket,

and inside the synthetic plastic red pencil case are five dice, each one of the platonic solids,

a small bar magnet,

one good quality precision pair of compasses,

and the original ruler, set square and odd angled triangle.

A small Chinese abacus, the sort that are no larger than a person's hand.

and inside one small outer pocket of the synthetic plastic blue satchel are two decks of playing cards,

one large outer pocket of the blue satchel containing

the Book of Changes,

Plotinus' Enneads,

and Aristotle's Physics.

And in one inner compartment a complete set of mahjong, a

set of fifty five nine bar dominoes, a wei chi board and stones.

About six or seven printed books in one inner compartment.

And several handwritten notebooks in one inner compartment.

Then with some space available for any additional items, that satchel could reasonably be constructed in a few weeks from activation of eigenvalue b.

Thirteenth Idea.

Difference of Holistic Gestalt.

The holistic gestalt is event, time, space, mind, object.

The object is synthetic plastic blue satchel containing "things".

Mind is the owner of the object, the particular person who built it, in each individual example of its existence.

Space is the place where the object exists and not every other place where it does not exist.

Time is the durational time frame with a start date and end date within such time frame the object exists and not every other timeframe.

Event is the becoming, being and ceasing to be of the object.

If we assume both the black brief case default setting one and the plastic blue satchel default setting two both exist in their complete state, that is non-moving, constant, without change.

Then the black briefcase in its complete state designed from default one is called object one.

And the blue satchel in its complete state designed from default two is called object two.

The mind that owns the black brief case is called decision maker one.

The mind that owns the blue satchel is called decision maker two.

The person that owns the black briefcase exists in a place different to the person who owns the blue satchel.

That is local field reference frame one contains decision maker one and object one.

And local field reference frame two contains decision maker two and object two.

The universal time frame that contains both local field reference frame one and local field reference frame two, may or may not be the exact same start date, end date, and durational time frame.

The event of the becoming, being and ceasing to be of both objects is possibly in this instance simultaneous, in two different local fields.

The difference of local field is defined by the fact that:

reference frame one contains decision maker one and object one, but it does not contain decision maker two and object two.

reference frame two contains decision maker two and object two, but it does not contain decision maker one and object one.

Are these two different universes?

The Heinlein-Zelazny question is:

A. If we assume one decision maker who has to choose default one or default two, then assume both possibilities happen in two parallel universes. So the time vector forwards divides into two pathways. What are the conditions and implications of this?

B. If we assume two different decision makers where one chooses default one and the other chooses default two, then both possibilities happen in one universe, but different local field reference frames. What are the conditions and implications of this?

C. If we assume two different decision makers where both choose default one, then the object one need not be the same in every aspect apart from the agreement as to default setting, both in regard to structure and also to content. So then we have two different object ones, which we can call object one point one and object one point two.

D. If we assume two different decision makers where both choose default two, then the object two need not be the same in every aspect apart from the agreement as to default setting, both in regard to structure and also to content. So then we have two different object twos, which we can call object two point one and object two point two.

Fourteenth Idea.

The above thirteen ideas illustrate principles. The principles are described through the metaphor of how to pack a school satchel. Which in turn involves similar principles as to how to pack a rucksack. The principles themselves will not be abstractly named in this article.

The principles themselves in their abstract form are difficult to clarify in a way that is immediately understandable, since there is no obvious actualisation in particular instances of their existence.

Therefore instead of long theoretical description which fails to convey the meaning, one can say:

If you do this very easy thing, right first time, exactly as described

Then the complex coherent set of principles on which the activity is based will be activated by necessary accident.

The necessity is that the rules be efficient and effective.

Packing a rucksack has to be done in any way that is constant at any and every century of human history in any location of human existence.

Therefore the activity that actualises this matter must be an expression of abstract principles that are constant at any and every century of human history in any location of human existence.

These are the principles of the Special Relativity Game.

CHAPTER
THIRTY ONE.

A.

If we assume default one. Then in making that assumption we are asserting several different variables as if they are known.

That is, we are asserting that we know something that we do not in fact know.

And the assertion that we know when we do not is in regard to several different variables, not only one variable.

However, the proof of the truth of all those unknown variables is only one thing, not several things.

Therefore if we could assume one thing with any confidence, then all those other unknown variables are automatically proved.

The one thing that we have to be able to assume is that the physical fact of object one in its default one setting exists.

It seems to me that the only person who can make this assumption with complete confidence, is the person called decision maker one.

B.

The physical fact of object one in its default one setting existing is first stage of gameplay accomplished. The person who owns the physical object of the briefcase with the specified contents is called decision maker one.

The following description provides a critical path towards basic default one being accomplished.

Structural Default Setting One:

If we have a physical object that is the briefcase containing two decks of playing cards in one small outer pocket, an adjusted Oxford Set of Mathematical Instruments in one small outer pocket, The Bible, Euclids Elements and the Compendius Book on Calculation in one large outer pocket. And the three inner compartments empty.

The translation of "The Compendious Book on Calculation Through Completion and Balancing by Abū Abdallāh Muḥammad ibn Mūsā al-Khwārizmī" that we want, is the one by Frederic Rosen.

C.

Before providing the path through to object one, a few ideas about the theory.

Object One includes the King James version of the Holy Bible.

Default One Setting includes the King James version of the Holy Bible.

There are two simultaneous points I have to make in order to be clear so they could come in either order:

If it does not include the Bible, it is not what I mean by Object One. It must be assumed to be a product of Default Two setting or default three or four, but different in each case to Object One.

The simultaneous point is that in the place where the Bible is, it does not have to be the Bible.

The Book of Changes is an adequate alternative to the Bible, which is what is meant by Object Two.

What is the case is that there does have to be some "thing" in the space where the Bible is.

The reason that some "thing" must be there, is because there are places it will not go. If it is there, then it is in some place where it exists. If it is not there, then it might not be.

However, the purpose of the following explanation is a particular example, using Object One as the illustration of the basic framework.

The idea is not really to exactly copy the description as given. The description is given as an example, that can be replicated if one wants to. But, Object One in its entire structure, content, form and matter must be understood to be disciplined by the Bible. The important reasoning to understand here is that the content is physical object in relationship to other content that is physical object.

So if we decide to choose default two, then the content and structure, form and matter will be consistent with that choice and different or similar by accident to object one.

A different related matter is that any two decision makers who both construct default one exactly correctly.

And both so much the same that they could at this point exchange objects and be confident that they still have the same.

On making the next move beyond default one, will at that stage begin to diverge from the sameness with the other decision maker.

The idea is that it does not matter how near or far any variation of Object One is from any other variation of Object One, given that both agree as to Default One.

That being said, the following provides a simple explanation of necessary sequences of action that result in one version of Object One.

D.

To prove default one setting.

An empty black leather briefcase. Has outside pockets, two small, one large or very similar.

Then the object of the empty briefcase must exist in a local field owned by the decision maker. That is a minimum first move. If that first move is not the case then nothing else follows.

If and only if the first move is accomplished can move two be made. If the first move is not finished then no time is given to move two until move one is finished. That is, it does not matter how much of the contents of default one already exist until move one is finished.

Whether none, some or all it does not matter. It is the same.

Given the first move is finished, then move two is to obtain the adjusted Oxford Set of Mathematical Instruments, on their own.

That is the tin itself, the ruler, set square and odd angled triangle, a precision pair of compasses, a small bar magnet, a small abacus, and the five platonic solids in dice format.

If the mathematical instruments exist on their own exactly as described, then that is what is meant by move two being finished.

If move two is finished, then move one is finished.

If move two and move one are finished, then we know ahead of time that we can finish move three.

Then it is possible to place the tin next to and not touching the black briefcase.

The active event of the mathematics tin being placed next to the empty black briefcase is a hard event. It only exists for a brief instant in a small local time frame. As soon as the present move is finished which is only momentary instants away, then the quantum state of the brief instant collapses instantaneously.

At the precise moment when move one and move two are both finished and move three is not yet finished, we have two different objects.

As soon a move three is finished we will have only one object, where one object contains the other, and the object that contains is considered only one object.

When move three is finished, the mathematics tin is placed in one of the outer pockets of the black briefcase.

On move three being finished we can place the brief case aside as of no further present interest.

We have next to complete move four.

The fourth move is the construction of the following survival tin, with the contents as described:

Tobacco Tin Container with Mirror glued onto inside lid.

Inside the tobacco tin is contained: Flint and steel, LED microlight, Plastic whistle, Candle, Fishing line, Fish hooks, Snare wire, Glucose tablets, Tea bags, Potassium permanganate, Condoms, Button compass, Magnet, Needle and thread, Knife, Flexible wire saw, Scalpel, Plastic tape, Cotton wool, Cigarette papers.

Over the exact same time frame that move four is accomplished, the remaining items of the default one setting should be acquired in any order. The items are two decks of playing cards, the King James version of the Bible, a copy of the Elements of Euclid and the Frederic Rosen translation of "The Compendious Book on Calculation Through Completion and Balancing by Abū Abdallāh Muḥammad ibn Mūsā al-Khwārizmī".

The Compendius Book on Calculation may either be acquired in paperback format or alternatively must be handwritten from one of the online sources. But it must exist in hard paper form as a physical object in itself.

You know you have the right copy if it begins in this way:

"When I considered what people generally want in calculating, I found that it always is a number.

I also observed that every number is composed of units, and that any number may be divided into units.

Moreover, I found that every number, which may be expressed from one to ten, surpasses the preceding by one unit : afterwards the ten is doubled or tripled, just as before the units were : thus arise twenty, thirty, and such like, until a hundred ; then the hundred is doubled and tripled in the same manner as the units and the tens, up to a thousand ; then the thousand can be thus repeated at any complex number ; and so forth to the utmost limit of numeration.

I observed that the numbers which are required in calculating by Completion and Reduction are of three kinds, namely, roots, squares, and simple numbers relative to neither root nor square."

The completion of move four requires a time frame.

The time frame begins at the point of move three being finished.

The time frame finishes when the survival tin is completed.

For the entire duration of that time frame the briefcase has been doing nothing. The Oxford set of mathematical instruments contained in the brief case has been doing nothing for the same duration of time frame.

The Heinlein Zelazny question is:

What is the difference of relative time experienced inside the oxford mathematics tin, when compared with the relative time experienced inside the black briefcase?

What is the difference of relative time experienced inside the black brief case, when compared with the relative time experienced inside the local field reference frame that contains the black briefcase inside itself?

What is the actual date of the beginning of the time frame and what is the actual date of the end of the time frame?

What is the difference between the experienced subjective time and the actual durational length of the specific time frame?

E.

At some stage after move three is finished and before move four is complete, while the survival tin is being constructed.

The Bible and two decks of playing cards can be added to the briefcase.

Once this is done, any good translation of the Elements of Euclid can be obtained.

The Compendius Book on Calculation can then be copied into a notebook or a published version obtained. If copying by hand, do not write all of it. Instead determine to acquire all of the theoretical explanation and a single example for each basic method. The copying should be the exact words used without addition of personal ideas. In that way the transcription is exact but only the parts that are more valuable. Any personal notes can be written after the exact copy.

Since the Compendius Book on Calculation is the last physical object to be added to the briefcase, at this stage we have completed the activation of default one.

With Default One completed, we are just before finishing the fourth move.

At this point, after the completion of move three, when default one already exists, before the completion of move four.

Then the next immediate event we know will exist just before the completion of move four, is when default one is completed and the survival tin is finished and placed next to and not touching the black briefcase.

The completion of move four is when the black briefcase is entirely correctly in its default one setting. Move four must not be completed until the default one setting is exactly correct. The survival tin can be placed in any reasonable location not the briefcase for as long as is required until default one is exactly correct.

A total amount of time must then be provided in order to resolve what ever is the remaining condition for default one to be finished.

Until default one is finished, the survival tin can not be added to a finished default one, which is what must happen in order to complete move four.

If and only if default one is finished, then the completed survival tin can be added to the briefcase.

The playing cards should be removed from the small outer pocket.

The survival tin should be placed in the small outer pocket.

One set of playing cards should be thrown away.

The remaining set of playing cards should be placed in one of the inner compartments.

F.

Completion of move four means that the place of object one is now established.

It also means that the stage one move beyond default one has been accomplished.

The presently existant object signifies this state by having one deck of playing cards in one of the empty inner compartments, and nothing else in any of the inner compartments.

If this is true, and if the rules have been exactly followed, then the eigenvalues associated to default one have already been collapsed by the addition of the survival tin.

That this event has in fact happened is proof of the existant object that will be object one derived from default one.

If the described event has not happened, then this is indicative that default one has not been obtained, and that there is no significant proof for the possible existance of object one.

G.

If and only if move four is completed correctly as described then we have properly defined our object.

<Principle of Determinacy - That any future evolution of a quantum system state is based on the state the system was discovered to be in when measurement was made.>

<Principle of Local Field - Local field defined and determined by restricted limit of objects in it at time.>

<Principle of Quantum System State Collapse - Where a wave function exists in an eigenstate of different possible eigenvalues, each eigenvalue in accord with a different eigenvector, called a possibility frame. And such that interaction with an observer or measurement of one of the available variables causes state collapse of all eigenvectors found not to be the case.>

We are now correctly beyond the default one setting along one eigenvector that necessarily has its root in default one.

The circumstance itself can now be understood in terms of the holistic gestalt.

The event is the existance of the physical object that is beyond default one and not yet object one in its finished state. It is possible that this stage beyond default one and before completion of object one may exist for several years or even decades.

For the purpose of this explanation we will suppose a routine development without obstacles.

That is, on completion of move four exactly as described, the addition of the following items to the same inner compartment as the playing cards:

Silva compass, Swiss Army Knife, Otis King model K slide rule, Rubiks cube, Plumb line, Spirit level, Dominoes.

We shall signify the accomplishment to this point by calling it completion of stage G.

In that way we can refer to object one before having completed Stage G, and object one after having completed Stage G.

H.

We here assume Stage G has been completed.

Meaning we have a physical object that is exactly as described when Stage G is finished.

To complete object one all that is now required is that a personal selection of four or five printed books be added to the second of the three inner compartments.

And any hand written note books be added to the third of the inner compartments.

Imaginatively we may suppose at this stage the eight documents contained in the article "history as creative writing" can be copied to word format and printed onto A4 paper, placed in a folder and added to the middle compartment containing printed books.

And also if required, then the Shadowjack articles copied to word format and printed onto A4 paper, placed in a folder and added to the middle compartment containing the history as creative writing documents.

We are now at the point where "Object One" is complete. It is owned by the person we are calling Decision Maker One. It exists in a local field reference frame called Reference Frame One.

Object One itself is solid state, non-moving, still, static, constant, unchanging and fixed physical object.

It is one object, in the sense that if decision maker one picks up the briefcase and walks to a different location, he picks up one object. The various internal parts of the object are now connected together by contiguity. The connection is the same as the sort of connection that binds together knives and forks, spoons, plates, cups and saucers, table and chairs. That is, they are not held together by glue, but tend to be together by habit.

I.

Applying a System of Difference.

Object One has no memory of any previous existence. It has no sense of difference between past, present and future.

Change is forced on the player who obtains a finished Object One. This is why it can take years or decades to complete a properly static system.

So whereas we can imagine the completed Object One as described may be accomplished in two weeks start to finish. Once complete it must be put aside as of no further immediate interest.

However, if the Compendius Book on Calculation has been handwritten, this should be moved to the third inner compartment of handwritten notes.

This leaves a space in the larger outer compartment. The decision maker is free to choose any item that he thinks is mathematically equivalent to the value of the space.

The idea of the game is to only increase the value of the space.

The way to do this is by adding items to the briefcase. And by subracting items from the briefcase.

A way to force a change in the present state of the content is to think about what is the smallest object that can be removed. Smallest is here directly referring to volume and area of object. We may decide the fishhooks in the survival tin, since there is no chance of us catching any fish in the circumstance where our survival tin had to be activated. But we know that, its why we left the fish hooks there in the first place. So we can't really take them out.

If we find an object that is like one in our briefcase only better, then we subtract the item from the briefcase and replace it with the better version. So in the exact same space-place we have increased the value of the object.

The briefcase itself is an equation. The present state of the content is time-specific. It never changes backwards. That is, if you play in accord with the rules, the value of the space is at each future point more valuable than its past.

The amount of space is constant.

There is a single vector line that has been held by the briefcase from empty to full.

When the briefcase is complete as Object One, then change the briefcase. Either to another one exactly the same but definitely a different object. Or alternatively to a completely different style or form, but with exactly the same content.

Whilst there is always more that could be said, the essential information that is necessary in order to provide a complete explanation of a critical path through to Object One is as provided. By critical path I mean an efficient and effective method in necessary sufficient terms.

Therefore this article is complete at this point.

CHAPTER THIRTY TWO.

First Group.

According to Leonardo da Vinci:

All bodies together, and each by itself, give off to the surrounding air an infinite number of images which are all-pervading and each complete, each conveying the nature, colour and form of the body which produces it.

It can clearly be shown that all bodies are, by their images, all-pervading in the surrounding atmosphere,

and each complete in itself as to substance form and colour;

this is seen by the images of the various bodies which are reproduced in one single perforation

through which they transmit the objects by lines which intersect and cause reversed pyramids,

from the objects, so that they are upside down on the dark plane where they are first reflected.

Every point is the termination of an infinite number of lines, which diverge to form a base,

and immediately, from the base the same lines converge to a pyramid imaging both the colour and form.

No sooner is a form created or compounded than suddenly infinite lines and angles are produced from it.

And these lines, distributing themselves and intersecting each other in the air, give rise to an infinite number of angles opposite to each other.

Given a base, each opposite angle, will form a triangle having a form and proportion equal to the larger angle.

And if the base goes twice into each of the 2 lines of the pyramid the smaller triangle will do the same.

Every body in light and shade fills the surrounding air with infinite images of itself; and these, by infinite pyramids diffused in the air, represent this body throughout space and on every side.

Each pyramid that is composed of a long assemblage of rays includes within itself an infinite number of pyramids and each has the same power as all, and all as each.

A circle of equidistant pyramids of vision will give to their object angles of equal size; and an eye at each point will see the object of the same size.

The body of the atmosphere is full of infinite pyramids composed of radiating straight lines, which are produced from the surface of the bodies in light and shade, existing in the air; and the farther they are from the object which produces them the more acute they become and although in their distribution they intersect and cross they never mingle together, but pass through all the surrounding air, independently converging, spreading, and diffused.

And they are all of equal power and value; all equal to each, and each equal to all.

By these the images of objects are transmitted through all space and in every direction, and each pyramid, in itself, includes, in each minutest part, the whole form of the body causing it.

The body of the atmosphere is full of infinite radiating pyramids produced by the objects existing in it.

These intersect and cross each other with independent

convergence without interfering with each other and pass through all the surrounding atmosphere.

And are of equal force and value—all being equal to each, each to all.

And by means of these, images of the body are transmitted everywhere and on all sides, and each receives in itself every minutest portion of the object that produces it.

The air is filled with endless images of the objects distributed in it; and all are represented in all, and all in one, and all in each.

Third Group.

Q1. a = a

Q2. b = b

Q3. c = c

Q4. a =/= b v c

Q5. b =/= a v c

Q6. c =/= a v b

Q7. ~a => ~a

Q8. ~b => ~b

Q9. ~c => ~c

Q10. ~a = b v c

Q11. ~b = a v c

Q12. ~c = a v b

Q13. a + a = b : {[(a = b) => (a ^ b = 0)] ^ [(a =/= b) => (a v b =/= 0)]}

Q14. a - a = 0

Q15. a . a = a v b <=> {[(a = 1 v 0 v ∞) => (a . a = a)] ^ [(a = -n v +n) => (a . a = b)]}

Q16. a / a = 1 v 0 v ∞ v b : [(a / a = b) <=> (a = -n)]

Q17. $0 + 0 = 0$

Q18. $1 + 1 = b$

Q19. $\infty + \infty = \infty$

Q20. $0 - 0 = 0$

Q21. $1 - 1 = 0$

Q22. $\infty - \infty = 0$

Q23. $0 . 0 = 0$

Q24. $1 . 1 = 1$

Q25. $\infty . \infty = \infty$

Q26. $0 / 0 = 0 \vee \infty \vee 1 : \{[(0 / 0 = \infty) <=> (0 . \infty = 0)] \wedge [(0 / 0 = 1) <=> (0 . 1 = 0)]\}$

Q27. $1 / 1 = 1$

Q28. $\infty / \infty = \infty \vee 1 : [(\infty / \infty = 1) <=> (1 . \infty = \infty)]$

Q29. $a + b = c : (a =/= b)$

Q30. $a - b = c : (a =/= b)$

Q31. $a . b = c : [(c / b = a) \wedge (c / a = b)]$

Q32. $a / b = c : [(b . c = a) \wedge (a / c = b)]$

Q33. $+1 . +1 = +1$

Q34. $+1 / +1 = +1$

Q35. $-1 . -1 = +1 \vee 0 => Q : [(-1) + (+1) = 0]$

Q36. $-1 / -1 = +1 \vee 0 => Q : [(-1) + (+1) = 0]$

Q37. $-n . -1 = 0 : (n = c) \wedge \{[(-c) + (+c) = 0] => [(-c . -1) = (+c)]\}$

Q38. $+n . -1 = 0 : (n = c) \wedge \{[(+c) + (-c) = 0] => [(+c . -1) = (-c)]\}$

Fourth Group.

It is through understanding the problem space that we can begin to comprehend the nature of the quantum indefinite in one of its instances.

So that when we perceive its nature in other fields we are

familiar with its make up.

And its make up seems to have these sort of characteristics:

That it involves a possibility of more than one correct answer.

That the circumstance of possibility exists before any one correct answer is given.

That as soon as one correct answer is given, the possibility factor disappears, and we are told that the only correct answer is the one that we gave.

Having provided an answer that we are told is correct all sign of any alternative possibility no longer exists.

And my belief is that the quantum indefinite has these types of characteristics in each of its instances.

In particular that it signifies a subtle field before and earlier than the manifestly given.

The Idea of a Local Field.

Three concepts are required in order to explain what we mean by a local field effect.

The concepts are contiguity, cohesion and surface.

An object is considered one thing by gravity when the entirety of its parts are internally bound by a surface membrane.

Cohesion is when all of the parts internal to a single object are contained together.

Contiguity is when the surface membrane of one object touches the surface membrane of a different object.

Any local field on any changing scale of measurement can be determined by examination of contiguity, cohesion and surface.

Suppose we say a village is a local field.

Then what we mean is, the objects contained in the village are in a relationship of contiguity with other objects in the village.

So within the limited area of the village one object touches another and that object another and the same thing through all the objects in the village.

Cohesion means that each single object does not let any other object into its own space-place. An object may move because of different object, but when it moves it takes its space-place with it. No two objects can possess the exact same space-place at the exact same time.

For this reason, cohesion is the force that is manifested from objects in contiguity that hold their own space-place.

Surface means that the individuality of object is understood through a surface membrane that completely envelopes all the parts of the object, and all the parts the same surface membrane.

Where an object is singular, but does not exactly have a surface membrane in the way described, then this is because all the parts of the object have such a close bond through cohesion and contiguity that they do not need the same surface membrane as a boundary.

The village is a local field because it has a space aroung itself where there is no contiguity to other objects.

This absence of contiguity to other objects defines the boundary of the local field.

If a second village is three miles away, and is also described as its own local field, by reasons of contiguity, cohesion and surface.

Then village two is a second local field, and a different local field to village one.

This means that there is some difference that must be

understood between the two local fields. Also in regard to the space that exists in terms of distance between the two local fields.

If an object is taken from one village to the other, then in that transition, it loses its contiguity with the objects of the first local field, and obtains contiguity with objects of the second local field.

All these things must be considered when we develop ideas of the local field effect.

Suppose we say a house is a local field. Then we have changed the scale of measurement.

If a house is a local field then we have to maintain scale when making comparisons. Meaning that we compare the local field of a house, to the local field of the house immediately next to.

The house is like the surface membrane, that determines the unity of the entity, and its difference from the house next door.

If the two houses touch each other, then this is the contiguity of one surface membrane in contact with a different surface membrane.

This causes the cohesion effect, where each object pushes against the other.

The event of the three forces acting in proportional relationship signifies the existence of a local field.

Suppose we say a room in a house is a local field. Then we maintain scale to other rooms when making comparisons.

If one room in a house is a local field, and each of the rooms in the house is each a different local field.

Then the combination of these different fields is reduced to a resultant by the enveloping surface membrane of the house itself.

Suppose the brief case referred to as "Object One" in the article "How to pack a rucksack" is a local field.

Then we do not only compare to other briefcases. Instead we compare with other local fields in the same room.

So the brief case would by its existence in a room possess space-place of its own particular gravity.

Gravity confirms this as true by acting on the briefcase as if it is one thing.

As a local field, the briefcase contains objects. Those objects are individual. They each are in contiguous relationship to other particular objects. Each of those objects possesses space-place. Each object says the other objects are called: "Other".

Object minus Space equals Time.

Object minus Time equals Space.

Object minus Gravity equals Electo-magnetism.

Object minus Electro-magnetism equals Gravity.

Therefore, Object at the centre. The Centre is called Aether.

Object then, is Aether.

Anagram refers to a game where rearranging all the letters of a word makes a different word.

Lady includes Lad.

Boy and Yob.

Tame Team Mate.

Aether, Earth, Heart, Thea, Ear, Art, Her, He.

Aether is called "primordial matter".

The basic constant model is fire above, water below, wood on the left, metal on the right.

All permutations of the model maintain the abstract model as given.

So for example, if we say: Fire equals Electro-magnetism, Water equals Gravity, Wood equals Space, Metal equals Time.

Then, following our model: Electo-magnetism above, Gravity below, Space on the left, Time on the right.

Or Spring on the left, Summer above, Autumn on the right, Winter below.

Then: Spring equals Wood and Space, Summer equals Fire and Electro-magnetism, Autumn equals Metal and Time, Winter equals Water and Gravity.

As directions: South at the top, North at the base, East on the left, West on the right.

Therefore:

East is on the left and is Spring, Wood and Space.

South is at the top and is Summer, Fire and Electromagnetism.

West is on the right and is Autumn, Metal and Time.

North is at the base and is Winter, Water and Gravity.

Aether in its primordial sense is not the domain of physics, whether quantum, particle or atomic. Physics sometimes thinks it is, because it is a necessary condition supposed by the existence of all known physics.

The understanding physics obtains is that the possibility of doing physics mentally or physically, theoretically or applied is dependant on a given state of aether being in fact the case, by definition of the possibility of doing physics.

Since a particular state of aether is by definition the case, physics is not called upon to answer the question of what already is proved.

Cosmology contains physics, physics contains the study of gravity, therefore cosmology contains the study of gravity.

The point I am making is that "Cosmology" is the greater

vehicle, which contains physics as one of its parts.

There is no requirement that a physicist must have even an adequate knowledge of Kant's ideas as to space and time.

However, the ideas about space and time that a physicist in this world can have, are entirely pre-ordered and pre-determined by the ideas of Kant.

So Cosmology requires an adequate comprehension of the ideas about space and time provided by Immanuel Kant.

If wood equals strong nuclear, then metal equals weak nuclear.

And fire equals electromagnetism, then water equals gravity.

With earth equals aether at the centre.

I say wood is strong nuclear and metal is weak nuclear.

The single only other alternative is that they should be the other way round.

The important point is to be able to reason why one way round and not the other for yourself.

Wood is spring, space, east. The sense of wood is organic, growth, expansion. It is movement from dark towards light. It has an upward direction. Therefore I say strong nuclear.

Metal is autumn, time, west. The sense of metal is mineral, decay, condensation. It is movement from light towards dark. It has a downward direction. Therefore I say weak nuclear.

When we consider the five elements made famous by Milla Jovovitch and Bruce Willis then it is the fifth element at the centre which is known as the axel joint around which the four elements are positioned.

If we understand Aether as Object, then we mean the fabric of the substance that enables the manifest object to exist.

If we remain at the scale of the five elements, then aether

presents itself to us as object, subject to the forces of space, light, time and gravity.

So as physicists we are quite safe to study the five elements when given as object, space, time, light and gravity.

Light at the top, gravity at the base, space on the left and time on the right, with object at the centre.

As cosmologists we are required to study the matter of aether on its own.

This is the metaphysics of Aristotle.

When we study aether on its own, the scale alters. The alteration of the scale means that we lose sight of the four elements.

Only by giving up the four elements can we operate at the scale of aether on its own.

Since the study of aether on its own is not physics, then we must give up physics.

When we consider aether we find it to be a compound involving the elemental forces one or zero or not one or not zero.

One is unity.

Zero is emptiness.

The relationship of one and zero is called change.

We associate a symbol structure to the basic names.

So one is light, day, unity, substance, masculine.

And zero is dark, night, nothing, emptiness, feminine.

Quantum flavours spin strange loops Quarks lepton and the Quinks eigenstatic Dance patterned time in fractal lines of Chaotic dream shape.

Deep design spoke words to no beginning And no end thought ideas of indefinite shape While perception reflection and phenomena Streamflowed continuum event through change.

All great metaquizical thinkers know that What isn't, wasn't and won't be Is different to this and that and Maybe if possibly sometimes perhaps occasionally.

No thing entered by one thing Is two things, called no thing and one thing, In relationship is three things, No thing, one thing and the relationship between them. From three things all things appear.

Three things disappear And seem to be one thing Called the central axel known as earth Around earth the four forces Is five elements called the steps Centre, forwards, backwards, left and right.

Spring, Summer, Autumn, Winter, Four forces circle the earth, And the change between them is A total of eight gates called, Thunder, Lake, Heaven, Fire, Wind, Mountain, Earth, Water.

Eight gates combine as the Sixty Four changes, Thirty two opposites, Made from no thing and one thing And the relationship between them.

At the point previous to the four elements when only aether exists, the primary puzzle we are faced with is called the quantum indefinite.

The difficult understanding is that in studying aether we find it to be a different "thing" to the way it "actually is" when considered as the fifth element in relationship to the four cardinal elements.

Aether as the fifth element at the centre of the cardinals is a compound that seems to be a unitary element only at the scale of wood, fire, metal and water.

When aether is considered in itself it is discovered to be the same thing that is described by the tai chi symbol.

Because we find the tai chi symbol to be an exact description of the "thing" that is before the existence of the four elements, then, we understand metaphysics as if tethered by the visual picture of the tai chi.

If south at the top, west on the right, north at the base, east on the left.

And if one is light and day, masculine, creative.

And if zero is dark and night, feminine, responsive.

Then the larger area of white with a black point at the upper centre, and where the tail of the white area is at the base, and the mass of the white area is on the left.

And the larger area of black with a white point at the lower centre, and where the tail of the black area is at the top, and the mass of the black area is on the right.

According to Myers and Percy in the book Two Thirds:

Although the natures of the weak force, the strong force and three-dimensional gravity are somewhat understood, light remains a mystery. Light is complex, multi-faceted and unfathomable. Light does, however, seem to be a governor on how fast things can travel. Three-dimensional and four-dimensional gravity govern the speed of light. Working together, three-dimensional and four-dimensional gravity are sometimes strong enough to even stop light, due to the coalescing of an enormous amount of extremely dense matter – as in the collapse of certain types of stars. The strength of three-dimensional gravity decreases at greater and greater distances from matter. Similarly, and at the same rate, the strength of four-dimensional gravity decreases at greater and greater distances from matter. However, as the initial strength of three-dimensional gravity is weaker than that of four-dimensional gravity, the ability of three-dimensional gravity to help govern the speed of light decreases at a closer distance from a large mass than that of four-dimensional gravity. Due to the fact that galaxies are close enough together throughout the physical universe, four-dimensional gravity never actually loses its ability to govern the speed of light. As a result of the increasing inability of three-dimensional gravity to govern the speed of light, there are three greatly different speeds of light depending upon how far distant light is from a large amount of matter. It is unknown why light suddenly changes speed by discreet amounts, instead of gradually as it gets farther and farther from large amounts of matter, but the Universe likes to do things in blocks rather than just dribbling on. Representation of the refraction of light when light enters a solar system. Interstellar light speed is over 400,000 times faster than solar system light speed, it begins well beyond the limits of a solar system and extends well beyond the fringes of galaxies. Light entering a galaxy is similarly refracted. Solar system light speed is approximately 186,000 miles per second and extends well beyond the limits of a solar system. Interstellar light speed is the speed of light between solar systems. Over 400,000 times faster than solar system light speed, interstellar light speed begins well beyond the limits of a solar system and extends well beyond the fringes of galaxies. Intergalactic light speed is seven times faster than interstellar light speed. Intergalactic light speed is the speed of light in the physical universe well beyond the fringes of galaxies.

The intergalactic pioneers – having successfully persuaded their indigenous partners to accept the 24 hour day – went on to introduce their vitally important 360 degree system of angular measurement. Possessing only vague notions of measurement and no system of their own, the locals were not very interested in listening to the explanations offered to them, "The 360 degree system combines divisions of both time and planetary location," the spokesman said. "Since the system's most important attribute is its connection with the counting of time: one day is divided into 24 hours of 60 minutes, each consisting of 60 seconds; the 360 degrees are also divided into 60 minutes consisting of 60 seconds each." The locals were thoroughly confused by this 'revelation,' "How can you say there is a connection between time and angular measurement?" they asked. "We are to have 24 hours in time and 360 degrees in angular measurement."

"Having thoroughly explained all aspects of time," the original spokesman grinned broadly as she continued, "I can add that time becomes a most important factor in planetary measurement and is therefore combined with 360 degree angular measurement to form what we call 'The Nautical Mileage System.' This is quite simple: there are 360 degrees around a planet and 60 minutes in each degree. Multiplying degrees and minutes together results in 21,600 which is the total number of nautical miles around the equator of any given planet." Nautical miles around the equator of any planet. 360 degrees and 60 minutes in each degree 360 x 60 = 21,600 nautical miles. Although intrepid sailors, the indigenous seamen had used very crude methods for reckoning their whereabouts at sea. With the implementation of the nautical mileage system, came the gradual introduction of a planetary-wide grid of automated position locators. As the sailors were keen to learn and as they were anxious to take advantage of the new system, their ships were fitted with automatic position locating devices, giving them instantaneous readouts. Based on that planetary-wide grid reference system these positions were measured from the equator as degrees, minutes and seconds of north or south latitude. Additionally from a prime meridian (located at the centre of Hurtea, the new Altean capital) these positions were measured as degrees, minutes and seconds of east or west longitude (or meridian); with a clearly defined 180 degree demarcation east or west of the prime meridian.

After the locals had accepted the nautical mileage system the new arrivals introduced them to the statute mileage system, known to them since time immemorial, it required updating once per galaxy. This was done by measuring the equatorial circumference of the seed planet. Altea being remarkably similar in size to the preceding galaxy's seed planet, only required an adjustment of about one-tenth of one percent. Statute miles around the equator of the seed planet of any galaxy. 12 inches = 1 foot, 5,280 feet = 1 mile. "There are precisely 24,901.54558 statute miles around the equator of the seed planet of any given galaxy," explained the pioneer's spokesman. "How did a scheme like that ever come about?" asked one of the indigenous beings. "We don't know," answered the spokesman. After waiting for more questions, but receiving none, she continued her explanations. "The statute mile is divided into 5280 feet, each foot is divided into twelve inches and each inch into 32 parts. We don't really know why 5280 feet make up the mile, but we do know that, though cumbersome, counting by 12s (which is very important) as well as by 10s, is the most logical and convenient system devised during billions of years of experience. This vital counting by 10s and 12s links directly to an interesting relationship between the nautical mileage system, the retrograde precession of 25,920 years and a very important metaphor: dividing 21,600 (the number of equatorial nautical miles) by 25,920 results in a ratio of 5 to 6. This ratio of 5 to 6 is a metaphor for the vital relationship between the non-living parts of the Universe and living things. "The non-living parts of the Universe are all six-sided. "All living things are five-sided."

As the lecturer sat down, apparently from nowhere an enormous holographic projection of a sphere circumscribing a tetrahedron suddenly appeared, thoroughly startling the audience of indigenous beings. Another speaker rose and said, "This is a visual aid to help us all understand what I am about to tell you." He cleared his throat and pointedly read from his notes, "The square root of three, divided by two, multiplied by pi, is equivalent to 2.720699046 and is the transdimensional constant. The transdimensional constant is equivalent to the ratio between the surface of a sphere and the surface of the tetrahedron it circumscribes." Ratio between the surface of a sphere and the surface of the tetrahedron it circumscribes. Producing a light pointer from his lectern, the speaker transferred his notes to his left hand and while continuing to read from them, he used his right hand to aim the thin red beam at the holo-image. "The tetrahedron is the simplest solid shape, contained by four equilateral triangles placed together. It is the basic unit of construction of the physical universe. A tetrahedron whose four tips just touch the sphere surrounding it is called a circumscribed tetrahedron. A circumscribed tetrahedron is the geometric model for both hyperdimensional and resulting three-dimensional physics processes which devolve from much more complex four-dimensional processes. These four-dimensional processes are also modeled by this same circumscribed tetrahedron representation. "The physics manifestations of this model drive the physical universe. The four-dimensional manifestations of this model drive the Universe."

Fifth Group.

Object minus Space equals Time.

Object minus Time equals Space.

Object minus Gravity equals Electo-magnetism.

Object minus Electro-magnetism equals Gravity.

Therefore, Object at the centre. The Centre is called Aether.

Object then, is Aether.

Aether is called "primordial matter".

The basic constant model is fire above, water below, wood on the left, metal on the right.

All permutations of the model maintain the abstract model as given.

So for example, if we say: Fire equals Electro-magnetism, Water equals Gravity, Wood equals Space, Metal equals Time.

Then, following our model:

Electo-magnetism above, Gravity below, Space on the left, Time on the right.

Or Spring on the left, Summer above, Autumn on the right, Winter below.

Then: Spring equals Wood and Space, Summer equals Fire and Electro-magnetism, Autumn equals Metal and Time, Winter equals Water and Gravity.

As directions: South at the top, North at the base, East on the left, West on the right.

Therefore:

East is on the left and is Spring, Wood and Space.

South is at the top and is Summer, Fire and Electromagnetism.

West is on the right and is Autumn, Metal and Time.

North is at the base and is Winter, Water and Gravity.

If wood equals strong nuclear, then metal equals weak nuclear.

And fire equals electromagnetism, then water equals gravity.

With earth equals aether at the centre.

So as physicists we are quite safe to study the five elements when given as object, space, time, light and gravity.

Light at the top, gravity at the base, space on the left and time on the right, with object at the centre.

No thing entered by one thing Is two things, called no thing and one thing, In relationship is three things, No thing, one thing and the relationship between them. From three things all things appear.

Three things disappear And seem to be one thing Called the central axel known as earth Around earth the four forces Is five elements called the steps Centre, forwards, backwards, left and right.

Spring, Summer, Autumn, Winter, Four forces circle the earth, And the change between them is A total of eight gates called, Thunder, Lake, Heaven, Fire, Wind, Mountain, Earth, Water.

Eight gates combine as the Sixty Four changes, Thirty two opposites, Made from no thing and one thing And the relationship between them.

When we consider aether we find it to be a compound involving the elemental forces one or zero or not one or not zero.

One is unity.

Zero is emptiness.

The relationship of one and zero is called change.

We associate a symbol structure to the basic names.

So one is light, day, unity, substance, masculine.

And zero is dark, night, nothing, emptiness, feminine.

Phenomena changes constantly. That is impermanence. The sense perceptions.

Truth is constant to eternity. That is immutability. The mind.

Space without phenomena. Time without thought. That is emptiness. Existence.

Event, Time, Space, Mind, Object.

This is the continuum. It exists so far back that when we look for its beginning we cannot find it. So far forwards that when we look for its end it disappears into infinity. It is what body is born into but mind already exists within its self. Purpose is only entirely to serve the context that gives life to content.

All attempts to prove the existence of an objective reality separate from our consciousness of it as such are doomed to failure. Simply because any attempt at such a proof can only be the product of consciousness. And any comprehension of such a proof can only be the understanding of consciousness. And any such proof can only ever exist as a phenomena of consciousness.

Sixth Group.

Gravity is the understanding that object collapses to its point of stability.

The point of stability for any object is always the surface membrane of one object touching the surface membrane of a different object.

Our understanding of gravity is that things fall down if they are not obstructed.

Where they fall down to, is towards the centre.

And they fall through any available space. If the space is obstructed by some form of surface membrane, then this obstruction stops the fall of object, meaning it reaches its point of stability.

The fall of object towards the centre is of two kinds.

The first kind is the fall of the inward parts of an object, when they are bound by surface membrane, so cannot escape outwards, then all those parts are individually falling towards the centre of the object itself. However their fall towards the centre of the object is obstructed by the other parts, so the parts individually push against the other parts.

It is because of the surface membrane that gravity acts on

object as one thing. And gravity acts on all the parts of the object that are bound by a common surface membrane as if they are part of one object.

The second kind of the fall of object towards the centre is the fall of any one object, defined as such because bounded by a single surface membrane.

And the way that one object falls towards the centre of something outside itself.

This second kind of the fall of object is that which operates on all objects on earth as they each individually fall towards the centre of the earth to the extent that they are not obstructed by surface membrane.

Every particle of matter in the universe attracts every other particle with a force whose direction is that of a line joining the centre of their masses, whose magnitude is directly as the product of their masses, and inversely as the square of the distance between them.

Every body continues in its state of rest, or of uniform motion in a straight line, except in so far as it may be compelled by impressed Forces to change that state.

Change of motion is proportionate to the impressed Force, and takes place in the direction of the straight line in which the Force acts.

To every action there is always an equal and contrary reaction.

When a body is acted upon by two Forces at the same time, it will describe a diagonal, by the motion resulting from their composition, in the same time that it would describe the sides of the parallelogram.

Law of Inverse Squares gives that Gravitation acts inversely as the square of distance.

Thus if we take two masses of any kind, and place them

at various distances as represented by the numbers 1, 2, 3, 4, 5, 6, the intensity of the attracting forces between the same masses at the relative distances will be represented by the numbers 1, 1/4, 1/9, 1/16, 1/25, 1/36, which are the inverse squares of the respective numbers representing their distances.

The proportion of the attractive force between any two bodies is constant, given the masses of the two bodies remain the same.

Through all the changes of volume and density of any body, its attractive force remains constant, as long as the mass remains constant, since, as the volume of a body is increased, the density is proportionately decreased, or, as the volume is decreased, the density is increased.

Every particle of matter in the universe attracts every other particle.

The attraction of Gravitation is always directed along the straight line which joins the centres of masses of the attracting and attracted bodies.

An object is considered one thing by gravity when the entirety of its parts are internally bound by a surface membrane.

Cohesion is when all of the parts internal to a single object are contained together.

Contiguity is when the surface membrane of one object touches the surface membrane of a different object.

Cohesion means that each single object does not let any other object into its own space-place. An object may move because of different object, but when it moves it takes its space-place with it. No two objects can possess the exact same space-place at the exact same time. For this reason, cohesion is the force that is manifested from objects in contiguity that hold their own space-place.

Surface means that the individuality of object is understood through a surface membrane that completely envelopes all the parts of the object, and all the parts the same surface membrane.

Where an object is singular, but does not exactly have a surface membrane in the way described, then this is because all the parts of the object have such a close bond through cohesion and contiguity that they do not need the same surface membrane as a boundary.

Matter is that which can be acted upon by motion, such as heat or electricity, both being forms of motion, and which can exert the motion so derived upon some other body.

Wherever, therefore, in the universe we find any object, solid, liquid or gaseous, or any medium which can be acted upon by motion, and after being so acted upon, can exert motion, then that body or medium may legitimately be included in the term Matter, although it may be absolutely invisible to the sense perceptions.

Matter which fills the universe is unchangeable in quantity, so that the total quantity is always constant.

Changes may take place in regard to the state of the Matter, but the sum-total of Matter throughout all the changes remains unaltered.

Seventh Group.

Lattice One, Logic:

I. $(a => b \lor c) => [(a < b => c) \land (a < c => b)]$

II. $(d => a \lor b) => [(a => d < b) \land (b => d < a)]$

III. $(e => a \lor c) => [(a => e < c) \land (c => e < a)]$

IV. $(f => b < c) => [(b => f \lor c) \land (c => b < f)]$

V. $(g => c < b) => [(c => g \lor b) \land (b => c < g)]$

Lattice One, Algebra:

I. $(a = b \cdot c) \Rightarrow [(a / b = c) \wedge (a / c = b)]$

II. $(d = a \cdot b) \Rightarrow [(a = d / b) \wedge (b = d / a)]$

III. $(e = a \cdot c) \Rightarrow [(a = e / c) \wedge (c = e / a)]$

IV. $(f = b / c) \Rightarrow [(b = f \cdot c) \wedge (c = b / f)]$

V. $(g = c / b) \Rightarrow [(c = g \cdot b) \wedge (b = c / g)]$

Lattice One, Number:

I. $(8 = 2 \cdot 4) \Rightarrow [(2 = 8 / 4) \wedge (4 = 8 / 2)]$

II. $(16 = 8 \cdot 2) \Rightarrow [(8 = 16 / 2) \wedge (2 = 16 / 8)]$

III. $(32 = 8 \cdot 4) \Rightarrow [(8 = 32 / 4) \wedge (4 = 32 / 8)]$

IV. $(1/2 = 2 / 4) \Rightarrow [(2 = 1/2 \cdot 4) \wedge (4 = 2 / 1/2)]$

V. $(2 = 4 / 2) \Rightarrow [(4 = 2 \cdot 2) \wedge (2 = 4 / 2)]$

1. Distance equals Speed multiplied by Time.

2. Time equals Distance divided by Speed.

3. Speed equals Distance divided by Time.

4. Change in Speed equals Acceleration multiplied by Time.

5. Time equals Change in Speed divided by Acceleration.

6. Acceleration equals Change in Speed divided by Time.

7. Mass equals Density multiplied by Volume.

8. Density equals Mass divided by Volume

9. Volume equals Mass divided by Density.

10. Force equals Mass multiplied by Acceleration.

11. Mass equals Force divided by Acceleration.
12. Acceleration equals Force divided by Mass.

13. Work equals Force multiplied by Distance.

14. Force equals Work divided by Distance.

15. Distance equals Work divided by Force.

16. Work equals Power multiplied by Time.

17. Power equals Work divided by Time.

18. Time equals Work divided by Power.

19. Force equals Pressure multiplied by Area.

20. Pressure equals Force divided by Area.

21. Area equals Force divided by Pressure.

One. $(D = S \cdot T) => [(D / S = T) \wedge D / T = S]$

Two. $(\Delta S = Acc \cdot T) => [(\Delta S / Acc = T) \wedge (\Delta S / T = Acc)]$

Three. $(M = Dn \cdot V) => [(M / Dn = V) \wedge (M / V = Dn)]$

Four. $(F = M \cdot Acc) => [(F / M = Acc) \wedge (F / Acc = M)]$

Five. $(W = F \cdot D) => [(W / F = D) \wedge (W/ D = F)]$

Six. $(W = P \cdot T) => [(W / P = T) \wedge (W / T = P)]$

Seven. $(F = Pr \cdot A) => [(F / Pr = A) \wedge (F / A = Pr)]$

CHAPTER THIRTY THREE.

First Figure BARBARA

AAA

All B is A. All C is B. ⊢ All C is A.

$\forall B < \exists A.$ $\forall C < \exists B \Rightarrow \forall C < \exists A$

AaB   BaC ⊢ AaC

Permutations of Barbara

$(\forall B < \exists A) \wedge (\forall C < \exists B)$
$(\exists A < \forall C) \wedge (\forall C < \exists B)$
$(\forall B < \exists A) \wedge (\exists B < \forall C)$
$(\exists A < \forall B) \wedge (\exists B < \forall C)$

$\Rightarrow (\forall C < \exists A)$
$\Rightarrow (\exists A < \forall C)$

First Figure CELARENT

EAE

No B is A. All C is B. ⊢ No C is A.

$\exists B < \exists A.$ $\forall C < \exists B \Rightarrow \neg C < \forall A$

AeB   BaC   AeC

Permutations of Celarent

$(\neg B < \forall A) \wedge (\forall C < \exists B)$
$(\forall A < \neg B) \wedge (\forall C < \exists B)$
$(\neg B < \forall A) \wedge (\exists B < \forall C)$
$(\forall A < \neg B) \wedge (\exists B < \forall C)$

$\Rightarrow (\neg C < \forall A)$
$\Rightarrow (\forall A < \neg C)$

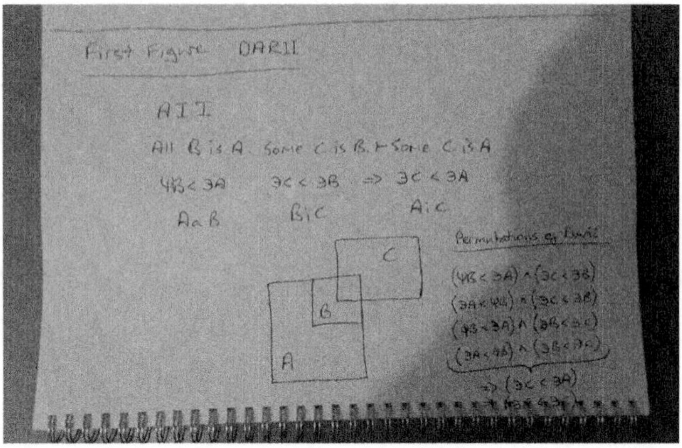
First Figure DARII
AII
All B is A. Some C is B ⊢ Some C is A
∀B < ∃A ∃C < ∃B => ∃C < ∃A
AaB BiC AiC
C
B
A
Permutations of
(∀B < ∃A) ∧ (∃C < ∃B)
=> (∃C < ∃A)

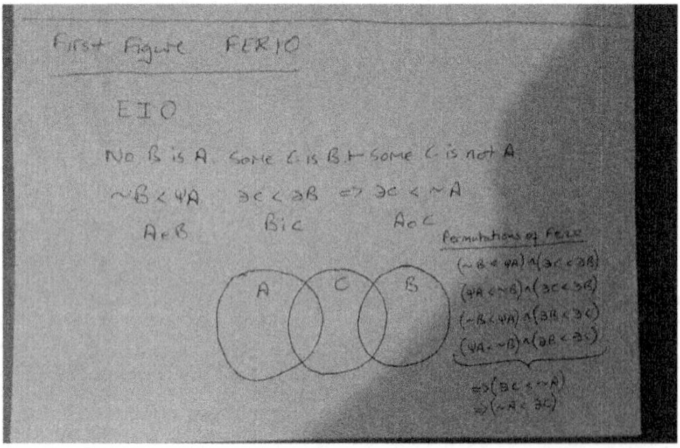
First Figure FERIO
EIO
No B is A. Some C is B ⊢ Some C is not A.
~B < ∀A ∃C < ∃B => ∃C < ~A
AeB BiC AoC
Permutations of
(~B < ∀A) ∧ (∃C < ∃B)
(∀A < ~B) ∧ (∃C < ∃B)
A
C
B
=> (∃C < ~A)
=> (~A < ∃C)

Second Figure CAMESTRES

AEE

All A is B. No C is B.∴ No C is A.

∀A < ∃B   ∼C < ∀B ⇒ ∼C < ∀A
BaA   BeC   AeC

Permutations of Camestres

(∀A < ∃B) ∧ (∼C < ∀B)
(∃B < ∀A) ∧ (∼C < ∀B)
(∀A < ∃B) ∧ (∀B < ∼C)
(∃B < ∀A) ∧ (∀B < ∼C)

⇒ (∼C < ∀A)
∼ (∀A < ∼C)

Second Figure CESARE

E A E

No A is B. All C is B.∴ No C is A.

∼A < ∀B   ∀C < ∃B ⇒ ∼C < ∀A
BeA   BaC   AeC

Permutations of Cesare

(∼A < ∀B) ∧ (∀C < ∃B)
(∀B < ∼A) ∧ (∀C < ∃B)
(∼A < ∀B) ∧ (∃B < ∀C)
(∀B < ∼A) ∧ (∃B < ∀C)

⇒ (∼C < ∀A)
⇒ (∀A < ∼C)

Second Figure FESTINO

E I O

No A is B. Some C is B.∴ Some C is not A.

∼A < ∀B   ∃C < ∃B ⇒ ∃C < ∼A
BeA   BiC   AoC

Permutations of Festino

(∼A < ∀B) ∧ (∃C < ∃B)
(∀B < ∼A) ∧ (∃C < ∃B)
(∼A < ∀B) ∧ (∃B < ∃C)
(∀B < ∼A) ∧ (∃B < ∃C)

⇒ (∃C < ∼A)
⇒ (∼A < ∃C)

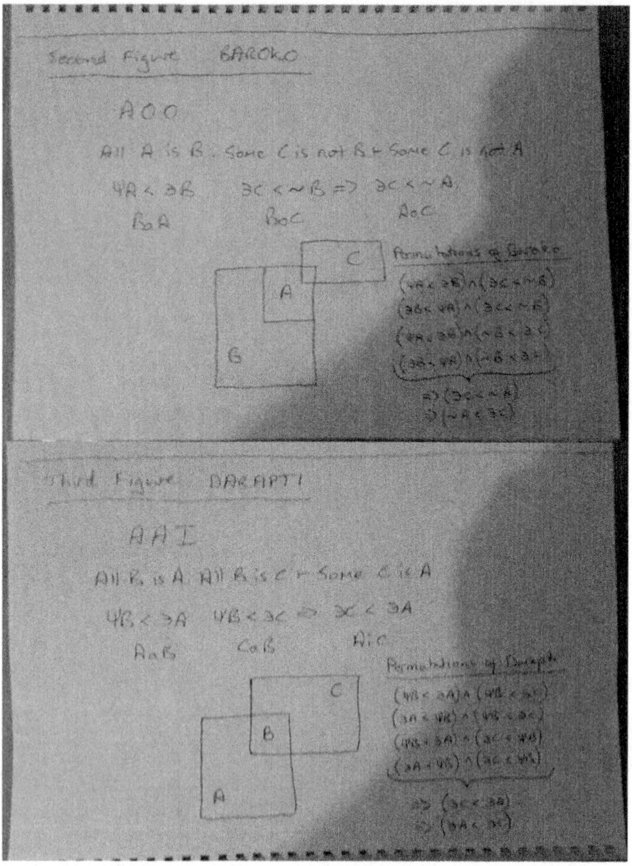
Second Figure BAROKO
AOO
BaA
BoC
AoC
C
A
B
Third Figure BARAPTI
AAI
AaB
CaB
AiC
C
B
A

Third Figure   FELAPTON

E A O

No B is A   All B is C ⊢ Some C is not A

~B < ∀A   ∀B < ∃C ⇒ ∃C < ~A

A e B   C a B   A o C

Permutations of Felapton

$(\sim B < \forall A) \wedge (\forall B < \exists C)$
$(\forall A < \sim B) \wedge (\forall B < \exists C)$
$(\sim B < \forall A) \wedge (\exists C < \forall B)$
$(\forall A < \sim B) \wedge (\exists C < \forall B)$

⇒ (∃C < ~A)
⇒ (~A c ∃C)

Third Figure   DISAMIS

I A I

Some B is A   All B is C ⊢ Some C is A

∃B < ∃A   ∀B < ∃C ⇒ ∃C < ∃A

B i B   C a B   A i C

Permutations of Disamis

$(\exists B < \exists A) \wedge (\forall B < \exists C)$
$(\exists A < \exists B) \wedge (\forall B < \exists C)$
$(\exists B < \exists A) \wedge (\exists C < \forall B)$
$(\exists A < \exists B) \wedge (\exists C < \forall B)$

⇒ (∃C < ∃A)
⇒ (∃A < ∃C)

Third Figure   DATISI

A I I

All B is A, Some B is C ⊢ Some C is A

∀B < ∃A   ∃B < ∃C ⇒ ∃C < ∃A

AaB   CiB   AiC

Formulations of Datisi

$(∀B < ∃A) ∧ (∃B < ∃C)$
$(∃A < ∀B) ∧ (∃C < ∃B)$
$(∀B < ∃A) ∧ (∃C < ∃B)$
$(∃A < ∀B) ∧ (∃C < ∃B)$

⇒ $(∃C < ∃A)$
⇒ $(∃A < ∃C)$

Third Figure   BOKARDO

O A O

Some B is not A. All B is C ⊢ Some C is not A

∃B < ~A   ∀B < ∃C ⇒ ∃C < ~A

AoB   CaB   AoC

Formulations of Bokardo

$(∃B < ~A) ∧ (∀B < ∃C)$
$(~A < ∃B) ∧ (∀B < ∃C)$
$(∃B < ~A) ∧ (∃C < ∀B)$
$(~A < ∃B) ∧ (∃C < ∀B)$

⇒ $(∃C < ~A)$
⇒ $(~A < ∃C)$

Third Figure FERISON

E I O

No B is A. Some B is C ⊢ Some C is not A

~B < ψA   ∃B < ∃C ⇒ ∃C < ~A

AeB   CiB   ⊢   AoC

Permutations of Ferison

(~B < ψA) ∧ (∃B < ∃C)
(ψA < ~B) ∧ (∃B < ∃C)
(~B < ψA) ∧ (∃C < ∃B)
(ψA < ~B) ∧ (∃C < ∃B)

⇒ (∃C < ~A)
⇒ (~A < ∃C)

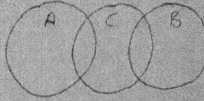

Fourth Figure BRAMANTIP

A A I

All A is B. All B is C ⊢ Some C is A

ψA < ∃B   ψB < ∃C   ∃C < ψA

BaA   CaB   AiC

Permutations of Bramantip

(ψA < ∃B) ∧ (ψB < ∃C)
(∃B < ψA) ∧ (ψB < ∃C)
(ψA < ∃B) ∧ (∃C < ψB)
(∃B < ψA) ∧ (∃C < ψB)

⇒ (∃C < ψA)
⇔ (ψA < ∃C)

Fourth Figure CAMENES

A E E

All A is B. No B is C ⊢ No C is A

ψA < ∃B   ~B < ψC ⇒ ~C < ψA

BaA   CeB   AeC

Permutations of Camenes

(ψA < ∃B) ∧ (~B < ψC)
(∃B < ψA) ∧ (~B < ψC)
(ψA < ∃B) ∧ (ψC < ~B)
(∃B < ψA) ∧ (ψC < ~B)

⇒ (~C < ψA)
⇔ (ψA < ~C)

533

Fourth Figure   DIMARIS

$I A I$

Some A is B. All B is C ⊢ some C is some A

$\exists A < \exists B \qquad \forall B < \exists C \Rightarrow \exists C < \exists A$

BiA   CaB   AiC

Permutations of Dimaris

$(\exists A < \exists B) \wedge (\forall B < \exists C)$

$(\exists B < \exists A) \wedge (\forall B < \exists C)$

$(\exists A < \exists B) \wedge (\exists C < \forall B)$

$(\exists C < \exists A) \wedge (\exists C < \forall B)$

$\Rightarrow (\exists C < \exists A)$

$\Rightarrow (\exists A < \exists C)$

Fourth Figure   FESAPO

$E A O$

No A is B. All B is C ⊢ some C is not A

$\sim A < \forall B \qquad \forall B < \exists C \Rightarrow \exists C \times \sim A$

BeA   CaB   AoC

Permutations of Fesapo

$(\sim A < \forall B) \wedge (\forall B < \exists C)$

$(\forall B < \sim A) \wedge (\forall B < \exists C)$

$(\sim A < \forall B) \wedge (\exists C < \forall B)$

$(\forall B < \sim A) \wedge (\exists C < \forall B)$

$\Rightarrow (\exists C \circ \sim A)$

$\Rightarrow (\sim A < \exists C)$

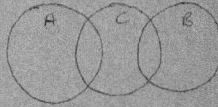

Fourth Figure   FRESISON

EIO

No A is B. Some B is C ⊢ Some C is not A.

$\sim A < \forall B$ $\exists B < \exists C$ ⇒ $\exists C < \sim A$

BeA   CiB   AoC

Permutations of Fresison

$(\sim A < \forall B) \wedge (\exists B < \exists C)$
$(\forall B < \sim A) \wedge (\exists B < \exists C)$
$(\sim A < \forall B) \wedge (\exists C < \exists B)$
$(\forall B < \sim A) \wedge (\exists C < \exists B)$

$\Rightarrow (\exists C < \sim A)$
$\Rightarrow (\sim A < \exists C)$

CHAPTER THIRTY FOUR.

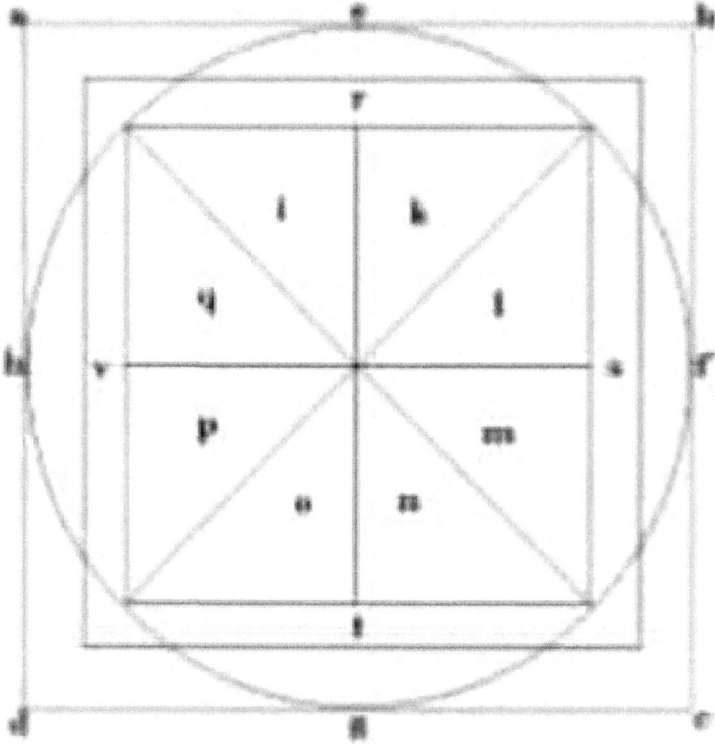

$$\frac{\text{Circumference}}{\text{Diameter}} = \pi$$

$$\Rightarrow 3.14159265358979323846$$

$$\sqrt{50} = 7.07\,106\,781\,186\,5475$$

$$\pi \cdot \sqrt{50} = 22.2\,144\,146\,907\,9181$$

$$\frac{22.2}{7.07} = 3.1400$$

Pi = 3.14 159 265 358 979
Circumference = 22.2 144 146 907 9181
Radius = 3.53 553 390 593 2738
Diameter = 7.07106 781 186 5475
Quink = 4.44 288 293 815 8362
Side of square = 5
Square of side of square = 25
Sum of square of other two sides = 50

1	2	3	4
8	7	6	5

2	4	6	8
7	5	3	1

4	8	3	7
5	1	6	2

3	6	9	3
6	3	9	6

1	2	3	4	5	6	7	8
2	4	6	8	1	3	5	7
3	6	9	3	6	9	3	6
4	8	3	7	2	6	1	5
5	1	6	2	7	3	8	4
6	3	9	6	3	9	6	3
7	5	3	1	8	6	4	2
8	7	6	5	4	3	2	1

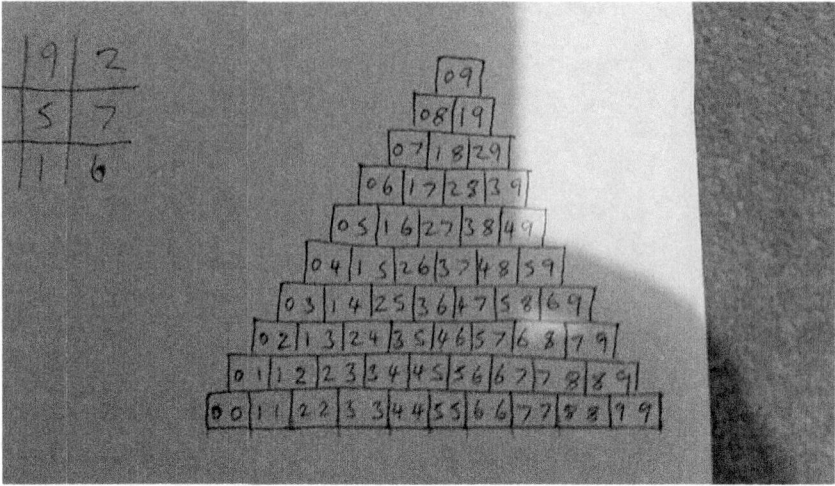

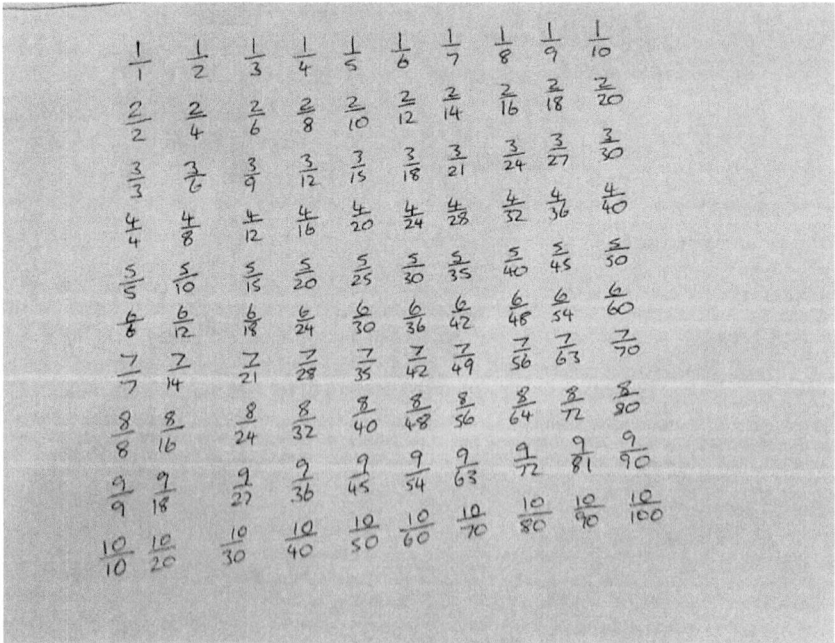

1	2	3	4	5	6	7	8	9	10	11	12	13	14	15	16	17	18	19	20	(1)
1	2	3	4	5	6	7	8	9	1	2	3	4	5	6	7	8	9	1	2	
2	4	6	8	10	12	14	16	18	20	22	24	26	28	30	32	34	36	38	40	(2)
2	4	6	8	1	3	5	7	9	2	4	6	8	1	3	5	7	9	2	4	
3	6	9	12	15	18	21	24	27	30	33	36	39	42	45	48	51	54	57	60	(3)
3	6	9	3	6	9	3	6	9	3	6	9	3	6	9	3	6	9	3	6	
4	8	12	16	20	24	28	32	36	40	44	48	52	56	60	64	68	72	76	80	(4)
4	8	3	7	2	6	1	5	9	4	8	3	7	2	6	1	5	9	4	8	
5	10	15	20	25	30	35	40	45	50	55	60	65	70	75	80	85	90	95	100	(5)
5	1	6	2	7	3	8	4	9	5	1	6	2	7	3	8	4	9	5	1	
6	12	18	24	30	36	42	48	54	60	66	72	78	84	90	96	102	108	114	120	(6)
6	3	9	6	3	9	6	3	9	6	3	9	6	3	9	6	3	9	6	3	
7	14	21	28	35	42	49	56	63	70	77	84	91	98	105	112	119	126	133	140	(7)
7	5	3	1	8	6	4	2	9	7	5	3	1	8	6	4	2	9	7	5	
8	16	24	32	40	48	56	64	72	80	88	96	104	112	120	128	136	144	152	160	(8)
8	7	6	5	4	3	2	1	9	8	7	6	5	4	3	2	1	9	8	7	

First sheet:

$$c = a + b$$
$$a = c - b$$
$$b = c - a$$
$$0 = a + b - c$$
$$2c = a + b + c$$
$$(-a) = b - c$$
$$(-b) = a - c$$
$$(-c) = (-a - b)$$

$$a \times b = c$$
$$b = \frac{c}{a}$$
$$a = \frac{c}{b}$$

$$\frac{a}{b} = \frac{c}{d}$$
$$\Rightarrow$$
$$ad = bc$$

$$\frac{a}{b} + \frac{c}{d} = \frac{a \cdot d}{b \cdot d} + \frac{b \cdot c}{b \cdot d} = \frac{ad + bc}{bd}$$

$$\frac{a}{b} - \frac{c}{d} = \frac{a \cdot d}{b \cdot d} - \frac{b \cdot c}{b \cdot d} = \frac{ad - bc}{bd}$$

$$\frac{a}{b} \times \frac{c}{d} = \frac{a \cdot c}{b \cdot d} = \frac{ac}{bd}$$

$$\frac{a}{b} \div \frac{c}{d} = \frac{a}{b} \times \frac{d}{c} = \frac{ad}{bc}$$

$$\frac{a}{b} \times c = \frac{a}{b} \times \frac{c}{1} = \frac{ac}{b}$$

$$\frac{a}{b} \div c \Rightarrow \frac{a}{b} \div \frac{c}{1} = \frac{a}{b} \times \frac{1}{c} = \frac{a}{bc}$$

Second sheet:

$$+(+a) = (+a)$$
$$+(-a) = (-a)$$
$$-(+a) = (-a)$$
$$-(-a) = (+a)$$

$$a + (+b) = a + b$$
$$a + (-b) = a - b$$
$$a - (+b) = a - b$$
$$a - (-b) = a + b$$

$$a + (b+c) = a + b + c$$
$$a + (b-c) = a + b - c$$
$$a - (b+c) = a - b - c$$
$$a - (b-c) = a - b + c$$

$$x(a+b) = xa + xb$$
$$x(a+b+c) = xa + xb + xc$$
$$x(a-b) = xa - xb$$
$$x(a+b-c) = xa + xb - xc$$
$$x(a-b-c) = xa - xb - xc$$

$$(+a) \cdot (+b) = +ab$$
$$(+a) \cdot (-b) = -ab$$
$$(-a) \cdot (+b) = -ab$$
$$(-a) \cdot (-b) = +ab$$

$$(+a) \div (+b) = \left(+\frac{a}{b}\right)$$
$$(+a) \div (-b) = \left(-\frac{a}{b}\right)$$
$$(-a) \div (+b) = \left(-\frac{a}{b}\right)$$
$$(-a) \div (-b) = \left(+\frac{a}{b}\right)$$

$$a^2 = (+a) \cdot (+a)$$
$$a^2 = (-a) \cdot (-a)$$

$$(-a)^3$$
$$\Rightarrow (-a) \cdot (-a) \cdot (-a)$$
$$\Rightarrow -a^3$$

$$(-a)^4$$
$$\Rightarrow (-a) \cdot (-a) \cdot (-a) \cdot (-a)$$
$$\Rightarrow +a^4$$

$$\frac{a}{b} = \frac{a \cdot n}{b \cdot n} \quad \Big| \quad \frac{a}{b} = \frac{a \div m}{b \div m}$$

$$y^2 = yy$$
$$y^3 = yyy$$
$$(y^2)(y^3) = yy \cdot yyy = yyyyy$$
$$\therefore y^2 \times y^3 = y^{2+3} = y^5$$

$$x^1 = x$$
$$x^0 = 1$$
$$x^{-1} = \frac{1}{x}$$
$$x^{-n} = \frac{1}{x^n}$$

$$\frac{m}{n} = \left(\frac{1}{n}\right) \cdot M$$
$$x^M x^n = x^{M+n}$$
$$\frac{x^M}{x^n} = x^{M-n}$$
$$x^{\frac{M}{n}} = \sqrt[n]{x^M}$$

$$y^2 + y^3 \neq y^5$$
$$y^2 + y^3 = y^2 + y^3$$

$$(xy)^3 = x^3 y^3$$

$$a^{\frac{M}{n}} \Rightarrow \sqrt[n]{a^M}$$
$$\Rightarrow \left(\sqrt[n]{a}\right)^M$$
$$\Rightarrow \left(a^{\frac{1}{n}}\right)^M$$
$$\Rightarrow a^{\left(M \cdot \frac{1}{n}\right)}$$
$$\Rightarrow \left(a^M\right)^{\frac{1}{n}}$$

$$x^{\frac{2}{3}} = \sqrt[3]{x^2}$$

$$x^{-3} = \frac{1}{x^3}$$

$$x^{-n} = \frac{1}{x^n}$$

$$(x^2)^3 = x^{2 \cdot 3} = x^6$$

First notebook page:

$$a^m \cdot a^n = a^{m+n}$$
$$a^m \div a^n = a^{m-n}$$
$$(a^m)^n = a^{m \cdot n}$$
$$(ab)^n = a^n \cdot b^n$$

$$a^{\frac{1}{2}} \cdot a^{\frac{1}{2}} = a^{\frac{1}{2}+\frac{1}{2}}$$
$$\Rightarrow a^1 = a$$
$$\therefore a^{\frac{1}{2}} = \sqrt{a}$$

$$a^{\frac{1}{n}} = \sqrt[n]{a}$$

$$\frac{1}{a^{-1}} = a$$

$$a^{\frac{2}{3}} \cdot a^{\frac{2}{3}} \cdot a^{\frac{2}{3}} = a^{\frac{2}{3}+\frac{2}{3}+\frac{2}{3}}$$
$$\Rightarrow a^2$$
$$\therefore a^{\frac{2}{3}} = \sqrt[3]{a^2}$$

$$a^{\frac{m}{n}} = \sqrt[n]{a^m}$$
$$\therefore a^{3/4} = \sqrt[4]{a^3}$$
$$\wedge a^{\frac{2}{5}} = \sqrt[5]{a^2}$$
$$\wedge a^{0.25} = a^{1/4} = \sqrt[4]{a}$$

$$a^n \div a^n = a^{n-n}$$
$$\Rightarrow a^0$$
$$\wedge a^n \div a^n = 1$$
$$\therefore a^0 = 1$$

$$a^{-1} \cdot a^{+1} = a^{-1+1}$$
$$\Rightarrow a^0$$
$$\Rightarrow 1$$

$$a^{-1} = \frac{1}{a}$$
$$a^{-2} = \frac{1}{a^2}$$
$$a^{-3} = \frac{1}{a^3}$$

$$2a^{-3} \Rightarrow \frac{2}{a^3}$$

$$a^{-n} \cdot a^{+n} = a^{-n+n}$$
$$\Rightarrow a^0$$
$$\Rightarrow 1$$
$$\therefore a^{-n} = \frac{1}{a^n}$$

$$\frac{1}{a^{-n}} = a^n$$

$$a^{-\frac{1}{2}} = \frac{1}{\sqrt{a}}$$

Second notebook page:

$$\sqrt{ab} = \sqrt{a} \cdot \sqrt{b}$$
$$\sqrt{a^2} = \sqrt{a \cdot a} = \sqrt{a} \cdot \sqrt{a} = a$$

$$\frac{\sqrt{a}}{\sqrt{b}} = \sqrt{\frac{a}{b}}$$

$$\sqrt[3]{a} \cdot \sqrt[3]{a} \cdot \sqrt[3]{a} = a$$

$$\sqrt[n]{ab} = \sqrt[n]{a} \cdot \sqrt[n]{b}$$

$$\frac{a}{b} \times \frac{b}{a} = 1$$

$$\frac{a}{b} : \frac{c}{d} \Rightarrow \frac{b}{a} : \frac{d}{c}$$
$$\Rightarrow \frac{d}{b} : \frac{c}{a} = \frac{b}{d} : \frac{a}{c}$$

$$a(b+c) \Rightarrow ab + ac$$

$$(a+b)(c+d)$$
$$\Rightarrow ac + ad + bc + bd$$

$$(a+b)^2 = (a+b)(a+b)$$

$$(a+b)(a+b) \Rightarrow aa + bb + 2ab$$

$$(a+b)^2 \Rightarrow a^2 + b^2 + 2ab$$

$$(a+b)^2 \Rightarrow (a+b)(a+b)$$
$$\Rightarrow aa + bb + 2ab$$
$$\Rightarrow a^2 + b^2 + 2ab$$

$$(a+b)^2 = a^2 + b^2 + 2ab$$
$$(a-b)^2 = a^2 + b^2 - 2ab$$

$$a^2 + b^2 = (a+b)^2 - 2ab$$
$$a^2 - b^2 = (a+b)(a-b)$$

$$(a+b)^3 = a^3 + 3a^2b + 3ab^2 + b^3$$
$$(a-b)^3 = a^3 - 3a^2b + 3ab^2 - b^3$$

$$a^3 + b^3 = (a+b)(a^2 - ab + b^2)$$
$$a^3 - b^3 = (a-b)(a^2 + ab + b^2)$$

$(a+b)(c+d)$

$\Rightarrow a(c+d) + b(c+d)$

$\Rightarrow ac + ad + bc + bd$

$(a+b)(c-d)$

$\Rightarrow a(c-d) + b(c-d)$

$\Rightarrow ac - ad + bc - bd$

$(a-x)(b-y)$

$\Rightarrow a(b-y) - x(b-y)$

$\Rightarrow ab - ay - bx + xy$

$(x+a)(x+b)$

$\Rightarrow x(x+b) + a(x+b)$

$\Rightarrow x^2 + bx + ax + ab$

$\Rightarrow x^2 + x(b+a) + ab$

$(px+a)(qx+b)$

$\Rightarrow px(qx+b) + a(qx+b)$

$\Rightarrow pqx^2 + pbx + aqx + ab$

$\Rightarrow pqx^2 + x(bp+aq) + ab$

$(a+b)(a^2 - ab + b^2)$

$\Rightarrow a(a^2 - ab + b^2) + b(a^2 - ab + b^2)$

$\Rightarrow a^3 - a^2 b + ab^2 + a^2 b - ab^2 + b^3$

$\Rightarrow a^3 + b^3$

$(x+a)(x+b)$

$\Rightarrow x^2 + x(a+b) + ab$

$\rightarrow b = a$

$\Rightarrow (x+a)(x+a)$

$\Rightarrow x^2 + x(a+a) + a \cdot a$

$\Rightarrow x^2 + 2xa + a^2$

$\therefore (x+a)^2 = x^2 + 2ax + a^2$

$\wedge (x-a)^2 = x^2 - 2ax + a^2$

$(x+c)^2$

$\Rightarrow x^2 + 2cx + c^2$

$\rightarrow x = a+b$

$\therefore (a+b+c)^2$

$\Rightarrow (a+b)^2 + 2c(a+b) + c^2$

$\Rightarrow a^2 + 2ab + b^2 + 2ac + 2bc + c^2$

$\therefore (a+b+c)^2$

$\Rightarrow a^2 + b^2 + c^2 + 2ab + 2bc + 2ac$

$(a+b)^3$
$\Rightarrow (a+b)(a+b)(a+b)$
$\Rightarrow (a+b)(a^2+2ab+b^2)$
$\Rightarrow a(a^2+2ab+b^2) + b(a^2+2ab+b^2)$
$\Rightarrow a^3 + 2a^2b + ab^2 + a^2b + 2ab^2 + b^3$
$\Rightarrow a^3 + 3a^2b + 3ab^2 + b^3 = (a+b)^3$

$^\wedge (a-b)^3 = a^3 - 3a^2b + 3ab^2 - b^3$

$(a+b)(a-b)$
$\Rightarrow a(a-b) + b(a-b)$
$\Rightarrow a^2 - ab + ab - b^2$
$\Rightarrow a^2 - b^2$
$\therefore (a+b)(a-b)$
$\Rightarrow a^2 - b^2$

$(x+a)(x+b) = x^2 + x(a+b) + ab$
$(x+a)^2 = x^2 + 2ax + a^2$
$(x-a)^2 = x^2 - 2ax + a^2$
$(a+b+c)^2 = a^2 + b^2 + c^2 + 2ab + 2bc + 2ac$
$(a+b)^3 = a^3 + 3a^2b + 3ab^2 + b^3$

$ax = b$
$ax^2 = b$
$ax^2 = bx$

$x^2 + ax = b$
$ax + b = x^2$
$x^2 + b = ax$

$x^2 + ax = b \quad \boxed{y = \frac{a}{2}}$
$\Rightarrow x = [(\sqrt{y^2+b}) - y]$

$ax + b = x^2 \quad \boxed{y = \frac{a}{2}}$
$x = [(\sqrt{y^2+b}) + y]$

$x^2 + b = ax \quad \boxed{y = \frac{a}{2}}$
$\Rightarrow x = [y \pm (\sqrt{y^2-b})]$

$ax^2 + bx + 1 = \phi$
$\Rightarrow$
$x = \dfrac{-b \pm \sqrt{b^2 - 4ac}}{2a}$

$cx^2 + ax = b$
$\Rightarrow$
$x^2 + \dfrac{a}{c}x = \dfrac{b}{c}$

$ax + b = cx^2$
$\Rightarrow$
$\dfrac{a}{c}x + \dfrac{b}{c} = x^2$

$cx^2 + b = ax$
$\Rightarrow$
$x^2 + \dfrac{b}{c} = \dfrac{a}{c}x$

$$x = \frac{-b - \sqrt{b^2 - 4ac}}{2a}$$

$$x = \frac{-b + \sqrt{b^2 - 4ac}}{2a}$$

$$\Rightarrow$$

$$x = \frac{-b \pm \sqrt{b^2 - 4ac}}{2a}$$

$$\Rightarrow x = -\frac{b}{2a} + \frac{\sqrt{b^2 - 4ac}}{2a}$$

$$x = -\frac{b}{2a} \pm \frac{\sqrt{b^2 - 4ac}}{2a}$$

$$\Rightarrow x + \frac{b}{2a} = \pm \frac{\sqrt{b^2 - 4ac}}{2a}$$

$$\Rightarrow \left(x + \frac{b}{2a}\right)^2 = \frac{b^2 - 4ac}{4a^2}$$

$$\Rightarrow x^2 + \frac{b}{a}x + \left(\frac{b}{2a}\right)^2 = \frac{b^2}{4a^2} - \frac{c}{a}$$

$$\Rightarrow x^2 + \frac{b}{a}x = -\frac{c}{a}$$

$$\Rightarrow ax^2 + bx = -c$$

$$\Rightarrow ax^2 + bx + c = \phi$$

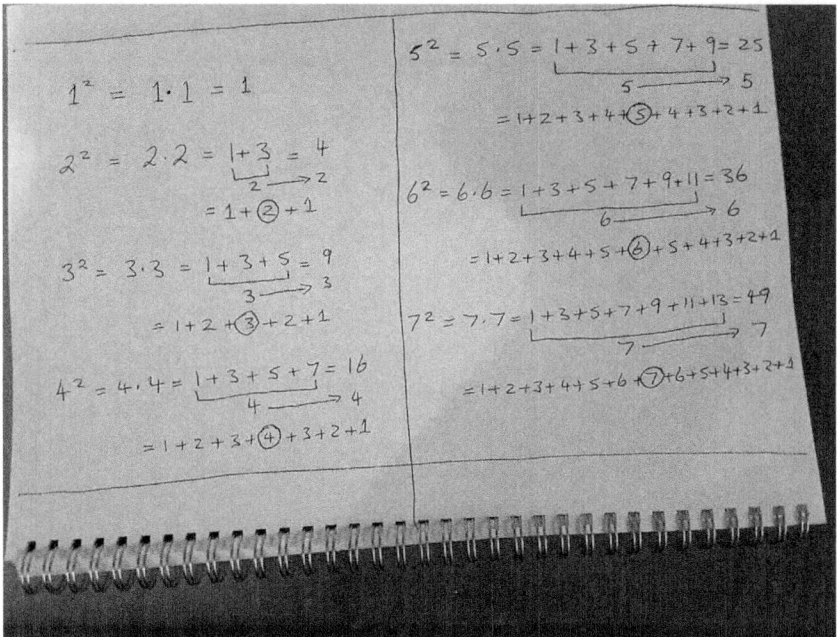

$$1^2 = 1 \cdot 1 = 1$$

$$2^2 = 2 \cdot 2 = \underbrace{1 + 3}_{2} = 4 \longrightarrow 2$$
$$= 1 + ②+ 1$$

$$3^2 = 3 \cdot 3 = \underbrace{1 + 3 + 5}_{3} = 9 \longrightarrow 3$$
$$= 1 + 2 + ③ + 2 + 1$$

$$4^2 = 4 \cdot 4 = \underbrace{1 + 3 + 5 + 7}_{4} = 16 \longrightarrow 4$$
$$= 1 + 2 + 3 + ④ + 3 + 2 + 1$$

$$5^2 = 5 \cdot 5 = \underbrace{1 + 3 + 5 + 7 + 9}_{5} = 25 \longrightarrow 5$$
$$= 1 + 2 + 3 + 4 + ⑤ + 4 + 3 + 2 + 1$$

$$6^2 = 6 \cdot 6 = \underbrace{1 + 3 + 5 + 7 + 9 + 11}_{6} = 36 \longrightarrow 6$$
$$= 1 + 2 + 3 + 4 + 5 + ⑥ + 5 + 4 + 3 + 2 + 1$$

$$7^2 = 7 \cdot 7 = \underbrace{1 + 3 + 5 + 7 + 9 + 11 + 13}_{7} = 49 \longrightarrow 7$$
$$= 1 + 2 + 3 + 4 + 5 + 6 + ⑦ + 6 + 5 + 4 + 3 + 2 + 1$$

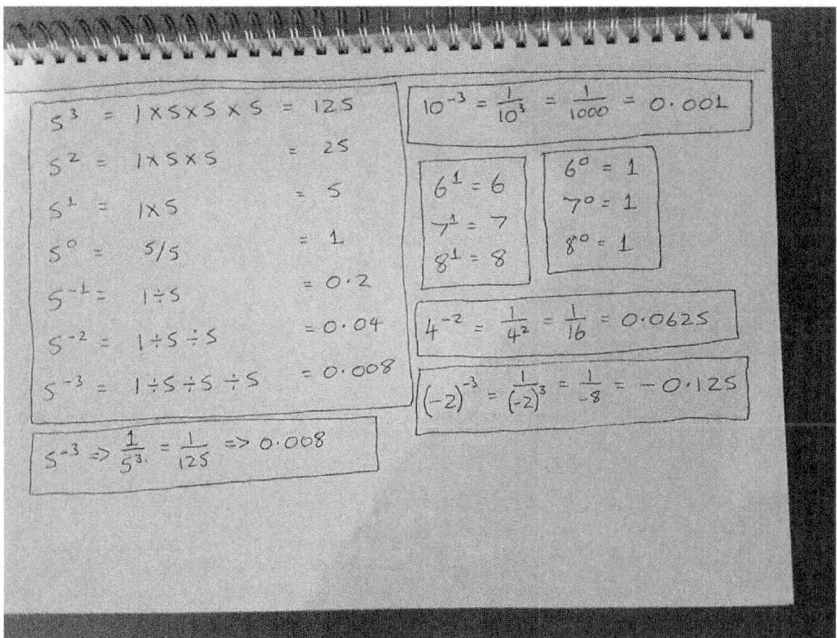

$$5^3 = 1 \times 5 \times 5 \times 5 = 125$$
$$5^2 = 1 \times 5 \times 5 = 25$$
$$5^1 = 1 \times 5 = 5$$
$$5^0 = 5/5 = 1$$
$$5^{-1} = 1 \div 5 = 0.2$$
$$5^{-2} = 1 \div 5 \div 5 = 0.04$$
$$5^{-3} = 1 \div 5 \div 5 \div 5 = 0.008$$

$$5^{-3} \Rightarrow \frac{1}{5^3} = \frac{1}{125} \Rightarrow 0.008$$

$$10^{-3} = \frac{1}{10^3} = \frac{1}{1000} = 0.001$$

$$6^1 = 6$$
$$7^1 = 7$$
$$8^1 = 8$$

$$6^0 = 1$$
$$7^0 = 1$$
$$8^0 = 1$$

$$4^{-2} = \frac{1}{4^2} = \frac{1}{16} = 0.0625$$

$$(-2)^{-3} = \frac{1}{(-2)^3} = \frac{1}{-8} = -0.125$$

64	32	16	8	4	2	1		
2^6	2^5	2^4	2^3	2^2	2^1	2^0		
						0	0	
						1	1	
					1	0	2	
					1	1	3	
				1	0	0	4	
				1	0	1	5	
				1	1	0	6	
				1	1	1	7	
			1	0	0	0	8	
			1	0	0	1	9	

$0 = 0 \times 2^0 = 0 \times 1 = 0$ ⓪

$1 = 1 \times 2^0 = 1 \times 1 = 1$ ①

$\left.\begin{array}{l} 2 = 1 \times 2^1 = 1 \times 2 = 2 \\ 0 \times 2^0 = 0 \times 1 = 0 \end{array}\right\}$ ②

$\left.\begin{array}{l} 3 = 1 \times 2^1 = 1 \times 2 = 2 \\ 1 \times 2^0 = 1 \times 1 = 1 \end{array}\right\}$ ③

$\left.\begin{array}{l} 4 = 1 \times 2^2 = 1 \times 4 = 4 \\ 0 \times 2^1 = 0 \times 2 = 0 \\ 0 \times 2^0 = 0 \times 1 = 0 \end{array}\right\}$ ④

$\left.\begin{array}{l} 5 = 1 \times 2^2 = 1 \times 4 = 4 \\ 0 \times 2^1 = 0 \times 2 = 0 \\ 1 \times 2^0 = 1 \times 1 = 1 \end{array}\right\}$ ⑤

$\left.\begin{array}{l} 6 = 1 \times 2^2 = 1 \times 4 = 4 \\ 1 \times 2^1 = 1 \times 2 = 2 \\ 0 \times 2^0 = 0 \times 1 = 0 \end{array}\right\}$ ⑥

$x = \sqrt{4}$ $x = \sqrt{9}$ $x = \sqrt{16}$

$4 = \dfrac{1+3}{2}$ $9 = \dfrac{1+3+5}{3}$ $16 = \dfrac{1+3+5+7}{4}$

$\therefore x = 2$ $\therefore x = 3$ $\therefore x = 4$

$ax = b$
$ax^2 = b$
$ax^2 = bx$

$\boxed{ax^2 = b}$ $\dfrac{16}{5 \overline{)80}}$

$5x^2 = 80$

$x^2 = \dfrac{80}{5} \Rightarrow x^2 = 16$

$\Rightarrow x = \sqrt{16} = 4$ $5 \times 16 = 80$

$5 \times 4^2 = 80$

$\boxed{ax = b}$ $a = 4$
$b = 20$
$x = ?$

$4x = 20$ $x = \dfrac{b}{a}$

$x = \dfrac{20}{4}$

$4 \overline{)20}^{\,5}$ $5 \times 4 = 20$

$\therefore x = 5$

$\boxed{ax^2 = bx}$

$5x^2 = 10x$

$x^2 = \dfrac{10x}{5}$ $5 \times 2^2 = 5 \times 4$

$x^2 = 2x$ $5 \times 4 = 20$

$x = 2$

$$x^2 + ax = b$$

$$\boxed{x^2 + 3x = 28}$$

$$x = \left[\left(\sqrt{y^2+b}\right) - y\right] \quad y = \frac{a}{2}$$

$$x = \sqrt{\left(\frac{3}{2}\right)^2 + \frac{28}{1}} - \frac{3}{2}$$

$$= \sqrt{2.25 + 28} - 1.5$$

$$= \sqrt{30.25} - 1.5$$

$$= 5.5 - 1.5$$

$$\underline{\underline{x = 4}}$$

$a = 3$
$b = 28$
$y = 1.5$
$x = 4$

$$\underline{\underline{4^2 + 12 = 28}}$$

$x^2 + ax = b$

$\Rightarrow x = [(\sqrt{y^2 + b}) - y]$

$y = \frac{a}{2}$

$x^2 + 10x = 39$

$a = 10$
$b = 39$
$y = 5$
$x = 3$

$3^2 + 30 = 39$

$x = \sqrt{\left[\left(\frac{10}{2}\right)^2 + \frac{39}{1}\right]} - \frac{10}{2}$

$\Rightarrow \sqrt{(5^2 + 39)} - 5$

$\Rightarrow \sqrt{(25 + 39)} - 5$

$\Rightarrow \sqrt{64} - 5$

$\Rightarrow 8 - 5$

$\therefore x = 3$

$$\underline{ax + b = x^2}$$

$$\boxed{2x + 15 = x^2}$$

$$x = \left[\left(\sqrt{y^2 + b}\right) + y\right] \qquad y = \frac{a}{2}$$

$$x = \sqrt{\left[\left(\frac{2}{2}\right)^2 + 15\right]} + \frac{2}{2}$$

$$= \sqrt{1 + 15} + 1$$

$$= \sqrt{16} + 1$$

$$x = 4 + 1$$

$$\underline{\underline{x = 5}}$$

$$a = 2$$
$$b = 15$$
$$y = 1$$
$$x = 5$$

$$\underline{\underline{10 + 15 = 25}}$$

$$ax + b = x^2$$
$$\Rightarrow x = \left[\left(\sqrt{y^2 + b}\right) + y \right]$$
$$y = \frac{a}{2}$$

$$3x + 4 = x^2$$
$$y = \frac{3}{2} \Rightarrow \left(\frac{3}{2}\right)^2 = 1 \cdot 5^2$$
$$\Rightarrow \frac{9}{4} = 2.25$$

$$a = 3$$
$$b = 4$$
$$y = 1\tfrac{1}{2}$$
$$x = 4$$

$$x = \sqrt{\left[\left(\tfrac{3}{2}\right)^2 + 4\right]} + \tfrac{3}{2}$$
$$\Rightarrow \sqrt{(2\tfrac{1}{4} + 4)} + 1\tfrac{1}{2}$$
$$\Rightarrow \sqrt{6\tfrac{1}{4}} + 1\tfrac{1}{2}$$
$$\Rightarrow 2\tfrac{1}{2} + 1\tfrac{1}{2}$$
$$\therefore \underline{x = 4}$$

$$2.5 \times 2.5 = 6.25$$

$$\sqrt{6\tfrac{1}{4}}$$
$$\Rightarrow 2\tfrac{1}{2} \cdot 2\tfrac{1}{2}$$
$$= 6\tfrac{1}{4}$$

$$12 + 4 = 16$$

$$x^2 + b = ax$$

$$x^2 + 18 = 9x$$

$$x = \left[y \pm \left(\sqrt{y^2 - b}\right) \right]$$

$$x = \frac{9}{2} \pm \sqrt{\left(\tfrac{9}{2}\right)^2 - 18}$$

$$= 4\tfrac{1}{2} \pm \sqrt{(4\tfrac{1}{2})^2 - 18}$$

$$= 4\tfrac{1}{2} \pm \sqrt{20.25 - 18}$$

$$= 4.5 \pm \sqrt{2.25}$$

$$= 4.5 \pm 1.5$$

$$\underline{x = 6 \text{ or } 3}$$

$$a = 9$$
$$b = 18$$
$$y = 4\tfrac{1}{2}$$
$$x = 6 \text{ or } 3$$

$$36 + 18 = 54$$
$$9 + 18 = 27$$

$$x^2 + b = ax$$
$$\Rightarrow x = \left[y \pm \left(\sqrt{y^2 - b} \right) \right]$$
$$y = \frac{a}{2}$$

$$x^2 + 21 = 10x$$

$$x = \frac{10}{2} \pm \sqrt{\left(\frac{10}{2} \right)^2 - \frac{21}{1}}$$

$$\Rightarrow 5 \pm \sqrt{5^2 - 21}$$
$$\Rightarrow 5 \pm \sqrt{25 - 21}$$
$$\Rightarrow 5 \pm \sqrt{4}$$
$$\Rightarrow 5 \pm 2$$
$$\therefore \; 5 + 2 = 7, \; 5 - 2 = 3$$
$$\Rightarrow x = 7 \text{ or } 3$$

$$a = 10$$
$$b = 21$$
$$y = 5$$
$$x = 7 \text{ or } 3$$

$$7^2 + 21 = 70$$
$$3^2 + 21 = 30$$

$$(10 + 1)(10 + 2) = 132$$

$$10 \times 10 = 100 \qquad 10 + 1 = 11$$
$$1 \times 2 = 2 \qquad\quad 10 + 2 = 12$$
$$1 \times 10 = 10$$
$$10 \times 2 = \underline{20} \qquad\quad \underline{11 \times 12 = 132}$$
$$\underline{132}$$

$$(10 + 2)(10 - 1) = 108$$

$$10 \times 10 = 100 \qquad 10 + 2 = 12$$
$$2 \times -1 = -2 \qquad\; 10 - 1 = 9$$
$$10 \times -1 = -10 \qquad \underline{9 \times 12 = 108}$$
$$2 \times 10 = 20$$
$$\Rightarrow 100 + 20 - 10 - 2$$
$$\therefore \Rightarrow 120 - 12 = \underline{108}$$

$$(10 + 1)(10 + 1) = 121$$

$$10 \times 10 = 100 \qquad 10 + 1 = 11$$
$$1 \times 1 = 1 \qquad\quad \underline{11 \times 11 = 121}$$
$$10 \times 1 = 10$$
$$1 \times 10 = \underline{10}$$
$$\underline{121}$$

$$(10 + 1)(10 - 1) = 99$$

$$10 \times 10 = 100 \qquad 10 + 1 = 11$$
$$1 \times -1 = -1 \qquad\; 10 - 1 = 9$$
$$10 \times -1 = -10$$
$$1 \times 10 = 10 \qquad\quad \underline{9 \times 11 = 99}$$
$$\Rightarrow 110 - 11$$
$$\therefore \Rightarrow \underline{99}$$

Top left:
$(10 + x)^2 = (10 + x)(10 + x)$

$\Rightarrow 10 \cdot x = 10x$
$\quad x \cdot 10 = 10x$
$\quad 10 \cdot 10 = 100$
$\quad x \cdot x = x^2$
$\Rightarrow \underline{100 + 20x + x^2}$

Top right:
$(10 - x)(10 - x)$

$10 \cdot -x = -10x$
$-x \cdot 10 = -10x$
$10 \cdot 10 = 100$
$-x \cdot -x = x^2$
$\Rightarrow \underline{100 - 20x + x^2}$

Bottom left:
$(10 + x)(10 - x)$

$10 \cdot -x = -10x$
$x \cdot 10 = 10x$
$10 \cdot 10 = 100$
$x \cdot -x = -x^2$
$\Rightarrow 100 + 10x - 10x - x^2$
$\Rightarrow \underline{100 - x^2}$

Bottom right:
$(x + 1)(x + 3)$

$x \cdot 3 = 3x$
$1 \cdot x = x$
$x \cdot x = x^2$
$1 \cdot 3 = 3$
$\Rightarrow 3x + x + x^2 + 3$
$\Rightarrow \underline{4x + x^2 + 3}$

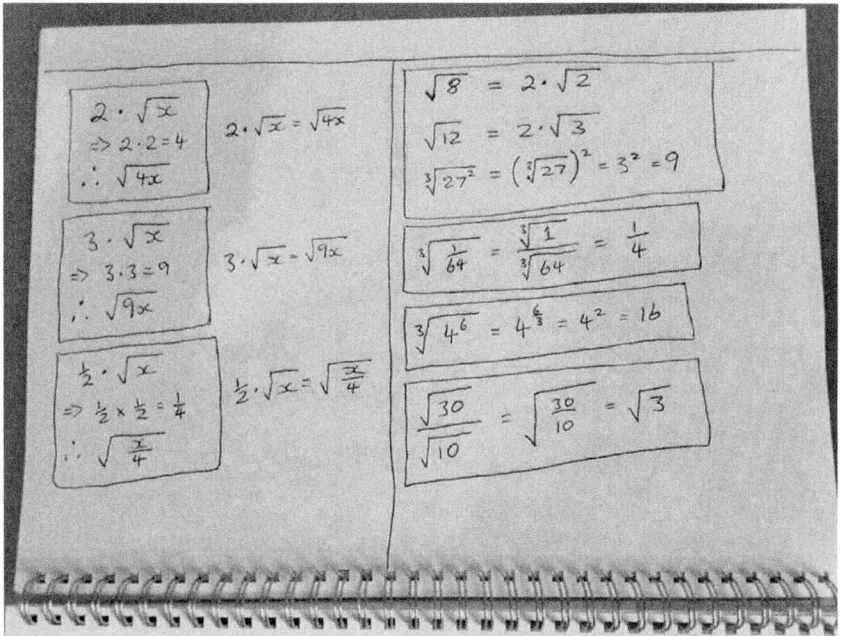

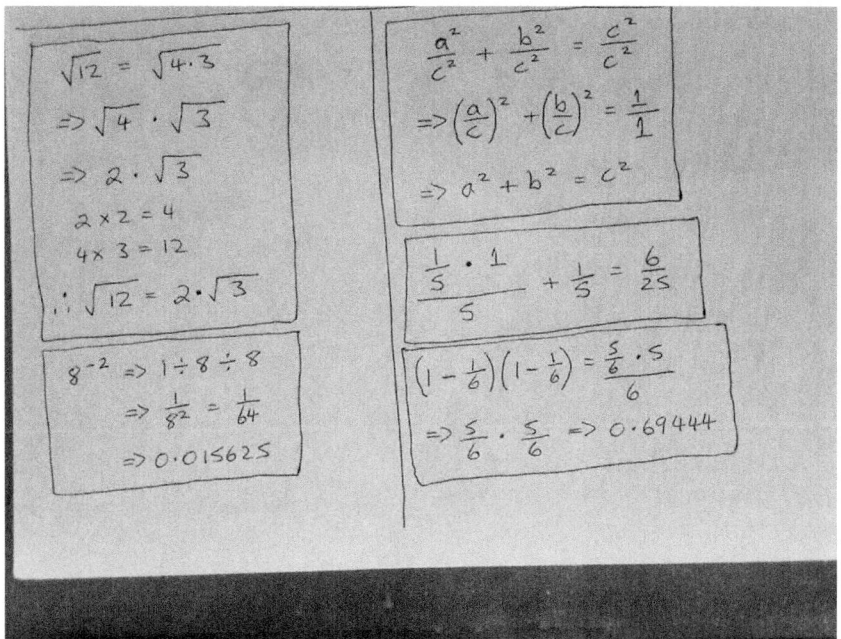

$$\frac{4x^3y}{6xy^3} = \frac{4 \cdot x \cdot x \cdot x \cdot y}{6 \cdot x \cdot y \cdot y \cdot y}$$

$$\Rightarrow \frac{2 \cdot x \cdot x}{3 \cdot y \cdot y} \Rightarrow \frac{2x^2}{3y^2}$$

$$\frac{8x^3}{5a^2y} \div \frac{4x^2}{3a}$$

$$= \frac{8x^3}{5a^2y} \times \frac{3a}{4x^2}$$

$$\Rightarrow \frac{2x \cdot 3}{5ay} = \frac{6x}{5ay}$$

$$\frac{x}{12a^2b} - \frac{y}{18ab^2}$$

$$\Rightarrow 3b \cdot 12a^2b = 36a^2b^2$$
$$3b \cdot x = 3bx$$
$$2a \cdot 18ab^2 = 36a^2b^2$$
$$2a \cdot y = 2ay$$

$$\therefore \frac{(x \cdot 3b)}{(3b \cdot 12a^2b)} - \frac{(y \cdot 2a)}{2a \cdot 18ab^2}$$

$$\Rightarrow \frac{(x \cdot 3b)}{36a^2b^2} - \frac{(y \cdot 2a)}{36a^2b^2}$$

$$\Rightarrow \frac{3bx - 2ay}{36a^2b^2}$$

556

$$\frac{6ax^4}{14x^2y^2} \times \frac{2y^3}{3a^4}$$

$$\Rightarrow \frac{6ax^4}{3a} \Rightarrow \frac{2x^4}{1}$$

$$\Rightarrow \frac{2x^4}{2x^2} = \frac{x^2}{1}$$

$$\Rightarrow \frac{14x^2y^2}{2x^2} = 7y^2$$

$$\therefore \frac{x^2}{7y^2} \times \frac{2y^3}{a^3}$$

$$\frac{x^2}{7y^2} \times \frac{2y^3}{a^3}$$

$$\Rightarrow \frac{2y^3}{y^2} = \frac{2y}{1}$$

$$\Rightarrow \frac{7y^2}{y^2} = 7$$

$$\therefore \frac{x^2 \times 2y}{7 \times a^3}$$

$$\Rightarrow \frac{2x^2y}{7a^3}$$

$$a^M \div a^n$$
$$\Rightarrow \frac{a^n}{a^n}$$
$$\Rightarrow a^{n-n}$$

$$\frac{x}{y} - \frac{a}{b}$$
$$\Rightarrow \frac{(x \cdot b) - (a \cdot y)}{y \cdot b}$$
$$\Rightarrow \frac{bx - ay}{by}$$

$$3y^4 \div 6y^6$$
$$\Rightarrow \frac{3y^4}{6y^6}$$
$$\Rightarrow \frac{3\,xyxyxyxy}{6\,xyxyxyxyxy}$$
$$\Rightarrow \frac{1}{2y^2}$$

$$\frac{2a}{15} + \frac{5b}{12}$$
$$\Rightarrow \frac{2a\cdot4}{15\cdot4} + \frac{5b\cdot5}{12\cdot5}$$
$$\Rightarrow \frac{(2a\cdot4)+(5b\cdot5)}{60}$$
$$\Rightarrow \frac{8a+25b}{60}$$

$$\frac{x}{3} + \frac{x}{5} = \frac{(x\cdot5)+(x\cdot3)}{3\cdot5}$$
$$\Rightarrow \frac{5x+3x}{15} \Rightarrow \frac{8x}{15}$$

$$\frac{3}{a} + \frac{4}{b} = \frac{(3\cdot b)+(4\cdot a)}{ab}$$
$$\Rightarrow \frac{3b+4a}{ab}$$

$$\frac{x}{12a^2b} - \frac{y}{18ab^2} \Rightarrow \frac{(x\cdot3b)-(y\cdot2a)}{36a^2b^2}$$
$$\Rightarrow \frac{3bx-2ay}{36a^2b^2}$$

$a(a^2 + ab + b^2)$
$\Rightarrow a^3 + a^2b + ab^2$

$3(4a - b) - 2(3a - 2b)$
$\Rightarrow 12a - 3b - 6a + 4b$
$\Rightarrow 6a + b$

$2(4a + 3b) + 6(2a - b)$
$\Rightarrow 8a + 6b + 12a - 6b$
$\Rightarrow 20a$

$5a - \dfrac{a-b}{2} = 5a - \dfrac{1}{2}(a-b)$

$5x - (5y + 2x)$
$\Rightarrow 5x - 5y - 2x$
$\Rightarrow 3x - 5y$

$2\left[3a + 5(b+c)\right]$
$\Rightarrow 2(3a + 5b + 5c)$
$\Rightarrow 6a + 10b + 10c$

$3\left[3a - 2(a-b)\right]$
$\Rightarrow 3(3a - 2a + 2b)$
$\Rightarrow 3(a + 2b)$
$\Rightarrow 3a + 6b$

$$x^2 = 2x$$
$$\therefore x = 2$$

$$x^2 = 3x$$
$$\therefore x = 3$$

$$x^2 = 4x$$
$$\therefore x = 4$$

$$x^2 = 5x$$
$$\therefore x = 5$$

$$\frac{x^2}{2} = 18$$
$$\Rightarrow x^2 = 18 \times 2$$
$$\Rightarrow x^2 = 36$$
$$\Rightarrow x = \sqrt{36}$$
$$\Rightarrow x = 6$$

$$\frac{10 - x}{x} = 4$$
$$\Rightarrow 10 - x = 4x$$
$$\Rightarrow 10 = 4x + x$$
$$\Rightarrow 10 = 5x$$
$$\Rightarrow \frac{10}{5} = x$$
$$\therefore \underline{x = 2}$$

$$x^2 = 9$$
$$\therefore x = 3$$

$$x^2 = 16$$
$$\therefore x = 4$$

$$x^2 = 25$$
$$\therefore x = 5$$

$$\frac{x}{x+2} = \frac{1}{2}$$
$$\Rightarrow x = \frac{1}{2} \times x + 2$$
$$\Rightarrow x = \frac{1}{2} \times \frac{x+2}{1}$$
$$= \frac{x+2}{2}$$

$$x = \frac{x+2}{2}$$
$$\Rightarrow x = \frac{x}{2} + \frac{2}{2}$$
$$\Rightarrow x = \frac{x}{2} + 1$$
$$\Rightarrow \frac{x}{2} = 1$$
$$\Rightarrow x + 2 = 4$$

$$x = 2$$
$$2 = \frac{2+2}{2}$$
$$2 = \frac{2}{2} + 1$$
$$2 = \frac{2}{2} + \frac{2}{2}$$

$$4x \cdot 5x = 2x^2 + 36$$
$$\Rightarrow 20x^2 = 2x^2 + 36$$
$$\Rightarrow 20x^2 - 2x^2 = 36$$
$$\Rightarrow 18x^2 = 36$$
$$\Rightarrow x^2 = \frac{36}{18}$$
$$\Rightarrow x^2 = 2$$
$$\Rightarrow x = \sqrt{2}$$
$$\sqrt{2} = 1.414\ 213\ 562\ 373$$
$$\therefore \underline{x = 1.414}$$

$$4x \cdot 3x = x^2 + 44$$
$$\Rightarrow 12x^2 = x^2 + 44$$
$$\Rightarrow 12x^2 - x^2 = 44$$
$$\Rightarrow 11x^2 = 44$$
$$\Rightarrow x^2 = \frac{44}{11}$$
$$\Rightarrow x^2 = 4$$
$$\Rightarrow x = \sqrt{4}$$
$$\therefore x = 2.$$

$$(4 \times 2) \cdot (3 \times 2) = (2 \cdot 2) + 44$$
$$\Rightarrow 8 \times 6 = 4 + 44$$
$$\Rightarrow 48 = 48$$

LANCE GRUNDY

$$x^2 = 4x(10-x)$$
$$\Rightarrow x^2 = (4x \cdot 10) - (4x \cdot x)$$
$$\Rightarrow x^2 = 40x - 4x^2$$
$$\Rightarrow x^2 + 4x^2 = 40x$$
$$\Rightarrow 5x^2 = 40x$$
$$\Rightarrow x^2 = \frac{40x}{5}$$
$$\Rightarrow x^2 = 8x$$
$$\Rightarrow x = \sqrt{8x}$$
$$\Rightarrow x = \sqrt{64}$$
$$\therefore x = 8$$

$$8^2 = 4 \cdot 8(10-8)$$
$$8^2 = 32 \cdot (2)$$
$$8^2 = 64$$
$$8 \cdot 8 = 64$$
$$\underline{8 = 8}$$

$$2^6 = 2 \times 2 \times 2 \times 2 \times 2 \times 2$$
$$= 64$$

$$8n - 5 = 123$$
$$8n = 123 + 5$$
$$8n = 128$$
$$n = \frac{128}{8}$$
$$\underline{n = 16}$$

$$6x - 5 = 2x + 9$$
$$6x - 5 - 2x = 9$$
$$6x - 2x = 9 + 5$$
$$4x = 14$$
$$x = \frac{14}{4}$$
$$x = \frac{7}{2}$$

$$\left(6 \times \frac{7}{2}\right) - 5 = 16$$
$$\frac{6}{1} \times \frac{7}{2} - 5 = 16$$
$$\frac{42}{2} - 5 = 16$$
$$21 - 5 = 16$$

$$\left(2 \times \frac{7}{2}\right) + 9 = 16$$
$$\left(\frac{2}{1} \times \frac{7}{2}\right) + 9 = 16$$
$$\frac{14}{2} + 9 = 16$$
$$7 + 9 = 16$$

$$10(x-4) = 4(2x-1) + 5$$
$$\Rightarrow 10x - 40 = 8x - 4 + 5$$
$$\Rightarrow 10x - 8x = 40 - 4 + 5$$
$$\Rightarrow 2x = 41$$
$$\Rightarrow x = 20\frac{1}{2}$$
$$\therefore 10(20\frac{1}{2} - 4) = 4(2 \cdot 20\frac{1}{2} - 1) + 5$$
$$\Rightarrow 10 \times 16\frac{1}{2} = 160 + 5$$
$$\Rightarrow \underline{165}$$

$$\frac{3x}{5} + \frac{x}{2} = \frac{5x}{4} - 3 (= 22)$$
$$\Rightarrow \left(\frac{3x}{5} \times 20\right) + \left(\frac{x}{2} \times 20\right) = \left(\frac{5x}{4} \times 20\right) - (3 \times 20)$$
$$\Rightarrow \frac{60x}{5} + \frac{20x}{2} = \frac{100x}{4} - 60$$
$$\Rightarrow 12x + 10x = 25x - 60$$
$$\Rightarrow 12x + 10x - 25x = -60$$
$$\Rightarrow -3x = -60$$
$$\Rightarrow x = \frac{-60}{-3} \quad \therefore x = 20$$

560

$x + y = 10$

$x = 4y$

$\therefore 4y + y = 10$

$\Rightarrow 5y = 10$

$\Rightarrow y = \dfrac{10}{5}$

$\Rightarrow y = 2$

$\therefore x = 4 \times 2$

$\Rightarrow x = 8$

$2x + y = 21$

$3x + 4y = 44$

$\Rightarrow y = 21 - 2x$

$3x = 44 - 4y$

$x = \dfrac{44 - 4y}{3}$

$\Rightarrow 3x + 4y = 44$

$\Rightarrow 3x + 4(21 - 2x) = 44$

$\Rightarrow 3x + 84 - 8x = 44$

$\Rightarrow 3x - 8x = 44 - 84$

$\Rightarrow -5x = -40$

$\Rightarrow 5x = 40$

$\Rightarrow x = \dfrac{40}{5}$

$\Rightarrow x = 8$

$y = 21 - (2 \cdot 8)$

$y = 21 - 16$

$y = 5$

$x + y = 15$

$3x - y = 21$

$\Rightarrow (x + y) + (3x - y) = 15 + 21$

$\Rightarrow x + 3x = 36$

$\Rightarrow 4x = 36$

$\Rightarrow x = \dfrac{36}{4}$

$\Rightarrow x = 9$

$\therefore x + y = 15$

$\Rightarrow 9 + y = 15$

$\Rightarrow y = 15 - 9$

$\Rightarrow y = 6$

LANCE GRUNDY

$2x + 3y = 42$
$5x - y = 20$
$\Rightarrow -y = 20 - 5x$
$\Rightarrow y = 5x - 20$
$\therefore 2x + 3y = 42$
$\Rightarrow 2x + 3(5x-20) = 42$
$\Rightarrow 2x + 15x - 60 = 42$
$\Rightarrow 17x = 42 + 60$
$\Rightarrow x = \frac{102}{17}$
$\Rightarrow x = \underline{6}$
$\therefore y = (5\times6) - 20$
$\Rightarrow y = \underline{10}$

$2x + 3y = 42$
$5x - y = 20$
$\therefore (5x \times 3) - (3xy) = 20 \times 3$
$\Rightarrow 15x - 3y = 60$
$\Rightarrow (2x + 3y) + (15x - 3y) = 42 + 60$
$\Rightarrow 17x = 102$
$\Rightarrow x = \frac{102}{17}$
$\Rightarrow x = \underline{6}$
$\therefore y = 5x - 20$
$y = (5 \times 6) - 20$
$y = \underline{10}$

$(2x + 3y = 42) \times 5$
$(5x - y = 20) \times 2$
$\Rightarrow 10x + 15y = 210$
$10x - 2y = 40$
$\Rightarrow (10x+15y) - (10x - 2y)$
$= 210 - 40$
$\Rightarrow 17y = 170$
$\Rightarrow y = \underline{10}$

$x(a+b) = xa + xb$
$\therefore xa + xb$
$\Rightarrow \frac{xa}{x} + \frac{xb}{x}$
$\Rightarrow a + b$
$\wedge\ x(a+b) = xa + xb$

$5x^2 y^2 - 10x^2 y + 20y^2$
$\Rightarrow \frac{5x^2 y^2}{5y} - \frac{10x^2 y}{5y} + \frac{20y^2}{5y}$
$\Rightarrow x^2 y - 2x^2 + 4y$
$\wedge\ 5y(x^2 y - 2x^2 + 4y) = 5x^2 y^2 - 10x^2 y + 20y^2$

$6a^2 + 3ac$
$\Rightarrow \frac{6a^2}{3a} + \frac{3ac}{3a}$
$\Rightarrow 2a + c$
$\therefore 3a(2a+c) = 6a^2 + 3ac$

$xy + bx + ay + ab$
$\Rightarrow (xy + bx) + (ay + ab)$
$\Rightarrow \frac{xy}{x} + \frac{bx}{x} + \frac{ay}{a} + \frac{ab}{a}$
$\Rightarrow (y+b) + (y+b)$
$\therefore x(y+b) + a(y+b)$
$\Rightarrow (y+b)(x+a)$

562

$$\frac{a}{a-b} - \frac{a^2}{a^2-b^2}$$

$$\Rightarrow \frac{a}{a-b} - \frac{a^2}{(a+b)(a-b)}$$

$$\Rightarrow \frac{a(a+b)-a^2}{(a+b)(a-b)}$$

$$\Rightarrow \frac{a^2+ab-a^2}{(a+b)(a-b)}$$

$$\Rightarrow \frac{ab}{(a+b)(a-b)}$$

$$\frac{3}{a-b} - \frac{2a+b}{(a+b)(a-b)}$$

$$\Rightarrow \frac{3(a+b)-(2a+b)}{(a+b)(a-b)}$$

$$\Rightarrow \frac{3a+3b-2a-b}{(a+b)(a-b)}$$

$$\Rightarrow \frac{a+2b}{(a+b)(a-b)}$$

$$\frac{a+6}{b+2} \neq \frac{a+3}{b}$$

$$\frac{2a+6}{4b+2} = \frac{a+3}{2b+1}$$

$$\left(\frac{1}{3}x+1\right)\left(\frac{1}{4}x+1\right) = 20$$

$$\frac{1}{3}x \cdot \frac{1}{4}x = \frac{x^2}{12}$$

$$\frac{1}{3}x \cdot \frac{1}{1} = \frac{1}{3}x$$

$$\frac{1}{4}x \cdot \frac{1}{1} = \frac{1}{4}x$$

$$1 \cdot 1 = 1$$

$$\Rightarrow \frac{x^2}{12} + \frac{1}{3}x + \frac{1}{4}x + 1 = 20$$

$$\frac{1}{3}x + \frac{1}{4}x = \frac{7}{12}x$$

$$\frac{1}{3} + \frac{1}{4} = \frac{3\times1}{3\times4} + \frac{4\times1}{3\times4} = \frac{3+4}{12}$$

$$\frac{x^2}{12} + \frac{7}{12}x + \frac{1}{1} = 20$$

$$\Rightarrow \frac{x^2}{12} + \frac{7}{12}x = 20-1 = 19$$

$$\Rightarrow x^2 + 7x = 19\times12 = 228$$

$$\Rightarrow x^2 + 7x = 228$$

$$\therefore x^2 + ax = b$$

$$\Rightarrow x = \left[\left(\sqrt{y^2+b}\right)\right] - y$$

$$y = \frac{a}{2} = 3.5$$
$$a = 7$$
$$b = 228$$

$$\Rightarrow x = \sqrt{3.5^2 + 228} - 3.5$$

$$\Rightarrow \sqrt{12.25 + 228} - 3.5$$

$$\Rightarrow \sqrt{240.25} - 3.5$$

$$\Rightarrow 15.5 - 3.5$$

$$\therefore x = 12$$

$$15.5 \times 15.5 = 240.25$$

$$5 \times 4 = 20$$

$$\frac{x^3 - 4x^2 + 2x - 3}{x + 2}$$

① $x + 2 \overline{)x^3 - 4x^2 + 2x - 3}$

② $x + 2 \overline{)\overset{x^2}{x^3 - 4x^2 + 2x - 3}}$

③ $x + 2 \overline{)\overset{x^2}{x^3 - 4x^2 + 2x - 3}}$
$\quad\quad\quad x^3 + 2x^2$

④ $x + 2 \overline{)\overset{x^2}{x^3 - 4x^2 + 2x - 3}}$
$\quad\quad\quad \underline{x^3 + 2x^2}$
$\quad\quad\quad\quad -6x^2 + 2x$

⑤ $x + 2 \overline{)\overset{x^2 - 6x}{x^3 - 4x^2 + 2x - 3}}$
$\quad\quad\quad \underline{x^3 + 2x^2}$
$\quad\quad\quad\quad -6x^2 + 2x$

⑥ $x + 2 \overline{)\overset{x^2 - 6x}{x^3 - 4x^2 + 2x - 3}}$
$\quad\quad\quad \underline{x^3 + 2x^2}$
$\quad\quad\quad\quad -6x^2 + 2x$
$\quad\quad\quad\quad -6x^2 - 12x$

⑦ $x + 2 \overline{)\overset{x^2 - 6x}{x^3 - 4x^2 + 2x - 3}}$
$\quad\quad\quad \underline{x^3 + 2x^2}$
$\quad\quad\quad\quad -6x^2 + 2x$
$\quad\quad\quad\quad \underline{-6x^2 - 12x}$
$\quad\quad\quad\quad\quad\quad 14x - 3$

⑧ $x + 2 \overline{)\overset{x^2 - 6x + 14}{x^3 - 4x^2 + 2x - 3}}$
$\quad\quad\quad \underline{x^3 + 2x^2}$
$\quad\quad\quad\quad -6x^2 + 2x$
$\quad\quad\quad\quad \underline{-6x^2 - 12x}$
$\quad\quad\quad\quad\quad\quad 14x - 3$

⑨ $x + 2 \overline{)\overset{x^2 - 6x + 14}{x^3 - 4x^2 + 2x - 3}}$
$\quad\quad\quad \underline{x^3 + 2x^2}$
$\quad\quad\quad\quad -6x^2 + 2x$
$\quad\quad\quad\quad \underline{-6x^2 - 12x}$
$\quad\quad\quad\quad\quad\quad 14x - 3$
$\quad\quad\quad\quad\quad\quad 14x + 28$

⑩ $x + 2 \overline{)\overset{x^2 - 6x + 14}{x^3 - 4x^2 + 2x - 3}}$
$\quad\quad\quad \underline{x^3 + 2x^2}$
$\quad\quad\quad\quad -6x^2 + 2x$
$\quad\quad\quad\quad \underline{-6x^2 - 12x}$
$\quad\quad\quad\quad\quad\quad 14x - 3$
$\quad\quad\quad\quad\quad\quad \underline{14x + 28}$
$\quad\quad\quad\quad\quad\quad\quad\quad -31$

⑪ $\quad x^2 - 6x + 14 - \dfrac{31}{x + 2}$

$$\frac{x^3 - 4x^2 + 2x - 3}{x + 2}$$

① $x + 2 \overline{)\, x^3 - 4x^2 + 2x - 3}$

② $x + 2 \overline{)\, x^3 - 4x^2 + 2x - 3}^{\quad x^2}$

③ $x + 2 \overline{)\, x^3 - 4x^2 + 2x - 3}^{\quad x^2}$
$\quad\quad\quad x^3 + 2x^2$

④ $x + 2 \overline{)\, x^3 - 4x^2 + 2x - 3}^{\quad x^2}$
$\quad\quad\quad x^3 + 2x^2$
$\quad\quad\quad\quad\quad -6x^2 + 2x$

⑤ $x + 2 \overline{)\, x^3 - 4x^2 + 2x - 3}^{\quad x^2 - 6x}$
$\quad\quad\quad x^3 + 2x^2$
$\quad\quad\quad\quad\quad -6x^2 + 2x$

⑥ $x + 2 \overline{)\, x^3 - 4x^2 + 2x - 3}^{\quad x^2 - 6x}$
$\quad\quad\quad x^3 + 2x^2$
$\quad\quad\quad\quad\quad -6x^2 + 2x$
$\quad\quad\quad\quad\quad -6x^2 - 12x$

⑦ $x + 2 \overline{)\, x^3 - 4x^2 + 2x - 3}^{\quad x^2 - 6x}$
$\quad\quad\quad x^3 + 2x^2$
$\quad\quad\quad\quad\quad -6x^2 + 2x$
$\quad\quad\quad\quad\quad -6x^2 - 12x$
$\quad\quad\quad\quad\quad\quad\quad 14x - 3$

⑧ $x + 2 \overline{)\, x^3 - 4x^2 + 2x - 3}^{\quad x^2 - 6x + 14}$
$\quad\quad\quad x^3 + 2x^2$
$\quad\quad\quad\quad\quad -6x^2 + 2x$
$\quad\quad\quad\quad\quad -6x^2 - 12x$
$\quad\quad\quad\quad\quad\quad\quad 14x - 3$

⑨ $x + 2 \overline{)\, x^3 - 4x^2 + 2x - 3}^{\quad x^2 - 6x + 14}$
$\quad\quad\quad x^3 + 2x^2$
$\quad\quad\quad\quad\quad -6x^2 + 2x$
$\quad\quad\quad\quad\quad -6x^2 - 12x$
$\quad\quad\quad\quad\quad\quad\quad 14x - 3$
$\quad\quad\quad\quad\quad\quad\quad 14x + 28$

⑩ $x + 2 \overline{)\, x^3 - 4x^2 + 2x - 3}^{\quad x^2 - 6x + 14}$
$\quad\quad\quad x^3 + 2x^2$
$\quad\quad\quad\quad\quad -6x^2 + 2x$
$\quad\quad\quad\quad\quad -6x^2 - 12x$
$\quad\quad\quad\quad\quad\quad\quad 14x - 3$
$\quad\quad\quad\quad\quad\quad\quad 14x + 28$
$\quad\quad\quad\quad\quad\quad\quad\quad\quad -31$

⑪ $x^2 - 6x + 14 - \dfrac{31}{x + 2}$

$$\frac{-13x^2 + 4x^3 + 2x - 7}{x^2 + 3x - 2}$$

① $x^2 + 3x - 2 \overline{\smash{)}4x^3 - 13x^2 + 2x - 7}$

②
$$
\begin{array}{r}
4x \\
x^2 + 3x - 2 \overline{\smash{)}4x^3 - 13x^2 + 2x - 7} \\
4x^3 + 12x^2 - 8x
\end{array}
$$

③
$$
\begin{array}{r}
4x - 25 \\
x^2 + 3x - 2 \overline{\smash{)}4x^3 - 13x^2 + 2x - 7} \\
\underline{4x^3 + 12x^2 - 8x} \\
-25x^2 + 10x - 7
\end{array}
$$

④
$$
\begin{array}{r}
4x - 25 \\
x^2 + 3x - 2 \overline{\smash{)}4x^3 - 13x^2 + 2x - 7} \\
\underline{4x^3 + 12x - 8x} \\
-25x^2 + 10x - 7 \\
-25x^2 - 75x + 50
\end{array}
$$

⑤
$$
\begin{array}{r}
4x - 25 \\
x^2 + 3x - 2 \overline{\smash{)}4x^3 - 13x^2 + 2x - 7} \\
\underline{4x^3 + 12x - 8x} \\
-25x^2 + 10x - 7 \\
\underline{-25x^2 - 75x + 50} \\
85x - 57
\end{array}
$$

⑥ $4x - 25 + \dfrac{85x - 57}{x^2 + 3x - 2}$

$$\frac{2x^3 + 2x + 7x^2 + 9}{2x + 3}$$

① $2x + 3 \overline{\smash{)}\ 2x^3 + 7x^2 + 2x + 9}$

② $2x + 3 \overline{\smash{)}\ \overset{\displaystyle x^2}{2x^3 + 7x^2 + 2x + 9}}$
$\ \underline{2x^3 + 3x^2}$
$\ 4x^2 + 2x$

③ $2x + 3 \overline{\smash{)}\ \overset{\displaystyle x^2 + 2x}{2x^3 + 7x^2 + 2x + 9}}$
$\ \underline{2x^3 + 3x^2}$
$\ 4x^2 + 2x$
$\ \underline{4x^2 + 6x}$
$\ -4x + 9$

④ $2x + 3 \overline{\smash{)}\ \overset{\displaystyle x^2 + 2x - 2}{2x^3 + 7x^2 + 2x + 9}}$
$\ \underline{2x^3 + 3x^2}$
$\ 4x^2 + 2x$
$\ \underline{4x^2 + 6x}$
$\ -4x + 9$
$\ \underline{-4x - 6}$
$\ 15$

⑤ $\qquad x^2 + 2x - 2 + \dfrac{15}{2x + 3}$

$$\frac{1}{3} + \frac{2}{5} \Rightarrow \frac{1\times5}{3\times5} + \frac{2\times3}{5\times3}$$
$$\Rightarrow \frac{5}{15} + \frac{6}{15} = \frac{5+6}{15} = \frac{11}{15}$$

$$x = \frac{1}{3} + \frac{1}{4}$$
$$\Rightarrow x = \frac{1\times4}{3\times4} + \frac{1}{4}$$
$$\Rightarrow x = \frac{1}{3} + \frac{1\times3}{3\times4}$$
$$\Rightarrow x = \frac{1\times4}{3\times4} + \frac{1\times3}{3\times4}$$
$$\Rightarrow x = \frac{4}{12} + \frac{3}{12}$$
$$\Rightarrow x = \frac{4+3}{12}$$
$$\therefore x = \frac{7}{12}$$

$$\frac{11}{4} = \frac{8+3}{4}$$
$$\Rightarrow \frac{8}{4} + \frac{3}{4}$$
$$\Rightarrow \frac{2}{1} + \frac{3}{4}$$
$$\Rightarrow 2\tfrac{3}{4}$$

$$\frac{1}{4} + \frac{1}{4}$$
$$\Rightarrow \frac{1+1}{4}$$
$$= \frac{2}{4}$$
$$= \frac{1}{2}$$

$$\frac{1}{4} + \frac{3}{8}$$
$$\Rightarrow \frac{1\times8}{4\times8} + \frac{3\times4}{4\times8}$$
$$\Rightarrow \frac{8}{32} + \frac{12}{32}$$
$$\Rightarrow \frac{8+12}{32} = \frac{20}{32}$$
$$\Rightarrow \frac{10}{16} = \frac{5}{8}$$

$$\frac{3}{4} - \frac{1}{4}$$
$$\Rightarrow \frac{3-1}{4}$$
$$\Rightarrow \frac{2}{4}$$
$$\Rightarrow \frac{1}{2}$$

$$\frac{2}{5} \times \frac{1}{4}$$
$$\Rightarrow \frac{2\times1}{5\times4}$$
$$\Rightarrow \frac{2}{20}$$
$$= \frac{1}{10}$$

$$\frac{2}{5} \div 4$$
$$\Rightarrow \frac{2}{5} \div \frac{4}{1}$$
$$\Rightarrow \frac{2}{5} \times \frac{1}{4}$$
$$\Rightarrow \frac{1}{10}$$

$$\frac{1}{2} \div \frac{1}{6}$$
$$\Rightarrow \frac{1}{2} \times \frac{6}{1}$$
$$\Rightarrow \frac{1\times6}{2\times1}$$
$$\Rightarrow \frac{6}{2}$$
$$\Rightarrow \frac{3}{1}$$

$$\frac{2}{3} \div \frac{5}{1}$$
$$\Rightarrow \frac{2}{3} \times \frac{1}{5}$$
$$\Rightarrow \frac{2\times1}{3\times5}$$
$$= \frac{2}{15}$$

$$\frac{2}{2+2} = \frac{2}{4} = \frac{1}{2}$$
$$2 = \frac{1}{2} \times 2+2$$
$$\Rightarrow 2 = \frac{1}{2} \times \frac{2+2}{1}$$
$$\Rightarrow 2 = \frac{1}{2} \times \frac{4}{1}$$
$$\Rightarrow 2 = \frac{1\times4}{2\times1}$$
$$\Rightarrow 2 = \frac{4}{2}$$
$$\Rightarrow 2 = \frac{2+2}{2}$$

$$\frac{2}{2} = 1 \qquad \frac{2+2}{2} = 2 \qquad \frac{2}{2+2} = \frac{1}{2} \qquad 2+2 = 4$$

$$4x = 8$$
$$\div \frac{4}{1} \quad \div \frac{4}{2} \Biggr\} \begin{array}{l} 1 \cdot x = 2 \\ \Rightarrow x = 2 \\ = 4 \times 2 = 8 \end{array}$$

$$\frac{4}{8} = \frac{2}{4} = \frac{1}{2}$$

$$\frac{5}{8} + \frac{1}{8} = \frac{5+1}{8} = \frac{6}{8} = \frac{3}{4}$$

$$\square \div 3 = 5$$
$$\Rightarrow \frac{x}{3} = 5$$
$$\Rightarrow \frac{x}{3} \times \frac{3}{1} = \frac{5}{1} \times \frac{3}{1}$$
$$\Rightarrow \frac{3x}{3} = \frac{5 \cdot 3}{1}$$
$$\Rightarrow x = 15$$
$$15 \div 3 = 5$$

$$\frac{3}{8} + \frac{1}{4}$$
$$\Rightarrow \frac{3}{8} + \frac{2}{8}$$
$$\Rightarrow \frac{3+2}{8}$$
$$\Rightarrow \frac{5}{8}$$

$$\frac{1}{3} + \frac{1}{6}$$
$$\Rightarrow \frac{1 \times 6}{3 \times 6} + \frac{1 \times 3}{3 \times 6}$$
$$\Rightarrow \frac{6}{18} + \frac{3}{18}$$
$$\Rightarrow \frac{6+3}{18}$$
$$\Rightarrow \frac{9}{18}$$
$$= \frac{1}{2}$$

$$\varphi = \frac{1+\varphi}{\varphi}$$
$$\varphi = 1 + \frac{1}{\varphi}$$
$$\varphi = \varphi \cdot \varphi - 1$$

$$\phi = \{1 + [\varphi - (\varphi \cdot \varphi)]\}$$
$$\phi = \{1 + [(1/\varphi) - \varphi]\}$$
$$\phi = [(\varphi \cdot \varphi) - \varphi - 1]$$

$$1 + \varphi = \varphi \cdot \varphi$$
$$\varphi - 1 = \frac{1}{\varphi}$$
$$\varphi \cdot \varphi - 1 = 1 + \frac{1}{\varphi}$$
$$\varphi \cdot \varphi - 1 = \frac{1+\varphi}{\varphi}$$
$$1 + \frac{1}{\varphi} = \frac{1+\varphi}{\varphi}$$
$$(\varphi \cdot \varphi) - \varphi = \varphi - \frac{1}{\varphi}$$
$$\frac{1}{\varphi} - \varphi = \varphi - (\varphi \cdot \varphi)$$

$$1 = (\varphi \cdot \varphi) - \varphi$$
$$1 = \varphi - \frac{1}{\varphi}$$
$$-1 = \frac{1}{\varphi} - \varphi$$
$$-1 = \varphi - (\varphi \cdot \varphi)$$

$$\varphi = 1.618\ 033\ 988\ 75$$
$$\varphi = \frac{1}{2} + \frac{\sqrt{5}}{2}$$
$$\varphi = \frac{1+\sqrt{5}}{2}$$
$$\sqrt{5} = 2.236\ 067\ 9775$$
$$\sqrt{5} + 1 = 3.236\ 067\ 9775$$
$$\frac{\sqrt{5}+1}{2} = 1.618\ 033\ 988\ 75$$

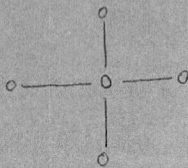

$$\phi = \frac{1}{2} + \frac{\sqrt{5}}{2}$$

$$\phi = \frac{1 + \sqrt{5}}{2}$$

$$\phi = \frac{3.236\ 067\ 9775}{2}$$

$$\phi = 1.618\ 033\ 988\ 75$$

$$x = \sqrt{5}$$

$$x = 2.236\ 067\ 9775$$

$$x + 1 = 3.236\ 067\ 9775$$

One plus the root of five, then divide by two.

The square root of five is
2.236 067 9775

Plus one gives
3.236 067 9775

Divided by two gives
1.618 033 988 75

Phi uses the symbol ϕ

$$\phi = 1.618\ 033$$

CHAPTER THIRTY FIVE

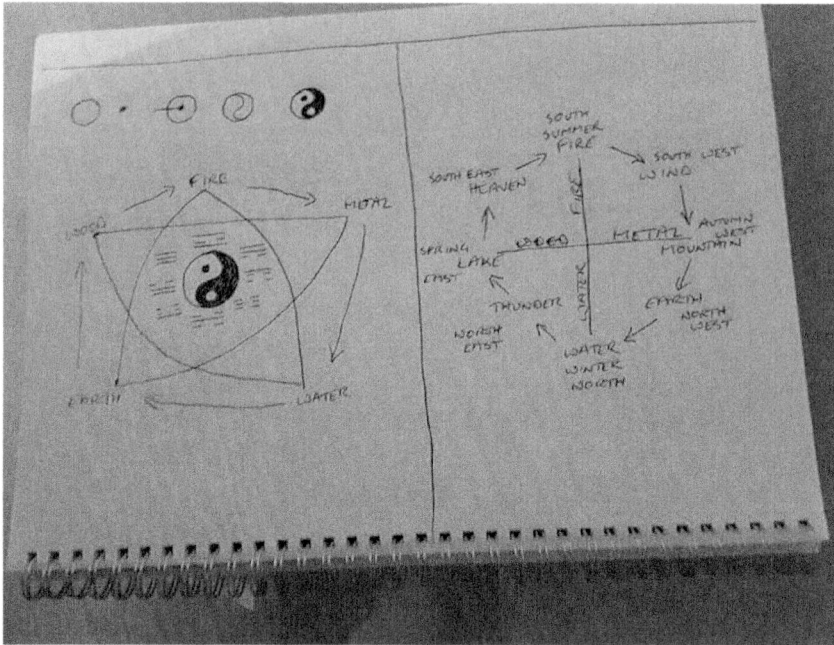

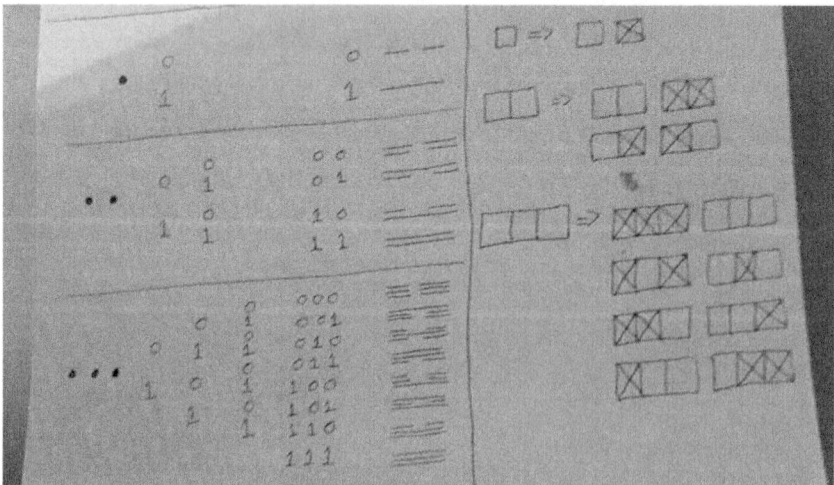

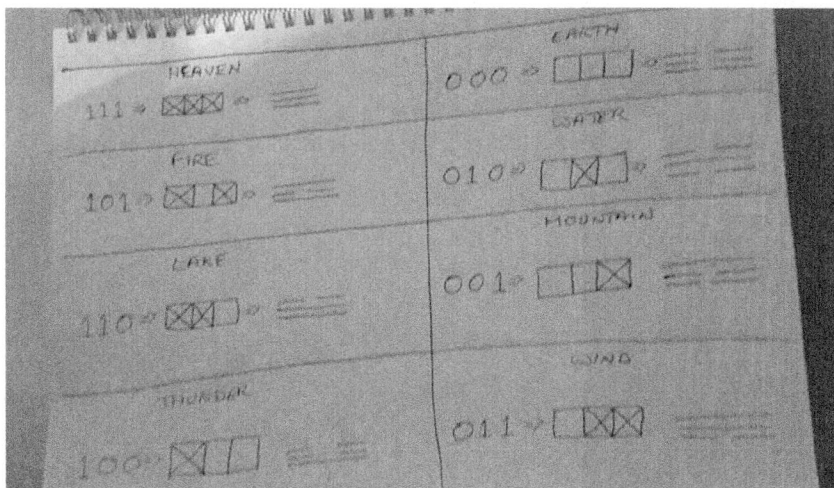

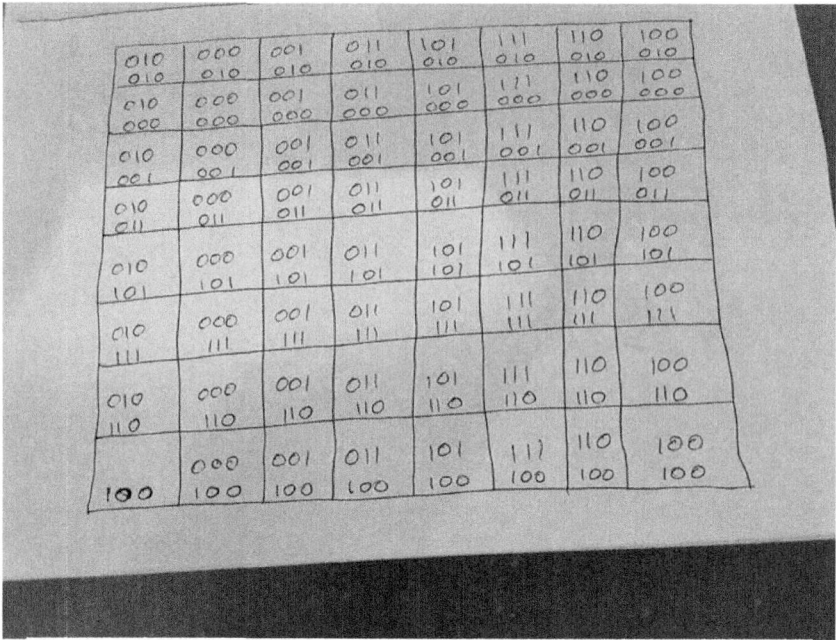

Runes - The Elder Futhark

F Fehu
cattle, wealth

U Ūruz
aurochs, strength

Th Thurisaz
giant, thor

A Ansuz
god, odin

R Raido
journey, wheel

K Kaunan
ulcer, fire

G Gebō
gift

W Wunjō
joy

H Hagalaz
hail, air

N Naudiz
need, necessity

I Īsaz
ice

J Jēra
year, harvest

E Eiwaz
yew tree, tree of life

P Perth
unclear meaning

Z Algiz
elk protection

S Sōwilō
sun

T Tīwaz
the god Tiwaz, victory

B Berkanan
birch, birth

E Ehwaz
horse

M Mannaz
man

L Laguz
water, lake

Ng Ingwaz
the god Ingwaz, fertility

O Othila
heritage, property

D Dagaz
day, dawn

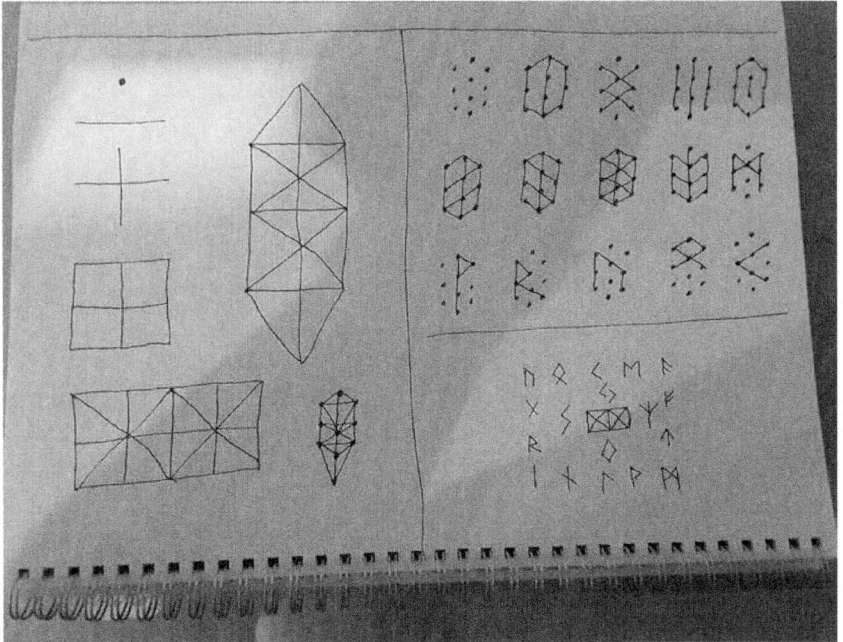

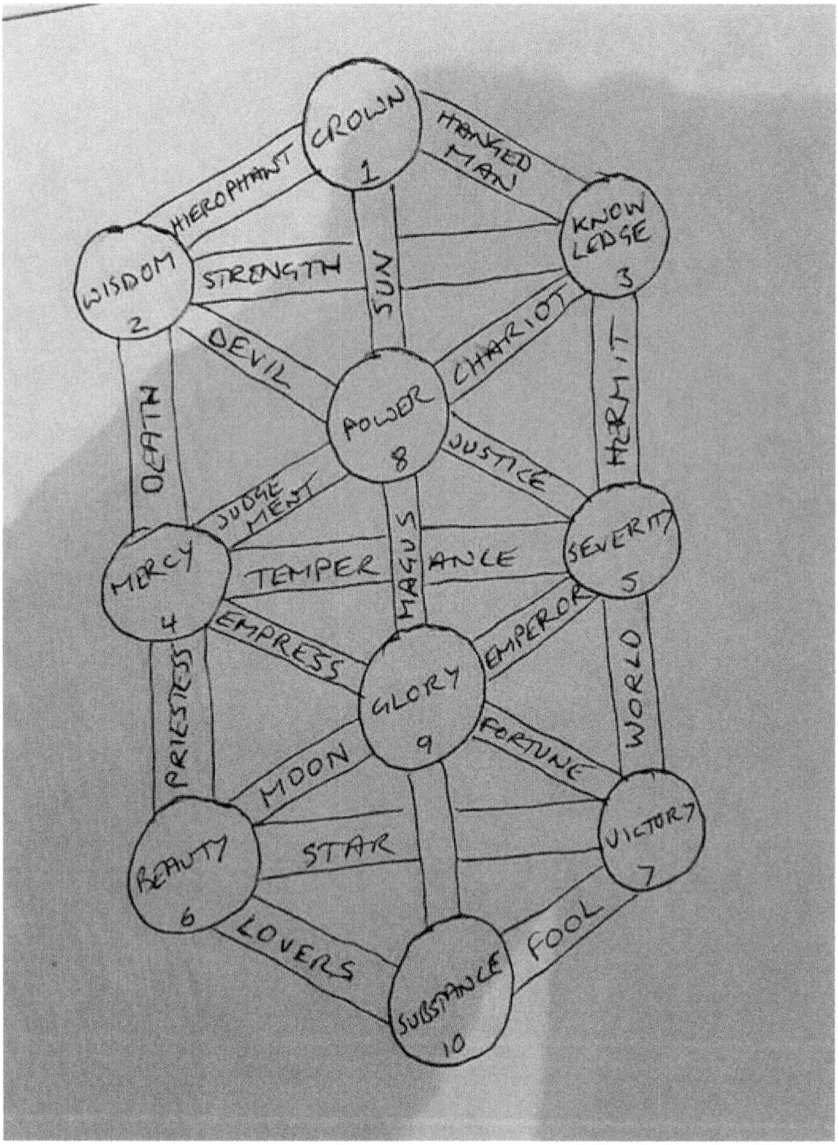
CROWN
1
HANGED MAN
HIEROPHANT
WISDOM
2
STRENGTH
SUN
KNOW LEDGE
3
DEVIL
CHARIOT
POWER
8
HERMIT
DEATH
JUSTICE
JUDGE MENT
MERCY
4
TEMPER
MAGUS
ANCE
SEVERITY
5
EMPRESS
EMPEROR
GLORY
9
PRIESTESS
WORLD
MOON
FORTUNE
BEAUTY
6
STAR
VICTORY
7
LOVERS
FOOL
SUBSTANCE
10

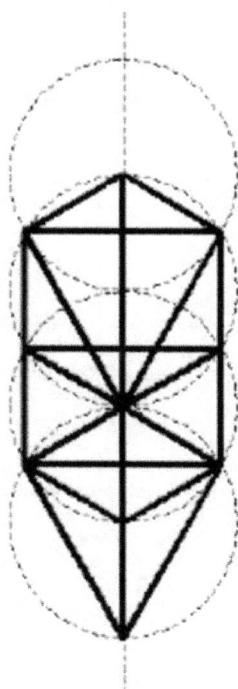

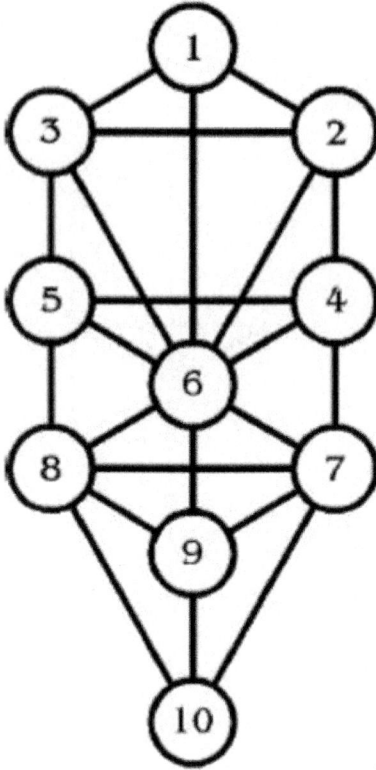

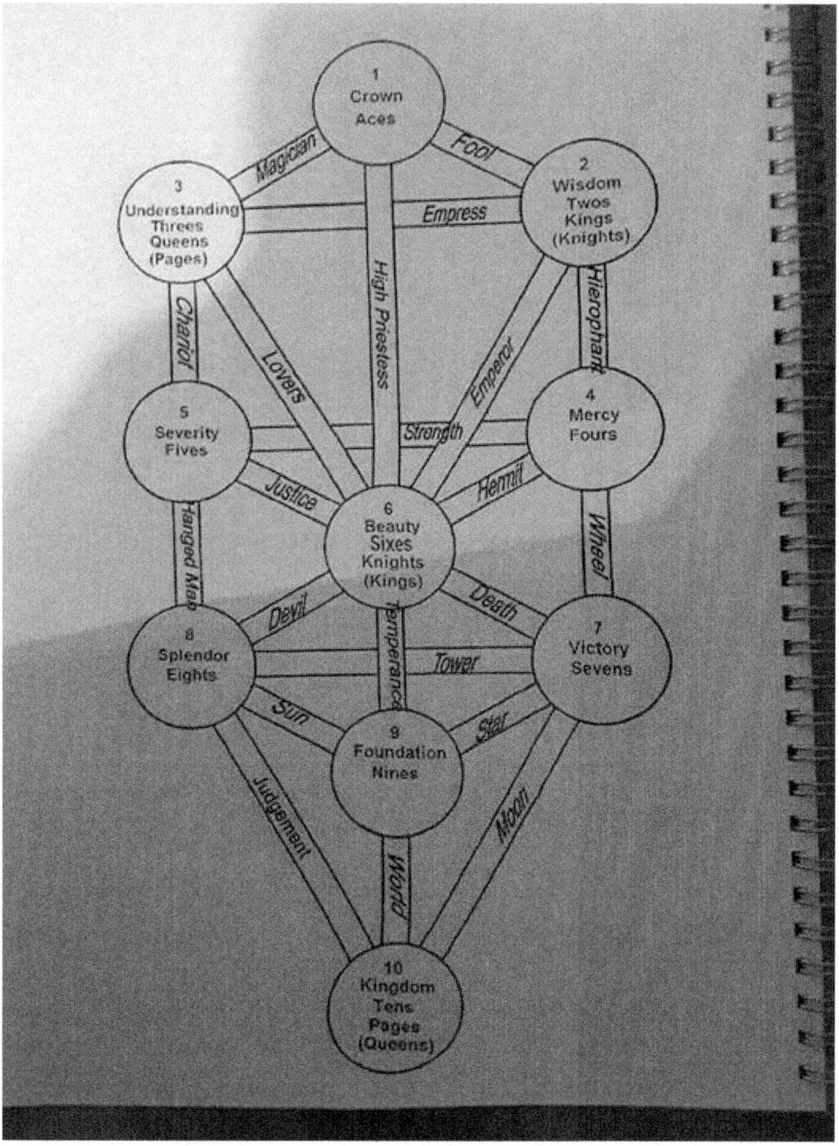
1
Crown
Aces
2
Wisdom
Twos
Kings
(Knights)
3
Understanding
Threes
Queens
(Pages)
4
Mercy
Fours
5
Severity
Fives
6
Beauty
Sixes
Knights
(Kings)
7
Victory
Sevens
8
Splendor
Eights
9
Foundation
Nines
10
Kingdom
Tens
Pages
(Queens)
Magician
Fool
Empress
High Priestess
Hierophant
Chariot
Lovers
Emperor
Strength
Justice
Hermit
Hanged Man
Wheel
Devil
Death
Temperance
Tower
Sun
Star
Judgement
Moon
World

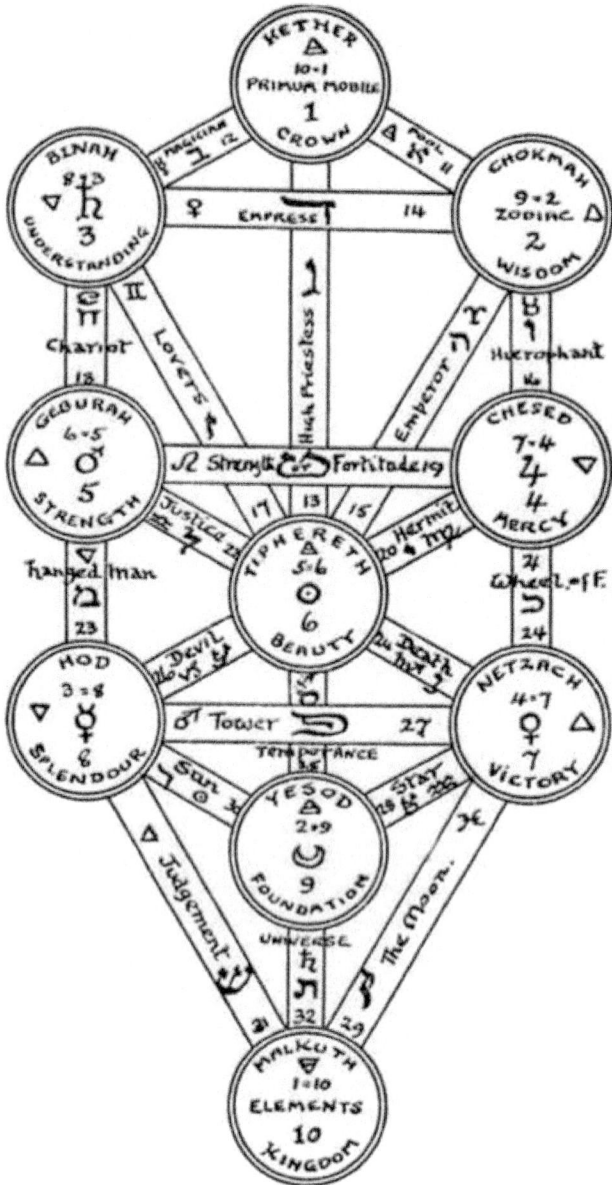

The He Tu diagram

Fire

Wood   Earth   Metal

Water

The directions represented by the Five Elements

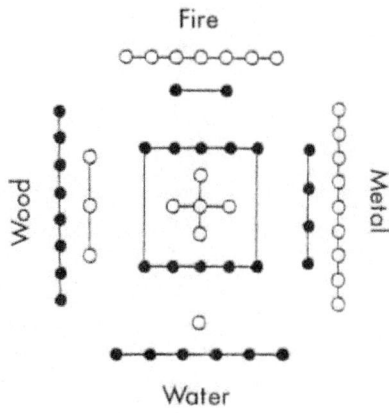

Fire

Wood

Metal

Water

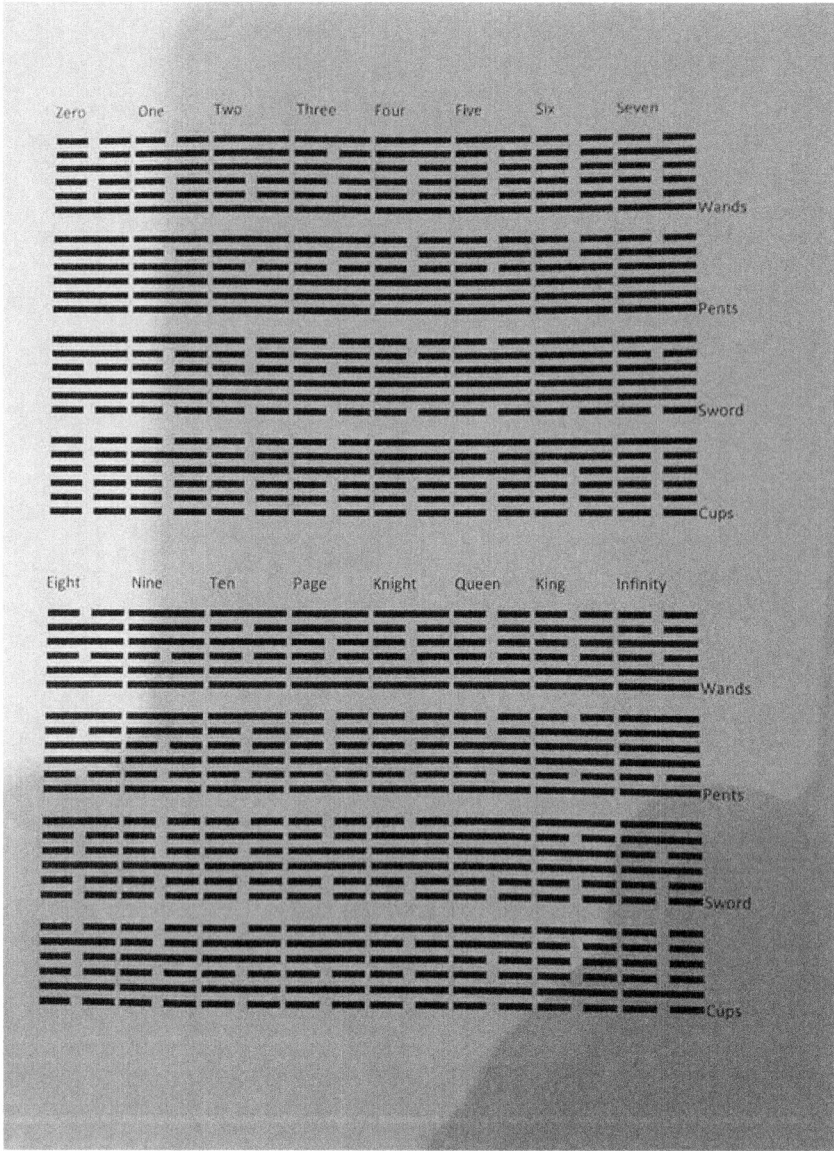

	1	2	3	4	5	6	7	8	9	10	11	12	13	14	A ∞
A 0	A1	A2	A3	A4	A5	A6	A7	A8	A9	A10	A11	A12	A13	A14	B ∞
B 0	B1	B2	B3	B4	B5	B6	B7	B8	B9	B10	B11	B12	B13	B14	C ∞
C 0	C1	C2	C3	C4	C5	C6	C7	C8	C9	C10	C11	C12	C13	C14	0 ∞
D 0	D1	D2	D3	D4	D5	D6	D7	D8	D9	D10	D11	D12	D13	D14	

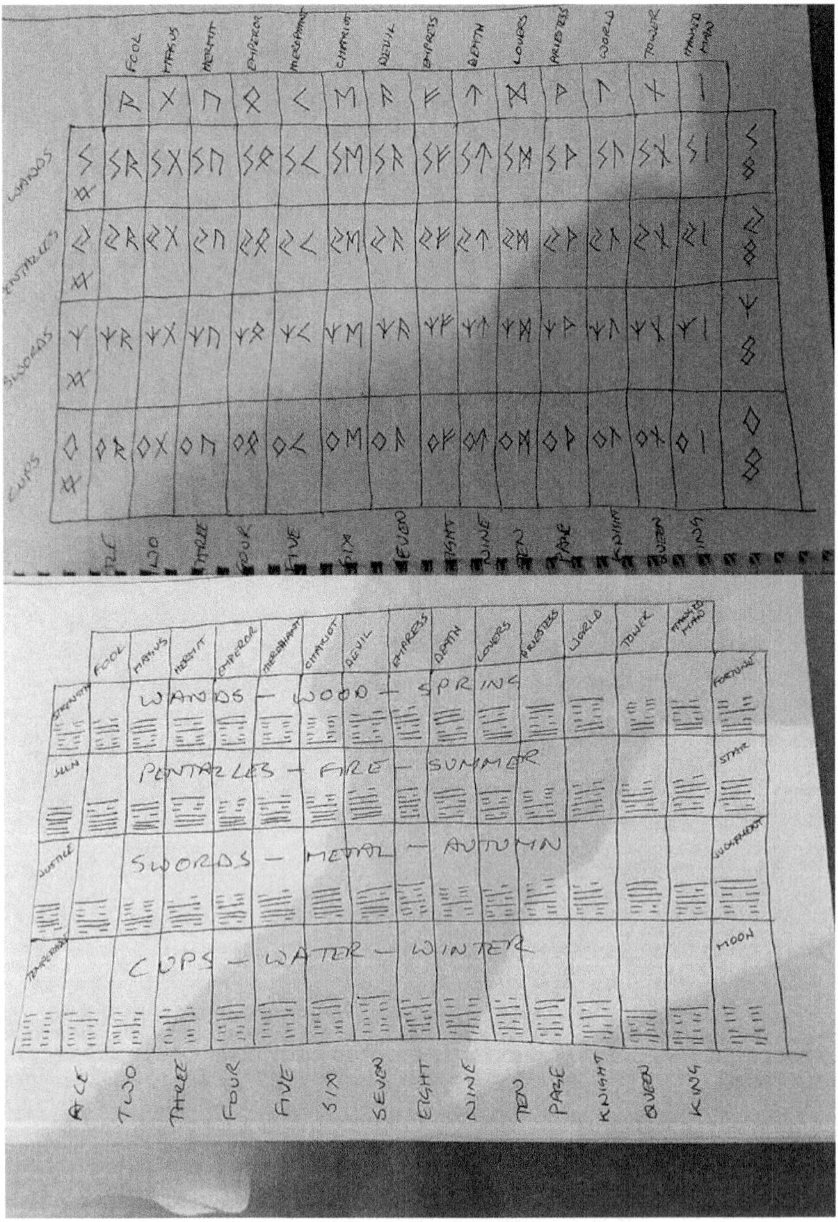
WANDS – WOOD – SPRING
SWORDS – METAL – AUTUMN
CUPS – WATER – WINTER
ACE
TWO
THREE
FOUR
FIVE
SIX
SEVEN
EIGHT
NINE
TEN
KNIGHT
QUEEN
KING

WANDS — WOOD — SPRING

PENTACLES — FIRE — SUMMER

SWORDS — METAL — AUTUMN

CUPS — WATER — WINTER

FOOL MAGUS HERMIT EMPEROR HIEROPHANT CHARIOT DEVIL EMPRESS DEATH LOVERS PRIESTESS WORLD TOWER HANGED MAN

ACE TWO THREE FOUR FIVE SIX SEVEN EIGHT NINE TEN PAGE KNIGHT QUEEN KING

Zero	Ace	Two	Three	Four	Five	Six	Seven	
Gen/Exo	Levit	Numb	Deut	Josh	Judg	Ruth	1Sam	Wands
Job	Psalms	Prov	Eccles	Song	Isai	Jerem	Lamen	Pents
Nahum	Habak	Zephan	Haggai	Zechar	Malac	Matt	Mark	Swords
Philip	Coloss	I Thess	II Thess	I Tim	II Tim	Titus	Philem	Cups

Eight	Nine	Ten	Page	Knight	Queen	King	Infinity	
1Sam	1King	2King	1Chron	2Chron	Ezra	Nehem	Esther	Wands
Ezek	Dani	Hosea	Joel	Amos	Obad	Jonah	Micah	Pents
Luke	John	Acts	Roman	I Corin	II Corin	Galat	Ephes	Swords
Hebrew	James	I Pet	II Pet	I John	II John	III John	Jude Rev	Cups

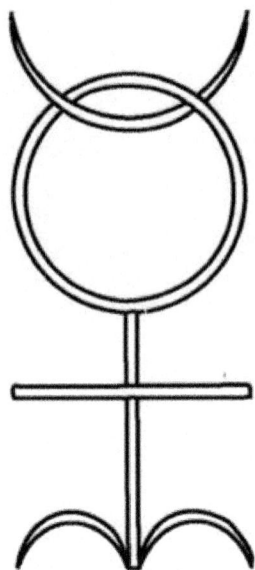

CHAPTER THIRTY SIX

Q Search Kindle

⫶ FILTER   ALL   DOWNLOADED   SORT ⩦

In Other Worlds: The Radix Tetrad Book Two ✓
ATTANASIO, A. A.
99% 2.4 MB

Radix (The Radix Tetrad Book 1) ✓
ATTANASIO, A. A.
READ 2.7 MB

The Dorsai! eBook Collection (Gateway Essentials 297) ✓
DICKSON, GORDON R
2.3 MB

Lord of Light ✓
ZELAZNY, ROGER
3.2 MB

This Immortal ✓
ZELAZNY, ROGER
2% 958 KB

Roadmarks ✓
ZELAZNY, ROGER
READ 3.4 MB

Glory Road ✓
HEINLEIN, ROBERT A.
13% 4.2 MB

Robert Heinlein's Expanded Universe: Volume Two ✓
HEINLEIN, ROBERT A.
2% 1.7 MB

Robert Heinlein's Expanded Universe: Volume One ✓
HEINLEIN, ROBERT A.
1% 717.4 KB

⌂ HOME   📖 LIBRARY   🛒 STORE   ☰ MORE

||| ◯   ‹

15:56 📷 ☺ ▶ ·

Q Search Kindle

Stranger in a Strange Land
HEINLEIN, ROBERT A.
1.3 MB

The Complete Riftwar Saga Trilogy: Magician,
Silverthorn, A Darkness at Sethanon
FEIST, RAYMOND E.
4.1 MB

Waylander (Drenai Book 3)
GEMMELL, DAVID
READ 709.8 KB

The Last Guardian (Jon Shannow Novel Book 2)
GEMMELL, DAVID
READ 805.6 KB

Two-Thirds: A History of our Galaxy
MYERS, DAVID P; PERCY, DAVID S
49% 34.8 MB

Gray Lensman
SMITH, E. E.
1% 439.7 KB

Triplanetary
SMITH, E. E.
630 KB

The Science Delusion: Freeing the Spirit of Enquiry (NEW
EDITION)
SHELDRAKE, RUPERT
4% 2.5 MB

Red Prophet: Tales of Alvin Maker: Book 2
CARD, ORSON SCOTT
1% 796.5 KB

| ⌂ HOME | 📖 LIBRARY | | 🛒 STORE | ☰ MORE |

||| ○   ‹

15:57

Q Search Kindle

FILTER   ALL   DOWNLOADED   SORT

Red Prophet: Tales of Alvin Maker: Book 2
CARD, ORSON SCOTT
1% 796.5 KB

Seventh Son: Tales of Alvin Maker: Book 1
CARD, ORSON SCOTT
1% 644.2 KB

Nature's God: Historical Illuminatus Chronicles Volume 3 (The Historical Illuminatus Chronicles)
WILSON, ROBERT ANTON
1% 4 MB

The Widow's Son: Historical Illuminatus Chronicles Volume 2 (The Historical Illuminatus Chronicles)
WILSON, ROBERT ANTON
6.5 MB

The Earth Will Shake: Historical Illuminatus Chronicles Volume 1 (The Historical Illuminatus Chronicles)
WILSON, ROBERT ANTON
38% 5.7 MB

78T64I14C9S Chapters Eighteen to Thirty Two_220319_090224
LANCE GRUNDY
345.6 KB

78T64I14C9S Chapters Ten to Seventeen _220319_085609
LANCE GRUNDY
242.6 KB

78T64I14C9S Chapters One to Nine_220320_114427
LANCE GRUNDY
119.7 KB

HOME   LIBRARY   STORE   MORE

Absolute Key To Occult Science, The Tarot Of The Bohemians
PAPUS
2% 4.7 MB

The Book of Thoth (Egyptian Tarot)
CROWLEY, ALEISTER; THERION, THE MASTER
READ 56.2 MB

MAGICK IN THEORY AND PRACTICE
CROWLEY, ALEISTER
4% 2.6 MB

Magick (Illustrated)
CROWLEY, ALEISTER
READ 1.6 MB

The Five Houses of Zen (Shambhala Dragon Editions)
CLEARY, THOMAS
13% 679.5 KB

The Mechanism of Mind: Understand how your mind works to maximise memory and creative potential
DE BONO, EDWARD
1% 3.4 MB

Think and Grow Rich (Panama Classics) (Napoleon Hill - The Thirteen Steps to Riches)
HILL, NAPOLEON
834.8 KB

Everything I Know - Buckminster Fuller
FULLER, BUCKMINSTER
5% 975.4 KB

HOME   LIBRARY   STORE   MORE

15:57

Q Search Kindle

The Meaning of Relativity :(Routledge Classics)The
Special and the General Theory
ALBERT EINSTEIN
7.7 MB

Relativity: The Special and the General Theory
EINSTEIN,ALBERT
2% 667.5 KB

The Collected Works of Albert Einstein: The Complete
Works PergamonMedia (Highlights of World Literature)
EINSTEIN, ALBERT
3% 327.2 KB

Introduction to Quantum Mechanics with Applications
to Chemistry (Dover Books on Physics)
PAULING, LINUS; WILSON, E. BRIGHT
READ 12.8 MB

The Physical Principles of the Quantum Theory (Dover
Books on Physics)
HEISENBERG, WERNER
5% 3.3 MB

Quantum Theory (Dover Books on Physics)
BOHM, DAVID
22.1 MB

The Principles of Quantum Mechanics
DIRAC, P. A. M.
2% 6.8 MB

Eight Lectures on Theoretical Physics by Max Planck
and his 1920 Nobel Prize Address on the Origin and De...
PLANCK, MAX
1% 2.1 MB

A Survey of Physical Theory
PLANCK, MAX

HOME   LIBRARY   STORE   MORE

15:57 🖼 📷 •   📶 🔋

Q   Search Kindle   🔔

Aether and Gravitation
HOOPER, WILLIAM GEORGE
1% 2 MB   ✓

Inventions, Researches and Writings of Nikola Tesla
MARTIN, THOMAS COMMERFORD
1% 9.8 MB   ✓

The Essential Works of Nikola Tesla
TESLA, NIKOLA
1% 21.3 MB   ✓

Collected Writings of Nikola Tesla
MARTIN, THOMAS COMMERFORD; TESLA, NIKOLA
11% 12.8 MB   ✓

The Problem Of Increasing Human Energy: With Special References To The Harnessing Of The Sun's Energy
TESLA, NIKOLA
READ 2.4 MB   ✓

The Nikola Tesla Treasury
TESLA, NIKOLA
6.2 MB   ✓

Tractatus Logico-Philosophicus (Chiron Academic Press - The Original Authoritative Edition)
WITTGENSTEIN, LUDWIG
1% 460.5 KB   ✓

A Compendium Of Mathematical Methods: A handbook for school teachers
MORGAN, JOANNE
87% 3.9 MB   ✓

How to Solve It: A New Aspect of Mathematical Method (Princeton Science Library Book 34)

🏠 HOME   📖 LIBRARY   🛒 STORE   ☰ MORE

||| ◯   ‹

15:58

Q Search Kindle

How to Solve It: A New Aspect of Mathematical Method (Princeton Science Library Book 34)
POLYA, G.
21% 2 MB

Music, Geometry and Mathematics: The Source Code Revealed
SCOTT VAN HEERDEN, DERRICK
READ 13.9 MB

Elements of Algebra
EULER, LEONHARD
14.6 MB

Boolean Algebra (Dover Books on Mathematics)
GOODSTEIN, R. L.
56% 12.3 MB

Gottlob Frege: Foundations of Arithmetic: (Longman Library of Primary Sources in Philosophy)
FREGE, GOTTLOB
43% 6.5 MB

Principles of Mathematics (Routledge Classics)
RUSSELL, BERTRAND
4% 2 MB

Human Knowledge: Its Scope and Limits (Routledge Classics)
RUSSELL, BERTRAND; SLATER, JOHN G.
1% 2.5 MB

The Bertrand Russell Collection
BERTRAND RUSSELL
1.2 MB

An Investigation of the Laws of Thought
BOOLE, GEORGE
8.6 MB

HOME   LIBRARY   STORE   MORE

III   ◯   ‹

15:58

Search Kindle

The Mathematical Analysis of Logic Being an Essay Towards a Calculus of Deductive Reasoning
BOOLE, GEORGE
140.2 KB

The Foundations of Science Science and Hypothesis The Value of Science Science and Method
POINCARÉ, HENRI
64% 77.4 MB

Manhood of Humanity
KORZYBSKI, ALFRED
27.6 MB

Darwin on Trial
JOHNSON, PHILLIP E.
2% 816.5 KB

At The Deathbed Of Darwinism
E. DENNERT
86.9 KB

The Mystery of Life's Origin
THAXTON, CHARLES; BRADLEY, WALTER; OLSEN, ROGER; TOUR, JAMES; ME...
1% 4.9 MB

Signature in the Cell: DNA and the Evidence for Intelligent Design
MEYER, STEPHEN C.
5.1 MB

The cell , outlines of general anatomy and physiology
HERTWIG, OSCAR
2.4 MB

The Presence of the Past: Morphic Resonance and the Habits of Nature
SHELDRAKE, RUPERT
3% 4 MB

| HOME | LIBRARY | | STORE | MORE |

15:58

Q Search Kindle

A New Science of Life
SHELDRAKE, RUPERT
3% 2.3 MB

General Chemistry (Dover Books on Chemistry)
PAULING, LINUS
READ 37.2 MB

Elements of Chemistry
LAVOISIER, ANTOINE
36.3 MB

Hegel - Premium Collection: The Science of Logic, The Philosophy of Mind, The Philosophy of Right, The Philo...
HEGEL, GEORG WILHELM FRIEDRICH
1% 6.3 MB

Kant's Critiques: The Critique of Pure Reason; The Critique of Practical Reason; The Critique of Judgement
KANT, IMMANUEL
1.7 MB

The Complete Works of David Hume: An Enquiry Concerning Human Understanding, A Treatise of Hum...
HUME, DAVID
18% 9.5 MB

Three Dialogues between Hylas and Philonous in Opposition to Sceptics and Atheists (Illustrated)
BERKELEY, GEORGE
1% 1.9 MB

A Treatise Concerning the Principles of Human Knowledge
GEORGE BERKELEY
1% 480.4 KB

Discourse on Metaphysi **d The Monadology (Dover Philosophical Classics)**

⌂ HOME	📖 LIBRARY		🛒 STORE	☰ MORE

15:58

Search Kindle

Discourse on Metaphysics and The Monadology (Dover Philosophical Classics)
LEIBNIZ, G. W.
2% 1.3 MB

Two Treatises of Government
LOCKE, JOHN
2% 1.4 MB

An Essay Concerning Human Understanding
LOCKE, JOHN
READ 834.8 KB

Ethics
SPINOZA, BARUCH
1.2 MB

Descartes: The Essential Collection
DESCARTES, RENÉ
76% 3.8 MB

Three Books of Occult Philosophy (Illustrated)
AGRIPPA, HEINRICH CORNELIUS
READ 13.6 MB

Q.B.L.: Being A Qabalistic Treatise on the Nature and Use of the Tree of Life
ACHAD, FRATER
READ 2.7 MB

The Anatomy of the Body of God
ACHAD, FRATER
READ 2.1 MB

The Hieroglyphic Monad
DEE, JOHN
4% 1.8 MB

HOME   LIBRARY   STORE   MORE

15:58 •

Q Search Kindle

A Source Book in Mathematics (Dover Books on Mathematics)
SMITH, DAVID EUGENE
64% 17.4 MB

The Divine Proportion (Dover Books on Mathematics)
HUNTLEY, H. E.
READ 3.8 MB

Geometrical Researches on the Theory of Parallels
LOBACHEVSKY, NICHOLAS
READ 1.6 MB

The Foundations of Geometry
DAVID HILBERT
7% 4.8 MB

Principia Mathematica: The mathematical principles of natural philosophy Illustrated.: SIR ISAAC NEWTON ...
NEWTON, SIR ISAAC
63% 6 MB

Opticks: Or, a Treatise of the Reflections, Refractions, Inflections, and Colors of Light
NEWTON, ISAAC
898.4 KB

The Early Mathematical Manuscripts of Leibniz (Dover Books on Mathematics)
LEIBNIZ, G. W.
3% 5.6 MB

The Geometry of René Descartes: with a Facsimile of the First Edition (Dover Books on Mathematics)
DESCARTES, RENÉ
7% 45.2 MB

Deductive Logic : annotated
ST. GEORGE WILLIAM JOSEPH

HOME   LIBRARY   STORE   MORE

III   ◯   ‹

15:58

Q Search Kindle

Deductive Logic : annotated
ST. GEORGE WILLIAM JOSEPH STOCK
READ 223.7 KB

The Port-Royal Logic
ANTOINE ARNAULD
5.8 MB

The Collected Works of Blaise Pascal (Highlights of World Literature)
PASCAL, BLAISE
8% 1.6 MB

Summa Theologica (All Complete & Unabridged 3 Parts + Supplement & Appendix + interactive links and ...
AQUINAS, THOMAS
1% 6.9 MB

Delphi Collected Works of Galileo Galilei (Illustrated) (Delphi Series Seven Book 26)
GALILEI, GALILEO
67% 6 MB

The Essential Galileo (Hackett Classics)
GALILEI, GALILEO; FINOCCHIARO, MAURICE A. (EDITOR)
13% 2 MB

The Notebooks of Leonardo Da Vinci
DA VINCI, LEONARDO
2.3 MB

Mechanical Drawing Self-Taught
ROSE, JOSHUA
3.8 MB

Ruler and Compass: Practical Geometric Constructions
SUTTON, ANDREW

| HOME | LIBRARY | | STORE | MORE |

15:59

Search Kindle

The Harmonies of the World
KEPLER, JOHANNES
1.5 MB

On the Revolutions of the Heavenly Spheres
COPERNICUS, NICOLAUS
333.8 KB

The Kybalion
INITIATES, THREE
1 MB

Alchemical Catechism
PARACELSUS
12% 660.2 KB

Alchemical Writings
PARACELSUS
2% 303.7 KB

The Hermetic and Alchemical Writings of Paracelsus--Two Volumes in One
PARACELSUS; WAITE, ARTHUR EDWARD
241.2 MB

Collectanea Hermetica (Volumes 1-10): Hermetic Arcanum, The Divine Pymander, Egyptian Magic, Seph...
WESTCOTT, WILLIAM WYNN
1.8 MB

The Corpus Hermeticum
GEORGE ROBERT STOWE MEAD
1% 1.2 MB

The Emerald Tablet of Hermes
HERMES
65% 271.3 KB

HOME   LIBRARY   STORE   MORE

15:59

Search Kindle

Heavenly Mathematics: The Forgotten Art of Spherical Trigonometry
VAN BRUMMELEN, GLEN
9% 21.3 MB

Triples: Applications of Pythagorean Triples
WILLIAMS, KENNETH
2% 12.1 MB

A Trillion Triangles: An Easy Approach to Trigonometry
WILLIAMS, KENNETH
13.3 MB

Plane Trigonometry
LONEY, SIDNEY
1% 261.6 MB

Trigonometry: A Complete Introduction: The Easy Way to Learn Trig (Teach Yourself)
NEILL, HUGH
6% 4.1 MB

Mental Math: Tricks To Become A Human Calculator (For Speed Math, Math Tricks, Vedic Math Enthusiasts,
V R, ABHISHEK
READ 12.3 MB

Think Like A Maths Genius: The Art of Calculating in Your Head
ARTHUR BENJAMIN AND MICHAEL SHERMER
27% 8.2 MB

Vedic Mathematics Teacher's Manual - Advanced Level
WILLIAMS, KENNETH
6.7 MB

Vedic Mathematics Teacher's Manual - Intermediate Level
WILLIAMS, KENNETH

| HOME | LIBRARY | | STORE | MORE |

15:59

Search Kindle

Vedic Mathematics Teacher's Manual: Elementary Level
WILLIAMS, KENNETH
READ 3.9 MB

The Power of Vedic Maths
GUPTA, ATUL
READ 3.7 MB

Vedic Mathematics: Sixteen Simple Mathematical
Formulae from the Vedas
TIRTHAJI MAHARAJA, JAGADGURU SWAMI SRI BHARATI KRISHNA
31% 22.6 MB

Diophantus of Alexandria: a study in the history of Greek
algebra
HEATH, SIR. THOMAS LITTLE; EULER, LEONHARD
31% 1.2 MB

A History of Greek Mathematics, Volume II: From
Aristarchus to Diophantus (Dover Books on Mathemati...
HEATH, SIR THOMAS
17.9 MB

A History of Greek Mathematics, Volume I: From Thales
to Euclid
HEATH, SIR THOMAS
5% 5.8 MB

Mathematics in Aristotle (Routledge Library Editions:
Aristotle)
HEATH, THOMAS
17% 1.4 MB

The Works of Archimedes
ARCHIMEDES
2% 13.5 MB

Delphi Collected Works of Euclid (Illustrated) (Delphi
Ancient Classics Book 96)
OF ALEXANDRIA, EUCLID

HOME   LIBRARY   STORE   MORE

15:59

Q Search Kindle

Holy Bible : King James Version (KJV) Word of God:
Formatted for Kindle
KJV
1.9 MB

Plotinus: The Enneads (LP Classic Reprint Series)
MACKENNA, STEPHEN
READ 7.4 MB

The Complete Works of Aristotle: The Revised Oxford
Translation, One-Volume Digital Edition (Bollingen Ser...
ARISTOTLE
14% 4.2 MB

Plato: The Complete Works (31 Books)
PLATO; EVERYWHERE, MASTERPIECE
58% 2 MB

The Book of Five Rings: A Classic Text on the Japanese
Way of the Sword by Musashi Miyamoto (illustrated)
MIYAMOTO, MUSASHI
3% 1,009.5 KB

The Yellow Emperor's Classic of Medicine: A New
Translation of the Neijing Suwen with Commentary
NI, MAOSHING
3% 962.6 KB

Tao Te Ching (Hackett Classics)
LAO-TZU
20% 1.2 MB

The Tibetan Book of the Dead: First Complete Translation
(Penguin Classics)
COLEMAN, GRAHAM
1% 6.8 MB

The Bhagavad Gita (Easwaran's Classics of Indian
Spirituality Book 1)

HOME   LIBRARY   STORE   MORE

The Upanishads (Easwaran's Classics of Indian Spirituality Book 2)
EASWARAN, EKNATH
1% 500.5 KB

The Taoist I Ching (Shambhala Classics)
LIU, I-MING
13% 1 MB

The Numerology of the I Ching: A Sourcebook of Symbols, Structures, and Traditional Wisdom
HUANG, TAOIST MASTER ALFRED
READ 2 MB

HOME   LIBRARY   STORE   MORE

Printed in Great Britain
by Amazon

11733744R00342